Viking Age
Aristocratic Residences
in Northern Europe

Viking Age Aristocratic Residences
in Northern Europe

Edited by
Mads Ravn

Aarhus University Press |

Viking Age Aristocratic Residences in Northern Europe
© The authors and Aarhus University Press 2024
Cover: Jørgen Sparre
Cover illustration:
1) The reconstructed King's Hall at Lejre Land of Legends.
Photo: Ole Malling, Sagnlandet Lejre.
2) Arabic silver dirhem found at Erritsø.
3) *Codex Vindobonensis 473, folio 153v*. The page is opening with the last part of entry on the invasion of Jutland. In the second line from the top the scribe left an empty space for the unknown place name of the location of the Frankish army's campsite in Jutland. Photo: Austrian National Library.

Layout, repro and typesetting: Narayana Press, Denmark
This book is typeset in Adobe Garamond Pro and LTSyntax and printed on 100g Munken White
Printed by Scandinavian Book
Printed in EU 2024
ISBN 978 87 7219 794 4 (printed book)
ISBN 978 87 7597 360 6 (e-pdf)
ISBN 978 87 7597 361 3 (epub)

Aarhus University Press
aarhusuniversitypress.dk

Published with the financial support of:
The Augustinus Foundation

International distributors
Casemate UK, casemateuk.com
ISD, isdistribution.com

PEER REVIEWED

/ In accordance with requirements of the Danish Ministry of Higher Education and Science, the certification means that a PhD level peer has made a written assessment justifying this book's scientific quality.

Contents

PART 1. THEORETICAL APPROACHES TO
POWER, SPACE AND PLACE   9

Chapter 1. Introduction
Viking Age Aristocratic Sites in Northern Europe – an Introduction to a Long Discussion   11
By Mads Ravn

Chapter 2
The Notion of Power in the Study of Metal-rich Archaeological Sites   20
By Trine Borake

Chapter 3
From Central Space to Urban Place   33
Growth and Centrality in the Fjord Landscapes of Aalborg and Odense from the 5th to 12th Century
By Mads Runge

Chapter 4
Gudme as First-Generation Central Place   48
– the Case of an Agrarian-Based, Non-Resilient Urban Trajectory
By Mads Dengsø Jessen, Mette Marie Hald, Morten Fischer Mortensen, Peter Steen Henriksen and Sofie Laurine Albris

Chapter 5
Jelling: a Central Place or a Royal Place, and what is the Difference in the 10th Century?   65
By Anne Pedersen

Chapter 6
Dynamic Changes of Society and Settlements in the Greater Jelling Area in the First Millennium AD   80
By Charlotta Lindblom & Katrine Balsgaard Juul

PART 2. POWER, WAR AND ARISTOCRATIC SITES IN NORTHERN EUROPE 105

Chapter 7
"Great Hall" and "Central Place": characterising power in the settlement geography of England in the fifth to eighth centuries 107
By Christopher Scull

Chapter 8
Borre – A Royal Manor with Halls, Mounds, Harbour and Ship Graves 120
By Terje Gansum

Chapter 9
Iron Age Monuments and Finds from the Tinghaug Plateau – a Synthesis 134
By Elna Siv Kristoffersen & Alf Tore Hommedal

Chapter 10
On Top of the World 157
An Aristocratic Settlement from the 7th-10th Century on Munkebo Bakke, Funen
By Malene Refshauge Beck

Chapter 11
A "Tissø Complex" at Birka 175
Birka-Korshamn and the Origins of the Viking Town
By Sven Kalmring & Johan Runer

PART 3. ATTACKS AND COMMUNICATION BY LAND AND SEA 195

Chapter 12
Failure or success? 197
The Frankish Invasion of Jutland in AD 815
By Kasper H. Andersen

Chapter 13
From Esesfelth to Echeho   211
– Continuity and change in a Nordalbingian landscape of power
By Thorsten Lemm

Chapter 14
**Unlocking the Mysteries of Erritsø Manor –
the Maritime Aspects**   231
By Morten Ravn

Chapter 15
Navigating past Erritsø during the Viking Age   246
By Jens Ulriksen

PART 4. THE ERRITSØ LOCATION, ITS CHRONOLOGY, CHOREOGRAPHY AND INTERPRETATIONS   263

Chapter 16
Radiocarbon dates and Bayesian modelling of the Erritsø site   265
By Bente Philippsen & Marie Kanstrup

Chapter 17
The Erritsø Excavations in a Bayesian Perspective   276
By Mads Ravn & Christian Juel

Chapter 18
Erritsø – the Production Area   303
By Morten Lyngkjær Jensen

Chapter 19
Synthesis of Central Places, Royal Places, Great Hall Complexes and Aristocratic Sites   322
By Mads Ravn

Authors   325

PART 1.
THEORETICAL APPROACHES TO POWER, SPACE AND PLACE

BY MADS RAVN

Chapter 1. Introduction

Viking Age Aristocratic Sites in Northern Europe – an Introduction to a Long Discussion

Were Danish kings itinerant and did they travel between the estates, the *Vicus Reges,* if you like, as known from contemporary Anglo-Saxon England with the court in Denmark already in the 7th, 8th and 9th centuries? Did the Carolingian Emperor Louis the Pious' troops approach the Erritsø royal hall in AD 815, possibly scorching it, while King Godfred's sons were hiding on what must have been Funen, 'an island 3 miles away', as the Frankish Annals report? It seems so and the function of the Erritsø, fortified manor thus seemed to change its emphasis from a royal *vicus,* based on tribute collection and religion in Erritsø, the name which from place name research is interpreted as the "supreme king's (i.e., Eirik's) hill", to a more militarized strategic defence-in-depth site of Jutland.[1] Is this a coincidence? And did the residents because of the 815 incidents, consequently, build a comprehensive moat and palisade before the impressive palisade in Jelling, 30 kilometres away in order to utilize the highly strategic landscape in a place where later military strategists of the 17th and 18th centuries found it imperative to place a garrison town like Fredericia before Fredericia?[2]

All hypotheses are substantiated by this array of papers in this volume that directly or indirectly elicit the use, multifunctionality, width and potential power related to such, for the lack of a better word, *aristocratic sites* in Northern Europe from AD c. 600-1000. The term, aristocratic, here defined in *Britannica* as: "Government by a relatively small, privileged class or by a minority consisting of those presumed to be best qualified to rule,"[3] needs to be meshed with new data and landscape analyses from the papers in this volume. The papers additionally bear perspectives that are more critical

---

1 https://arcnames.w.uib.no/2019/11/04/a-name-fit-for-a-king/
2 Fredericia here referring to the nearby garrison town founded in 1650 only four km away, as a means to defend the country against an attack and invading armies in the flank when they invaded deeper into the Jutland hinterland.
3 https://www.britannica.com/topic/aristocracy

to an unilateral evolutionary, top-down and power-related perspective of central places (Chapter 2). In that I agree that the terms need to be better contextualised to regional but also interregional contexts and seen in a less 'medieval-centric' perspective as also outlined by Scull, distinguishing between 'overlapping social geographies' (Chapter 7).[4] It also needs to be seen in a larger geographic perspective as outlined in Chapter 6.

The term manor, defined in Britannica as: "During the European Middle Ages, the dwelling of the lord of the manor or his residential bailiff and administrative centre of the feudal estate", may be problematic as it is a high medieval, feudal term applied to a slightly earlier phenomenon in Denmark, unless we accept that the problematic terms feudalism and lord-vassal relations were already instated in Denmark in the 8th century. We need to discuss the usefulness and archaeological content of these terms, as many of the authors do in relation to geography, archaeological finds and localities and time, as done by for example Lemm in Chapter 13.

At first glance, it seems that the early Danish kingdoms were weaker, more volatile, than in the south but also peripatetic, maybe compatible to changing patterns of power of warlords in Afghanistan or Hawaii.[5] Under these circumstances the function of the sites also changed over time.

Background

The project Royal Landscape and Power came about when Vejle Museum undertook a rescue excavation in 2006 and came across a very similar-looking hall to the ones then known in Lejre[6] and Tissø[7] in Zealand. As this was the first in Jutland of its type, we thought it appropriate to get a better understanding of the nature and dates around this phenomenon of second-generation central places. The project has from 2016 when the first research excavations started collected numerous C-14 dates and made stratigraphical observations combined with dendrodates that has not been possible to the same extent on other earlier excavations in Lejre and Tissø. Therefore, the general house chronology without many fixed dates have been a recurring problem. Due to extensive development in the area, we were also lucky to combine rescue excavations in the area and the surroundings, making it much more profitable in terms of data quantity and extent of research areas, than previously expected. The fact that the C-14 dates from Erritsø now exceed all other compatible sites in quantity makes it possible also to make Bayesian modulation on the high-resolution settlement history of the location, as three papers in this volume will reveal (Chapters 16, 17 and 18).[8] It is now possible to trace

---

4   Ravn 2018
5   Bath, 2008; Ravn 2018; See also Graeber and Wengrow 2021, 4. See also Skre 2020
6   Christensen 2015
7   Jørgensen 2001
8   C-14 dates from a recent excavation in 2023 have not yet been fully processed, but dendrochronology suggest that too, as also the typology of houses do, (see also Ravn and Juel this volume and Lyngkjær Jensen this volume).

the Erritsø halls back to at least the early 8th century, and by proxy maybe even earlier back to the 7th century. What is perhaps more surprising is that the location also seems to continue when Jelling appears in the 10th century, suggesting that the two sites were contemporary, at least some of the time. Whether it can explain 'the missing link' in habitation history in the Jelling area proper from AD 550-900 is discussed elsewhere (Chapter 6) but could offer one element of an explanation. What this implicates in terms of the wider history and position among the emerging ringforts in the late 10th century, supposedly for the purposes of a national defence, remains to be deciphered. We shall here focus mainly on the so-called second-generation central places in Scandinavia and Northern Europe as a phenomenon, and leaving the 10th century for a later elaboration by the contributors, with the exception of Chapter 5.

The papers in this volume were first presented in 2021 in a workshop in *Kongernes Jelling*, at the Royal Viking seat of Jelling (Denmark) in-between two waves of COVID. The aim was to discuss the advent of aristocratic and possible royal sites in the late Iron Age and Viking Age. It so far concludes the research project '*Royal Power and Landscape*', a diachronic research project by Vejle Museums together with the National Museum, initiated already back in 2016. The approach we have taken is an international and contextualised approach, where both place name evidence, archaeological evidence, metal detecting as well as landscape analyses in various regions of Northern Europe have been included, an approach that has developed out of a number of seminal projects in Scandinavia and abroad since the 1990s.[9]

Research question

The main research question of the project was: was there a royal seat nearby Jelling before, during or after the advent of Jelling in the middle of the 10th century; and if so, what characterised it? (See also Chapter 5). In other words, did Jelling rise in importance when Erritsø, only 30 km to the south-east, faded out, before Jelling was established in the middle of Jutland? Because according to written sources and several archaeological finds in Zealand, such as Lejre and Tissø, there certainly were aristocratic places and kings long before Jelling.[10] Therefore, in order to solve the riddle as to why Jelling suddenly appeared, and as the specific investigations from the Jelling Project have come to a close, the results from it paving the way for this project, it became pertinent to look into the meaning and content of aristocracy in the greater region of South Jutland and Denmark.[11] One take-away from the workshop is that the term royal seat needs to be expanded, to include aspects of wealth, religion and assembly sites (especially in Norway, Sweden and England) production of some items, Grubenhäuser, war and kings (England and Denmark). But it is also obvious that geographical differences between Norway, Denmark, Sweden and England do matter, as does the exposed military posi-

---

9   E.g., Fabech & Ringtved eds. 1999
10 E.g., Christensen 2015
11 Pedersen, Dengsø Jessen & Holst eds. 2023

tion of Erritsø in Jutland in times of war, in comparison to the less defended sites of Tissø and Lejre in Zealand.

Methodological approach

We chose to take a broader perspective inviting scholars from Denmark, Britain, Sweden, Norway, and Germany into the discussion. This revealed regional similarities, but also where there were differences (Chapters 8, 9, 11). Comparisons with the British find patterns, one firstly discovers that the English 'Great Hall Complexes' appear earlier and fade our earlier, but that the organization and use of such royal places are compatible, despite a different history in the region (Chapter 7). It is striking and confirms my hypothesis that the Anglo-Saxon analogy for the development of Scandinavia remains a useful tool to work with, whilst it is also important to look for differences.

This anthology tries to do so, looking for similarities and explain the differences. One must admit that some of the same aspects regarding royal estates, conspicuous consumption, workshops and numerous sunken featured buildings (here called Grubenhäuser) seem to appear earlier in Britain (except for the Grubenhäuser) and end earlier there too (see also chapter 18).[12] Also, first generation central places or low-density urban sites, in for example Gudme and metal rich sites in Zealand, still remain a riddle to be explored further (chapter 2 and chapter 4), with parallels to be found. However thus far, Gudme seems to distinguish itself as having been connected to more extensive, supra-regional trade routes, more than the so-called second-generation central places that seem to contain more luxury production and exchange at a more local scale, related to the needs of the particular elite and its conspicuous consumption and tribute collection.[13] In any respect none of them can be referred to as urban centres, which incidentally also involved international trade (see also Chapter 3 and 11), and the relationships between such phenomena and towns remain somewhat unclear (see however Chapters 3 and 11). Possibly the function of many of the second-generation sites may be summarized as follows by the Stanford historian Ian Morris:

> By 650, though, markets were putting new options on the table. Instead of just turning up and eating everything, a king or lord could install an agent on his farm, confiscate the lion's share of its output and then take his cut to Norwich or some similar market to swap for more durable goods. Continental merchants wanted food and drink (and slaves) to sell in the cities back home; Anglo-Saxon elites wanted Continental ornaments, clothes, and weapons to distinguish themselves from their poorer peers. Everybody gained, except the slaves.[14]

---

12 As arose during the workshop the term 'pit-house' often used by Danish archaeologists does not make sense in English.
13 Jørgensen 2001.
14 Morris 2022, 164

If one accepts this highly likely analogy and exchanges Norwich with Ribe, or more likely Hedeby, and Anglo-Saxons with Danes, and the 7th century with the 8th and 9th centuries in Denmark, it is most likely that the same happened here.

Terminologies

It is now 10 years since the seminal volume *Wealth and Complexity* was published.[15] Relevant to this volume is that it summed up a number of models for understanding centrality and central places in Scandinavia in the late Iron Age, a period that is as relevant to understand as the Viking Age proper.[16] Here, it was pointed out that the geographical models presented by Walter Christaller did not apply well to the Scandinavian and Northern European past reality (see also Chapter 7). Neither of the continental models were relevant, as they are intertwined with the early towns that were not present in large numbers in the late Iron Age and Early Viking Age in Scandinavia. This claim has only been substantiated during the last 10 years of extensive excavations and research in Scandinavia, where numerous sites and metal detector finds have changed the picture of what constitutes an important site in general and an elite site in particular.[17] And as it is revealed in this volume, rich metal finds do not necessarily comprise the only good indication for a central place, let alone an elite site *per se*, as the find record currently is so extensive that we need to redefine the importance of such sites (For more on this see Chapter 2 and 7). In contrast we need to explore the usefulness of different terminologies, among others defined in the Wealth and Complexity volume, and get a better understanding of what the term aristocratic sites holds, archaeologically and historically, in general in Northern Europe and specifically at the Erritsø site, which is the focus of this volume in particular.

Karen Høilund Nielsen has, drawing from Harrison, distinguished between **centripetal** and **centrifugal** sites, and the question is whether these two terminologies are applicable to current data.[18] Before we explore that, the definitions presented are as follows. Centripetal sites "… outline[s] functions of controlling a superregional area. Such sites constitute: "… rituals, solution of judicial disputes, marriage, exchange of livestock and 'economic specialities' … and defence of the region."[19] They should also: "have a catchment area and service the local population" and … "be evenly spread relative to the general pattern of settlement;"[20] This is not the case for centrifugal sites which within a network: "are supra-regional and related to inter-regional contacts and

---

15 Stidsing, Høilund Nielsen & Fiedel 2014
16 For a historical review of the concepts see Høilund Nielsen 2014, 11.
17 See also Fabech and Ringtved eds., 2000.
18 Harrison 1997, 25
19 Wolf 1966, 40
20 Høilund Nielsen 2014, 23

are therefore not centres in a regional perspective, but nodes in a supra-regional network (centrifugal centres)."[21]

By challenging the recent results of the papers present in this volume with these two definitions, there seem to be some empirical facts that are defying a rigid archaeological definition of aristocratic sites. There also seems to be new elements we need to add to the equation to understand this phenomenon. But as a working hypothesis the Erritsø site seems more like a centripetal site than a centrifugal site, in that we suggest that it served an interregional function where the king could visit on occasions in order to keep an unstable kingdom with centrifugal tendencies together, by ruling and performing conspicuous rituals and collecting tribute, elements the finds seem to support. In that perspective it almost equals the term defined here by Runge as "space" (Chapter 3). An important factor as also identified by Runge is that the convergence of several transport routes is essential for all the sites, as also seen at Lisbjerg further north[22]. It does not seem that a king was present all the time, judging from the few metal finds and the lack of an extensive array of craft production, contrary to for example at Gudme-Lundeborg, a first generation central place, where supra-regional trade seemed to play a more significant role (Chapter 4).

The itinerant king's road to Ribe and/or Hedeby?

Therefore, I suggest the contention that as an explanation for those phenomena, we consider the perspective of a peripatetic kingdom; that this was an institution in operation already in the 7th and 8th century, perhaps earlier, as indeed Ian Wood suggests among the Franks in the 5th and 6th centuries[23] and Rosamund McKitterick does for the Carolingians, in the 9th century.[24] Also Anne Pedersen suggests this for the 10th century in Jelling in this volume (Chapter 5). This sort of institution with a leader who was present, as any modern leader knows, was necessary in both Danish and European kingdoms up until the 17th century[25], when an administration could take over: A phenomenon seen in compatible societies around the world such as Hawaii and among the Incas.[26]

Taking this perspective, the recently found site at Munkebo (Chapter 10) and possibly Fæsted/Harreby make better sense.[27] They may be stops on the way. Now we only need to find the "in-between-sites" that may have been reached by the peripatetic king within one day, considering a day's ride to be approximately 20-30 km, as Andersen does in

---

21 Hoilund Nielsen 2014, 23
22 Jeppesen 2005
23 Wood 1994, 65
24 McKitterrick 2008, 178 discusses this and suggests that it is problematic but likely present from the reign of Louis the Pious.
25 Porsmose 2023
26 For Hawaiians see Ravn 2018; for Incas see Schjellerup 2021.
27 Although they need more publication and datings of the hall, see Grundvad & Albris 2020.

this book (Chapter 12).[28] In this respect, if the king was not going to Jelling, 30 km to the northwest, the king could travel to Almind, some 20 km to the west, which is seen as a Thing place by some place name scholars, and there next further on to Dollerup, some 20 km further to the southwest, the latter incidentally known all the way back into the Roman Iron Age for its rich chiefly grave.[29] They could both be stops on the way to Fæsted/ Harreby, further 30 km to the west along the hypothesized great Faris forest and ultimately making way to Ribe or Hedeby.[30] Future research and detailed landscape analyses assessing the routes may substantiate this hypothesis.

This hypothesis of a peripatetic kingdom would reconcile two opposing traditions in Danish Viking Age scholarship, the one suggesting that Denmark was not united before the 10th century[31] an analogy which looks very much towards the Anglo-Saxon, diversified internally competing kingdoms, and others that suggest that Denmark was a united realm already back in the 6th-7th century, an analogy that looks very much towards the Frankish societal development and possibly also is influenced by a teleological, national romantic perspective.[32] With a peripatetic kingdom it was both and neither, depending on time and place.

In order to explore this hypothesis, we will in future studies need to focus on whether there was habitation all year in the Erritsø locality, or whether the site functioned as a seasonal site, when the court of up to 300 persons potentially arrived on occasions.[33] The hypothesis that there were peripatetic kings that early would furthermore explain that despite almost identical halls on Zealand and in Erritsø, grubenhäuser and workshop areas and despite great effort, we find fewer metal finds in Erritsø and also only selected evidence of production[34]. A compatible case is presented from a mid-Swedish area (Chapter 11). We have in Erritsø indications of iron- and textile production only, but no clear evidence of other sorts of specialised craft production. It simply does not seem that the itinerant kings would stay very long here, only as long as goods could be collected to sell on in either contemporary Ribe or Hedeby, and until other ritual and juridical functions were taken care of, as the overrepresentation of barley for ritual ale seem to suggest was important.[35] It would thus explain difference in intensity of metal finds in contemporary Lejre and Tissø with the Erritsø site.

---

28 Grundvad & Albris 2020
29 Hartvig & Sørensen 2021. For Iron Age Dollerup, see Mikkelsen and Davidson 1989, 183.
30 Grundvad & Albris 2020, 20
31 Sawyer & Olsen 1988; Holst 2014
32 Näsman 2006. See also Skre 2020
33 Here, I refer to a Carlsberg funded project we participate in, with exactly that focus by Dr. Sarah Croix, Aarhus University.
34 By the look at the metals in Erritsø it also seems the metal finds are less well-preserved.
35 Henriksen and Stevnsvig 2020, 4. Indeed one charred barley seed with a sprout suggesting production of ale was located at the site.

The military aspect

Another thing that is different at the Erritsø site, compared to similar types of sites in Zealand and Scania, is the emphasis in Erritsø on defence (Chapter 14; Chapter 15; chapter 16 and Chapter 17). It certainly seems that the moat and palisade complex are fit for a king, at least in 9th or 10th century; we also see from landscape analyses that the site was strategically very well situated in a landscape, making it a crucial area in terms of defence, something later historical events all the way up until 1864 also suggest was the case, where south meets north and east meets west in terms of transport routes by land and sea. That this area was a focal point in the defence of a royal realm a number of times, during the course of the 17th to 19th centuries, makes it even more likely that this was also the case in earlier times, as also Andersen suggest in a pivotal paper in this volume (chapter 12). He here suggests that an event in AD 815 could have taken place in this area, as it corresponds well with an army's seven-day journey from the river Eider.

The Erritsø site was not an early town, as Ribe. Whether it was, as indicated by Jessen et al. (Chapter 4 and Chapter 7) a low intensity non-urban settlement is a question only future research may help solve and put into a larger perspective. In this case I believe that we need to look at the entire region from another perspective, as in Chapter 13, looking at the North Albingian area. Additionally, the Erritsø aristocratic royal hall was more about ritual, defence, and royalty, whereas the few towns we know of were more about supra-regional trade, as explained by Runge (Chapter 3). That it was fit for a king is however beyond doubt.

Acknowledgements

This project and book would not have been possible without the support of the Beckett Foundation and the Augustinus Foundation and without the advice from the National Museum, especially Anne Pedersen, Mads Dengsø Jessen and Peter Steen Henriksen. I also thank all the contributors for their patience during numerous waves of COVID and other delays. Your contributions are exceptionally useful as navigating points of reference for a further understanding of the phenomenon of aristocratic sites in Northern Europe.

Bibliography

Electronic sources
Albris, L. https://arcnames.w.uib.no/2019/11/04/a-name-fit-for-a-king/ [Accessed 09.06.2024]

Secondary sources
Bath, F. 2008: *Afghanistan og Taliban*. Pax Forlag: Oslo.
Fabech, C. & J. Ringtved (eds.). 1999: *Settlement and Landscape. Proceedings of a conference in Aarhus, Denmark, May 4-7 1998*. Jutland Archaeological Society, Aarhus University Press.
Christensen, T. 2015: *Lejre bag myten. De arkæologiske udgravninger*. (Jysk Arkæologisk Selskabs Skrifter 87). Aarhus: Jysk Arkæologisk Selskab.
Graeber, D. & D. Wengrow. 2021: *The Dawn of Everything. A new History of Humanity*. London: Allan Lane.

Grundvad, L.& L. Albris. 2020: "Afdækning af fænomenet hørg fra yngre jernalder og vikingetid. Nye udgravninger ved Harreby", *By, Marsk og Geest*, 32, 17-43.

Harrison, D. 1997: "Centralorter i historisk forskning om tidig medeltid", in *"... Gick Grendel att söka det höga huset..." Arkeologiska källor til aristokratiska miljöer i Skandinavien under yngre järnålder*, edited by J. Callmer & E. Rosengren (Rapport från ett seminarium i Falkenberg 16-17 november 1995). Halmstad, 25-29.

Hartvig, A. & M. Sørensen. 2021: "Et indblik i den ældre og højmiddelalderlige bebyggelsesstruktur i Sønderjylland", in *Landbebyggelsen bebyggelsesstruktur. Middelalderens rurale Danmark,* edited by M. Svart & L.C. Bentsen. Aarhus: Jysk Arkæologiske Selskab, 33-50.

Henriksen, P.S. & A.M. Stevnsvig. 2020: "Erritsø VKH 6810. Naturvidenskabelige undersøgelser. Miljøarkæologi og materialeforskning bevaring og naturvidenskab", Nationalmuseet. *Rapport 65/2020. NNU j-nr. A9280.*

Høilund Nielsen, K. 2014: "Key issues concerning Central Places", in *Wealth and Complexity. Economically Specialised sites in Late Iron Age Denmark,* edited by E. Stidsing, K. Høilund Nielsen & R. Fiedel. Aarhus: Aarhus University Press, 11-50.

Holst, M.K. 2014: "Warrior aristocracy and village community", in *Wealth and Complexity. Economically Specialised sites in Late Iron Age Denmark,* edited by E. Stidsing, K. Høilund Nielsen & R. Fiedel. Aarhus: Aarhus University Press, 179-198.

Jeppesen, J. 2004: "Stormandsgården ved Lisbjerg kirke – Nye undersøgelser". *Kuml, 53*(53), 161-180. https://doi.org/10.7146/kuml.v53i53.97497

Jørgensen, L. 2001: "From tribute to the estate system, 3rd-12th century. A proposal for the economic development of the magnates' residences in Scandinavia based on settlement structure from Gudme, Tissø and Lejre", in *Kingdoms and Regionality. Transactions from 49th Sachsensymposium 1998 in Uppsala,* edited by B. Arrhenius. Stockholm: Archaeological Research Laboratory, Stockholm University (Theses and papers in Archaeology B:6.), 73-82.

McKitterick, R. 2008: *Charlemagne: The Formation of a European Identity.* Cambridge: Cambridge University Press.

Mikkelsen, D.K., & Davidson, J. 1989: "To ryttergrave fra ældre romersk jernalder -den ene med tilhørende bebyggelse." *Kuml, 36*(36), 143-200. https://doi.org/10.7146/kuml.v36i36.110932

Morris, I. 2022: *Geography is Destiny. Britain and the world. A 10.000- year history.* London: Profile Books.

Näsman, U. 2006: "Danerne og det danske kongeriges opkomst – Om forskningsprogrammet "Fra Stamme til Stat i Danmark"", *Kuml, 55*(55), 205-241. https://doi.org/10.7146/kum..v55i55.24694

Pedersen, A., M. Dengsø Jessen & M.K. Holst (eds.) (2023): *Jelling – Monuments and Landscape: Publications from the National Museum. Studies in Archaeology & History Vol. 20:4 1-2 Jelling Series.* (Publications from the National Museum. Studies in archaeology & history Bind 20 Nr. 4; 1-2 Jellinge Series Bind 20 Nr. 4, 1-2). Odense: Syddansk Universitetsforlag.

Porsmose, E. 2023: *Magtfuld gennem Riget. Rejsekongedømmet i Danmark o. 960-1660.* Odense: University of Southern Denmark studies in History and the Social sciences. Vol. 647.

Ravn, M. 2018: "Roads to complexity: Hawaiians and Vikings compared", *Danish Journal of Archaeology,* 7, 119-132. https://doi.org/10.1080/21662282.2018.1468147

Sawyer, P. & O. Olsen (eds.) 1988: *Gyldendals og Politikens Danmarkshistorie,* Bind 3. København: Gyldendal og Politiken.

Schjellerup, I. 2021: *Stenenes Magi. Tawantinsuyu – Inkaernes rige.* København: Gads Forlag.

Stidsing, E., K Høilund Nielsen & R. Fiedel (eds.). 2014: *Wealth and Complexity. Economically Specialised sites in Late Iron Age Denmark.* Aarhus: Aarhus University Press.

Skre. D. 2020: Rulership and Ruler's sites in 1st-10th century Scandinavia. In Skre, D. ed., *Rulership in 1st to 14th century Scandinavia. Royal Graves and sites at Avaldsnes and beyond.* Berlin/Boston, s. 193-234.

Wolf, E.R. 1966: *Peasants.* Englewood Cliffs. New Jersey: Prentice Hall.

Wood, I. 1994: *The Merovingian Kingdoms 450-751.* New York: Routledge. Taylor and Francis.

BY TRINE BORAKE

Chapter 2
The Notion of Power in the Study of Metal-rich Archaeological Sites

ABSTRACT
This article explores the concept of power in archaeological studies from the Late Iron Age to the Middle Ages, particularly in Denmark. It is here argued that power is not only exercised top-down by kings and aristocrats but also bottom-up by the rural population. New metal detector finds indicate that power and resources were widely distributed among rural communities, challenging traditional hierarchical models. It is also here highlighted how local networks and collective actions played a central role in social organisation and development. Borake calls for a broader, more nuanced understanding of power structures in archaeological studies.

Archaeological research on social organisation from the Late Iron Age to the Middle Ages particularly in Denmark but also in other Scandinavian countries has been inspired by a grand narrative pursuing a national identity and the formation of kingdoms and nation-states in the last 40 years.[1] Monuments, sites, and artefacts are spellbound within this interpretive frame and 'aristocratic environments', 'king's manors' and 'elite residences' are pivotal in the discussions.

However, detector finds uncovered in the last decades, particularly in Denmark now show ambiguous patterns that are difficult to comprehend in a traditional narrative. Artefacts that were once rare or prestige are now found in numbers in rural sites suggesting widespread use among a diverse rural population.[2] The amount, distribution and composition of detector finds have modified perceptions of centres and peripheries, of resources and relations. They challenge the notion of central institutions, domains, and monopolies and call for alternate and nuanced explanations. An accumulated and ambiguous body of rare, imported and prestige detector material in rural locations in Western Zealand, inspired my research and made me question the notion of a top-down social structure. It motivated and contributed to a general discussion on the discourse

---

1   Skre 2022
2   Christiansen and Sarauw 2014; Feveile 2018

of power, and an exploration of complementary ways to understand social organisations in a wider debate.³ Is our notion of power based on a top-down perception of social organisation adequate and satisfactory as an interpretive frame to understand the signs of an empowered rural population? How can other forms of organisation and power nuance perceptions? I will explore the following departing from Denmark in the Late Iron Age to the Middle Ages, but will make explanatory detours in time and space. I will argue that collective and network-based organisations, actions, and counteractions are equal agents to kings and elites in the formation of social organisation and development.

Ambiguous evidence

My research is motivated by an accumulated and ambiguous body of detector material in rural locations in Western Zealand. I analysed the detector material from sites surrounding the Tissø-complex and Ringsted based on a variety of criteria that express function, status, and relations: chronology; trade; production; weapons; riding gear; prestige artefacts; imports, and amulets. For the sites around the Tissø complex, I found a long chronology and no disruption with the decline of the Tissø complex around 1050; even locations with a close relation to the complex; Melby, Dalby Hals and Bakkendrup continued to develop into the Middle Ages. There were no signs of extensive colonising of vacant land with the decline of the complex, indicating that extensive landholding by the complex was not given. Most of the rural sites showed a diverse composition; demonstrating signs of both trade and handicraft; weapons and riding gear, prestige artefacts and amulets. The results suggest a strong local network able to organise trade, access to raw material and know-how independently or in congruence with the complex; an aristocratic presence if we regard weapons and riding gear to express just that; and individual cultic expression leaving no signs of cultic monopoly. Based on the analysis, I found socioeconomic independence and socio-political influence in the rural sites surrounding the Tissø-complex.⁴

The Ringsted region showed a different dynamic. Here, one site stood out. Kildeagergård demonstrated a long continuity and a conspicuous composition. It flourished at the same time as royal powers tried to establish a power base in Ringsted. I have suggested that Kildeagergård served as an antagonist, preventing Ringsted to develop into an important town thus decentralising royal institutions.⁵

From the results, it was essential to grant the rural population significant influence and power, if you like, in the social organisation and the processes forming it.⁶ Consequently, I found that a top-down notion of power framed in models of a hierarchical social organisation was inadequate to understand the social organisation and dynamics suggested in my analysis. However, examples of alternative organisational forms, coun-

---

3   Borake 2019a; Furholt et al. 2020; Lund et al. 2022
4   Borake 2019b
5   Borake 2022
6   Borake 2019b

teractions, and bottom-up power mechanisms in social science research nuanced my perceptions and facilitated a better understanding of the role of the rural population.

An empowered rural population

There are multiple examples of an empowered rural population serving as agents in social dynamics.

For example, things or assemblies sustained the appreciation. This system assigns influence to networks and communal organisations. It served several administrative functions, political and legal: resolving disputes; measuring punishment; discussing and agreeing on laws; and accepting elections of both royal and ecclesiastic character.[7] The system provides a decentralising institution with various levels of control systems to minimize dominion. But apart from administrative and legal functions, it also offered a stage for alliances, marriage, display of status and skills, and exchange, all equally important in constituting social organisation.[8] Social, administrative, and legal regulations are essential to procure self-government and influence, and the things served as the glue that tied societies together. The election of King Haakon the Good in return for the right to woodlands illustrates the empowerment of the community.[9]

Another example of empowered network organisation is suggested in connection to Danevirke. Like few other monuments, it serves a nationalistic narrative of early state formation testifying to a centralised royal institution capable of initiating the massive construction work.[10] However, based on a thorough analysis of the archaeological remains in their own right, and not as a stage for written evidence, Andres Dobat (2008) concludes that each phase represents a short-term investment pointing to 'the type of leadership found in societies who have a form of centralised leadership when it is needed'.[11] No evidence points to a standing army permanently posted at Danevirke to control the southern frontier of a rising kingdom, and as the monument is not continuously maintained, there is little support for a centralised institution behind the establishment. By contrast, new excavations demonstrate a foundation period in the 5th century that, along with numerous reworks points to various interests and organisational structures.[12] Dobat along with Andersen sees the labour investment as a need for communal protection from external stress from the Frankish Empire.[13]

A new perspective on the Ring Fortress from Denmark, monuments of King Harold Bluetooth's imperialistic ambitions, is also offered. Their construction, chronology

---

7   Brink 1998; Sanmark 2009, 205; Semple and Sanmark 2013; Olsen 2015, 49
8   Sanmark 2017, 52
9   Storm 1900, ch. 1
10 Andersen, H.H. 2004; Dobat 2008, 33-35; Andersen, K.H. 2016, 153
11 Dobat 2008, 60
12 Witte 2015
13 Andersen 1998, 11-12; Dobat 2008, 55-58

and find material fits poorly with popular ideas of a network of royal strongholds.[14] Subsequently, based on evidence from *Borgring* found and excavated in 2014, Søren Sindbæk (2017) suggest 'they were a means of protecting the portion of the rest of the population in times when the primary fighting force was called elsewhere by the king'. He asks: 'What support could be gathered from an army of warriors, who worried for the home regions, they had left behind?'.[15] Accordingly, to motivate armed men to fight, a defence system for the families left behind was initiated. This demonstrates how the desires, needs and ambitions of the local population had to be indulged and fulfilled by kings and aristocrats.

The list pointing to bottom-up influence and empowerment of the local community can be continued. For example, we find the peasant rebellion against King Cnut in 1085 where the enforcement of unjust taxation with overwhelming pressure resulted in a violent uprising, eventually leading to his murder.[16] The migration to Iceland in the middle of the ninth century can likewise be understood as a deliberate evasion of centralising powers although the causal explanations vary.[17] Another collective mechanism to counter centralised power can be found in common farming.[18] It implies strong communities capable of organising beside centralised institutions. Ethnographic studies offer multiple examples of decentralising mechanisms as well. Studies from Vanuatu in Polynesia show how a lavish ceremonial performance and feast were required to be elected chief. This would, subsequently, grant him status and prestige but at the same time limit his economic position and thereby decentralise power. At the same time, this social mechanism would channel resources back to the community.[19] For the Prehistoric Southwest, Randall McGuire and Dean Saitta (1996) see 'pueblo hierarchies as responsive to, rather than exploitative of, the commune', and find that elites were subsumed to the commune. 'Subsumed elites are limited by kin and civil obligations'.[20] These multiple and interdisciplinary examples of an empowered rural population, inspire to discuss the challenges of the nation-state as an imperative frame.

The state as an interpretive frame

Influential studies on social organisation are often framed by evolutionary state-formation theories based on top-down and hierarchical perspectives.[21] However, state formation is not a linear evolutionary process with a fixed end goal: the nation-state as a formalistic entity, but an ambiguous process inferring multiple consequences of

---

14 Christiansen 1971; Randsborg 1980, 99
15 Sindbæk 2017, 539-540
16 Fenger 1989, 65-67
17 Olsen 2015, 52
18 Hoff 1997, 173; Fritzbøger 2006
19 Earle and Spriggs 2015, 522-525
20 Saitta 1994; McGuire and Saitta 1996, 202
21 Lund and Sindbæk 2021, 29-32; Iversen 2013; Andersen, K.H. 2016, 170

social relations, networks and agencies with variating levels and scales of centrality and spatiality influenced by multiple internal and external motivations.[22] An evolutionary perception inevitably adheres to a top-down line of command in control of widespread bureaucracies.[23] A national narrative will therefore tell the tales of kings and lords holding the power to mobilise and take advantage of resources in a centralised system.[24] When the nation-state becomes the interpretive frame, the sources are biased and monumental earthwork, written sources and metal-rich sites willingly lent themselves to the investigation. This way we end up doing circular endings. For instance, central places are seen as a sign of centrality, and the layout and material composition become the constituting element placing the site in a social hierarchy. However, what metal-rich compositions, large hall buildings and ritual performances as evident at the Tissø complex merely represent, is the fruit of centrality, a place where functions and relations meet and unite.[25] Accordingly, when the nation-state becomes the interpretational frame, other organisational forms are shadowed. As noted by David Graeber and David Wengrow (2021): 'exceptional islands of political hierarchy, surrounded by much larger territories whose inhabitants, if visible to the historians' eyes, are described […] as 'segmentary societies''.[26]

However, there are plenty of examples of societies that organise, trade, interact, fight, and evolve without state structures. Research demonstrates: '… how hundreds of small villages, competing for wealth, slaves and prestige are able to manage their intervillage affairs[?]' without waiting for centralisation and decision-making to be placed in the hands of chiefs.[27] Likewise, in his analysis of nodal points in early Viking Age Scandinavia, Sindbæk (2007) suggests that trading systems emerged and developed outside political organisations or centralised institutions: 'Regardless of the political situation, each participant in a long-distance exchange will have had a significant incentive to seek out what he considered the most favourable, safe and active places for trading'.[28] Furthermore, he states that '[o]ne can think of many other periods and parts of the world in which this type of non-political initiative may well have proved pivotal'.[29] Christopher Loveluck reaches the same conclusion for liminal coastal sites in northwest Europe suggesting that living conditions and social practises were of greater importance in shaping social organisation than tenurial demands.[30] James Flexner points to: '… the Piaroa from the Orinoco basin in South America, the Tiv from Nigeria, and the Malagasy of Madagascar as examples of anarchic societies that actively prevent anything resem-

22 Furholt et al. 2020
23 Graeber and Wengrow 2021, 360
24 Näsman 2006, 211
25 Lihammer 2003, 74
26 Graeber and Wengrow 2021, 382
27 Tollefson 1987; Angelbeck and Grier 2012
28 Sindbæk 2007, 128
29 Sindbæk 2007, 119
30 Loveluck 2013, 361

bling state power from emerging. One way is by simply moving away or disappearing whenever something like state power appears …'.[31] Marcel Mauss studied economies and markets without money and argued that for moral reasons, a gift-giving economy was a preferred and conscious model avoiding profit and, accordingly, inequality.[32] Likewise, Pierre Clastres offered an analysis of politics, demonstrating political organisations in Amazonian societies with distinct counteractions toward political powers.[33] Central to these analyses are systems that consciously function besides, outside or instead of state structures.

The Notion of Power

As argued, a strong focus on state formation has given prime agency to kings and magnates, resulting in a homogeneous identification of power and insufficient exploration of the notion of power.[34] Two interpretive lines can be followed; one imagines power as dominion – as a coercive or violent force or the threat or fear of such; another line focus on symbolic display, performances and sacred ancestral connections used to explain tributary relations.[35] Both, however, are spun in a discursive web of kings and chiefs, male dominion, aristocracy, and warrior elite with the objective to either force, deceive or manipulate a population to fulfil the goal of the individual, and both have a top-down perspective.[36] This may partly be caused by a lack of definition or assessment of the concept of power leaving the range of mechanisms involved in any power relation unaccounted for. For example, the fortification at the Erritsø hall dating to the 9th century excavated recently (Ravn et al.), is suggested to serve a clan 'who obtained the power but did not yet hold a strong powerbase'.[37] Likewise, cultural landscape analysis 'strongly suggests an area of aristocratic power'.[38] Further, … 'the Jelling dynasty now extent its power to the rest of Denmark'.[39] These examples should urge us to ask what kind of power? Dagfinn Skree (2010) has questioned Lars Jørgensen's (2010) model for the economic basis for the Tissø-complex pointing to practical difficulties in executing dominion over the local community due to the lack of accommodation for armed forces at the complex.[40] His comment illustrates how the range and execution of power and responses to such are often shadowed by a fixed and unfolded premise of power; in this case anticipating that the subjugated would willingly participate in corvée labour in a dominate manorial system. With a much more complex understanding of state forma-

---

31   Graeber 2004, 26-29; Flexner 2014, 84
32   Mauss 1925
33   Clastres 1989
34   Lund and Sindbæk 2021, 197-200
35   Jørgensen 2010; Dobat 2015
36   Lund, Furholt, and Austvoll 2022, 2
37   Therkildsen 2018, 186
38   Juel and Ravn 2016, 23
39   Nielsen 2010, 140, my translation
40   Jørgensen 2010; Skre 2010, 187

tion and power, we may begin to identify and understand a variety of agents, relations, actions and counteractions that are normally shadowed.

Alternative encounters to dominion

Michel Foucault makes clear that there are irreducibly multiple and heterogeneous forms of power flowing in every direction within the social fabric, offering multiple points of resistance.[41] The ontology of power is a philosophic subject of its own, and this is not the place to engage in discussion on the range of definitions. However, it illustrates that when dealing with power in any setting, it cannot be perceived as one-sided and formalistically. Reactions and receptions in the surrounding community, in wider social groups or by individuals being the subject of dominion whether in the form of cohesion, deception, manipulation or control will, subsequently, be overlooked. Furthermore, it leaves little room for counteractions, decentralisation, structural lability and network organisation and neither for transboundary behaviour nor conscious actions. The focus on discontinuity, non-linear developments and unexpected changes and actors are diminished, constricting our interpretive frame.[42] However, plenty of theoretical frameworks are posing nuanced perceptions of power. The archaeological evidence, likewise, supports a more nuanced notion of power than yet explored as demonstrated above. However, a theoretical glaze at some organisational alternatives to centralised power will help to expand our interpretive frame.

An anarchistic perspective has been introduced in recent years pointing to legitimised leaders, network organisation and decentralisation as powerful mechanisms in social organisation and has inspired my theoretical approach.[43] The idea is that legitimate leaders are accepted and useful in specific settings, but unjust dominion is met with decentralisation in the form of revolt, migration, resistance, or negotiations obtainable through network organisation. It stresses mutual aid, collectiveness and cooperation as structuring mechanisms holding a desire for self-government and liberty as the premise.[44] Graeber advances the concept of counterpower as a social mechanism and defines it as 'a collection of social institutions set in opposition to the state and capital: from self-governing communities to radical labour unions to popular militias'.[45] Likewise, a notion of counterpower is fundamental to Collective Action Theory, but here the means are identified as control over own resources in the form of labour, know-how and local knowledge; a collective resource that can be exercised in negotiations.[46] Carole Crumley (1995) proposes heterarchy as an alternative perspective suggesting that heterarchy and

---

41 Medina 2011, 10
42 Lihammer 2007, 23; Morgren 2013, 75; Furholt et al. 2020
43 Angelbeck and Grier 2012; Borake 2019a
44 Angelbeck and Grier 2012; Borake 2019; Furholt et al. 2020, 5
45 Graeber 2004, 27
46 Blanton and Fargher, 2008

hierarchies are not oppositional phenomena, but coexist in societies.[47] She argues for a multiscale and multirange social structure allowing multiple hierarchies in different contexts and settings operating from multiple interests and in multiple forms. Finally, an attempt to meet critique on a political economy approach for being centred on top-down processes has recently been put forward. It is argued that social segments with countervailing interests and strategies fundamental to political economies confront, limit, and co-opt elite power.[48] Common for these perspectives is an appreciation that people oppose unjust dominion but approve legitimised leaders, seeking self-government and liberty; that power also comes from the bottom up or from the outside in; and that power relations are dualistic and dichotomous.

Discussion

Having argued that state formations are multiscale, pointing to power based on collectivity and counteractions, and demonstrating how the archaeological material concedes bottom-up interpretations, it will be reasonable to ask what enables people to make their influence successful and to resist unjust dominion. Is it at all relevant to suggest such actions and agents when discussing state formation and power?

Questioning the primacy of hierarchy as the desired model for a complex society is counter-intuitive to westerners for whom the hierarchical organisation is deeply ingrained, and for whom concepts of cultural complexity are typically welded in ideas of progressive, social evolution[49]. From childhood, we are socialised into a grand national narrative, where national monuments and events are pivotal.[50] This also accounts for historians and archaeologists and thus for interpretations in human and social sciences. We must be conscious of this pitfall, and one way is critically exploring the notion of states and powers. In a new social history, Wengrow and Graeber (2021) ask with references to a critique of European civilisation from indigenous North Americans, when Europeans turned wealth, freedom, and faith into power. They propose that people we like to imagine as primitive and innocent perhaps were more imaginative than us when choosing to organise without rulers and bureaucracies.[51] This is thought-provoking, but agents, relations, actions, and counteractions that are normally shadowed may offer new conceptions. We must be critical as to what the ruling class claim they can do, what they are actually able to do, and the discourse in which we frame our interpretations.

I have argued that network organisations and communities held collective resources that enabled common actions but what means were at play? Firstly, knowledge is commonly understood as a means to power. The superior knowing expert is believed to serve as the prime agent, and others are ignorant, passive recipients or objects of this

---

47 Crumley 1995, 4
48 Furholt et al. 2020
49 Rathbone 2017, 2
50 Andersen, K.H. 2016, 48-50; Jenkins 2011
51 Graeber and Wengrow 2021, 65-73

knowledge.⁵² Using this argument, the value of local knowledge becomes vital. The local community was the superior knowing expert in a local or regional setting having access to raw material, infrastructure and mutual aid, granting them the upper hand in any conflict with long-distance chiefs or lords. Secondly, the notion of collective memory has seen increased recognition in recent years, although, mainly interpreted from a power perspective, in which authority over the past is seen as a means of social control.⁵³ However, collective memories have been recognised e.g., in grave goods, typology and monuments and the social identity and self-perceptions they offer may serve to identify and support different social interests and groupings. It can be argued that collective memories, accordingly, empower a local population or multiple social groups and relations. Thirdly, a phenomenon that likewise has seen increased interest in recent years due to economic and environmental crises is that of radical care. It builds on the idea that care is an efficient approach to push back structural disadvantages and to make community resiliency. Radical care inspires people to work together across class, race, ethnicity, religion, and state boundaries toward a common cause, and in the present day, grass-roots medical and dietary health support services remain a cornerstone of political movements that critique state and environmental racism. Care can be viewed as a set of acts, ideologies, and strategies that offer possibilities for living through uncertain times.⁵⁴ This way, care becomes a community resource and a pushback to unjust dominion. Further, technological innovation and development sustain influence. Development and adaption to new technologies are prone to rural sites arguably leaving rural communities in a favoured position. Signs of iron smelting are concentrated in Western Zealand whereas an Iron Age kingdom is proposedly identified in Eastern Zealand.⁵⁵ Ceramic kilns introduced in Denmark by the 12th century are all found in rural sites.⁵⁶ Other elements such as the wheel plough with great impact on agriculture production are likewise bound to rural sites with no obvious connection to elites.⁵⁷ Many technological advantages are rural prodigies unlikely to have favoured only the elite. Finally, in his work on Danish identity, Andersen (2016) concludes that around 800-900 the Danes had a certain sense of identity belonging to a common group or territory.⁵⁸ It must be understood as an imagined community feeling rather than a concrete one and a sense of common identity may have sustained collective actions.

But why are these agents and actions so difficult to grasp? Why do history and archaeology not lend themselves to a more nuanced perspective? The material leaves only very little opportunity to give the whole population a voice. Many people; women,

52 Focault 1980; Hobart 1993, 4
53 Pedersen 2006; Lund and Sindbæk 2021, 179-180
54 Hobart and Kneese 2020; Fredengren 2020
55 Lund Hansen 1995; Voss 2002
56 Koch 2001
57 Larsen 2015
58 Andersen, K.H. 2016, 387

children; peasants and slaves are lost in the material and historical records. However, it may be deliberate. Staying outside the institutionalised spotlight might be a useful strategy to avoid repression, consequently leading to an absence from the historical record. Moreover, resistance and decentralisation might not be historically recorded as they do not favour the strategy of an institutionalised organisation, and only when they succeed or fail dramatically do such actions enter the record.[59] Furthermore, the focus is biased: the most sustained fieldwork efforts in Northern Europe have been directed at supposedly royal monuments and for long in the hands of the primary male researcher.[60] Likewise, the majority of sites and monuments on UNESCO's world heritage list have a royal connotation[61]. Local communities and counteractions are granted very little attention.

Conclusion

If we target monumental and royal sites and pursue grand narratives in the quest for fixed notions of a state, we 'entail a risk of embracing existing narratives rather than challenging the equilibrium of research'.[62] Social conflict leads to the suspension of old organisational forms but restates a new social organisation on the ruins. Subsequently, we experience short- or long-term oscillations in manifestation and emphasis 'with shifts from autonomy to domination, from involuntary identifications to free associations, from cooperation to competitiveness, from hierarchy to heterarchy, and from imposed to justified authorities'.[63] Various trans-historical and trans-geographical and trans-disciplinary examples of collective and democratic forms of decision-making, resources, influences, and counteractions as demonstrated above, suggest that archaeological research will benefit from a wider perspective. Defining power as a complex set of relations rather than as cohesive or manipulative domination will help interpret accumulated and ambiguous evidence. Lewis Borck and Matthew Sanger (2017) suggest that: 'Instead of being constructed by purposeful actions of elite individuals, these top-down societies may grow like weeds from cracks spreading in the social processes meant to limit aggrandizement'.[64] Human history is not about equal access to resources; land, calories, infrastructure, knowledge and so on, although these elements are not without value, but rather about our capacity to contribute to decisions about how we live together.[65] The overall problem with a grand narrative favouring an excessive focus on power and prestige and centralisation and institutionalisation is that it evades and excludes other perspectives. I believe that the notion of collec-

---

59 Scott 1985, 350; 2009, 34; 2012, 12-13
60 Lund and Sindbæk 2021, 27, 32
61 Jensen 2009
62 Lund and Sindbæk 2021, 26
63 Angelbeck and Grier 2012, 568
64 Borck and Sanger 2017, 11
65 Graeber and Wengrow 2021, 8

tive or consensus-based powers will expand the interpretive potential, and by gazing beyond 'aristocratic environments', 'king's manors' and 'elite residences' will bring new reflections to archaeological research.

Bibliography

Andersen, H.H. 1998: *Danevirke og Kovirke: arkæologiske undersøgelser 1861-1993*. Moesgård Museums Skrifter. Århus: Jysk arkæologisk Selskab.

Andersen H.H. 2004: *Til Hele Rigets Værn: Danevirkes Arkæologi Og Historie*. Højbjerg: Moesgård.

Andersen, K.H. 2016: "Da Danerne Blev Danske. Dansk Etnicitet Og Identitet Til ca. År 1000." Upubliceret Ph.D.-afhandling, Institut for Kultur og Samfund, Historisk afdeling: Aarhus Universitet.

Angelbeck, B. & C. Grier 2012: "Anarchism and the Archaeology of Anarchic Societies: Resistance to Centralization in the Coast Salish Region of the Pacific Northwest Coast." *Current Anthropology* 53 (5), 547-87. https://doi.org/10.1086/667621.

Blanton, R.E. & L. Fargher 2008: *Collective Action in the Formation of Pre-Modern States*. Fundamental Issues in Archaeology. New York, N.Y.: Springer.

Borake, T. 2019a: "Anarchistic Action. Social Organization and Dynamics in Southern Scandinavia from the Iron Age to the Middle Ages." *Archaeological Dialogues* 26 (2): 61-73. https://doi.org/10.1017/S1380203819000151.

Borake, T. 2019b: "No Man Is an Island – Anarchism and Social Complexity in Western Zealand 550-1350." PhD-dissertation, Aarhus: Aarhus Universitet.

Borake, T. 2022: "Affiliated and Antagonistic Actions." *Tings Tale, Tidsskrift for Materiel Kultur*. 2022 (4), 27-44.

Borck, L., & M.C. Sanger. 2017: "An Introduction to Anarchism in Archaeology." *The SAA Archaeological Record: The Magazine of the Society for American Archaeology* Vol. 17 (1): 9-16.

Brink, S. 1998: "Land, Bygd, Distrikt Och Centralorter i Sydsverige. Några Bebyggelseshistoriska Nedslag." In *Centrala Platser, Centrala Frågor: Samhällsstrukturen under Järnåldern: En Vänbok till Berta Stjernquist*, edited by Birgitta Hårdh and Lars Larsson. Acta Archaeologica Lundensia. Series in 8:O, Nr. 28. Stockholm: Almquist & Wiksell.

Christiansen, T.E. 1971: "Træningslejr Eller Tvangsborg", *Kuml. Årbog for Jysk Arkæologisk Selskab* 1970: 43-63.

Christiansen, T.T. & T. Sarauw. 2014: "Central Places in Abundance? The Eastern Lim-Fjord Area in the Late Iron Age and Viking Age", in *Wealth and Complexity: Economically Specialised Sites in Late Iron Age Denmark*, edited by E. Stidsing, K. Høilund Nielsen & R. Fiedel. East Jutland Museum Publications; Vol. 1. Randers: East Jutland Museum, 127-142.

Clastres, P. 1989: *Society against the State: Essays in Political Anthropology*. New York: Zone Books.

Crumley, C.L. 1995: "Heterarchy and the Analysis of Complex Societies", *Archaeological Papers of the American Anthropological Association* 6 (1): 1-5. https://doi.org/10.1525/ap3a.1995.6.1.1.

Dobat, A.S. 2008: "Danevirke Revisited: An Investigation into Military and Socio-Political Organisation in South Scandinavia (c AD 700 to 1100)." *Medieval Archaeology* 52 (1): 27-67. https://doi.org/10.1179/174581708X335431.

Dobat, A.S. 2015: "Viking Stranger-Kings: The Foreign as a Source of Power in Viking Age Scandinavia, or, Why There Was a Peacock in the Gokstad Ship Burial?: Viking Stranger-Kings", *Early Medieval Europe* 23 (2): 161-201. https://doi.org/10.1111/emed.12096.

Earle, T. & M. Spriggs. 2015: "Political Economy in Prehistory: A Marxist Approach to Pacific Sequences", *Current Anthropology* 56 (4): 515-44. https://doi.org/10.1086/682284.

Fenger, O. 1989: *Kirker Rejses Alle Vegne: 1050-1250*. Gyldendal, København 1989.

Feveile, C. 2018: "Nordøstfyn – Fra Ingen Til Mange Metalrige Pladser På Få År", in *Viele Funde – Grosse Bedeutung?, Potenzial Und Aussagewert von Metalldetektorfunden Für Die Siedlungsarchäologische Forschung Der Wikingerzeit, Bericht Des 33. Tværfaglige Vikingesymposiums, 9. Mai 2014, Wikinger Museum Haithabu*, edited by Volker Hilberg and Thorsten Lemm. Kiel: Ludwig: 29-48.

Flexner, J.L. 2014: "The Historical Archaeology of States and Non-States: Anarchist Perspectives from Hawai'i and Vanuatu", *Journal of Pacific Archaeology* Vol. 5 (2): 81-97.

Foucault, M. 1980: *Power/Knowledge: Selected Interviews and Other Writings, 1972-1977*, edited by C. Gordon. New York, N.Y.: Pantheon Books.

Fredengren, C. 2020: "Radical Cultural-Environment-Care", Nordic Tag, Oslo. 2020.

Fritzbøger, B. 2006: "Fællesskabstiden – Fra Middelalderen Til 1800-Tallet", in *Naturen i Danmark*, edited by Kaj Sand-Jensen. København: Gyldendal.

Furholt, M., C. Grier, M. Spriggs & T. Earle. 2020: "Political Economy in the Archaeology of Emergent Complexity: A Synthesis of Bottom-Up and Top-Down Approaches." *Journal of Archaeological Method and Theory* 27 (2): 157-91. https://doi.org/10.1007/s10816-019-09422-0.

Graeber, D. 2004: *Fragments of an Anarchist Anthropology*. Paradigm; 14. Chicago: Prickly Paradigm Press.

Graeber, D. & D. Wengrow. 2021: *The Dawn of Everything: A New History of Humanity*. London: Allen Lane, an imprint of Penguin Books.

Hobart, H.J.K. & T. Kneese. 2020: "Radical Care: Survival Strategies for Uncertain Times." *Social Text* 38 (1): 1-16. https://doi.org/10.1215/01642472-7971067.

Hobart, M. 1993: *An Anthropological Critique of Development: The Growth of Ignorance*. EIDOS Series. London: Routledge.

Hoff, A. 1997: *Lov og landskab: landskabslovenes bidrag til forståelsen af landbrugs- og landskabsudviklingen i Danmark ca. 900-1250*. Aarhus: Aarhus Universitetsforlag.

Iversen, F. 2013: "Big Bang, Lordship or Inheritance? Changes in the Settlement Structure on the Threshold of the Merovingian Period, South-Eastern Norway", in *Hierarchies in Rural Settlements,* edited by J. Klápště. Brepols Publishers, Turnhout, 341-358.

Jenkins, R. 2011: *Being Danish: Paradoxes of Identity in Everyday Life*. København: Museum Tusculanum.

Jensen, M.B. 2009: "Royal Jelling: Danish National Heritage Reinvented." *Archaeological Review from Cambridge. 2009*. Vol. 24 (No. 1): 77-93.

Jørgensen, L. 2010: "Gudme and Tissø. Two Magnates' Complexes in Denmark from the 3rd to the 11th Century AD," in *Trade and Communication Networks of the First Millennium AD in the Northern Part of Central Europe: Central Places, Beach Markets, Landing Places and Trading Centres*, edited by B. Ludowici. (Neue Studien Zur Sachsenforschung, 1). Stuttgart: Theiss, 273-286.

Juel, C. & M. Ravn. 2016: "Erritsø – A Fortified Early Viking Age Manor near Lillebælt," in *Fortified Settlements in Early Medieval Europe: Defended Communities of the 8th-10th Centuries*, edited by N. Christie & H. Herold. Oxford: Oxbow Books.

Koch, J. 2001: "Projekt Middelalderlige Pottemagerovne", *Hikuin*, Middelalderlige pottemagerovne, 28 (28): 7-9.

Larsen, L.A. 2015: "Muldfjælsplovens tidlige historie – Fra yngre romersk jernalder til middelalder." *Kuml*, 165-200.

Lihammer, A. 2003: "Kungen Och Landskapet. Funderingar Kring Förändringar i Västra Skåne under Sen Vikingatid Och Tidig Medeltid," in *Landskapsarkeologi Och Tidig Medeltid: Några Exempel Från Södra Sverige*, edited by J. Thomasson and M. Anglert. (Acta Archaeologica Lundensia. Series in 8°, 41). Department of Archaeology and Ancient History, Lund University, 71-114.

Lihammer, A. 2007: *Bortom riksbildningen: människor, landskap och makt i sydöstra Skandinavien*. (Lund studies in historical archaeology, 7). Lund: Institutionen för arkeologi och antikens historia, Lunds universitet.

Loveluck, C. 2013: *Northwest Europe in the Early Middle Ages, c. AD 600-1150: A Comparative Archaeology*. Cambridge; Cambridge University Press.

Lund Hansen, U. 1995: *Himlingøje – Seeland – Europa: Ein Gräberfeld Der Jüngeren Römischen Kaiserzeit Auf Seeland, Seine Bedeutung Und Internationalen Beziehungen*. (Nordiske Fortidsminder. Serie B, Band 13). Kbh: Det Kongelige Nordiske Oldskriftselskab.

Lund, J., M. Furholt & K.I. Austvoll. 2022: "Reassessing Power in the Archaeological Discourse. How Collective, Cooperative and Affective Perspectives May Impact Our Understanding of Social Relations and Organization in Prehistory." *Archaeological Dialogues*, 1-18. https://doi.org/10.1017/S1380203822000162.

Lund, J. & S.M. Sindbæk. 2021: "Crossing the Maelstrom: New Departures in Viking Archaeology." *Journal of Archaeological Research* 30 (2) 2021: 169-229. https://doi.org/10.1007/s10814-021-09163-3.

Mauss, M. 1925: *The Gift: Forms and Functions of Exchange in Archaic Societies*. Faksimile udgave. Miami: HardPress Publishing.

McGuire, R.H. & D.J. Saitta. 1996: "Although They Have Petty Captains, They Obey Them Badly: The Dialectics of Prehispanic Western Pueblo Social Organization." *American Antiquity* 61 (2), 197-216. https://doi.org/10.2307/282418.

Medina, J. 2011: "Toward a Foucaultian Epistemology of Resistance: Counter-Memory, Episte-Mic Friction, and Guerrilla Pluralism." *Foucault Studies,* 2011 (12), 9-35.

Morgren, M. 2013: "The First Sparks and the Far Horizons Stirring up the Thinking on the Earliest Scandinavian Urbanization Processes – Again", *Lund Archaeological Review* 2013 (18), 73-88.

Näsman, U. 2006: "Danerne og det danske kongeriges opkomst: om forskningsprogrammet 'Fra stamme til stat i Danmark'", *Kuml* 2006, 205-241.

Nielsen, H. 2010: *Middelalderen bag tallene. Middelalderens befolkningsudvikling, landbrug, bebyggelse og økonomi belyst ud fra listerne i Kong Valdemars Jordebog og andre kilder.* København.

Olsen, A.B. 2015: "Courtyard Sites in Western Norway. Central Assembly Places and Judicial Institutions in the Late Iron Age," in *Viking Worlds: Things, Spaces and Movement*, edited by M. Hem Eriksen, U. Pedersen, B. Rundberget, I. Axelsen & H. Lund Berg, Oxford: Oxbow Books, 43-55.

Pedersen, A. 2006: "Ancient Mounds for New Graves: An Aspect of Viking Age Burial Customs in Southern Scandinavia", in *Old Norse Religion in Long-Term Perspectives: Origins, Changes and Interactions, An International Conference in Lund, Sweden, June 3-7, 2004*, edited by A. Andrén, K. Jennbert & C. Raudvere. Vagar till Midgård 8. Lund: Nordic Academic Press, 346-353.

Randsborg, K. 1980: *The Viking Age in Denmark: The Formation of a State.* London: Duckworth.

Rathbone, S. 2017: "Anarchist Literature and the Development of Anarchist Counter-Archaeologies", *World Archaeology* 49 (3): 291-305. https://doi.org/10.1080/00438243.2017.1333921.

Saitta, D.J. 1994: "Class and Community in the Prehistoric Southwest", in *The Ancient Southwestern Community: Models and Methods for the Study of Prehistoric Social Organization*, edited by W.H. Wills. Albuquerque: Univ. of New Mexico Press.

Sanmark, A. 2009: "Administrative Organisation and State Formation: A Case Study of Assembly Sites in Södermanland, Sweden." *Medieval Archaeology* 53 (1), 205-241. https://doi.org/10.1179/007660909X12457506806289.

Sanmark, A. 2017: *Viking Law and Order: Places and Rituals of Assembly in the Medieval North.* Edinburgh: Edinburgh University Press.

Scott, J.C. 1985: *Weapons of the Weak: Everyday Forms of Peasant Resistance.* New Haven: Yale University Press.

Scott, J.C. 2009: *The Art of Not Being Governed: An Anarchist History of Upland Southeast Asia.* Yale Agrarian Studies Series. New Haven, Conn.: Yale University Press.

Scott, J.C. 2012: *Two Cheers for Anarchism: Six Easy Pieces on Autonomy, Dignity, and Meaningful Work and Play.* Princeton: Princeton University Press.

Semple, S., & A. Sanmark. 2013: "Assembly in North West Europe: Collective Concerns for Early Societies?", *European Journal of Archaeology* 16 (3), 518-542. https://doi.org/10.1179/1461957113Y.0000000035.

Sindbæk, S.M. 2007: "Networks and Nodal Points: The Emergence of Towns in Early Viking Age Scandinavia." *Antiquity* 81 (311): 119-32. https://doi.org/10.1017/S0003598X00094886.

Sindbæk, S.M. 2017: "Borgring and Harald Bluetooth's Burgenpolitik", In *Viking Encounters*, edited by A. Pedersen & S.M. Sindbæk. Proceedings of the Eighteenth Viking Congress, Denmark, August 6-12, 2017. Aarhus University Press, 529-543.

Skre, D. 2010: Review of *Comment on: Gudme and Tissø. Two Magnates' Complexes in Denmark from the 3rd to the 11th Century AD*, by L. Jørgensen. Edited by B. Ludowici. *Trade and Communication Networks of the First Millennium AD in the Northern Part of Central Europe: Central Places, Beach Markets, Landing Places and Trading Centres*, (Neue Studien zur Sachsenforschung, 1), 273-86.

Skre, D. 2022: "Scandinavian Kingship AD 500-1000", *Neue Studien Zur Sachsenforschung.* 2022 (11): 117-131.

Storm, G. 1900: *Norges Kongesagaer, 1914-Utgaven.* Snorre Sturlasøn: Heimskringla, Bd. 1-2. Kristiania: I.M. Stenersen, i Hovedkommission.

Terkildsen, K.F. 2018: "Yngre jernalders eliteresidenser i Jylland", *Kuml*, 171-213.

Tollefson, K.D. 1987: "The Snoqualmie: A Puget Sound Chiefdom." *Ethnology* 26 (2), 121-136. https://doi.org/10.2307/3773450.

Voss, O. 2002: "Jernalderproduktionen i Danmark i Oldtid Og Middelalder – Status Og Fremtid", in *Drik – Og Du Vil Leve Skønt: Festskrift Til Ulla Lund Hansen På 60-Årsdagen 18. August 2002*, edited by J. Pind, A. Nørgård Jørgensen, L. Jørgensen, B. Storgaard, P.O. Rindel, and J. Ilkjær, 139-148. Publications from the National Museum, Vol. 7. Cph: The National Museum of Denmark, Danish Collections.

Witte, F. 2015: "Danevirke – udgravninger ved porten", *Fund & fortid* 2015, nr. 2/3. Jubilæumsudgave (2015): 86-88.

BY MADS RUNGE

Chapter 3
From Central Space to Urban Place
Growth and Centrality in the Fjord Landscapes of Aalborg and Odense from the 5th to 12th Century

ABSTRACT

This article examines the early urbanisation in southern Scandinavia from AD 400-1100. The project, involving multiple museums and universities, explores the origins of the towns Aalborg and Odense, analysing their relationship with their hinterlands. The study identifies different organizational entities, such as primary vills and hundreds, and assesses whether towns developed from local elite environments or through top-down processes. The research highlights how local magnates and royal power interacted, and it emphasizes the importance of local networks, trade, military, and religious factors in the urbanisation process.

In the research project, *From Central Space to Urban Place*, funded by the VELUX FOUNDATION and conducted over the years 2017-2021, the early urbanisation in southern Scandinavia was analysed based on the relationship between town and hinterland within the period AD 400-1100. The project involved archeology, history, place names and natural sciences. In the project Museum Odense, Museum of North Jutland, Museums of Eastern Funen, Moesgaard Museum, National Museum of Denmark, University of Southern Denmark, University of Copenhagen and Aarhus University participated. The project's research is presented in a major anthology and at two international seminars, the presentation of which have been published.[1] In addition, several reports with background knowledge about the many scientific analysis and description of dissemination and education initiatives are presented.[2] A comprehensive overview of the project's results can be seen and downloaded from Museum Odense'

---

1 Hansen and Runge 2018; Bjerregaard et al. 2022
2 Mogensen et al. 2021

webpage.[3] The following article is a summary of the analysis presented *in toto* in the main research publication of the project.[4]

From Central Space to Urban Place and Aristocratic residences of Northern Europe

In the centuries predating their urbanisation, the areas around Aalborg and Odense have several localities and artefacts of an elite calibre. Sites and objects can be grouped within different spheres, such as trade and specialized crafts, military and religion. By assessing these indicators within an organizational framework corresponding to the hundreds, it is possible to approach elite environments, which contain elements from all the central spheres.

In the project, the analyses are used to assess whether the towns originate in the elite environments of the Late Iron Age and the Viking Age or whether the towns instead are established via top-down and externally initiated processors. It must be stressed that the project supports the idea that from around AD 600 there is a Danish kingdom and an almost fully divided landscape.[5] Thus, it is in this context that the relationship between independent magnates and royal power must be addressed.

The analyses do not go into detail with regard to specific "aristocratic residences", but instead look at general trends. The trends can help to clarify the resource and social background for the elite environments and the towns, just as they can help understand the extent to which the local magnates have been able to act independently or vice versa, when a royal control becomes more visible.

Space and place

Theoretically, a fundamental aspect of the project is the *space* and *place* perspective. In this project, *space* and *place* are primarily used in a structural sense. Structurally, *space* is perceived as an "open" organisational form, whereby the various functions in a specific unit, for example a magnate's residence, are situated in several different locations distributed over a large geographical area – i.e. the residential area in one place, military functions in another, trade and crafts in a third place, and so on (Fig. 1). *Space* can thereby be equated in many ways with central-place complexes as exemplified by such as Gudme-Lundeborg and Uppåkra in the Late Iron Age – Viking Age.[6] The term *place*, on the other hand, is perceived here as a "closed" organisational form, for example a town, combining the range of functions that in a *space* are distributed across several

---

[3] https://odensebysmuseer.dk/en/research/research-projects/from-central-space-to-urban-place/
[4] Runge et al. 2021, especially Runge 2021a
[5] E.g., Näsman 2006; Hansen 2021b
[6] Brink 1999a, 37ff.; Fabech 1999

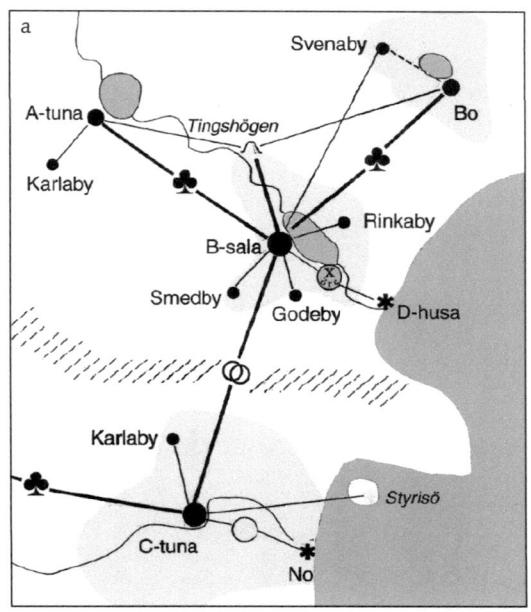

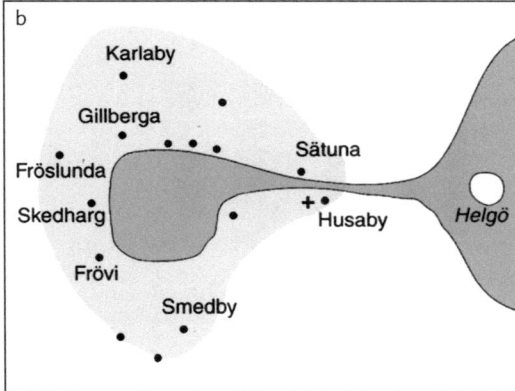

Fig. 1. Model of a hierarchical central-place complex, with an illustration of the presumed relationship between the sites. Large dots: major hall. Medium dots: minor hall. Small dot: farm/hamlet. Asterix: port of trade. Interlocking rings: alliance by marriage. Clover: alliance by gifts etc. Coin: "customs". b: An idealised place-name environment. Brink 1999b: 434 (25).

locations. *Space* and *place* are terms which support the central-place theory and the growth-centre theory, which are other fundamental elements of the project.[7]

By isolating the central functions that each of the organisational forms contain, it is possible to compare the towns with the predecessors in the central spaces. Against this background it can be analysed whether towns may have an origin in a local hinterland or whether the earliest urbanisation is a result of an external influence. It is also possible to establish which societal spheres have had the greatest impact on the individual urbanisation process.

---

7   Christaller 1968; Perroux 1971; Christensen 2016, 21ff.; Runge 2021b, 21f.

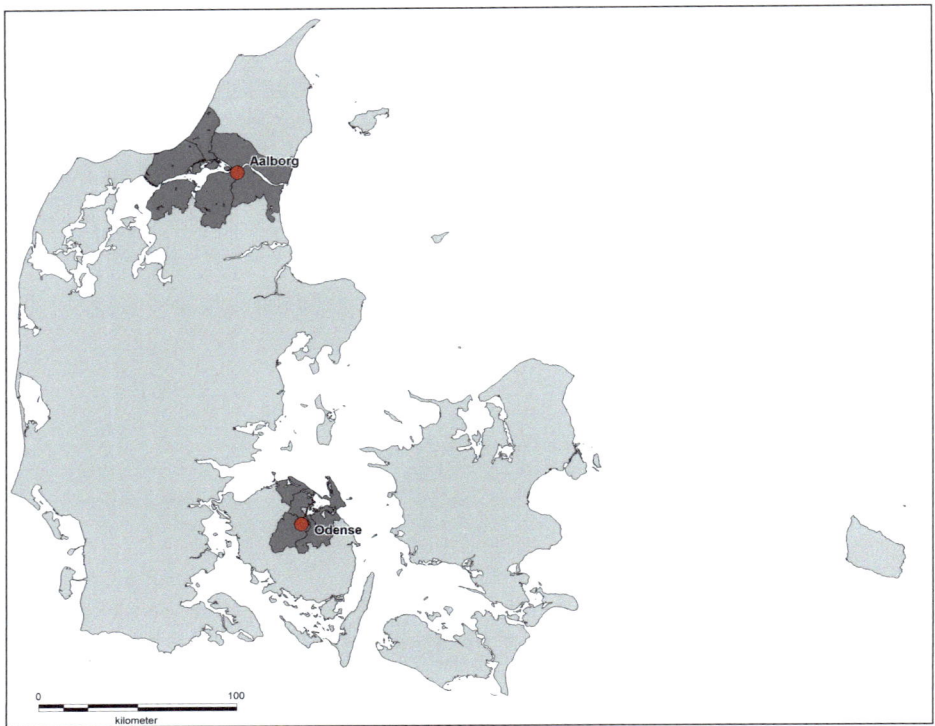

Fig. 2. The two study areas and their hundreds. Graphics: Mads Runge. (15).

The timeframe for the project, is divided up into three phases: 1) c. AD 400-600, 2) c. AD 600-900, 3) c. AD 900-1100. The three phases reflect marked development stages within the study's range of topics and across the various spheres it examines. The following focus will be on phases 2 and 3.

Various organisational entities have been identified that are assumed to coincide with different levels in the pre-urban central spaces. Around AD 600, the so-called primary vills appear as part of a general agro-economic reorganisation, with the spatially fixed villages as foundation stones, and as representatives of an individual village's resource area.[8] At a level above this system was a layer of a greater organisational entity which presumably corresponded to the hundreds. The dating of the hundreds is much debated, but it is argued that they can probably be extended back to the Late Germanic Iron Age.[9]

In conclusion, organisationally and geographically, the central spaces are in the project understood in a framework corresponding to the hundreds. Thus, it is possible to conceive of a central magnate placed in one of the primary vills in a hundred and the other central functions distributed across other primary vills in that hundred. Of

---

8   Hansen 2015, 146; 2021b
9   Hansen 2015, 177; 2021b, 175f.

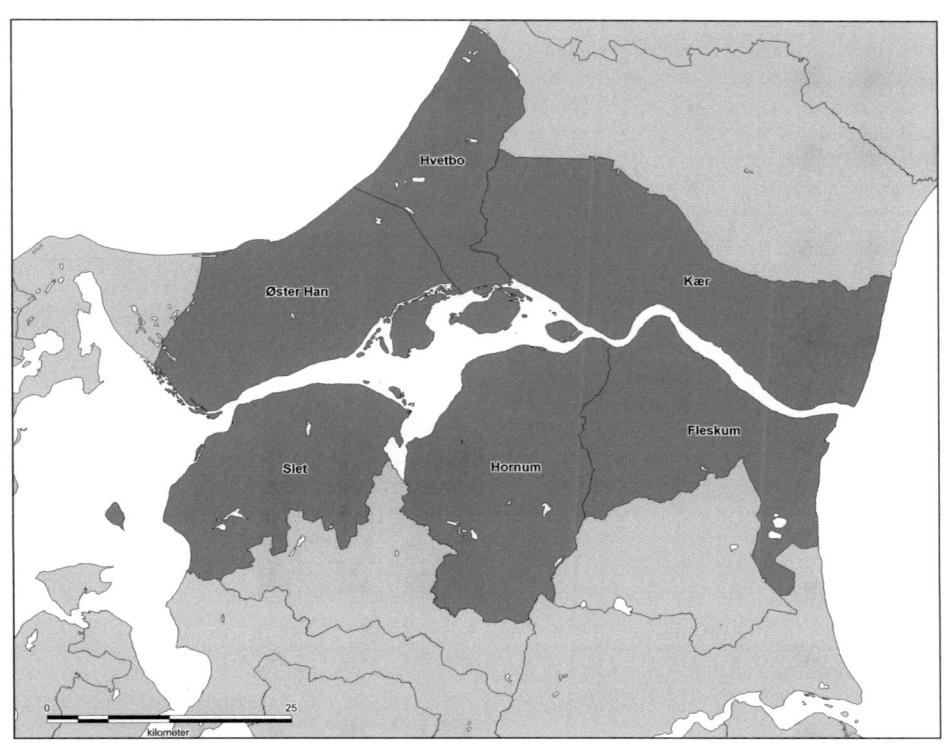
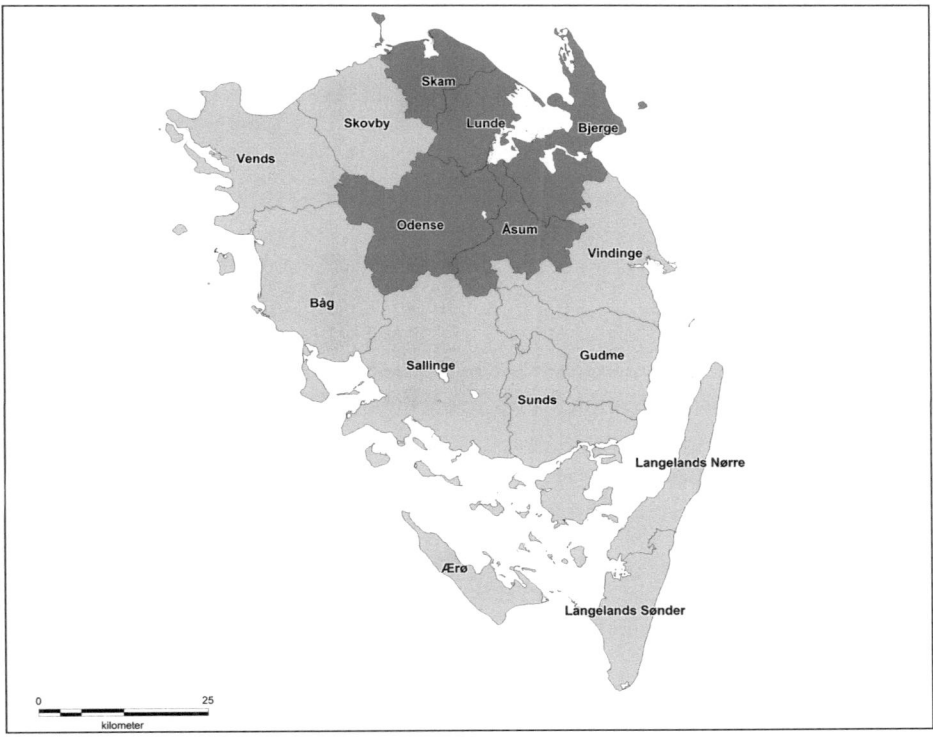

Chapter 3 • From Central Space to Urban Place   37

Fig. 3. *Relief map of the landscape around the eastern Limfjord. © The Danish Geodata Agency (22).*

the study areas, the Bjerge hundred on Northeast Funen is the best-known example of a central space in terms of sources.[10]

Landscape, settlement and logistics

The study areas consist of the hundreds around the eastern Limfjord in northern Jutland, and Odense Fjord – Kertinge Nor on the island of Funen (Fig. 2).

The terrain of the eastern Limfjord is characterised by large hill islands alternating with the low-lying plain of the raised Stone Age seabed (Fig. 3). Throughout prehistoric and historical times, settlement has been almost exclusively limited to these hill islands, while lower-lying areas would have been exploited for grazing. Large heathland expanses have also characterised the area and constituted a significant resource.[11]

Throughout a major part of prehistory, the Limfjord has been a main waterway with important functions for E-W traffic, and not just at a regional level.[12] Together with the unusual character of the hinterland's topography and several N-S-oriented watercourses extending back from the Limfjord deep into the hinterland, this has led to activities being oriented towards the fjord.[13] The land traffic was consequently N-S-oriented, at the obvious crossing places over the fjord at Aggersborg and Aalborg. Aalborg's late classification as a bishopric could be due, among other things, to the road links northwards

---

10   Christensen 2016; Runge 2021b, 301f.
11   Beck et al. 2021b, 32ff.
12   Sarauw 2019, 246
13   J.N. Nielsen 1999, 215

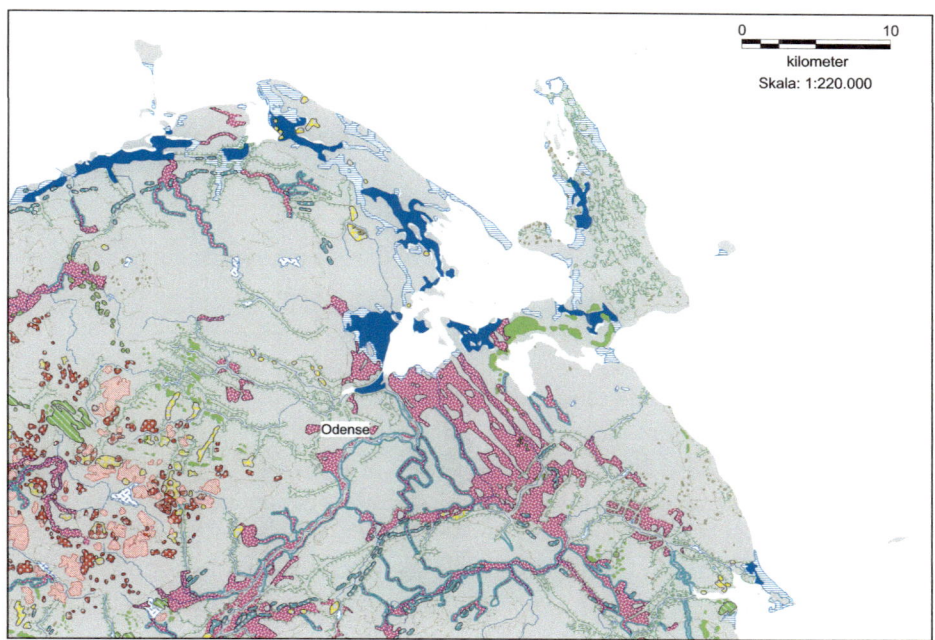

The geomorphology of the Funen archipelago. Digitalised by Adam Schacke after Smed (1962) (16). Fig. 4.

not being developed earlier. Until the Early Middle Ages, Aalborg's urbanisation appears to have been oriented towards the south.[14]

Northeast Funen is characterised by good agricultural soils with no marked differences in the terrain. The exception to this is the hilly landscape in the northern part of the Hindsholm/Bjerge hundred, where Fyns Hoved and Munkebo Bakke stand out as conspicuous landscape formations (Fig. 4). Up until the Early Iron Age, the heavy soils here were presumably difficult to cultivate and characterised by smaller settlements.[15] The new, improved cultivation forms and implements that were introduced in the Late Iron Age resulted in a higher degree of cultivation, and villages became a dominant element.[16]

The waterscapes of Odense Fjord and Kerteminde Nor/Kerteminde Fjord offer a number of natural harbours, and barrages indicate that these facilities have been important. It has not been possible to sail larger vessels up the Odense river and, therefore, the town was oriented to a greater degree towards the interior and land traffic.[17] The land-traffic situation, as shown on historical maps of the late 18th century, appears to have been established already in the Late Iron Age as there is major coincidence between

---

14 Møller and Haue 2021, 65ff.
15 Runge 2014, 169ff.
16 Hansen 2017, 171ff.
17 Beck et al. 2021b, 24ff.

the locations of metal-rich sites, and the historical road network.[18] At the same time, northeast Funen occupied an important strategic position relative to the Kattegat and the Great Belt.

Growth factors and manifestations of power

Trade and specialised crafts
The Limfjord region was a central transit and trade waterway throughout the entire study period and, consequently, specialised crafts appear to have played a significant role as a growth factor. The large metal-rich sites on the hill islands bordering the Limfjord have to a great extent been in continual use, though a degree of displacement in their location over time can be detected. After around AD 600, the metal-rich complexes were oriented in relation to the stationary villages.[19]

Several of the metal-rich sites have large clusters of sunken-featured buildings (hereafter called Grubenhäuser). These localities became more common and more extensive from the Late Roman Iron Age and up through the Germanic Iron Age. From the 8th century, they were linked to the emergence of the warp-weighted loom and extensive sailcloth production. It is obvious here to link the sailcloth production with the Viking campaigns and expeditions and the Limfjord's role as an anchorage and mustering place prior to the raids westwards.[20] The production of sail cloth was an important growth factor, which, with time, rendered the area attractive to the central power.

From the 8th century AD, a concentration of grubenhäuser appeared in the area that later became Aalborg. These buildings are perceived as being a seasonally occupied trading place on a par with other similar occurrences along the Limfjord. But around AD 900, the town was fortified, and a series of plots were laid out, presumably as a parcelling out of a market area, as seen for example at the Ribe emporium. The plots or parcels were established on a minor, raised area alongside the S-N course or the river Østerå, which together with an E-W-oriented street alongside the fjord, the later Algade, formed the axis in the earliest Aalborg.[21] By this time, at the latest, Aalborg stood out from the other trading places along the Limfjord.

An important reason for this development was presumably that of location, as an obvious crossing place over the central and eastern parts of the Limfjord, supported the steadily increasing trade which characterised the region at that time. This is evident from the coupling to a major trade network, the second phase of emporia in southern Scandinavia, with trade in goods such as soapstone etc. from Norway.[22] The opportunity to settle close to the coast was presumably another significant factor, as this has given more direct access to trade.

---

18   Møller and Haue 2021
19   Hansen 2021b, 175ff.
20   Sarauw 2021, 155f.
21   J.N. Nielsen 1999
22   Søvsø 2020, 241ff.

It is suggested that this new trade pattern, which featured long-distance trade of everyday goods, resulted in a direct progression from space to place, in that people living on the chalk hill islands around Aalborg saw an advantage in moving to the coastal Aalborg.[23] The place's fortification, and perhaps also the parcelling out, may reflect the presence of the central power from around AD 900.[24]

The number of artefacts representing long-distance trade in everyday goods is much less prominent in Odense compared with Aalborg, probably reflecting a more inland-based, regional trading pattern.[25] These differences between Odense and Aalborg are presumably attributable to their distance from Norway, where most of these artefacts originated. Long distance goods are more normal at the metal-rich sites of Odense's hinterland; probably due to the latter having a closer connection to the sea. A large body of archaeological material from Odense in the Middle Ages support the theory of a primarily locally oriented trading pattern also in the Viking Age.[26]

Trade and specialised crafts do not feature prominently in the place-name evidence in Northeast Funen, while the archaeological record reveals traces of trade and specialised crafts at all metal-rich sites through phase 2.[27] In Odense, on the other hand, it is not until phase 3 that traces of specialised crafts, and thereby indirectly trade, become evident.[28] Thus, except for the later part of phase 3, it cannot be concluded that trade and specialised crafts were of any special focus in Odense.

Military

In the Aalborg area the military elements are not quite as prominent as on Northeast Funen. In phase 2, the military indicators in the North Jutland area are both few and uncertain. Minor war booty depositions at central settlements may, however, suggest the existence of a structure corresponding to military structures concentrated in a few magnate environments.

In phase 3, a couple of central structures become evident by the Limfjord: The urban fortifications in Aalborg and the ring fortress of Aggersborg in, respectively, the early and the late 10th century. Several potential beacon sites are also evident, distributed along both sides of the fjord, from its eastern opening towards its central part. Although the beacon names are later than the Middle Ages, they can perhaps provide indications of defence systems further back in time.[29] The placement of a fortified town and a ring fortress in the eastern and central part of the fjord should probably be perceived as the central power's attempts to control the two most important crossing places over the

---

23 J.N. Nielsen 1998, 299
24 Vrængmose Jensen 2017, 83
25 Runge 2021b, 294f.
26 Brandt et al. 2018; Dam et al. 2021, 63ff.
27 Albris and Christensen 2021, 44f.; Beck 2021; Beck et al. 2021a
28 Jensen 2021; Runge and Henriksen 2018, 16f.
29 Christiansen et al. 2018; Albris and Christensen 2021, 41ff.

fjord as well as the E-W water route. Aalborg's urban fortifications were also intended to protect an important trading place.

In the Funen area, in phase 2, a clustering of military elements is evident around the centres of Glavendrup, Rosenlund/Rønninge and Ladby. These comprise rich weapon graves and references on runestones. Their location in affluent environments distinguishes them from the ordinary warrior stratum. The three areas lie equidistant from Odense.[30] Refuges, presumably constructed on the initiative of the local community and therefore a bottom-up development, are supplemented by actual military structures such as Munkebo Bakke, with palisade from the 7th-8th centuries AD.

In phase 3, a large collective military system is evident on Northeast Funen, with Nonnebakken centrally placed in the hinterland, barrages in Kerteminde Fjord, potential naval harbours and possible beacon warning systems along Odense Fjord and, not least, out towards Fyns Hoved and perhaps Munkebo Bakke. Fyns Hoved was well-placed in relation to being able to monitor shipping routes towards the Kattegat and the Great Belt/Baltic. This part of Funen also has the greatest concentrations of beacon names.[31] Munkebo Bakke had a central position in this respect. A hypothetical fortification of Viking Age Odense can also be mentioned.[32] The development probably reflects the central power's desire to dominate larger areas, partly to unite the realm, partly to protect against now more evident external threats.[33]

Military developments should primarily be seen as a response to changes in external threats as well as general military-technological advances. Regardless of the reasons behind the development in the military sphere, the sector would have functioned as a growth factor, but to varying extents. The ring fortress at Nonnebakken e.g., must, to some degree, create lasting growth while other elements – barrages and other military elements without staffing – perhaps did not have a long growth effect.

Religion
In phase 2 a number of place names referring to the pagan religion are evenly distributed south of the Limfjord. While there are several *vi* names on Funen, indicating specific religious areas, the structure in northern Jutland was possibly different. Consequently, the Gudum place name refers more to an area than to a specific cult site and is probably linked to phase 1. There are a few other religious place names in the area; these are *Thor* names and may refer to phase 2 shrines.[34]

In phase 3, in the first half of the 11th century, St. Clement's church was built in Aalborg, possibly in association with a royal residence. Several other churches followed later. Aalborg did not become the bishopric for northern Jutland until the Reformation.

---

30   Beck et al. 2021, 229ff.
31   Crumlin-Pedersen 1996, 191
32   Lauritsen 1974
33   Runge 2021c, 11ff.
34   Albris and Christensen 2021, 47f.

Instead, the bishopric was placed in Børglum in Vendsyssel.[35] In the 12th century, there were unsuccessful attempts to have the two Norwegian throne pretenders canonised.[36]

In Odense, a possible *hörgr* (altar or cult site) has been investigated; this may even be the eponymic Odin's vi. The structure is undated.[37], but shows great similarity to corresponding structures, for example at Lejre.[38] The interpretation as *hörgr* is based on the design – a larger pit with burned stones and animal bones as well as the location close to the river Odense Å at the most obvious crossing point of the river. The site at the same time is placed immediately north of Nonnebakken. A physical connection between pagan shrines and the Christian fortresses of Harald Bluetooth is not unknown.[39] The place-name analyses have identified several pagan names which could indicate pagan central places. These are evenly distributed across the hundreds in the study area.[40]

During the course of the 10th century, Christianity was acknowledged in the town by its so-called "birth certificate" of AD 988, in which Odense is referred to as a bishopric. The Christian fortress Nonnebakken and Christian graves in St. Alban's churchyard with ^{14}C dates prior to AD 1000 point in the same direction.[41] Also, new ^{14}C dates from St Alban's Church support a date of the church earlier than AD 1000.[42] In AD 1086, Canute IV was murdered and his canonisation AD 1100 heralded Odense's subsequent development as a regular place of pilgrimage, where religion became a significant growth factor. The building up of a memorial culture around Canute, associated with a pilgrimage church, monasteries and written sources, is reminiscent of Harald Bluetooth's construction of the Jelling complex in honour of his parents and himself.[43]

Secular and sacral powers have been tightly interwoven throughout prehistory, and religion therefore has constituted a growth factor. It is, however, with the special structures and mythological thinking of the Late Iron Age that central religious institutions can more closely be linked to the archaeological record. It is argued that a certain degree of institutionalised religion emerged during this phase and provided an opportunity to accumulate an economic surplus.[44] These aspects evolved with the introduction of Christianity. Correspondingly, churches and monasteries attain great significance for new urban ideals and are important as steps in the development of ideological religious urban environments. Thereby, religion developed further as a growth factor.[45]

That the church was a growth factor is evident from its power to attract people from rural to urban areas and within towns, too. Accordingly, it is evident that the coupling of

---

35 Kristensen 2013; Møller 2021
36 Møller 2021
37 Jensen and Sørensen 1989, 326ff.
38 Olsen 1966, 103ff.; Christensen 2015, 173ff.
39 Dobat 2013, 54ff.
40 Albris and Christensen 2021, 44
41 Runge and Henriksen 2018, 64f.
42 Kirstine Haase, personal communication.
43 Christensen 2021, 282ff.
44 Hansen 2021a
45 Christensen 2021; Møller 2021

ecclesiastical institutions to the existing towns of Odense and Aalborg gradually shifted the town centre from the originally secular or pagan core towards the area hosting the ecclesiastical institutions. It is also evident though, that the religious centralisation in Odense is clearer than in Aalborg, where cathedral status was first granted much later.

Conclusion

Odense and Aalborg are situated at the centre of major fjord systems and possess urban elements which around AD 900 attain a character such that they can be identified as towns. From the turn of the 1st millennium AD, Odense and Aalborg transformed into royal and ecclesiastical towns. The ultimate result was in many ways the same but the route leading to this destination differed. For both areas, all the growth factors mentioned are present, but their significance varies (Fig. 5).

Aalborg's foundation is rooted in new patterns in trade and crafts and the Limfjord's general position as a trade-related transit route. Aalborg was one of a series of localities on the hill islands along the fjord, where trade and crafts were significant elements and saw expression in large metal-rich sites, which had their roots back in the Late Roman Iron Age. A grubenhäusersettlement in the later Aalborg, with dates extending back to the 8th century, was one of the later sites in this system. It was not until its incorporation into the system of royal emporia in the late 9th century that it acquired its central position in the region. Aalborg's coastal location, in combination with its location by a central crossing place, conferred advantages relative to the other metal-rich sites. Conversely, the region's central functions in relation to religion, the military and administration, which can be traced from the late 10th century, were placed elsewhere – respectively at Børglum, Aggersborg and Viborg: This further suggests that Aalborg's central significance did not have a long temporal depth. Thus, Aalborg's role as sacral and secular administrative centre was not added until after the Middle Ages.

Odense as the central place on Funen on the other hand has very deep temporal roots and a foundation in religion, administration, and military, but rests only to a minor degree on trade and crafts. In the town's first centuries – up until the 11th century – the latter activities took place to an equal extent at the hinterland's more coastal, metal-rich sites, which lay close to the main maritime trade routes of the time. An important factor was Odense's central position in relation to the predominant land-traffic routes and the town can, despite its relationship with the fjord, be perceived as an inland place. The interpretation of the town's name – *Odin's vi* – may indicate a supra-regional, religious significance in pagan times. This is succeeded by the placing of the bishopric in the town in the late 10th century. Odense's central position on the island of Funen also made it the obvious choice as the regional thing stead from the 11th century, and perhaps the Odin's vi function also indicates a thing stead function, which extended further back in time. Finally, Odense's position rendered it an important bastion in the fortification systems of the time.

Thus, both towns are established based on the central functions on which the preceding elite environments also founded their power and on a varying degree of bottom-up

Odense	Aalborg
Great time depth as centre	Small time depth as centre
Local orientation	External orientation
Religious centre in phases 2 and 3	Religious centre in phase 1
Bottom-up	Top-down
Land-traffic orientation	Water-traffic orientation
Administration	Trade
Religion	Crafts
Military	

General characteristics of Odense and Aalborg and their backgrounds. Graphics: Mads Runge (216). **Fig. 5.**

and top-down processes. Odense's primary central markers – land traffic, religion and administration – are important in the time before, during and after urban formation and seem independent of external factors. These markers are further developed after the central power's marked entry in the form of the fortress Nonnebakken (the function related to internal control) and the ecclesiastical institutions. Aalborg's central markers – trade and specialized crafts – seem to be more dependent on external, top-down processes in the form of evolution in trade routes and goods. For these reasons, the placing of the area's central location was over a shorter time span than that at Odense. The central place must simply be moved to where it makes most sense in relation to the changing trade routes. The increased importance that the trade acquires further means that the central power draws attention to the place and builds a fortification to protect the place.

Bibliography

Albris, S.L. & L.E. Christensen. 2021: "Place names and centrality around Odense and Aalborg in the Iron Age and Viking Age", in Runge et al. 2021, 3849.

Beck, M.R. 2021: "Specialisation of metal crafts", in Runge et al. 2021, 157-166.

Beck, M.R., C.V. Jensen & M. Runge 2021: "The military expression and organisation of power", in Runge et al. 2021, 199-240.

Beck, M.R., T.T. Christiansen & M.B. Henriksen 2021a: "Metal-rich sites in the hinterland of Odense and Aalborg", in Runge et al. 2021, 69-128.

Beck, M.R., T.T. Christiansen and M.B. Henriksen 2021b: "Topography. Landscape and seascape in the hinterland of Aalborg and Odense", in Runge et al. 2021, 23-35.

Brandt, L.Ø., K. Haase & M.J. Collins 2018: "Species identification using ZooMS, with reference to the exploitation of animal resources in the medieval town of Odense", *Danish Journal of Archaeology* 7, 139-153.

Brink, S. 1999a: "Fornskandinavisk religion – förhistoriskt samhälle. En bosättningshistorisk studie av centralorter i Norden", in *Religion och samhälle i det förkristna Norden. Ett symposium*, edited by U. Drobin. Odense, 11-55.

Brink, S. 1999b: "Social order in the early Scandinavian landscape", in *Settlement and Landscape. Proceedings of a conference in Århus, Denmark, May 4-7 1998*, edited by C. Fabech & J. Ringtved. Højbjerg, 423-439.

Christiansen, T.T., L. Feveile, N. Knudsen, T. Ljungberg & M. Runge 2018: "Lyskommunikation i vikingetiden", *Skalk* 2018:5, 3-7.

Christaller, W. 1968: *Die Zentralen Orte in Süddeutschland. Eine ökonomisch-geografische Untersuchung über die Gesetzmäßigkeit der Verbreitung und Entwicklung der Siedlungen mit städtischen Funktionen*. Repographischer Nachdruck der 1. Auflage, Jena 1933. Darmstadt.

Christensen, J.T. 2021: "The urban monastery in the Early Middle Ages – actor or sleeping partner? A discussion of urban monastic institutions based on the monasteries in Odense, Randers and Aalborg", in Runge et al., 268-284.

Christensen, L.E. 2016: "Centralpladsrelevante stednavne og centrale pladser på Fyn – Nye fund og mulige strukturer", in *Navn og navnebærer. Rapport fra NORNAs 45. symposium i Skagen 1.-4. oktober 2014*, edited by M.S. Danielsen, B. Eggert & J.G.G. Jakobsen. Uppsala, 7-33.

Christensen, T. 2015: *Lejre bag myten. De arkæologiske udgravninger*. Højbjerg.

Crumlin-Pedersen, O. 1996: "Kystforsvaret", in *Atlas over Fyns kyst i jernalder, vikingetid og middelalder*, edited by O. Crumlin-Pedersen et al. Odense, 182-193.

Dam, P., K. Haase, L.B. Lundø, M.S. Mogensen & J. Hansen 2021: "Årtusinders råvarer – ressourcernes geografi. Et indsamlings- og forskningsprojekt ved Odense Bys Museer", *Odense Bys Museer*, 60-69.

Dobat, A.S., 2013: *Kongens Borge. Rapport over undersøgelserne 2007-2010*. (Jysk Arkæologisk Selskabs skrifter 76). Højbjerg.

Fabech, C. 1999: "Centrality in sites and landscapes", in *Settlement and Landscape: proceedings of a conference in Århus, Denmark, May 4-7 1998*, edited by C. Fabech & J. Ringtved. Gylling, 455-473.

Hansen, J. 2015: *Landsbydannelse og bebyggelsesstruktur i det 1. årtusinde – et bebyggelseshistorisk regionalstudie*. Unpublished PhD thesis. University of Southern Denmark.

Hansen, J., 2017. "Fynske landsbyer fra arilds tid", in *Museumsleder, forsker og netværksskaber. Torben Grøngaard Jeppesen. 40 år ved Odense Bys Museer,* edited by H. Plechinger, A. Lorentzen, J. Toftgaard & M. Schultz. Odense, 168-179.

Hansen, J. 2021a: "Accumulating wealth in pre-Christian religious Scandinavia", in Runge et al. 2021, 242-253.

Hansen, J. 2021b: "From Space to place in a rural perspective", in Runge et al. 2021, 167-179.

Hansen, J. & M. Runge (ed.) 2018: *From Central Space to Urban Place, seminar 1. Social organisation of land in South Scandinavia AD 400-1100. Methods, challenges and possibilities. Report from an international seminar in Odense, 24th May 2018*. (Archaeological & Historical Studies in Centrality, vol. 2). Research Centre Centrum – Odense Bys Muser – University Press of Southern Denmark.

Jensen. C.V. 2017: *En kritisk analyse af Aalborgs ældste bebyggelse før ca. 1000 på grundlag af de arkæologiske kilder*. Unpublished master's thesis, Aarhus University.

Jensen, C.V. 2021: "Settlement in Aalborg and Odense", in Runge et al., 133-147.

Jensen, N.M. & J. Sørensen 1990: "Nonnebakkeanlægget i Odense. En ny brik til udforskningen", *KUML* 1988-89, 325-333.

Kristensen, H.K. 2013: "Børglum Domkirke og Kloster i middelalderen", Hjørring, 9-14.

Lauritsen, Aa., 1974. "Volden omkring vikingetidens Odense", *Fynske Minder* 1974, 140-154.

Mogensen, M.S., L.B. Lundø, N. Knudsen, C. Vrængmose & M. Runge 2021: "Vikingegys, spøgelsesskibe og bål i lange baner. Kompleks formidling omsat til nærværende formidling", *Odense Bys Museer* 2021, 124-135.

Møller, P.G. & N. Haue 2021: "Road Network", in Runge et al. 2021, 50-68.

Møller, S.B. 2021: "Crown and Church in early Aalborg and Odense", in Runge et al. 2021, 254-267.

Nielsen, J.N. 1998: "Det ældste Aalborg", in *Variation og enhed omkring Limfjorden,* edited by J. Lund & J. Ringtved. Limfjordsprojektet. Rapport nr. 8:II, 293-302.

Nielsen, J.N. 1999: "Maritime influences on the foundation and early history of Aalborg, Denmark", in *Maritime Topography and the Medieval Town,* edited by J. Bill & B.L. Clausen (Publications from The National Museum. Studies in Archaeology & History Vol. 4). Copenhagen, 213-220.

Näsman, U. 2006: "Danerne og det danske kongeriges opkomst. Om forskningsprogrammet 'Fra Stamme til Stat i Danmark'". *KUML* 2006, 205-241.

Olsen, O. 1966: 'Hørg, Hov og Kirke. Historiske og arkæologiske vikingestudier'. *Aarbøger for Nordisk Oldkyndighed og Historie 1965*. Copenhagen.

Perroux, F. 1971: 'Note on the Concept of "Growth Poles"', in *Economic policy for development,* edited by I. Livingstone. Michigan, 278-289.

Runge, M. 2014: Forskning på museerne. Ph.d.-projektet "Dannelsen af regionale bebyggelsesmønstre i sen bronzealder og ældre jernalder". *Odense Bys Museer,* 161-179.

Runge, M. 2021a: "From central place to town – dynamics and drivers in the early urbanisation process", in Runge et al. 2021, 290-315.

Runge, M. 2021b: "Introduction", in Runge et al. 2021, 20-22.

Runge, M. 2021c: "Revitalizing the Danish Viking Age ring fortress Nonnebakken", *Landscapes,* vol. 20, issue 2, 1-22.

Runge, M. & M.B. Henriksen 2018: "The origins of Odense – New aspects of early urbanization in southern Scandinavia", *Danish Journal of Archaeology* 2018, 2-68.

Runge, M., M.R. Beck, M.M. Bjerregaard & T.B. Sarauw (eds.) 2021: *From Central Space to Urban Place. Urbanisation processes in Viking Age and Medieval Odense and Aalborg, Denmark.* University Press of Southern Denmark.

Sarauw, T. 2019: *Bejsebakken – en nordjysk bebyggelse fra yngre jernalder og vikingetid.* Copenhagen.

Sarauw, T. 2021: "Large-scale production? Pit-houses and urbanization", in Runge et al. 2021, 148-156.

Søvsø, M. 2020: *Ribe 700-1050: From Emporium to Civitas in Southern Scandinavia. Ribe Studies 2.* (Jysk Arkæologisk Selskabs skrifter 113). Højbjerg.

BY M.D. JESSEN, M.M. HALD, M.F. MORTENSEN,
P.S. HENRIKSEN, A. PIHL & L. ALBRIS

Chapter 4

Gudme as First-Generation Central Place
– the Case of an Agrarian-Based, Non-Resilient Urban Trajectory

ABSTRACT

This paper examines the Gudme-Lundeborg complex on Funen, Denmark, as an early urban settlement with significant ritual and economic activities from the Late Roman Iron Age to the Early Germanic Iron Age. We propose that Gudme functioned as a low-density agrarian-based urban centre, characterized by dispersed farmsteads, significant metalworking activities, and ritual functions centred around monumental buildings. We suggest that Gudme's decline in the 6th century AD was due to its reliance on external trade networks and lack of resilience to environmental and economic changes.

Since the 1980s the so-called central places of the Scandinavian Iron Age have been an important focus of debates about the social structures and ritual life of the first millennium AD. There have been several attempts to describe the character of these types of sites,[1] but none have offered a satisfactory description, nor been able to describe the dynamic structure of these sites. Although the division of first- and second-generation central places as proposed by Jørgensen (2001) seems to have attained general academic acceptance, this does not contain a detailed description of the individual generations. The only characterisation available touches upon the manorial type of subsistence economical structure that the second-generation central places seem to represent. This was done with specific reference to the settlement organisation as it has been unearthed at the Tissø site in its Bulbrogård and Fugledegård phases, and the derived aristocratic and

---

1   Such as Brink 2000; Fabech 1994; 2006, see also Reiersen 2017 for a thorough critique

elite presence the many exceptional finds and structures at these sites may represent.[2] For the first-generation sites (mainly Uppåkra and Helgö in Sweden, and Gudme-Lundeborg and Sorte Muld in Denmark, and potentially also the very recent find area at Stavsager Høj/Fæsted in Southern Denmark), the descriptions are vaguer. In this paper, we propose a new description of the Gudme-Lundeborg complex by evaluating the distribution and frequency of detector finds, and the dynamic organisation of the settlement in combination with onomastic and paleo-ecological data. We explore the possibility of recognising Gudme-Lundeborg as an early version of a settlement set on an (eventually unsuccessful) urban trajectory, and how applying the concept of low-density, agrarian-based urbanism can be beneficial to understanding the dynamic biography of the Gudme-Lundeborg complex, including how the settlement may have coped with possible low internal resilience.

The Gudme settlement as central place

The emergence of central places in South Scandinavia with associated cultic activities should be seen in the context of a general shift in the ritual pattern from the Roman Iron Age onwards. The traditional pre-Christian ritual activities in bogs and lakes were clearly continued, as seen for example at Götavi and Frösvi, in Sweden, and likewise in the large war booty offerings as they can be recognised at Illerup, Alken Enge, Vimose or other sites.[3] It is equally clear, however, that a new type of ritually loaded settlement areas now appeared, that also became central to the performance of the pre-Christian cult. In the process, certain large settlements came to function as core locations, where the most extensive and probably most essential ritual activities were staged – these have been described as first-generation central places. The reasons for this change in the ritual and social landscape are unclear; they extend over a very long period, and the sites exhibit various new features, wherefore '… there was probably no single function that determined the rise of these sites, but rather that the political, religious and economic domains were tightly interwoven and interdependent factors'.[4]

In the case of the Gudme-Lundeborg complex on Funen (Fig. 1), the transition seems to begin just before AD 200, where a succession of small buildings was constructed on the northern slope of a small hill on the western shore of the small Gudme lake. One building succeeded another and the initial one had remarkable architectural features, including a prominent wall trench, a substantial entrance section and no internal roof-bearing posts, thereby providing almost 60 m² of internal open space, free of interrupting structures. This innovative type of construction was to become common later, but in much bigger houses, and could very well have served as a signifier of a special building with special functions. Remarkably, in the up to five subsequent phases of smaller buildings the entrance was kept in the exact same place, attesting to a continuity of place and

---

2   Jørgensen 2010
3   Engelhardt 1869, Ilkjær 2000, Lindqvist 1910, Løvschal, Iversen and Holst 2020, Svensson 2008
4   Rau 2020, 634

Fig. 1. *The Gudme-Lundeborg complex is situated on the south-eastern part of the island Funen, and virtually in the middle of present-day Denmark.*

movement that transcended the otherwise differing characters of each new building. Below the earliest of these entrance-posts a gold pin was unearthed, perhaps put there as a form of foundation deposit for the first building.[5] Just north of the small buildings a monumental hall was erected, overlooking the settlement. Being 47 m long and 10 m wide with eight pairs of enormous roof-supporting posts carrying a roof of nearly 500m^2 and dated to the 3rd-4th centuries AD, this building has completely changed the perception of southern Scandinavian Early Iron Age architecture as well as the academic understanding of the capacities of the craftsmen at the time.[6] The post-holes contained fragments from several unique Roman objects such as a gilded diadem, a silver dish and Roman bronze vessels, as well as several silver denarii and glass sherds.[7] Two large contemporaneous pits, containing large amounts of pottery and various fragments of high-status objects such as fibulae, swords, lances, belt equipment, coins, a bull figurine, glass beads, vessels and even the remains of a carriage (otherwise mainly found as burnt remains in ritual wet-land deposits thus underlining the ambiguous character or Early Iron Age rituality), is placed right outside the buildings. The dating of the finds covers a period from the transition between the Early and Late Roman Iron Age and reaches into the second half of the 3rd century, making the pits contemporaneous with the early phases of small buildings, and the construction of the Great Hall. Furthermore,

---

5   Sørensen 2022, 13-16
6   Jessen 2021, Sørensen 1994
7   Sørensen 2022, 22-30

all finds seem to have been deposited in one or two events, perhaps in unison with the demolition and erection of the small buildings.[8] Conclusively, the central buildings at Gudme appear to have been used for functions and activities that lay outside normal everyday life, which suggests, in combination with their conspicuous architecture, that they housed ritual functions. This situation is also reflected in the nature of the artefacts recovered with metal detectors from the same area, which include gilt objects and glass drinking vessels, bracteates and gold foil figurines.

In the surrounding area, virtually all excavated areas that are located on dry ground show evidence of settlement.[9] However, rather than a chaotic meander of buildings, they were palimpsests of rebuilt farmsteads within their own individual (often fenced) croft, and lots of them – we estimate that there must have been around 50 farmsteads during the Gudme heydays.[10] The individual crofts follow a recognisable organisation that is known from the rest of Southern Scandinavia, with a larger longhouse of 6-10 roof-supporting posts, often accompanied by a smaller building, and placed inside a fenced area usually smaller than 3,500 m². Still, the number of 10-post longhouses, which also often appear well-built, is noteworthy and hints at a settlement of considerable economic prowess and capability.[11] Furthermore, at the individual farmsteads the production of ferrous and non-ferrous metal objects has often been registered, and crucibles, moulds, forge-stones and slag often form part of the find material indicating that even if the basic economy was agrarian, there was an obvious incentive in crafting and trading precious metals.[12] In addition, even at these 'ordinary' farmsteads imported goods, glass sherds, and Roman coins appear regularly.[13]

The development of the Gudme-Lundeborg complex

Albris (2017) has analysed the long-term development of the Gudme area through archaeology, place names and pollen data. To estimate the general degree of human activity in the Gudme region through the First millennium AD, a series of maps present changing densities of registered archaeological sites through time.[14] As no definite site categories could be singled out, the mapping included all archaeological localities in Gudme, and its surroundings (Fig.2). In a resolution of 25 × 25 m, each cell was given a value indicated in registrations per square kilometre, with calculations based on the number of registrations within a radius of two kilometres. By comparing values from

---

8   Sørensen 2022, 16-22
9   Jørgensen 2010
10 In this connection, note the very large contemporary cemetery Møllegårdsmarken with more than 2,400 graves placed right between Gudme and Lundeborg, by far the largest cemetery from this period (Albrectsen 1971). The sheer size of Møllegårdsmarken attests to the large number of people inhabiting the area during the Roman Iron Age.
11 Sørensen 2022, 348-352
12 Ibid., 230-232, 325-326
13 See example: ibid., 286-289
14 Fig. 2, see Albris 2017, 111-117 for a thorough methodological discussion.

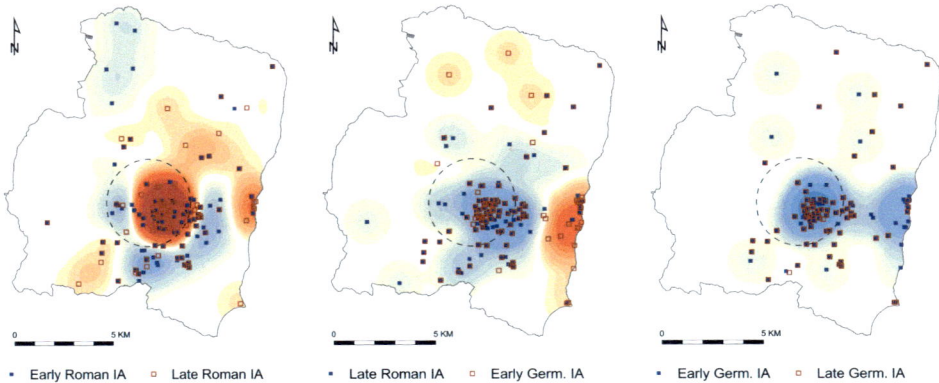

Fig. 2. *Maps showing all registered archaeological localities in the Gudme region (blue and orange squares) and the relative intensity of human activity from the Early Roman Iron Age through to the Late Germanic Iron Age increases (red) or decreases (blue). Places with neither growth nor decline, appear white but are shown with squares. A clear centralisation process is apparent in the Late Roman Iron Age, followed by intensified activity at Lundeborg on the coast in the Early Germanic Iron Age and a general drop in activity all over the region in the Late Germanic Iron Age. The encircled area marks the range of the pollen data. Maps by Pihl and Albris after Albris 2017.*

one archaeological period to another, an index was obtained that indicates whether the find density increases or decreases.

The maps show that activity in the Gudme area was already growing in the Early Roman Iron Age, but a dramatic increase and centralisation process is seen between the Early Roman Iron Age and the Late Roman Iron Age. The further development from the Late Roman to the Early Germanic Iron Age seems to be characterised by increased activities at Lundeborg on the coast, while the intensity of finds in the central Gudme area decreases slightly. There are still many sites, as can be seen from the squares on the map, but overall, there is a decline in the core area. This may be partly due to the fact that there is an over-representation of objects that have been registered within the Late Roman Iron Age, although many coins, for example, could have been in circulation for even longer. However, the reality of a decline in the Early Germanic Iron Age is also shown by the fact that the sizes of the longhouses on the individual farms in Gudme are reduced, and the large hall is closed down or moved.[15] The wider region has many gold finds dated to this period, which may reflect a continued economic ability, but their deposition could also reflect strategies to deal with crisis (whether they are sacrifices in the hope of better times or values tucked away). The activity in Lundeborg seems to have been declining around AD 500-550, possibly because of reduced imports that

15   Sørensen 2022, 348

started decreasing already during the end of the 4th century.[16] Most remarkable is the decline in the level of activity between the Early and Late Germanic Iron Ages, where the social structure of East Funen as a whole almost seems to be collapsing. Although we should be aware that there are also many places with settlement continuity, and that there is never a complete abandonment, it is significant that the craft activities at Lundeborg cease at the end of the 7th century.[17]

The level of activity in the Gudme area increases again in the Viking Age, but this happens inland, at a distance from the coast, along a stretch of forest.[18] A more extensive expansion only occurred later in the Middle Ages, when people moved back closer to the coast.

Landscape development and subsistence economy

Palaeo-environmental data can be compared with the levels of human activity as reflected in archaeological finds and place names to show the development of settlement in the area. Pollen data obtained from Gudme Lake[19] has been used to reconstruct the landscape development and human activity within a zone of approximately two kilometres.[20]

With the use of Landscape Reconstruction Algorithm (LRA) it is possible to estimate the relative coverage of trees, grasses, and cereals. This method has been applied by using a LOVE model (Local Vegetations Estimation) that quantifies the vegetation cover within a few kilometres of the lake.[21] Iron Age landscape development was rooted in processes occurring between the Early and Late Bronze Age, when a large part of the forested landscape of eastern Denmark was transformed into pastures and grazing areas. From the Late Bronze Age up until around AD 100, there was a relatively stable situation with a small degree of cereal cultivation and some tree cover. In the second century AD, we see a small increase in cereal growth and a corresponding small drop in grasses and trees. However, a more marked development happened after *c*. AD 200. Woodland expanded, with a clear peak around AD 300. This expansion mainly involved beech trees on upland soils.[22] Woodlands however declined markedly again in the 4th and 5th centuries leading to a low point around AD 500. This decline particularly concerns alder trees, indicating clearing of wetlands to create meadows for hay. This decline corresponds with accelerated soil erosion and higher levels of algae in the lake around AD 400-500, as well as a higher level of cereal pollen and some growth in grass pollen.[23] All this indicates that the 4th and 5th centuries saw intensified arable farming. In this period, there is also a

---

16 Thomsen 1994, 28
17 Thomsen 1994, 28
18 Jakobsen 2013, 127
19 Andersen et al. 1991, 101 ff.
20 Rasmussen and Olsen 2009
21 Fig. 3. Nielsen and Odgaard 2010, 382-383
22 Nielsen and Odgaard 2010, 38
23 Rasmussen and Olsen 2009, 38-39

Fig. 3. *Selected taxa (below) and reconstructed cover (above) based on pollen investigations from Gudme Lake. In red frame the period under investigation. After Nielsen and Odgaard 2010.*

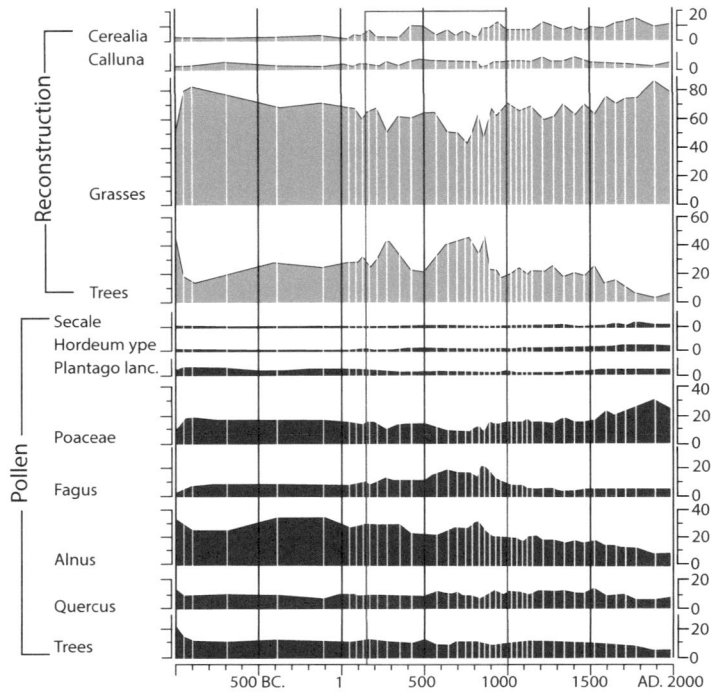

high level of pollen from *Cannabis* in Gudme Lake, indicating that the lake was used for retting hemp.[24] Then, between *c.* AD 600 and AD 900 there was less soil erosion as well as less non-arboreal pollen and almost no traces of hemp. Woodlands were now on the rise again, mainly with the growth of beech and alder showing a reforestation of both the dry upland and the wet meadows. After AD 900, the data shows a new wave of deforestation and hitherto unseen intensified arable farming.[25]

The pollen data matches the development in archaeological find material described above, which indicates a heyday of the Gudme settlement in the 4th and 5th centuries and a marked decline in the 6th to 8th centuries. It indicates that grazing is at its highest in the period *c.* A.D. 300-500 and again in the Viking Age. Animal husbandry thus seems to have played a key role in Gudme's economic growth in the Late Roman and Early Germanic Iron Age. This is supported by the fact that nearly 75% of the large number of animal bones from Lundeborg are from cattle.[26]

The plant remains from the Gudme settlement suggests an agricultural composition that looks very much like ordinary and everyday activities and corresponds broadly to the picture known from the rest of the country in the Late Roman and Early Germanic

---

24   ibid. 39
25   ibid.
26   Hatting 1994

Iron Ages.[27] However, a conspicuous amount of charred hulled barley (*Hordeum vulgare*) from a single house (house XIX at Gudme IV) with a clay-built oven placed in the main room, could be interpreted as the recurring drying and/or kilning of barley to produce malt, and essentially the brewing of beer.[28] This would fit with the ritual performances and feasting taking place in the Great Hall as they can be recognised in the old Norse literature.[29] Furthermore, products such as livestock, animal skins, furs, and salted meats, may have been some of the main goods that were traded out of Gudme-Lundeborg.[30]

The Gudme landscape and the onomastic record

From a place name perspective, Gudme is situated in an area with a remarkable lack of the oldest types of settlement names,[31] supporting the notion that Gudme itself dominated the area. In the very central settlement area, we find the sacral names Gudme, 'home of the gods' and Gudbjerg, 'hill of the gods', both likely linked to religious activities in the Iron Age (Albris 2017: 89-95). Although sacral interpretations have been suggested for two other nearby names ending in -*bjerg*, 'hill', *Albjerg* (1473 Albiergh) is most likely is composed with the tree name *alder* and *Galdbjerg* (1462 Gialdbergh) contains the word *giald*, 'payment, debt, fee'. The latter may have relevance for the economic organization of the Gudme complex.

In the onomastic record of the historical villages surrounding Gudme, we mainly find place names indicating outfields and grazing areas.[32] These place names correspond with areas where finds decrease from the Early to the Late Germanic Iron Age. An example is *Oure* (1408 Aarde, 1436 Øræ), meaning 'pasture or uncultivated area'. The names *Brudager* and *Hesselager* both have the generic -*ager*, with the common Germanic meaning 'cultivated land', but however with an older meaning 'pasture', which may be the most relevant interpretation here.[33] *Hesselager* (1183 (1450-1500) Heslaker) contains the tree name *hazel* and *Brudager* (1286-1300 Bruthaker), a word *brut*, 'break', indicating newly broken soil. These names came to function as settlement names when these areas were re-settled in the Viking Age and Medieval Period.

Forest is indicated by forest-related place names and place names denoting clearances that were formed in the new settlement expansions in the Viking Age and Medieval Period, and not during the Iron Age. On a regional level, these types of names are mainly found in the periphery of Gudme to the south, west and north, where forest can also be seen on early modern maps.[34]

---

27 Robinson & Harrild 1997
28 Henriksen (in press)
29 Lund Hansen 2011; Sundqvist 2011; 2015; Nygaard 2018
30 Michaelsen 2015, 123-25
31 Holmberg 1996, 59-60
32 Albris 2017, 107-110
33 Jørgensen 2008, 18; Dam 2015, 245
34 Albris 2017, Fig. 13; Dam 2015, 129, 142-44

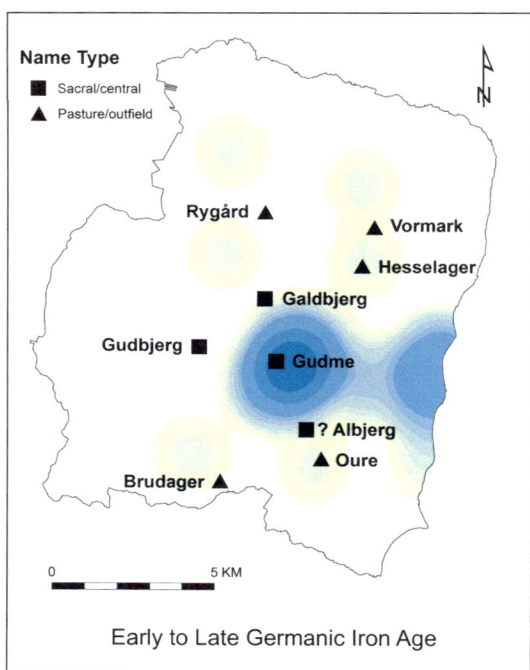

Fig. 4. *Sacral names in the centre surrounded by 'pastoral' names in the Gudme region mapped with the changes in human activity between the Early and Late Germanic Iron Age. Colours as for Fig. 2. Map by Pihl and Albris, Albris 2017.*

The Gudme area thus appears as a central core area with extensive settlement and sacral names, surrounded by pastures with a dispersed settlement structure again surrounded by a forested zone (Fig. 4).

The timing of the changes

The various stages of activities that can be recognised for the Gudme area seem to indicate that the development of the settlement did not follow any kind of linear trajectory. We suggest that the settlement underwent several, often drastic, changes, and that at least four different stages can be distinguished (Fig. 5).

Changes in the Gudme environment	
2nd cent. (ERIA)	Clustering and forest growth
3rd–5th cent. (LRIA, EGIA)	Growth in core area. Clearings without new settlements
6th–8th cent. (LGIA)	Decline in settlements. Rapid forest regrowth and reduction of arable land
9th–11th cent. (VA)	Regeneration and dispersed expansion

Fig. 5. *The main stages of the Gudme settlement.*

Basically, in the pollen diagram, it appears as if the initial stage of the Gudme settlement is based on the establishment of new farmsteads on the eastern side of Gudme lake – perhaps at the expense of nearby settlements encroaching on the Gudme-Lundeborg complex – and shortly thereafter, deforestation taking place.

After this stage, from *c.* AD 200 to 500 a pronounced growth of the Gudme settlement seems to take place within an environment surrounded by a wide circle of pastures or outfields, and, apparently, no new settlements. Thus, the course of events may be that the hinterland is drawn in and these abandoned areas are used in the process of establishing new pastures from Gudme outwards, eventually making them a periphery.

In the areas immediately surrounding Gudme, words that refer to clearings and 'landnam' or wetlands and pastures were used in the naming of new settlements in the Viking Age. These settlements represent the later and second stage of deforestation which can also be seen in the pollen diagram. A possible revitalisation and increase in activities may be an after-effect of the former glory of the site but is ill-understood and needs to be clarified by further excavation and investigation.[35]

Low-density agrarian urbanism

Before going deeper into the interpretation of the dynamic development of the Gudme-Lundeborg settlement we would like to introduce the ideas presented in the writings of Roland Fletcher and his model describing low-density urbanism and the diverse criteria for understanding the dynamics and non-linear developments of different types of urban environments. Whereas most western researchers have focused on describing urbanity via the examination of urban settlements from the Mediterranean and the Levant, as well as from the Roman Empire (see for example the famous ten urban criteria as they were proposed by Gordon Childe (1950)), Fletcher derives his model mainly from studying Asian sites. As case in point, he describes the development of Greater Angkor as it rose to a megacity with more than a million inhabitants in the 12th-13th century AD. However, Greater Angkor covered the same area in the 12th century as industrial Sydney did in Australia in 1945 (i.e., around 1.000 km^2); it was not an industrial city but rather had an extensive subsistence economy based on traditional agriculture of the lowlands of the Indochinese Peninsula.[36] Similar very large settlements, such as the Mayan city-states, the Tripillyan sites of the Neolithic Carpathians or the large Celtic oppida, remind us that the densely populated (proto)industrial townscape of the western world might not be the only way urban settlements have developed. Consequently, Fletcher has underlined the problematic character of the traditional understanding of urban development and instead stressed the need for acknowledging for alternative, multistranded developments of urbanity, where both population density as well as the socio-economic organisation, can take different forms. Therefore, he points to a series

---

35 Jessen & Majland 2021; see also Beck 2019; Beck, Christiansen & Henriksen 2019 for Funen in its entirety.
36 Fletcher 2019

of measures[37] that should be considered when evaluating the population density of individual settlements, and their urban character, such as:

1. Such sites should be regarded as primate settlements (following McGee 1967).
2. They should have a high degree of demographic heterogeneity (i.e., it cannot be expected for the urban environment to evolve in any kind of linear manner).
3. The socio-economic system should be non-defining (i.e., the same type of administration and socioeconomic setting can result in different types of urban organization).
4. The decoupling of wealth and social integration is noticeable in dispersed urban settings (i.e., in theory, the differentiation between the periphery and the centre should be larger in a low-density community. However, it is not just the rich getting richer, but more along the lines of the social fabric getting richer).
5. And finally, central areas of the settlements are often characterised by monumental buildings.

Importantly, Fletcher notes a tendency for certain sites to be non-stable and highlights that networks of larger, low-density, agrarian-based urban settlements are unlikely to survive severe decline within the network.[38] By contrast, the networks in which *compact* urban settlements are embedded endure even though the settlements may deteriorate. Even though it is now clear why, history has shown that the density pattern of settlements may be highly consequential for their ability to respond to external changes, and that low-density settlements seem to be inherently vulnerable to change and to hold a low degree of internal resilience.

Gudme-Lundeborg as a low-density urban settlement

Returning to the Scandinavian Iron Age, the Gudme-Lundeborg complex exhibits some very interesting characteristics that merit it being included as an example of a low-density urban environment. The Gudme settlement itself has a pronounced core area where there is a marked cluster of finds (Fig. 6).

As mentioned above, the settlement has its early beginnings in the Late Pre-Roman Iron Age but is particularly find rich in the Late Roman and Early Germanic Iron Ages, where it dominates an area of ca. 2.5 by 1.5 km (i.e., 375 ha), and, in comparison with the entire island of Funen, with a surrounding zone that is less find-rich and almost empty.[39] Therefore, if we address Fletcher's measures mentioned above, the Gudme Settlement can, firstly, be considered the primate settlement in its area. Therefore, if using the estimate of 50 households placed inside the central area and accepting that a household would comprise between 8-14 people, there would have been between 400-700 people in Gudme, which amount to between 1.1-1.9 persons per hectare. When

---

37 Fletcher 2012; 2019
38 Fletcher 2019, 12-18
39 Henriksen 2009, 307

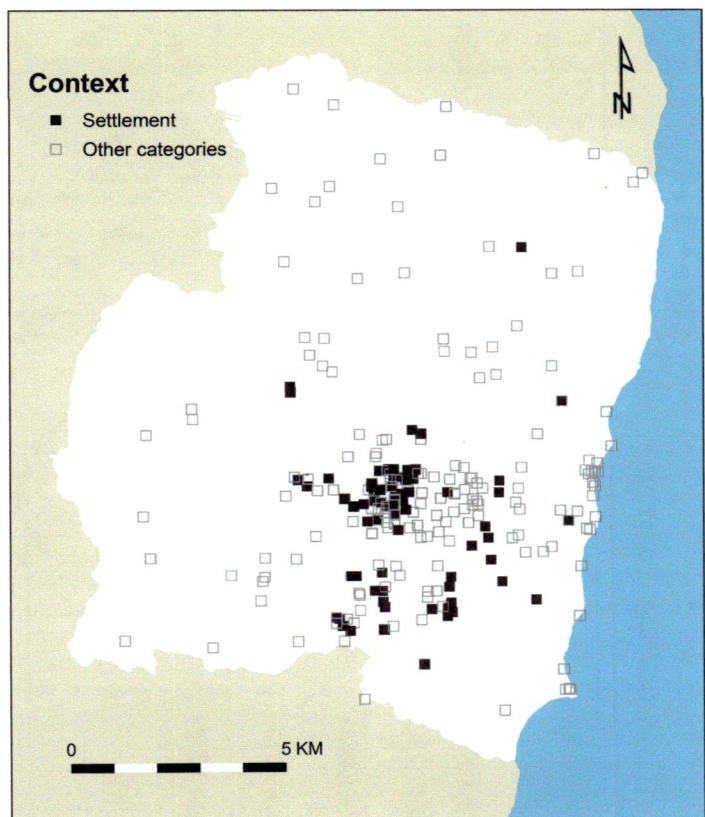

Fig. 6. First Millennium archaeological localities in the Gudme Region registered in Albris 2017. Black squares mark registered settlements, whereas open squares mark other types of find categories.[41]

comparing the level of population density to the urban matrix proposed by Roland Fletcher, the settlement is positioned below the threshold that would potentially classify it as a high-density settlement.[40] Therefore, with regards to population density, Gudme potentially has a settlement structure that resembles an (urban) environment with a low-density organisation (Fig. 7).

Secondly, the development of the Gudme-Lundeborg complex reveals periods of increase in settlement size as well as depopulation, and both types of changes seem to be happening at a rather fast pace as shown by pollen data and find frequency. In particular, the settlement organisation and community structure of the second stage (Fig. 5) indicate that a trajectory towards a low-density, agrarian-based urbanism has started, but presumably did not reach any prolonged, stable level before increase turned to decrease.

Thirdly, the buildings at the individual farmsteads do not differ in any significant way from the general house typology from the Early Roman Iron Age, nor does the organisation and size of the individual crofts, which emphasises that the basic economy

---

40 Fletcher 2019, Fig. 15
41 After Albris 2017

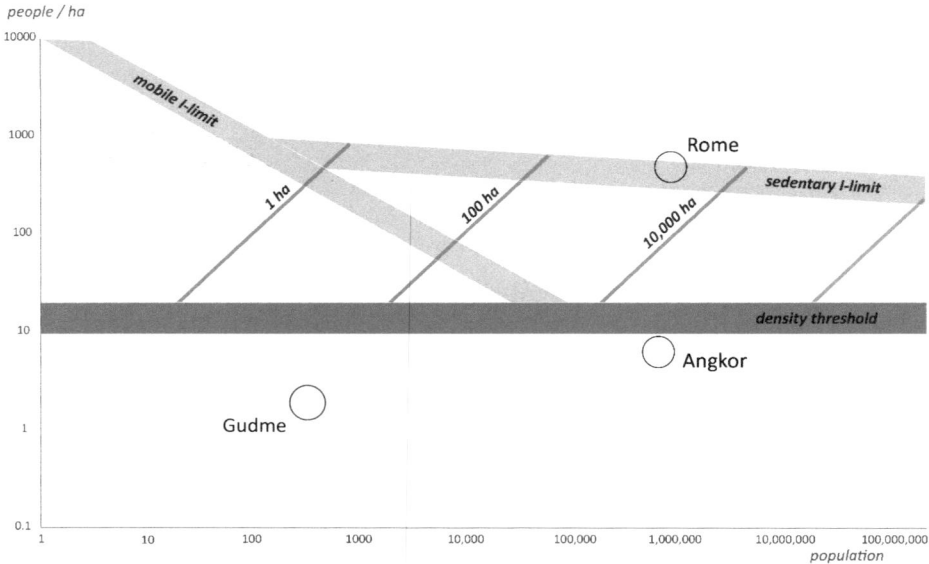

Fig. 7. *The position of the Gudme settlement within Fletcher's matrix of population density vs population size, is below the density threshold and therefore to be understood as a low-density settlement. After Fletcher 2019.*

must be agrarian. Nevertheless, the substantial evidence for local use of (mostly) non-ferrous metalworking at Gudme and at Lundeborg point towards a hybrid economy beginning to take form.

Fourthly, the actual 'wealth' of the site and its distribution inside the settlement is indeed almost impossible to assess. However, it is worth noting that the Great Hall *cum* small building does not show obvious signs of residence or dwelling and could have been buildings attached to communal functions, wherefore a possible co-operative system of redistribution and sharing of power cannot be ruled out.

Finally, the large, monumental Great Hall erected around AD 200 marks the centre of Gudme. The small temple-like side-house that is placed next to it and in its initial form even pre-dates the Great Hall is the first building erected here, thus indicating a ritual origin of the entire central area. Accordingly, we seem to recognise a structure and organisation for the Gudme settlement that complies with several of the characteristics Fletcher mentions as important for low-density, agrarian-based settlements.

Lack of Resilience?

Another main purpose of the paper is to evaluate how this type of settlement managed changes in its established trade network and how resilient it was towards external pressure, such as climatic and/or social fluctuations. In this regard, a preliminary interpretation of the data deriving from Gudme, would be that the dependency on external networks (such as trade) may have led to loss of local control and a decrease in resilience; dependency on external networks could be expected to have a negative impact on Gudme when, for example, these external networks are disrupted. Essentially being a 'world economy' at the time, the fall of the Roman Empire (often coupled to the fall of Emperor Romulus Augustulus in AD 476), would inevitably have influenced the trade networks coupled to the Gudme-Lundeborg complex, and could have led to an increase in vulnerability as the established flow of goods and produce decreased. Accordingly, the possibility of attaining exotic imports as well as trading produce from the settlement could have been affected negatively. The decrease in the number of finds (especially imported goods) from the Early to the Late Germanic Iron Age for the entire area indicates a downward spiral that eventually leads to the ending of the trade and production area at Lundeborg during the 7th century, which indicate a marked drop in external contact.

Our assessment of the onomastic and archaeological record as well as the pollen data suggest a similar drop at the Gudme settlement. In fact, the indication of forest growth in the arable zone surrounding Gudme suggests that the level of activity decreased, just as several farmsteads become smaller – both in individual house size and in the number of buildings at each croft – and some are even abandoned at the beginning of the 6th century, where even the area with the monumental hall is transferred into being used for more ordinary functions.[42]

An important point here is the oft-mentioned interconnectedness between ritual events and large assemblages where trading seems to have been an integral activity taking place at the same time as large ritual gatherings occur.[43] At the Gudme-Lundeborg complex the advent of the central ritual area and Lundeborg seem to happen in unison and diminished activities in one of the two spheres could very well impact the other. Consequently, if the ritual attractiveness of Gudme dwindled, perhaps the level of trade would lessen as well. A possible interpretation could be that Gudme as central ritual locality declined as the external contacts broke, and the complex entered a negative feedback loop where fewer people visited the site, and less trade took place. In combination with the possible strenuous decades following the volcanic eruptions in AD 536 and possibly also AD 540[44], or perhaps even the Justinian plague or smallpox[45], the resilience of the Gudme settlement seems to have been inadequate for coping with the social and economic disruptions southern Scandinavia might have faced in the wake of a fading Roman Empire and large-scale environmental upheaval.

---

42   Sørensen 2022, 47ff., 195, 291
43   Theuws 2004, Jørgensen, Jørgensen & Thomsen 2011, Sanmark 2015
44   Axboe 1999, van Dijk et al. 2023, Gräslund 2007, Mortensen, Henriksen & Olsen 2019
45   Mordechai & Eisenberg 2019, Mühlemann et al. 2020, Sarris 2022

Concluding remarks

In the case of the Gudme-Lundeborg complex, the description of low-density, agrarian urban organisation provides a new way of interpreting this first-generation central place, especially with regard to understanding the internal dynamics of the site and as an explanatory model for its dissolution as a primate settlement. The process of becoming a large, agrarian-based low-density settlement seemingly influenced the resilience of the site and could have made it more vulnerable to different kinds of external pressure. According to the composition of the finds with many Roman imports and precious objects already present early in its development, the Gudme-Lundeborg complex was highly attuned to long-distance contact, and presumably less integrated into the local environment of south-eastern Funen.[46] The consequence was that the combination of a dispersed settlement and an empty periphery that had been poorly integrated into the complex socio-ritual organization of Gudme-Lundeborg seemingly led to a severely reduced internal resilience when the crisis seems to have hit during the transition from the Early to the Late Germanic Iron Age in the 6th century. In effect, even if Gudme is a primate settlement the actual extent of its geographical powerbase remains unclear, and ought to form part of future research in Iron Age central places.

Acknowledgements

Funding was provided by the Independent Research Fund Denmark, Resilience & Breakpoints (Grant DFF 7013-00078) and the Carlsberg Foundation project Landscape of the Gods (Grant CF20-0437). The funders had no role in study design, data collection and analysis, decision to publish, or preparation of the manuscript.

Bibliography

Albrectsen, E. 1971: *Fynske jernaldergrave. Gravpladsen på Møllegårdsmarken ved Broholm* I-II. Odense: Odense Bys Museer.

Albris, S.L., 2017: *Stednavne og Storgårde i Sydskandinavien i 1. årtusind*. PhD dissertation, University of Copenhagen, Department of Scandinavian Research.

Andersen, S.T., B.V. Odgaard & P. Rasmussen. 1991: *Pollenanalytiske undersøgelser 1988/89/90 i gravhøje, Hassing Huse Mose, Skånsø, Gudme Sø, Kragsø og Kobbelhøje Mose*. Miljøministeriet, Skov- og Naturstyrelsen, Hørsholm.

Axboe, M. 1999: "The Year 536 and the Scandinavian Gold Hoards", *Medieval Archaeology* XLIII, 186-188.

Beck, M.R. 2019. "Vikingetid på Munkebo Bakke", *Fynboer og Arkæologi* nr. 1 2019, 27-29.

Beck, M.R., T.T. Christiansen & B.M. Henriksen. 2019: Fynske og nordjyske metalrige pladser 400-1100 e.kr. *Catalogue; From Central Space to Urban Place CENTRUM,* Rapport nr. 7. Odense Bys Museer.

Brink, S. 2000: "Social order in the early Scandinavian landscape", in *Settlement and landscape. Proceedings of a conference in Århus, Denmark 4-7 May 1998*, edited by C. Fabech & J. Ringtved. Jutland Archaeological Society, 423-439.

Childe, V.G., 1950: "The Urban Revolution", *The Town Planning Review*, Vol. 21(1), 3-17.

Dam, P. 2015: *Bebyggelser og stednavnetyper* (Navnestudier nr. 44). Copenhagen.

van Dijk, E., I.M. Gundersen, A. de Bode, H. Høeg, K. Loftsgarden & F. Iversen. 2023: "Climate and societal impacts in Scandinavia following the 536 and 540 CE volcanic double event", *Climate of the Past*, 19(2), 357-398.

---

46 See also Rau 2020, 635

Engelhardt, C. 1869: *Vimose Fundet.* (Fyenske Mosefund. No. II). Kjøbenhavn: G.E.C. Gad.

Fabech, C. 1994: "Reading Society from the cultural Landscape. South Scandinavia Between Sacral and Political Power", in *The archaeology of Gudme and Lundeborg*, edited by P.O. Nielsen, K. Randsborg & H. Thrane (Arkæologiske Studier 10). København, 169-183.

Fabech, C. 2006: "Centrality in Old Norse mental landscapes: a dialogue between arranged and natural places?", in *Old Norse religion in long-term perspectives*, edited by A. Andrén, K. Jennbert & C. Raudvere. Lund: Nordic academic Press, 26-32.

Fletcher, R. 2009: 2009: "Low-Density, Agrarian-Based Urbanism: A Comparative View", *Insights*, 2(4), 2-19.

Fletcher, R. 2012: "Low-Density, Agrarian-Based Urbanism: Scale, Power and Ecology", in *The Comparative Archaeology of Complex Societies*, edited by M.E. Smith. Cambridge: Cambridge University Press, 285-320.

Fletcher, R. 2019. "Trajectories to Low-Density Settlements Past and Present: Paradox and Outcomes", in *Where Do Cities Come from and Where Are They Going? Modelling Urbanism in the Past, Present, and Future*, edited by F. Fulminante, J.W. Hanson, S.G. Ortman & L.M.A. Bettencourt (Frontiers in Digital Humanities vol. 6), 1-21.

Gräslund, B. 2007: "Fimbulvintern, Ragnarök och klimatkrisen år 536-537 e. Kr.", *Saga och Sed* 2007, 93-123

Hatting, T. 1994: "The animal bones from Lundeborg", in *The Archaeology of Gudme and Lundeborg. Papers presented at a Conference at Svendborg, October 1991*, edited by P.O. Nielsen, K. Randsborg, H. Thrane (Arkæologiske Studier, Volume X). Copenhagen, 94-97.

Henriksen, M.B. 2009: *Brudager Mark – en romertidsgravplads nær Gudme på Sydøstfyn. Fynske Jernaldergrave* bind 6. (Fynske studier 22). Odense Bys Museer 2009.

Henriksen, P.S. (in press): "Macrofossil analysis from Gudme IV – Hus XIX", in *Gudme* vol. II, edited by M.D. Jessen & M.L. Bendtsen (Pre-Christian Cult Sites, volume 4), Oxford: Oxbow Books.

Holmberg, B. 1996: "Stednavne som historisk kilde", in *Atlas over Fyns kyst i jernalder, vikingetid og Middelalder*, edited by O. Crumlin-Pedersen, E. Porsmose & H. Thrane. Odense Universitetsforlag, 53-60.

Illkjær, J. 2000: *Illerup Ådal – et arkæologisk tryllespejl*. Aarhus: Aarhus Universitetsforlag.

Jakobsen, J.G.G. 2013: "Kystskov i vikingetidens og middelalderens Danmark: Onomastiske og andre historisk-geografiske spor efter et sagnomspundent kystskovsbælte", in *Nøvn í strandamentanini – Navne i kystkulturen*: *Forelæsninger fra det 41. NORNA-symposium i Tórshavn 2.-4. juni 2011*, edited by T.K. Jakobsen, K. Magnussen, A. Johansen & E. Weyhe. Uppsala: NORNA-förlaget (NORNA-rapporter, Vol. 89), 112-130.

Jessen, M.D. 2012: Tissø og Gudme: stormandsresidenser og førkristen kult. In *Togtet: På rejse i vikingernes verden*, edited by J. Varberg & P. Pentz. København: Strandberg Publishing, 106-111.

Jessen, M.D. & K.R., Majland. 2021: "The sovereign seeress. On the use and meaning of a Viking Age chair pendant from Gudme, Denmark", *Danish Journal of Archaeology* (10), 1-23.

Jørgensen, B. 2008: *Danske Stednavne*. 3rd edition Copenhagen: Gyldendal.

Jørgensen, L. 1995: "Stormandssæder og skattefund i 3.-12. århundrede", *Fortid og nutid. Tidsskrift for kulturhistorie og lokalhistorie*. Dansk historisk Fællesråd. 1995:2, 83-110.

Jørgensen, L. 2001: From tribute to the estate system, 3rd-12th century. A proposal for the economic development of the magnates' residences in Scandinavia based on settlement structure from Gudme, Tissø and Lejre. In: *Kingdoms and Regionality. Transactions from 49th Sachsensymposium 1998 in Uppsala*, edited by B. Arrhenius. Stockholm: Archaeological Research Laboratory, Stockholm University (Theses and papers in Archaeology B:6.), 73-82.

Jørgensen, L. 2010: Gudme and Tissø. Two magnate's complexes in Denmark from the 3rd to 11th Cent. AD. In: *Trade and Communication Networks of the First Millennium AD in the northern part of Central Europe: Central Places, Beach Markets, Landing Places and Trading Centres*, edited by B. Ludowici, H. Jöns, S. Kleingärtner, J. Scheschkewitz und M. Hardt. (Neue Studien zur Sachsenforschung Band 1). Hannover, 273-286.

Jørgensen, L. 2011: "Gudme-Lundeborg on Funen as a model for northern Europe?", in *The Gudme/Gudhēm phenomenon: papers presented at a workshop organized by the Centre for Baltic and Scandinavian Archaeology (ZBSA) Schleswig, April 26th and 27th, 2010*, edited by O. Grimm and A. Pesch (Schriften des Archäologischen Landesmuseums. Ergänzungsreihe, Bd. 6). 77-90.

Jørgensen, A.N., Jørgensen L. & Thomsen L.G. 2011: "Assembly Sites for Cult, Markets, Jurisdiction and Social Relations Historic-ethnological analogy between North Scandinavian church towns, Old Norse assembly sites and pit house sites of the Late Iron Age and Viking Period", *Archäologie in Sclesmig* 2010, 95-112.

Lindqvist, S. 1910: "Ett 'Frös-vi' i Nerike", *Fornvännen* 1910, 119-138.

Lund Hansen, U. 2011: "New Analyses of the Helgö drinking-glass fragments", in *Excavations at Helgö XVIII, Conclusions and New Aspects,* edited by B. Arrhenius & U. O'Meadhra. Kungl. Vitterhets-, historie- och antikvitetsakademien, Stockholm, 97-139.

Løvschal, M., R.B. Iversen and M.K. Holst (eds.) 2020: *De dræbte krigere i Alken Enge – Efterkrigsritualer i ældre jernalder.* Jysk Arkæologisk Selskab.

McGee, T.G. 1967: *The Southeast Asian City. A Social Geography of the Primate Cities of Southeast Asia.* London: Bell.

Michaelsen, K.K. 2015: *Den romerske forbindelse. Gudme-Lundeborg og Romerriget i jernalderen.* Odense Bys Museer.

Mordechai, L. & M. Eisenberg 2019: "Rejecting Catastrophe: The Case of the Justinianic Plague", *Past & Present*, Volume 244(1), 3-50.

Mortensen, M.F., P.S. Henriksen & A-L.H. Olsen. 2019: "Da Fenrisulven kom til Thy", *Historisk Årbog Thy: Historisk Samfund 2019,* 7-15.

Mühlemann B., Vinner L., Margaryan A., Wilhelmson H., de la Fuente Castro C., Allentoft M.E., de Barros Damgaard P., Hansen A.J., Holtsmark Nielsen S., Strand L.M., Bill J., Buzhilova A., Pushkina T., Falys C., Khartanovich V., Moiseyev V., Jørkov M.L.S., Østergaard Sørensen P., Magnusson Y., Gustin I., Schroeder H., Sutter G., Smith G.L., Drosten C., Fouchier R.A.M., Smith D.J., Willerslev E., Jones T.C., Sikora M. 2020: "Diverse variola virus (smallpox) strains were widespread in northern Europe in the Viking Age", *Science,* 369 (6502), pubmed.ncbi.nlm.nih.gov/32703849/

Nielsen, A.B. & B.V. Odgaard. 2010: "Quantitative landscape dynamics in Denmark through the last three millennia based on the Landscape Reconstruction Algorithm approach". *Vegetation History and Archaeobotany,* vol. 19(4), 375-387.

Nygaard, S. 2018: "… nú knáttu Óðin sjá: The Function of Hall-Based, Ritualised Performances of Old Norse Poetry in Pre-Christian Nordic Religion", In *The Fortified Viking Age. 36th Interdisciplinary Viking Symposium,* edited by J. Hansen & M. Bruus. Odense: Syddansk Universitetsforlag, 26-34.

Rasmussen P. & J. Olsen. 2009: "Soil erosion and land-use change during the last six millennia recorded in lake sediments of Gudme Sø, Fyn, Denmark", Geol Surv Den Greenl Bull 17, 37-40.

Rau, A. 2020: "Southern Scandinavia in the Migration Period – an Overview", in *The Migration Period between the Oder and the Vistula (2 vols),* edited by A. Rau *(East Central and Eastern Europe in the Middle Ages, 450-1450, Vol. 59).* Leiden: Brill, 627-648.

Reiersen, H. 2017: *Elite milieus in Western Norway AD 200-550.* Ph.d.-thesis, University of Bergen.

Sanmark, A. 2015: "At the Assembly – A study of ritual space", In *Power of Practice. Rituals and Politics in Northern Europe c. 650- 1350,* edited by W. Jezierski, L. Hermansson & H.J. Orning. Turnhout: Brepols Publishers, 79-112.

Sarris, P. 2022: "Viewpoint New Approaches to the 'Plague of Justinian", *Past & Present,* 254(1), February 2022, 315-346.

Sundqvist, O. 2011: "Gudme on Funen: A Central Sanctuary with Cosmic Symbolism?", in *The Gudme-Gudhem Phenomenon: Papers Presented at a Workshop Organized by the Centre for Baltic and Scandinavian Archaeology (ZBSA), Schleswig, April 26th and 27th, 2010,* edited by O. Grimm & A. Pesch. Neumünster: Wachholtz, 63-76.

Sundqvist, O. 2015. *An Arena for Higher Powers: Ceremonial Buildings and Religious Strategies for Rulership in Late Iron Age Scandinavia.* Leiden: Brill Academic Publishers.

Svensson, K. 2008: "Götavi – en vikingatida kultplats", in *På väg genom Närke, ett landskap genom historien,* edited by A. Lagerstedt. (Rapporter från Arkeologikonsult 2008), 197-210.

Sørensen, P.Ø. 1994: "Gudmehallerne. Kongeligt byggeri i jernalderen", *Nationalmuseets Arbejdsmark* 1994, 25-39.

Sørensen, P.Ø. 2022: *Gudme. Iron Age Settlement and Central Halls.* (Pre-Christian Cult Sites, vol. 1.). Oxford: Oxbow Books.

Theuws, F. 2004: "Exchange, religion, identity and central places in the early Middle Ages", *Archaeological Dialogues* 10(2), 121-138.

Thomsen, P.O. 1994: "Lundeborg – an Early Port of Trade in South-East Funen", In *The Archaeology of Gudme and Lundeborg,* edited by P.O. Nielsen et al. *(Arkæologiske Studier.* Vol. X). Copenhagen, 23-29.

Ward-Perkins, B. 2005: *The Fall of Rome and the End of Civilization.* Oxford: Oxford University Press.

BY ANNE PEDERSEN

Chapter 5
Jelling: a Central Place or a Royal Place, and what is the Difference in the 10th Century?

ABSTRACT

The first known references to Jelling are by the Danish chroniclers Sven Aggesen (c. 1185) and Saxo (c. 1200). By then, two centuries had passed since the death of King Harald and it cannot be of any wonder if details of events were omitted or forgotten, and the narratives adapted to suit the agenda of their authors. Jelling has long been perceived as a place of burial and royal commemoration, and the monuments have played a key role in discussions of the process of state formation and religious transition, lending name to both the Jelling dynasty and the Jelling centre. The results of the most recent excavations have added both scale and complexity to the site, and it has proved even more impressive in terms of the knowledge and the resources required for its construction. The extravagant dimensions and stringent layout of the site and its components have given rise to new questions, and this paper will present the most recent suggestions for interpretations of the function and purpose of the place in the socio-political milieu of 10th-century Scandinavia and northern Europe.

The monument complex at Jelling has been mentioned several times in recent years in connection with the manor site at Erritsø. While Erritsø is situated on the east coast of Jutland, facing the Little Belt, Jelling lies further inland north of the Vejle River Valley. The two places are only about 30 km apart, and there are evident similarities between them, not least in the remarkable geometric stringency of their layout: the straight lines and the clearly defined corners of the main enclosures. Yet, the sites are not identical. Unlike Erritsø which was identified during a rescue excavation in 2006, Jelling is an old site in research terms, and much has been said and written about the place and its significance in the Viking Age.[1] Scientific interest in Jelling was rekindled in 2006/2007 by the discovery of the remains of a huge palisade and two buildings of

---

1   See for instance, Pedersen 2006; Holst et al. 2013

Fig. 1. A modern visualization created in 2013 by the sculptor Ingvar Cronhammer in collaboration with Arkitekt Kristine Jensens Tegnestue. In the background the North Mound and Jelling Church. Photo Anne Pedersen, 2015.

Viking Age type, which added previously unknown and unexpected components to the monument area (Fig. 1). Subsequent investigations from 2009-2013, initiated as a joint venture between the National Museum, Vejlemuseerne (Vejle Museums) and participants from the universities of Aarhus and Copenhagen, have accentuated several key questions. What was Jelling apart from a monumental burial site and a place of royal commemoration? The two rune stones in front of the present Romanesque stone church refer to two generations of the royal family in the 10th century, but was Jelling as such a central place and if so central to whom; and at what level of society? What was the function of the complex; how did it work? The aim of the following chapter is to present the new discoveries at Jelling and their implications.

A royal residence?

The first known references to Jelling are from the Danish chroniclers Sven Aggesen (*c.* 1185) and Saxo (*c.* 1200). Two centuries had passed since the death of King Harald and his parents King Gorm and Queen Thyra, and details of life and events in Jelling had probably been long forgotten or were perhaps deemed less relevant by the chroniclers to potential readers and the persons who commissioned their work. Yet, some form of memory or tradition was still alive. Both Aggesen and Saxo refer to the twin burial mounds of King Harald's parents, which according to Aggesen were placed close to the royal residence, the *regis curiam*, and between which a church (*sacrarium*) could be seen according to Saxo.[2] A few decades later, Jelling was recorded as royal property in the Cadastre of King Valdemar (*Kong Valdemars Jordebog*) from 1231, a status, it could have acquired in earlier centuries and which would seem to indicate a royal estate in the area.

Interest in the mounds and rune stones as relics of the past was awakened in the late 16th and 17th centuries.[3] The early antiquarians showed little interest in the surroundings of the monuments, apparently taking for granted that Jelling had been a royal residence in ancient times. Although local legends relating to the royal family were reported to Professor Ole Worm at Copenhagen University, the description of Jelling in his epic work *Danicorum monumentorum Libri Sex* (Monuments of Denmark in Six Books) from 1643 only includes the standing monuments, i.e. the two mounds associated with King Gorm and Queen Thyra, the two rune stones and the stone church. Worm's approach to Jelling is thus very different from the one he applied to ancient Lejre in Zealand where other local monuments and the surrounding landscape formed an integrated part of the narrative.[4]

In the early 19th century, J.J.A. Worsaae, who was to become deeply involved in the excavations initiated by King Frederik VII at Jelling in 1861, pointed to the remarkable lack of Viking Age finds from the area, thus questioning a general assumption at his time that Jelling in view of its significance must have been a densely populated place.[5] According to the ancient chronicles and attested by the two great mounds and rune stones, King Gorm and Queen Thyra were buried here and there was once a royal estate in the vicinity. Worsaae argued, however, that there was no written evidence to confirm that Jelling was the main residence of King Harald or indeed any other Danish king, and it was not possible to determine where the king had preferred to stay nor how often.[6]

The main purpose of the investigations in 1861 was to determine whether King Gorm might be buried in the South Mound in a chamber comparable to the presumed resting place of Queen Thyra discovered in the North Mound in 1820. No attempts were made to locate a royal residence; nor did investigations conducted in the 1940s by the architect and archaeologist Ejnar Dyggve meet with any success in this respect. In addition to excavations in the two mounds as well as in and around the church, he opened a trench east of the North Mound, towards the former Bailiff's farm (*Fogedgården*) which he believed would be the most likely location for a residence. This hypothesis was based upon his experience in the eastern Mediterranean area, where a royal residence

2 Aggesøn, ch. VII; Saxo Book 10, ch. 6
3 Jacobsen and Moltke 1942, 65-81
4 Worm 1643
5 Worsaae 1841, 146-147
6 Worsaae 1842, 276-280; 1843, 262-263

(*palatium*) would often be linked to a sanctuary and a royal burial.[7] No remains were identified, however, and after severe critique from among others Olaf Olsen[8], Dyggve's controversial proposal of a pagan temple and sanctuary in Jelling was abandoned, and with it also the search for the residence of the royal family.

Since then, focus has gradually shifted from Jelling as a place of residence towards Jelling as a high-profile venue for important events associated with the development of kingship and the consolidation of the Church. In the 1980s, Klavs Randsborg introduced terms such as "the Jelling centre" and "the west Danish Jelling state", and assigned Jelling a major, even decisive role in the state formation process of the Viking Age.[9] Worth noting was its easily defendable and central position "like a spider" in a net with comparatively short distances to other important centres in western Denmark. It was not a city but rather a "gigantic estate centre or manor house, even a palace … adequately positioned for the king".[10] Other interpretations stressed the communicative qualities of the monuments which emphasized Jelling as "a place of power and of dynastic memory", well suited as a place for major thing meetings at which royal power and legitimacy could be visually demonstrated within a framework of law and religion.[11]

Buildings and palisade

The initial excavations by Vejle Museum in 2006/2007 revealed the remains of a wooden palisade and a building of Trelleborg-type, named after the well-known ring fortresses, associated with King Harald. Several large stones and a posthole to the north of the North Mound were assumed to mark the northern end of a huge ship setting, twice the length of the monument proposed by Knud J. Krogh after his excavations at Jelling in the 1970s.[12] As part of the subsequent research campaign of the Jelling Project, trial trenches covering an area of about 12 hectares north of the palisade were investigated in 2009. A single building of Viking Age type was uncovered about 350 m northeast of the palisade (and, a few years later, a second building next to this) but contrary to expectations, no workshop areas or subsidiary buildings were identified, and there was no evidence of trade or craft activities on a scale which could indicate a permanently or intensively occupied site. Excavations in the following years, covering an area of about 21,000 m2 in total within the enclosure, revealed traces of further buildings of Trelleborg-type which clearly were associated with the palisade (Fig. 2). The buildings provided an approximate date for the complex in the second half of the 10th century, and as such during the reign of King Harald. This was confirmed by dendrochronological analysis of palisade timbers recovered in 2013 from the pond Smededammen in the southern

---

7   Dyggve 1959, 116-122; Pedersen and Madsen 2023
8   Olsen 1966, 230-232, 244-267
9   Randsborg 1980, 125-133, 167-169; 1991
10 Randsborg 2008, 1
11 Roesdahl 2011, 353-358
12 Krogh 1993, 252-253; Andersen 2009

Fig. 2. A Trelleborg-type building uncovered in June 2010, seen from the south. Two porches placed diagonally opposite one another on the long sides of the building are yet to be uncovered. Photo: The Jelling Project.

part of the enclosure (Fig. 3). Of the samples, falling within a date range of 958-985, one of the planks came from a tree most likely felled around 968.[13] The palisade was therefore constructed shortly after the burial in the North Mound, possibly even while the mound was being completed.

Surprisingly few Viking Age artefacts were recovered in the initial surveys and excavations of the enclosure, and notably nothing in the Jellinge style defined by the animal motifs of the small silver cup discovered in the North Mound in 1820.[14] The lack of material finds forms a strong contrast to the evidence from, for example, the manor site immediately west of lake Tissø in Zealand, where literally thousands of metal artefacts have come to light, including a gold neck ring weighing almost 2 kilos.[15] Although it cannot be ruled out that remains of settlement activity have been destroyed by the present town, it is worth noting that the private collections of Worsaae from the early 19th century (now held in the British Museum) contain several prehistoric finds but no

---

13 Jessen et al. 2014
14 Krogh and Leth-Larsen 2007
15 Jørgensen 2003

Fig. 3. *Palisade timbers in the pond Smededammen, seen from the west. The line of oak planks with a row of oak posts along either side corresponds to the post outlines and patterns observed elsewhere along the palisade. Photo Peter Jensen Maring, 2013.*

Viking Age artefacts from the Jelling area, and that little has been discovered in more recent excavations in the town and its immediate outskirts to the south.[16]

The most striking feature of the Jelling complex is perhaps its layout and use of space. The enclosure covers about 12.5 hectares – far more than any known contemporary "manor site". The four sides, each measuring c. 360 m in length, appear to run in almost completely straight lines; minor deviations are probably due to slight inaccuracies in the surveying methods used when laying out the palisade in the uneven terrain, rather than any lack of attention to detail. The North Mound (with its burial chamber) lies at the exact centre of the enclosure, and three near identical Trelleborg-type buildings

---

16   Lindblom 2020

in the northeast quadrant appear to be laid out according to a very precise plan.[17] The distance between the palisade and the nearest wall of each building corresponds to roughly half the length of the main building corpus, and the distance of the southern building and its counterpart to the northwest in the quadrant to the northeast corner of the palisade is the same. This controlled use of space formed the inspiration for an initial, but unverified interpretation presented in the newspaper *Jyllands-Posten*, 29th August 2010, which emphasized a military perspective with identical buildings along all sides of the palisade.

Subsequent excavations in the northwest quadrant revealed no traces of similar buildings although the line of the palisade was confirmed, and the layout of the southern half of the enclosure remains uncertain. This area was heavily built-up in modern times and is still partly covered by the present town. In 2020, a building (not of Trelleborg-type) was identified in the gardens of the farm Anesminde in the western part of the enclosure. Unlike those in the northeast quadrant, this building is very close to the line of the palisade and appears to deviate slightly in orientation. The area of potential overlap between the building and palisade was not available for excavation, and the stratigraphical relationship between the two structures could therefore not be verified and it is uncertain whether they could be contemporary.[18] Neither could the exact nature of an opening in the palisade to the west be determined, and although it seems likely that an enclosure of this size would have had several entrances, no other openings apart from a gate to the north have yet been identified.

The orientation of the western and eastern sides of the enclosure does not correlate with the main axis running through the ship setting and the North and South Mounds. This could indicate two phases, i.e. that the ship setting predates the enclosure. Nevertheless, they do appear to be closely related in that the North Mound forms the centre of both the ship setting and the enclosure, and the estimated length of the ship setting is close to the length of the sides of the enclosure. It is therefore possible that the rhombic shape of the enclosure was adapted to accommodate the length of the ship setting and leaving space for movement between its northern and southern ends and the timber palisade.

Inspired master builders

The monument complex is in many ways unique, but parallels and inspiration from other sources are evident, and it would be a mistake to view the place in isolation. The new discoveries (the straight lines of the palisade and the buildings behind it) tie the monuments even closer than before to other building works associated with King Harald in the second half of the 10th century: the well-known bridge at Ravning Enge in the Vejle River Valley only 10 km south of Jelling, the ring fortresses of Trelleborg-type (Aggersborg and Fyrkat in Jutland, Nonnebakken in Funen, Trelleborg and Borgring in

---

17 Jessen et al. 2014
18 Pers. comm. Charlotta Lindblom

Zealand; possibly also Borgeby in Scania), and parts of the Danevirke rampart system at the southern border of the Danish kingdom in present-day Germany. Other building works such as an extension of the rampart around the town of Aarhus (*Aros*) are possibly also associated with royal, perhaps economic interest.[19]

Construction or at least planning probably took place at several of these sites at the same time, and they bear witness to a similar degree of technical knowledge and command of both human and material resources. The *c.* 760 m long Ravning bridge was built around 980.[20] It runs in a completely straight line, set out with "surveyor's sticks" of hazelwood. Within an overall range from 24 to 34 cm, more than two thirds of the examined oak bridge posts measure *c.* 30 × 30 cm in cross section.[21] This may be compared to the planks of the Jelling palisade, which on average measure *c.* 30 × 10 cm although with considerable variation probably due to variations in the available source material.[22] The ring fortresses were constructed in the period *c.* 970 to *c.* 980.[23] They vary in detail but conform to a common template which includes a circular rampart (with full or partial concentric moat) and a strictly organised interior layout. Worth noting are the dimensions: an inner diameter of 120 m at Fyrkat and 240 m at Aggersborg compared with the side length of *c.* 360 m of the Jelling palisade. The straight line of the Ravning Bridge and the V-shaped moat of the ring fortresses recur at Kovirke, an independent line of defence south of the main Danevirke ramparts. Based on ^{14}C determinations and similarities in construction, Kovirke is probably contemporary with the fortresses[24], whereas dendrochronological dating results from the Danevirke indicate that the Main Wall was renovated and the Connecting Wall to Hedeby established at the time when the enclosure at Jelling was being built.[25]

The scale of these building works has been associated with royalty and military power, and as mentioned above, the massive nature of the Jelling palisade gave rise to the suggestion that the enclosure was intended as a fortress along the lines of the Trelleborg fortresses. There are, however, significant differences. A circular form is easier to control and defend than the long straight lines of the palisade, and where the fortresses appear to aim for maximum utilization of all available space, the goal in Jelling seems to have been to create an imposing structure where space and room for movement were essential. The visual experience of the places would also have been different. People approaching Jelling would find their vision and path blocked by the long sides of the palisade, whereas in the case of the fortresses the closer they came to the gate, the less they would see of the circular rampart. There is no evidence of other defensive structures in Jelling, giving the impression that the palisade was first and

19 Skov 2010
20 Christensen 2003
21 Jørgensen & Møller 1999, 72-73
22 Andersen et al. 2023
23 Roesdahl & Sindbæk 2014, 208
24 Andersen 1998, 153-168
25 Ibid., 89-90

foremost intended for visual display and demarcation of space, implying also control of access to and from the enclosure.

The well-defined units of measurement and geometric stringency observed at Ravning and the fortresses as well as at Jelling probably contributed to an effective construction process while at the same time creating an easily recognizable and powerful expression. The sites suggest that the architectural principles were transferrable (and thus could be communicated) and that the scale could be adjusted to fit the individual structures, their purpose and natural setting. Like the fortresses and the bridge at Ravning, the Jelling enclosure was a short-lived manifestation and appears to have been abandoned around AD 1000, when the northern line was cut by a new building.

Based on the dendrochronological results, the Jelling enclosure preceded the ring fortresses. It is therefore likely that structures elsewhere such as in the rural settlements of the time provided models for the buildings as well as inspiration for the overall layout and organization of space. Numerous excavations of settlements since the 1970s have revealed common features such as four-sided enclosures with buildings and outhouses located close to the main, surrounding fences and the main house or hall placed in the central focal area. In the case of Jelling, this was the area to the south of the North Mound, where traces of several wooden building phases, the earliest following a traditional "hall" architecture, have been identified beneath the present stone church, and where the impressive memorial to King Harald's parents stood.

The Jelling enclosure is, however, much larger than any known farmstead or "manor site", and the time depth here seems to be much shallower than at other sites, including Erritsø to the southeast. This does not imply that there was a settlement void in Jelling before construction of the monuments but that the settlement pattern of the Iron Age and Early Viking Age differed, for instance, from that of Erritsø, Tissø and Lejre in Zealand or Uppåkra in Scania where high-status presence, significant ritual practices and activities such as extensive trade appear to have been maintained through centuries. In the case of Erritsø, the importance of the surrounding region of Elbo Herred is supported also by the place name evidence whereas no place names indicative of special administrative (royal), military or religious functions at Jelling have been identified.[26] Judging by the current picture, the enclosure and monument complex were new features in an otherwise undistinguished rural community similar to many others in the region, and there is a conspicuous lack of structures or finds related to agriculture, husbandry, or production – with the reservation that any necessary supplies, manpower or materials may have been provided by farmsteads located at some distance from the enclosure and perhaps managed by royal stewards. One such steward *(bryde)* could be the man Tófi who raised a rune stone in memory of his wife at Store Rygbjerg, just over 15 km southwest of Jelling.[27] Tófi is possibly the same man as Hrafnunga-Tófi who is named on two rune stones at Læborg and Bække another 15 km further to the southwest, both

---

26 Lindblom 2023; Christensen 2023
27 Imer 2023, 170-187; Imer et al. 2023

of which mention a lady named Thyrvé (Thyra); the stone from Bække even recording that Tófi together with two other men built Thyrvé's mound.

The purpose of Jelling

According to Ejnar Dyggve, the North Mound and the stone setting in Jelling can be regarded as archaic features, deliberately chosen in order to create the most magnificent stage for the kingdom and the king to act upon – allowing the king or rather kings, Gorm and Harald and perhaps later generations, to demonstrate and in this way strengthen their authority and their rights on a level corresponding to that of other contemporary rulers, or even the neighbouring Ottonian Empire.[28] In this respect, the location south of the ancient mound group Mangehøje would be very appropriate.

The exaggerated scale and the choice of monument types in Jelling may have served the additional purpose of establishing a link to other legendary places in Scandinavia, such as Gamla Uppsala in Uppland, Sweden, where raised halls and great mounds dominated the landscape.[29] Viewed in this light, the purpose of the South Mound, which appears never to have contained a grave, may have been to create two clearly identical monuments, two "burials" (Harald's parents), and together with the ship setting a series of monuments and thus also a visual impression of "time-depth" implying ancestral legitimacy. Only a short section of the stone ship has survived beneath the South Mound, whereas the tradition of two burial mounds was alive at the time of Sven Aggesen and Saxo.

The stone setting and impressive mounds were well-known forms of monumental expression but were combined at a scale not previously seen and truly worthy of an ambitious dynasty striving for power in competition with other prominent families in Scandinavia and perhaps also in a wider European perspective. The Jelling Monuments have been compared to Carolingian Aachen and the Carolingian-Ottonian palatinate of Paderborn in Germany.[30] Both Aachen and Paderborn include multiple components. From around AD 780 Charlemagne extended the Aachener Pfalz with a royal hall (*aula regia*), the Pfalz chapel, a residential tower, garrison and court facilities. Similar components are present in Paderborn in the royal residence (and *aula regia*), the cathedral, and facilities for the attending clergy. The different building phases at Paderborn are an indirect reflection of the shifting balance of power between secular authority and the Church. Although the physical form of Jelling was very different, the monumental architecture and the defined space probably served similar purposes, by providing an official "stage" or setting for significant political/social/religious events while also visually emphasizing the status and authority of the king.

As said, it would be a mistake to view Jelling as an isolated site or *the* centre of the kingdom. In an age of itinerant kingship, it would have functioned in conjunction with

---

28 Dyggve 1955, 140; 1959, 108
29 Ljungkvist & Frölund 2015
30 Meier 2002; Wemhoff 2014

other sites, including estates that could generate the necessary revenue and resources for the maintenance of the royal court. Exactly how this would have worked in 10th-century Denmark, is less easy to determine but neighbouring countries may again offer useful models. Aachen was a favoured place of Charlemagne, and it was chosen as the place to mark the election of Otto I as king in 936 – a demonstration of legitimacy and heritage. The travels of Otto I across his dominion are documented in the written sources.[31] Sites with political significance include Memleben where both Henry the Fowler, the father of Otto I, and he himself died, and Quedlinburg where Henry and Queen Mathilda, the mother of Otto I, were buried side by side. In March 973, the Easter court assembly was held here, a major political and cultural event, in which a delegation from the Danes, probably on behalf of King Harald, took part. Court assemblies, in Latin *conventus*, were held at regular intervals, when the king/emperor gathered all the leading secular and ecclesiastic powers of the realm for *auxilium et consilium*, help and advice (consultation) on matters of life and death, rights and careers.

A similar situation may be envisaged for England in the early 10th century, where in 924 Aethelstan (grandson of Alfred the Great and half-brother of Edgith, the first wife of Otto I) succeeded to a vastly expanded kingdom including all the Anglo-Saxon kingdoms south of the Humber River. New strategies had to be devised for ruling a kingdom covering a much wider geographical area than before. This included the need to find mechanisms to ensure the continued loyalty of the nobility dispersed across the king's realm. Aethelstan appears to have held his council meetings mostly in Wessex. This would require many leaders to travel to attend, making the royal council meetings larger and more diverse than before – a new form of assembly.[32] The administrative and legal systems of Athelstan's rule were matched with new expressions in word and image of his conceptions of royal power and authority. Scribes and artists invented discourses suitable for his assumption of kingship over the English and the unification of England, while leading men, meeting with the king in council at different places, worked strategically to further the acceptance and maintenance of the king's authority and obedience to his law.[33] Their efforts laid the foundations for his successors in the 10th century.

Following the patterns from the Ottonian empire and Anglo-Saxon England, more royal sites would probably have existed in Denmark, including meeting points that could be reached by many people at given times. The Jelling complex exhibits many of the features and qualities of a major assembly site.[34] It demonstrates a deliberate use of landscape that would have enhanced the visual and bodily experience of the site, and it is situated close to areas where land and sea routes converged. The final passage from the main traffic arteries such as the Army Road from the south required only a short journey through a very distinct landscape – Jelling Heath to the west, and Vejle River and Grejs Valley to the south and east. The timber palisade radiated power and

---

31 Müller-Mertens 2001, 193-195
32 Foot 2012, 128-136
33 Ibid., 10-11
34 Sanmark 2015

Fig. 4. *King Harald's rune stone with the image of Christ. The full inscription reads "King Haraldr ordered this monument made in memory of Gormr, his father, and in memory of Thyvé, his mother; that Harald who won for himself all of Denmark – and Norway – and made the Danes Christian". Photo: Roberto Fortuna, 2010.*

authority, and the monuments would have rivalled anything travellers might have seen at time-honoured places elsewhere in Scandinavia. The king and others of high-status were probably accompanied by armed men, and the enclosure could provide additional protection not only of people but of the royal burials and monuments, and it would separate those who were permitted to enter (and participate in the significant events and rituals) and others who would be left outside.

As an *ad hoc* royal assembly site, Jelling may have been one, perhaps the most important, of the places, where King Harald's succession was officially recognised and commemorated for the future. Exactly what this entailed is not known but sagas from the following centuries suggest that it would have been a highly ritualised process witnessed by leading members of the elite and possibly delegates from foreign powers.[35] Apart from the official acts and ceremonies, events at such an assembly might include banquets, processions, gift-giving, perhaps entertainment in the form of games or hunts, as well as recitals of poetry and song – activities that are reflected in high-status burials and finds of the 10th century such as the hoards from Fejø, Ribe Nørremark and Terslev which contain small silver drinking cups, in Fejø and Ribe combined med a silver *pyxis* of Frankish origin.[36]

To conclude, Jelling does not appear to have been a centre in the sense of an economic or administrative centre serving a region or the kingdom as a whole, nor a major production unit characterized by extensive trade and craft activity, and although the place incorporated many of the monuments and architectural components seen at other sites, it could not have functioned as a self-sustaining unit. The king and royal family would have had other places of residence and need not have stayed at Jelling for any considerable length of time. Events here probably relied on local resources, both human and material, but it is unlikely that the enclosure was intended for use by the local population. Instead, the place could have functioned as a royal assembly site on a higher geo-political level, possibly extending beyond the king's immediate sphere of interest in southern Scandinavia. It demonstrated the success of the royal family, its power and command of resources. On the rune stone commemorating his parents, King Harald claimed that he had won for himself all of Denmark and Norway (his succession and rule may have been confirmed in Jelling). The importance of family (legitimacy by calling upon ancestry and continuity between generations) is stressed and the image of Christ evokes religion as a significant component of the king's rule (Fig. 4).

Jelling lived on, not as an economic, political, or ecclesiastic centre which catered to a steadily growing population, but as a place of memory which could be recalled and reinterpreted in new contexts, a place where people congregated for one reason or another. It is not known how events affected the local population. The stone church with its impressive frescoes continued in use, and the deceased associated with the mounds and rune stones became the subject of legend. The most recent campaign has opened new avenues of research, with new questions as to how and where Jelling fits into the increasingly diverse picture of contemporary settlement, social order and complexity.

---

35 Sundqvist 2014; 2016, 476-502; Pedersen et al. 2023
36 Wamers 2005, 90, 178-181

Bibliography

Aggesøn, Sven. 2017: *Kortfattet Historie om Danmarks Konger.* Edited by M.Cl. Gertz. (Sven Aggesøns Historiske Skrifter). Copenhagen, 31-90.

Andersen, H.H. 1998: *Danevirke og Kovirke. Arkæologiske undersøgelser 1861-1993.* Højbjerg.

Andersen, S.W. 2009: "Bautasten og kæmpehegn", *Skalk* 2009/1, 11-15.

Andersen, S.W., M.D. Jessen, C. Lindblom & A. Pedersen. 2023: "The palisade and gate", in *Jelling – Monuments and Landscape,* edited by A. Pedersen, M.D. Jessen & M.K. Holst (Publications from the National Museum. Studies in Archaeology & History vol. 20.4. 1 Jelling Series). Odense, 161-192.

Christensen, K. 2003: "Ravning-broens alder", *Kuml,* 213-226.

Christensen, L.E. 2023: "Places and place names", in *Jelling – Monuments and Landscape,* edited by A. Pedersen, M.D. Jessen & M.K. Holst (Publications from the National Museum. Studies in Archaeology & History vol. 20.4. 2 Jelling Series). Odense, 61-94.

Dyggve, E. 1955: "Jellingkongernes mindesmærker", in *Jelling. Det gamle kongesæde. Vejle Amts historiske Samfunds Festskrift 1905 – 6. januar – 1955,* edited by A. Hansen, N. Jacobsen & J. Jakobsen. Copenhagen, 127-197.

Dyggve, E. 1959: "Om vore ældste Kongsgårde. Om deres forudsætninger", *Septentrionalia et Orientalia. Stvdia Bernhardo Karlgren. A.D.III Non.Oct.Anno MCMLIX dedicata.* Stockholm, 107-122.

Foot, S. 2012: *Æthelstan. The first king of England.* New Haven and London.

Holst, M.K., M.D. Jessen, S.W. Andersen & A. Pedersen. 2013: "The Late Viking Age Royal Constructions at Jelling, Central Jutland, Denmark. Recent investigations and a suggestion for an interpretative revision", *Praehistorische Zeitschrift* 87/2, 2012 (2013), 474-504.

Holst, M.K. & A. Pedersen (forthcoming): "The Jelling Project – readdressing a national icon", in *Returning to Gokstad: The art and science of revisiting monumental burials in Scandinavia,* edited by J. Bill & H. Skalleberg Gjerde. Aarhus.

Imer, L. 2023: *Danmarks runesten. En fortælling.* Revised edition. Copenhagen.

Imer, L., L. Kitzler Åhfeldt and H. Zedig 2023: "A lady of leadership: 3D-scanning of runestones in search of Queen Thyra and the Jelling Dynasty", *Antiquity* 97/395, 1262-1278.

Jacobsen, L. & E. Moltke 1941-42: *Danmarks Runeindskrifter.* Vols 1-2. Copenhagen.

Jessen, M.D., M.K. Holst, C. Lindblom, N. Bonde & A. Pedersen 2014: "A Palisade Fit for a King: Ideal Architecture in King Harald Bluetooth's Jelling", *Norwegian Archaeological Review* 47(1), 42-64.

Jessen, M.D., A. Pedersen and M.K. Holst. 2023: "The buildings and chamber burial beneath the stone church", in *Jelling – Monuments and Landscape,* edited by A. Pedersen, M.D. Jessen and M.K Holst (Publications from the National Museum. Studies in Archaeology & History vol. 20.4. 1 Jelling Series). Odense, 275-312.

Jørgensen, L. 2003: "Manor and Market at Lake Tissø in the Sixth to Eleventh Centuries: The Danish 'Productive' sites", in *Markets in Early Medieval Europe. Trading and 'Productive' Sites, 650-850,* edited by T. Pestell and K. Ulmschneider. Bollington, 175-207.

Jørgensen, M. Schou & J.T. Møller. 1999: "Landskabet som historiens scene. Ravning Enge i vikingetid og middelalder", *Vejle Amts Årbog* 1999, 67-82.

Krogh, K.J. 1993: *Gåden om Kong Gorms Grav. Historien om Nordhøjen i Jelling.* Vikingekongernes monumenter i Jelling 1. Herning.

Lindblom, C. 2020: "Jelling: The Royal Monuments in their Regional Setting", in *Viking Encounters. Proceedings of the Eighteenth Viking Congress,* edited by A. Pedersen & S.M. Sindbæk. Aarhus: Aarhus University Press, 481-494.

Lindblom, C. 2023: "Jelling and Surroundings – The archaeological evidence", in *Jelling – Monuments and Landscape,* edited by A. Pedersen, M.D. Jessen & M.K. Holst (Publications from the National Museum. Studies in Archaeology & History vol. 20.4. 2 Jelling Series). Odense, 9-59.

Ljungkvist, J. & P. Frölund 2015: "Gamla Uppsala – the emergence of a centre and a magnate complex", *Journal of Archaeology and Ancient History* 16, 2015, 1-29. http://uu.diva-portal.org/smash/get/diva2:885236/FULLTEXT01.pdf Accessed 20.12.2022.

Meier, T. 2002: "Magdeburg zwischen Aachen und Jelling: Repräsentationsarchitektur als semiotisches System", in *Europa im 10. Jahrhundert. Archäologie einer Aufbruchszeit,* edited by J. Henning. Mainz, 311-322.

Müller-Mertens, E. 2001: "Verfassung, Reichsstruktur und Herrschaftspraxis unter Otto I", in *Otto der Grosse. Magdeburg und Europa I. Essays,* edited by M. Puhle. Mainz, 189-198.

Olsen, O. 1966: *Hørg, Hov og Kirke. Historiske og arkæologiske vikingetidsstudier.* Aarbøger for Nordisk Oldkyndighed og Historie 1965. Copenhagen.

Pedersen, A. 2006: "The Jelling Monuments – Ancient royal memorial and modern world heritage site", in *Runes and their Secrets. Studies in Runology,* edited by M. Lerche Nielsen, M. Stoklund, G. Fellows-Jensen. Copenhagen, 283-313.

Pedersen, A., M.D. Jessen & M.K. Holst. 2023: "Royal Jelling", in *Jelling – Monuments and Landscape,* edited by A. Pedersen, M.D. Jessen & M.K. Holst (Publications from the National Museum. Studies in Archaeology & History vol. 20.4. 2. Jelling Series). Odense, 127-180.

Pedersen, A. & P.K. Madsen. 2023: "Ejnar Dyggve, Jelling and the Mediterranean", in *Vikings in the Mediterranean, Proceedings of International Conference Co-organized by the Norwegian, Swedish, and Danish Institutes at Athens, Athens, 27-30 November 2019,* edited by N. Price, M. Hem Eriksen & C. Jahnke (Papers and Monographs from the Norwegian Institute at Athens, vol. 14). Athens, 263-278.

Randsborg, K. 1980: *The Viking Age in Denmark. The Formation of a State.* London/New York.

Randsborg, K. 1991: *The First Millennium AD in Europe and the Mediterranean. An Archaeological Essay.* Cambridge.

Randsborg, K. 2008: "King's Jelling. Gorm & Thyra's palace – Harald's monument & grave – Svend's Cathedral", *Acta Archaeologica* 79, 1-23.

Roesdahl, E. 2011: "Scandinavia in the Melting-pot, 950-1000", in *Viking Settlements & Viking Society. Papers from the Proceedings of the Sixteenth Viking Congress, Reykjavík and Reykholt, 16th-23rd August 2009,* edited by S. Sigmundsson. Reykjavik, 347-374.

Roesdahl, E. & S.M. Sindbæk. 2014: "The dating of Aggersborg", in *Aggersborg. The Viking-Age settlement and fortress,* edited by E. Roesdahl, S.M. Sindbæk, A. Pedersen & D.M. Wilson (Jutland Archaeological Society, vol. 82). Højbjerg, 203-208.

Sanmark, A. 2015: "At the Assembly: A Study of Ritual Space", in *Rituals, Performatives and Political Order in Northern Europe c. 650-1350,* edited by W. Jezierski, L. Hermanson, H.J. Orning & T. Småberg (Ritus et Artes 7). Turnhout, 79-112.

Saxo Grammaticus: Gesta Danorum. The History of the Danes Vol. I. Ed./transl. by K. Friis-Jensen & P. Fischer. Oxford 2015.

Skov, H. 2010: "The defence and town fortifications of Århus from the 8th to the 15th century", in *Lübecker Kolloquium zur Stadtarchäologie im Hanseraum VI: Die Befestigungen,* edited by M. Gläser. Lübeck, 883-897.

Sundqvist, O. 2014: "Religious and ideological aspects of hall interiors in the Late Iron Age", in *Runsa borg – Representative Life on a Migration Period Hilltop Site – a Scandinavian Perspective,* edited by M. Olausson (Papers from the project Runsa Borg, Uppland 2). Tallin, 111-145.

Sundqvist, O. 2016: *An arena for higher powers. Ceremonial buildings and religious strategies for rulership in Late Iron Age Scandinavia.* (Numen Book Series. Studies in the History of Religions 150). Leiden/Boston.

Wamers, E. 2005: *Die Macht des Silbers. Karolingische Schätze im Norden.* Regensburg.

Wemhoff, M. 2014: "Der Platz des Königs – Eine Studie zur Nutzung des unbebauten Raumes an Orten königlicher Repräsentation", *Acta Praehistorica et Archaeologica* 46, 161-170.

Worm, O. 1643: *Danicorum Monumentorum Libri Sex.* Hafniæ (Copenhagen).

Worsaae, J.J.A. 1841: "Undersøgelse af Gravhöie i Danmark", *Annaler for Nordisk Oldkyndighed* 1840-41, 137-163.

Worsaae, J.J.A. 1842: "Hvorvidt man kan antage, at det i Haraldskiærmosen (1835) opgravede Liig er den norske Dronning Gunhildes?", *Historisk Tidsskrift* 3, 249-92.

Worsaae, J.J.A. 1843: "Endnu nogle Bemærkninger angaaende den norske Dronning Gunhildes formeentlig opdagede Liig", *Historisk Tidsskrift* 4, 253-272.

BY CHARLOTTA LINDBLOM & KATRINE BALSGAARD JUUL

Chapter 6
Dynamic Changes of Society and Settlements in the Greater Jelling Area in the First Millennium AD

ABSTRACT

The monument area of Jelling is recognized as one of the most important sites from the Viking Age in Denmark. Since the 1980s, several archaeological excavations have been carried out in the greater Jelling area. Investigations such as Haughus, Hvesager, Syrenlunden, Rønnelunden and Grangaard Allé revealed numerous houses and settlements from the First Millennium AD. According to archaeological research in the southern outskirts of modern Jelling, this was the preferred location for the settlements from roughly 500 BC–500 AD. Although new knowledge about the greater Jelling area is still being added, it is related to an overall narrative of that area and period. That narrative has not really changed for decades.

Based on selected settlements in the greater Jelling area this paper discusses the need for adjusting the overall longhouse chronology according to regional similarities and differences. By doing so, we may reach a slightly different narrative of the greater Jelling area in AD 0-1000, where the societal changes are apparent in terms of the dynamic changes of location, size, and duration of the settlements.

Likewise, our knowledge about the Viking Age settlement in the greater Jelling area is deeply rooted in the 10th century royal Jelling. The question of continuity between the settlement from the first and second halves of the First Millennium is interesting and important for understanding the establishment of the royal Jelling.

A narrative of settlements

Due to the iconic Viking Age monuments surrounding the church in Jelling, the area has attracted the attention of scholars for centuries.[1] The area still does, and the combination of centuries of scholarly attention and numerous excavations of sites from the Iron Age and Viking Age has resulted in an immense data set. Therefore, the archaeological record of Jelling between AD 0-1000 is extraordinary.[2] We can all agree on how important it is to investigate dynamic changes in the First Millennium AD and this research will be applied to the Jelling area due to the vast amount of research conducted here, making it necessary with new investigations of the old discussions of the emergence of tribes and states during AD 0-1000.[3] However, it is outside the scopes of the current article to do more than raise awareness of the possibilities for new research.

In particular, the numerous excavations of the burial mounds and the excavations and research conducted within the Jelling Project emphasising the palisade of the Viking Age has brought new knowledge about the site.[4] Furthermore, numerous investigations in the southern outskirts of modern Jelling due to rescue excavations have been conducted by Vejle Museum since the 1980s and ongoing.[5] In particular, the Grangaard Allé site is a new piece in the puzzle for understanding Jelling as well as it is highly relevant in terms of revisiting the Danish longhouse chronology.[6]

As such Jelling is defined as a core site located in a core area (Fig. 1). The core area is defined by the immediate surroundings with a distance up to approximately 5 kilometres. According to the numerous settlements from the Iron Age in the core area of Jelling it should perhaps be defined as a core site and area for AD 0-1000 taking into consideration that the area has been inhabited ongoing from AD 0-550 and AD 950-1050.[7] All investigated sites are illustrated in Fig. 3 and a more thorough introduction to the development of settlements over time is available in Balsgaard Juul & Lindblom updating Christiansen (1999).

As we see it, the area of Jelling has been investigated so thoroughly leading to an amazing data set ready to be applied in much new research of the First Millennium in relation to the development of settlements and society. The use of the area has varied greatly during AD 0-1000 and the amount of archaeological data from the different

---

1   Balsgaard Juul & Lindblom 2022: 277ff; see also Pedersen et al. 2023; Jessen et al. 2014; Holst et al. 2012; Christiansen 1999; Roesdahl 2011; 2008; Randsborg 2008, 1980; Krogh & Leth-Larsen 2007; Hvass 1998; Krogh 1993; Dyggve 1956; 1948; Brøndsted 1940: 316ff; Müller 1897: 649ff; Kornerup 1875
2   Balsgaard Juul and Lindblom 2022, 277
3   See Mortensen & Rasmussen 1988, 1990
4   Pedersen et al. eds. 2024
5   Balsgaard Juul (forthcoming); Balsgaard Juul & Lindblom 2022, 277ff; Lindblom & Balsgaard Juul 2018: 9ff; Juel 2013; 2013b; Måge 2006a, 2006b; Christiansen 1999; Hvass 1989; Hvass 1988; Kaldal Mikkelsen 1988/89; Kaldal Mikkelsen 1987
6   Balsgaard Juul 2022: 4ff; Balsgaard Juul (forthcoming)
7   See Fig. 3, 4, and 5 updating Christiansen 1999

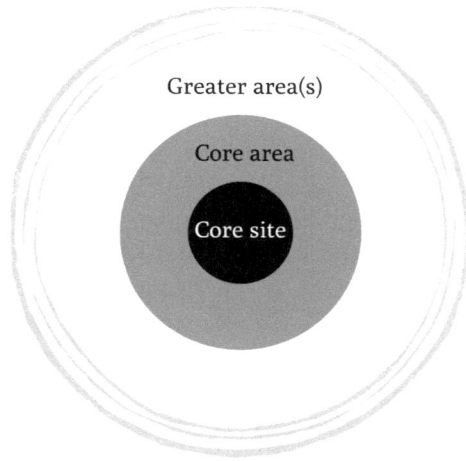

Fig. 1. A theoretical illustration of the terms core site, core area, and greater area(s).

Fig. 2. Adjusting the figure above to fit the conditions of the core site of Jelling in the First Millennium AD located in the core area of Jelling within the greater area(s).

settlements gives us a unique insight into the dynamic changes covering a large time span.[8]

Another analytical spatial division is the greater area(s) surrounding the core site and area. The greater area(s) is a dynamic term with very dynamic geographical boundaries (see Figs. 1 and 2).

The large data set will make it possible to investigate core aspects such as longhouse chronology revisited, societal developments in times of continuity and discontinuity, narratives of (Danish) state formation as well as new theoretical perspectives and methodological developments. With this article we wish to address the possibilities to use the numerous excavations in the Jelling area as stepping stones towards a new under-

---

8 Balsgaard Juul and Lindblom 2022, 270ff.

The Jelling area with the sites of 1: Grangaard Allé (AD 250-550). 2: Rønnelunden (AD 200-400). 3: Syrenlunden (AD 0-400). 4: Haughus 1 (AD 0-500). 5: Haughus 2 (AD 0-200). 6: Skovgade (AD 600/700-950). 7: Søndergård 1 (AD 200-600). 8: Skinbjerg (AD 200-500). 9: Søndergård 2 (AD 500-0). 10: Fårupvej (AD 0-200). 11: Hvesager (AD 0-200). 12: Plantagevej (AD 0-200). 13: Fårup (AD 0-200). 14: Møllegade (AD 400-600). 15: Church, burial mounds and palisade.[10]

Fig. 3.

standing of the 'tribe to state' discussion that has been ongoing in Danish archaeology for many decades.[9]

As we see it, the Jelling area is perfect to investigate new theoretical perspectives, to develop new methodological approaches and to investigate research questions that have been ongoing in Danish archaeology. To do so, we apply a holistic approach combining as many aspects as possible like the contextual archaeology described by I. Hodder.[11] To widen the debate,[12] we suggest the use of a holistic approach described as *helhedsarkæologi*

---

9   See for instance Mortensen and Rasmussen (eds.) 1991, 1998
10 After Lindblom and Balsgaard Juul 2018, 10; updating Christiansen 1999, 182
11 1986, 121
12 See Hodder 2002, 77ff.

Fig. 4. *Adjusting the figure above to fit the conditions of the core site of Jelling in the First Millennium AD located in the core area of Jelling (in dashes).*

in the research strategy developed at the archaeological department at Vejle Museum.[13] This approach emphasises the need to investigate as many aspects as possible to increase the knowledge of a particular site.[14] The way forward is combining the theoretical, and methodological knowledge with more data from the excavations.[15] Hence, a place such as Jelling should not only be understood as a core site or area of the Viking Age, but rather as an important archaeological site and area of the First Millennium AD with investigations of numerous settlements, cultural landscape, the palisade and monument area, scientific analyses of pollen, empty areas and burial sites combined with appropriate theoretical perspectives. In the end, this will lead to a strengthened understanding of the dynamic changes of society and settlements in the greater Jelling area in AD 0-1000.

13   Ravn et al. 2022
14   Balsgaard Juul (forthcoming)
15   Hodder 2002, 87

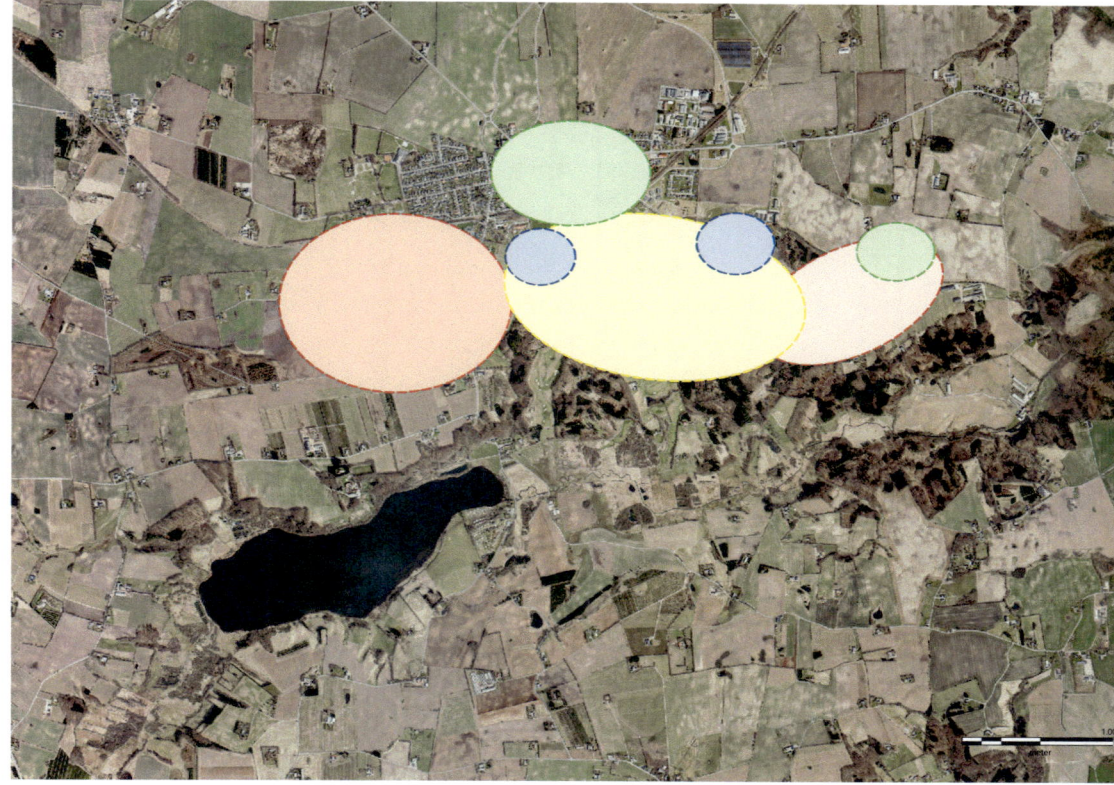

The Jelling area with settlements dated to AD 0-200 in red, AD 200-400 in yellow, AD 400-550 in blue and AD 950-1050 in green. After Balsgaard Juul & Lindblom 2022: Figure 6, p. 284.

Fig. 5.

Re-visiting the Danish longhouse chronology

To reach crucial new knowledge of the area investigated from the First Millennium AD, one approach is to revisit the Danish longhouse chronology. We have suggested this previously in relation to the site of Grangaard Allé, excavated in the south-eastern outskirts of Jelling by Vejlemuseerne (Vejle Museums) in 2016-2017.[16] This article aims to introduce preliminary thoughts and ideas leading to a future research project.

The Grangaard Allé site was an excavation of a very complex Iron Age settlement covering almost 60.000 m2. Here a total of 20.337 features were registered with most of them being postholes.[17]

A total of 21 farmsteads and two larger areas filled with pits have been recognized. 84 three-aisled longhouses, 168 economy buildings, 293 fences and fragments of fences

---

16   Balsgaard Juul (forthcoming); Balsgaard Juul 2022; Balsgaard Juul & Lindblom 2022, 279ff.
17   Balsgaard Juul 2022, 4ff.; Balsgaard Juul (forthcoming); Balsgaard Juul & Lindblom 2022, 279; Lindblom & Balsgaard Juul 2018, 9ff.

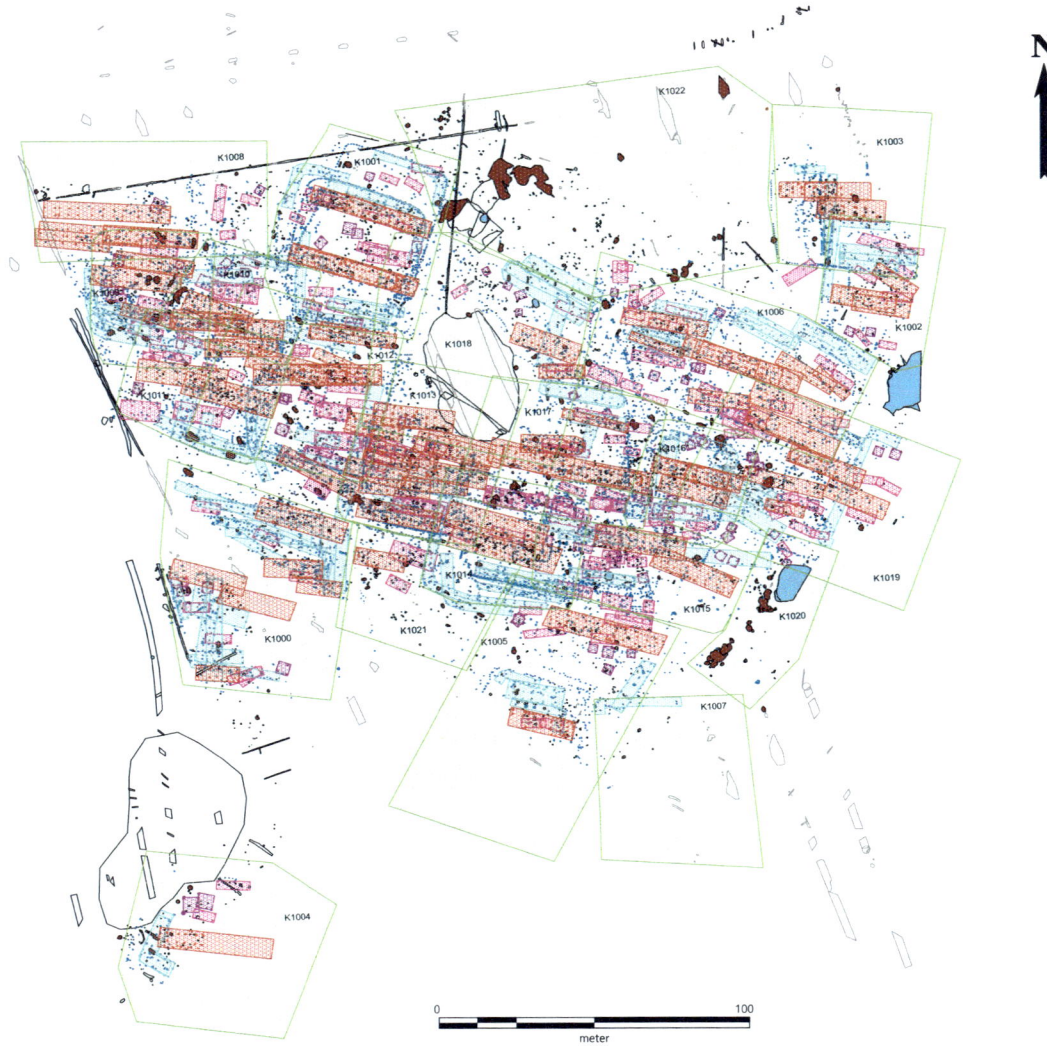

Fig. 6. *The site of Grangaard Allé with farmsteads marked in green, longhouses marked in red, economy buildings in pink, Grubenhäuser in purple, pits in brown, and fences and fence houses in blue. After Balsgaard Juul 2022.*

along with numerous fence houses, 84 granaries, 15 C-houses, three two aisled longhouses. Also, a house with assumed hall function has been recognized.[18] So far, it has not been possible to separate the farmsteads in total in terms of stratigraphy due to the fact that the number of postholes very seldom overlapped.[19] In other words, it is

---

18   Balsgaard Juul 2022, 4ff.
19   Balsgaard Juul 2022, 21; Balsgaard Juul (forthcoming)

necessary to compare the chronological observations of the longhouse development with the results of the C-14 dating.

Initially we expected the settlement of Grangaard Allé to be dated to AD 300-500 according to the Danish longhouse chronology. Later, the preliminary dating expanded to AD 300-700 still related to this chronology. The first C-14 dating took us by surprise seeing that they revealed an overall dating of the site to be AD 250-530.[20] The results from the longhouse chronology and the C-14 dating did not correlate as well as expected. To reach enhanced comprehension of the Danish longhouse chronology based on the Grangaard Allé excavations, we would suggest a large research project including all settlements from the Jelling area combining the longhouse chronology with the C-14 results to adjust the results of the chronologies of longhouse development and C-14 dating.

In total 33 house structures have been C-14 dated.[21] These results tell us that the settlement at Grangaard Allé was founded around AD 200-250 and most of the farmsteads have at least one posthole from this period. Around AD 400 there is a change in continuity of the settlement meaning that many farmsteads come to an end. However, other farmsteads were founded at this period. This suggests that the settlement was restructured and most likely downsized around AD 400.[22]

The settlement comes to an end around AD 530-550[23], which means that the settlement was inhabited for more than 300 years from AD 200/250-550.[24] The lack of settlements from the middle of the 6th century and onwards is a familiar challenge within Danish archaeology[25] where we lack the high number of settlements known from the previous centuries.[26] However, whether this is caused by the consequences of the Late Antique Little Ice Age (*LALIA*)[27] or a rapid change in the house and settlement structures resulting in difficulties to recognize them at archaeological excavations is debatable.[28]

By comparing the current knowledge of Danish longhouse chronology with the C-14 dating of Grangaard Allé it is very likely that there were two phases of settlement[29] Phase one is from AD 250-400 and contains between 10 farmsteads according to longhouse chronology and 14-17 farmsteads according to C-14 dating. Phase one is by far the largest phase with most simultaneous farmsteads with a total of 10-17 farmsteads for two centuries.

Phase two is from AD 400-550 and contains at least six farmsteads. In total 13 farmsteads were terminated around AD 550. Phase two is by far the smallest and this makes

---

20 Balsgaard Juul & Lindblom 2022, 281ff.
21 Balsgaard Juul (forthcoming); Balsgaard Juul 2022, 28ff.
22 Balsgaard Juul (forthcoming); Balsgaard Juul 2022, 33ff.
23 Balsgaard Juul (forthcoming); Balsgaard Juul 2022, 34f.; Balsgaard Juul & Lindblom 2022
24 Balsgaard Juul (forthcoming); Balsgaard Juul 2022, 35
25 See for instance Hansen 2015; Hvass 1989; Hvass 1988
26 Balsgaard Juul (forthcoming)
27 See Büntgen et. al 2016; Gräslund & Price 2012; Axboe 2001
28 Balsgaard Juul (forthcoming)
29 ibid.

it likely that a very slow termination took place during this phase leading towards AD 550 where the settlement was abandoned.

The overall understanding of society in Denmark from AD 250-550 follows the two settlement phases from Grangaard Allé, meaning that it is possible to move from postholes to society. The first phase fits our understanding of societal development in the Late Roman Iron Age, where the size of farmsteads and an increase in the number of economy buildings followed a more intensive cultivation strategy with the result of greater yield from farming and new technologies such as the rotary quern stone was introduced.[30] Traces of ordinary quern stones and rotary quern stones have been found at Grangaard Allé.[31] These aspects indicate the possibility to use Grangaard Allé and the greater Jelling area as a new way of understanding the societal changes during AD 0-1000. By looking closer at the contemporary material from the excavated settlements south of Jelling (Figs. 3-4), it becomes clear that there is an expansion of wealth. This was reflected in the grave material, where an especially rich furnished grave from the 2nd century AD was excavated at Hvesager. A grave with weaponry showing early military engagement.[32]

Furthermore, the C-14 datings demonstrate that there has been an extensive use of the area for several centuries resulting in the soil being contaminated and mixed. This will be a major issue in relation to reaching a more convincing longhouse chronology of this region as well as the overall Danish area. Almost all farmsteads have at least one house structure initiating around AD 250, but does that mean that the entire settlement always contained up to 20 simultaneous farmsteads? The answer to this is very likely no, seeing that there was a very dynamic structure within the settlement differing according to use and number of dwellers over almost 300 years from AD 250-550.[33]

The C-14 datings indicate that there were two overall phases of the settlement, but contemporary farmsteads are not yet clear to distinguish. To reach this conclusion, it could be fruitful with a similar approach of correspondence analyses as applied by M. Kähler Holst on Nørre Snede (2004), S. Vestergaard Laursen & Kähler Holst on Hummelure (2017) and finally Vestergaard Laursen & R. Birch Iversen on Hummelure and Eastern Jutland (2020). The authors all apply correspondence analysis to reach expanded knowledge of the finer chronology of the settlement as well as longhouse chronology. A similar approach would be worthwhile with the Grangaard Allé settlement in terms of three analytical steps investigating the core site, the core area and in time in the investigated area. This would in the end lead to expanded knowledge of the dynamic regionality of the societies within the Jelling area in times of continuity and change over a millennium.

Summing up, this matter becomes like the paradox of the chicken or the egg. We need a better longhouse chronology to understand the society of the First Millennium

---

30 Hedeager 1992, 169 ff.
31 Balsgaard Juul 2022, 2867 ff.
32 Dengsø Jessen; Lindblom and Pedersen 2023
33 Balsgaard Juul (forthcoming)

better, but to create a more convincing longhouse chronology we need an improved C-14 dating strategy. As the Grangaard Allé settlement demonstrates, settlements with a long use are difficult to approach due to the mixture of the cultural soil over centuries resulting in broad C-14 dating. These will not be useful to finetune the longhouse chronology, so which approach should we apply to do so? Before moving on to these questions, it is relevant to move on and look closer at Jelling as a location for the national narrative.

Local preconditions

Jelling has it all – kings, queens, and myths, based on written sources from the early Middle Ages, King Gorm and his son Haralds' statements on the two runic stones in Jelling, and the interpretations of the great monuments found here. The earlier excavations contributed to these myths.[34] These monuments are symbols of the early history of the nation, and as hereby, occupy a special position.

Taking Jelling's obvious importance into consideration, the lack of mention in contemporary written sources seems strange. The myths of Jelling are launched by the two mediaeval historians – Svend Aggesen and Saxo Grammaticus, around the year 1200.[35]

Nevertheless, the physical appearance of the site did not become visible and known by people, until King Frederik II, had a road built between Koldinghus and Skanderborghus via Jelling, around 1571. Furthermore Haralds' rune stone was raised and cleaned from dirt in 1586, also at the king's command. This is the start of a 400 year old interest in Jelling in scientific research.[36] Among the early archaeological discoveries, the discovery of a chamber grave in the northern mound in 1820-21, was probably the most significant. At the time it was believed to be the final resting place of King Gorms' queen – Thyra. In 1861, after digging a system of tunnels into the southern mound without any traces of Gorm's chamber grave, the chamber grave in the northern mound was reinterpreted as being the grave of both King Gorm and Queen Thyra.[37] Nonetheless another attempt to find Gorm's grave was made by Ejnar Dyggve in 1941, where the core and huge parts of the southern mound was removed. No grave was found. Instead, two rows of bautastones in a V-shape appeared under the mound. After further investigations in the northern mound and under the church, Dyggve was able to present a model of the presumed spatial development of the monuments.[38] At the excavations underneath the floor in the church, a layer of clay was interpreted as a floor belonging to a pagan temple. Immediately over this layer of clay, several postholes, huge stones and burned material from a floor were observed and interpreted as the subsequent stave church. He later describes the chronological transition from a pagan memorial to a Christian

---

34 Dyggve 1955, Krogh 1993
35 Aggesøn; Saxo 1917
36 Pedersen 2014
37 Kornerup 1875
38 Dyggve 1948; 1956

place of worship.³⁹ At later excavations in the church by Knud Krogh, it would become clear that there were in fact three wooden buildings underneath the present church and Dyggve's hypothesis of a pagan temple was discarded. An important and astonishing find beneath the church was the location of a chamber grave containing the remains of a middle-aged man. Unfortunately, the grave was plundered and contained very few artefacts. Nevertheless, the sparse findings from the chamber grave had a resemblance with the findings from the chamber grave previously found in the northern mound.⁴⁰ The two rows of bautastones were also reinterpreted, as a trench into the southern mound clearly showed that the two rows were slightly curved and strengthened the idea of a stone setting formed as a ship. Knud Krogh therefore published a revised theory for the development of the monument area.⁴¹ The remains of a man found in the chamber grave under the church, fit well into the story of the conversion of Harald Bluetooth and him transferring his father Gorm to sacred ground. This became the core in a new narrative of the spatial development in the monument area in the 10th century. A story about King Harald Bluetooth moving the earthly remains of his father Gorm into sacred space. This is a strong narrative still used by many. And who is to blame? It has an enormous potential for a good story, though there are obvious problems.⁴²

However, the location of Harald Bluetooth's royal estate was never a part of these discussions, though Svend Aggesen mensions it in 1185.⁴³ Excavations in the 1980s and 1990s revealed contemporary settlement areas nearby, but still 1 km from the monument area.⁴⁴

The narratives and interpretation did not really change, until 2006-7 when Vejle Museum unearthed parts of a huge palisade surrounding the monument area with an entrance to the north, a huge ship setting and parts of a Trelleborg-type house (Fig. 7). This was a game changer and within the frames of the Jelling-project (a research project between the National Museum, Aarhus University and Vejle Museum – 2008-2013), the existing narratives have been revised through research, excavations, and empirical analysis.⁴⁵

As the impressive structures within the monument area came to light, so did the questions as how to understand and interpret the relation between the monument area and surrounding areas as well as the question regarding if there were any local preconditions for the royal estate in this area.

One may say that the narrative is more fragmented today. Queen Thyra's grave is more a myth than a fact. There is no grave in the southern mound and no pagan temple

---

39 ibid. 1956
40 Pedersen 2014
41 Christensen/Krogh 1987; Krogh 1983; 1993, 260-265
42 Staecker 2005
43 Aggesøn 1917
44 Hvass 1998; Lindblom 2023
45 Kähler Holst et al. 2012; Dengsø et al. 2014

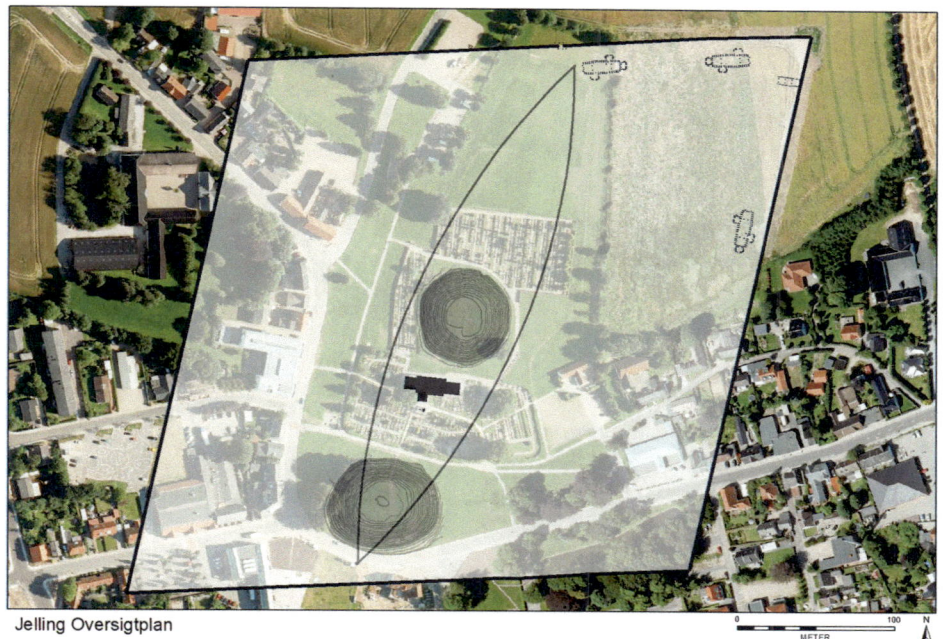

Jelling Oversigtplan

The monument area in Jelling seen in the second half of the 10th century.

Fig. 7.

underneath the church. Furthermore, the identity of the person buried in the chamber grave underneath the church is not certain either.

Instead, the latest excavations have revealed that there is still more to find in Jelling. The comprehensive structures of a settled area within the palisade and the huge stone setting surrounding the mounds, shows a larger complexity of the area than expected.[46]

As previously described, the settlement from AD 0-500 in Jelling is dense, but after the middle part of the 6th century, the traces of settlements become sparse. However, there are quite a few remarkable detector findings from this otherwise rather empty period.

In 2004, an imitation of a golden Tremessis from Dorestad was found in the vicinity of the northern mound in Jelling. This is a rare group of coins in Denmark and previously found in the southwestern and western parts of Jutland. The coin is dated to 650-675 AD.[47] In 2014 another golden Tremessis was found in Thyregod, only 18 km north of Jelling. As the coins were pierced at the rim, it is likely though that the deposition dates to the last part of the 7th or the 8th century and perhaps even somewhat later due to postponed circulation.[48]

Another remarkable detector find is the gold hoard deposited in the first half of

---

46 Dengsø Jessen, Kähler Holst, Lindblom, Bonde and Pedersen 2014
47 Moesgaard 2003
48 Lindblom 2023

the 6th century AD. The treasure was found in Vindelev, roughly 7 km northeast from Jelling. The treasure contains three roman medallions, one solidus, 13 bracteates, one pendant with stamp ornamentation and inlays with glass and a golden scabbard mount from a sword or dagger. The artefacts in the treasure cover a period of time from the middle of the 4th century to the first half of the 6th century.[49] Treasures on this scale have been found in Gudme, Funen and several of the bracteates from Vindelev show clear connection with bracteates from the area around Odense and Gudme.[50]

The following excavation revealed that the treasure had been deposited in a building, as a part of a settlement area.[51] This indicates that the treasure can be linked to a powerful elite.

Even though there are 400 years between the deposition of the Vindelev treasure and the reign of the Jelling dynasty, it may tell us something about an important area – an area with a rich and powerful heritage.

The latest excavations within the monument area in Jelling

The chapter of uncovering constructions within the monument area (i.e., within the palisade complex), was not over after the important discoveries in 2007-13. In 2019-20 Vejle Museum had the opportunity to excavate the north-western part of the area – the area around the present-day Anesminde. This is one of the "blank spaces" in the area, due to accessibility to the area. An area that the Jelling-project did not have access to in previous years. The consequences were that the only settlement that could be documented was the one in the north-eastern part of the area. As Vejle Municipality bought the area, an opportunity was suddenly gained to search the Anesminde area for traces of settlement. Some of the most important questions asked were – could we expect traces of settlement, traces of human activity and could we locate a western entrance to the monument area? The presence of a western entrance would be logical to assume, as the ancient army road is situated merely a couple of kilometres to the west. The question regarding settlement and traces of activity were highly relevant, as the earlier excavations in the north-eastern part of the monument area yielded three longhouses of Trelleborg-type as well as a minor building close to the palisade. Despite extensive analysis of the soil in the postholes there were no traces of human activity, except from microscopic traces of metalworking.[52]

The 2019-2020 excavation area was limited due to the location in a garden with several existing trees. When unearthing the area, we followed the western side of the palisade from north to south. The northernmost part of the palisade is located underneath the existing farmhouse at Anesminde, but in the rest of the area it was possible to follow the palisade southwards. The area contained several disturbances from modern

---

49   Laursen and Ravn 2022
50   Axboe 2021
51   Laursen 2021
52   Dengsø 2023

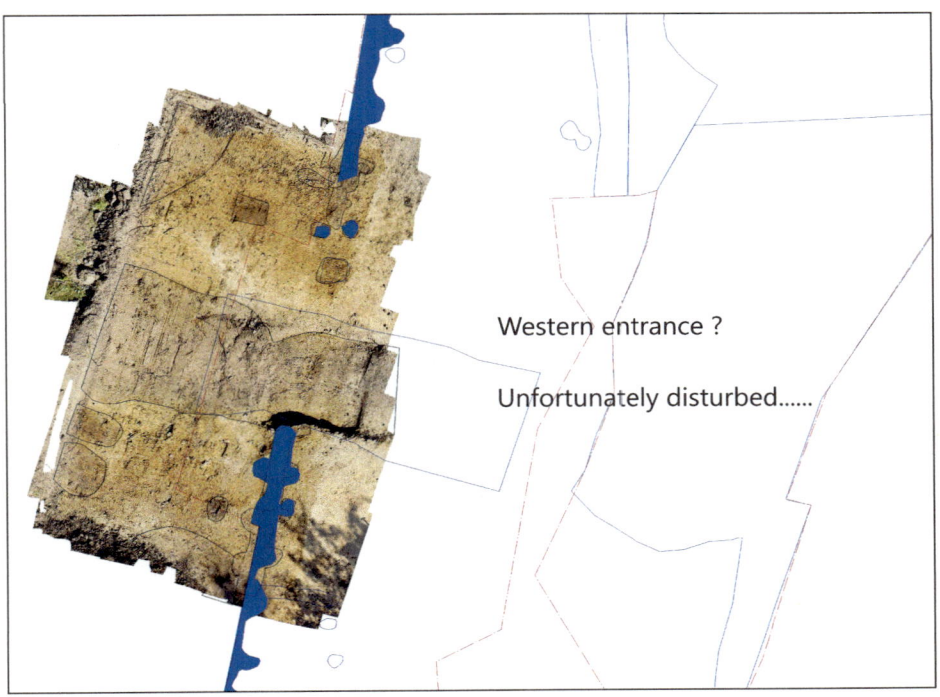

The western entrance. Photo: Arkæologisk IT, AU.

Fig. 8.

times and the 16th-17th centuries. In the southern part of the area an interruption in the palisade construction was seen, (Fig. 8) The same area was unfortunately also disturbed by a modern-day waste hole. There were no postholes indicating a superstructure, like traces of posts holding a roof over the entrance, as was the case in the northern entrance. Despite this, it was clear that the palisade was interrupted here.

In the northernmost area and immediately east of the existing farmhouse a building located seemingly parallel with the palisade was unearthed. Unfortunately, the excavation area was very limited which meant that we were not able to uncover the entire house (Fig. 9). The building measured approximately 19 m in length, but the northern gable is yet uncovered under the present garden with trees and a hedge to the north. Regarding the width, we were only able to uncover parts of the eastern wall. An approximated width would be 8.5-9 m. The present limitations mean that we are not able to establish with any certainty what type of a building this might have been. Samples from the roof-bearing posts were taken to C-14 dating, but the results were unfortunately not precise enough: AD 670-774, AD 889-989, and AD 1047-1220.[53] Although it places the building in the "right period" of time, it is not possible to place them in the same window of time as the buildings of "Trelleborg-type", from the second half of the 10th

---

53   AMS Direct, 2021

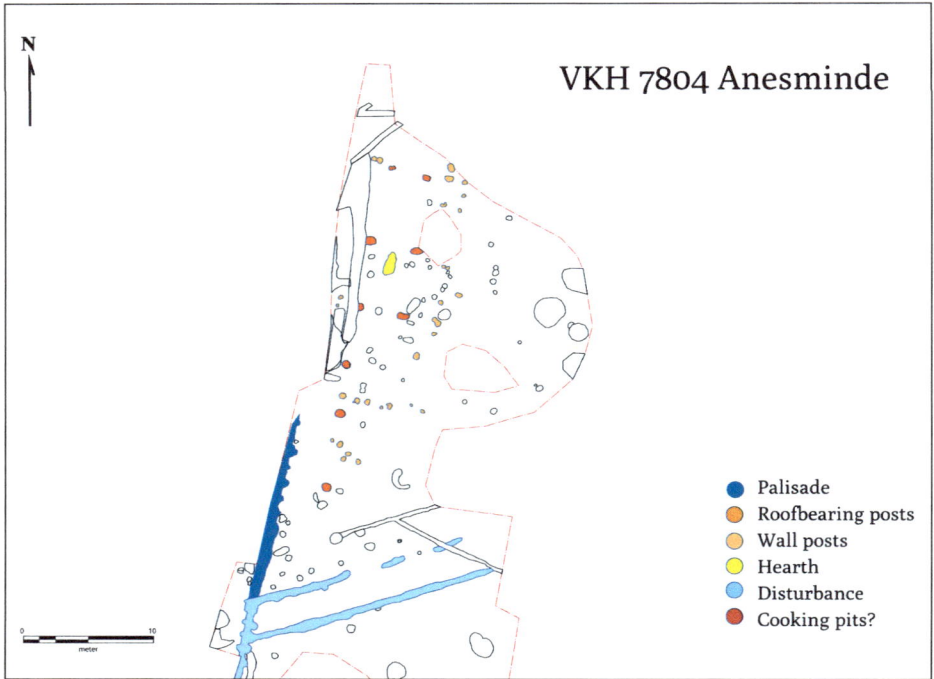

Fig. 9. *The unearthed part of a building in the northern part of the excavation area at Anesminde. Graphics: Vejle Museum.*

century. Nevertheless – the location of a building in the north-western part of the palisade, is exciting news. This also regards the dating of oblong pits with fire-cracked stones in this area. Samples were taken from two pits with the following results: AD 781-980, and AD 994-1154.[54] It í important to demonstrate an activity zone in this area.

Was Jelling densely populated in the 10th century?

From the central parts of present-day Jelling, an oval brooch of Berdal-type was found during an excavation. The brooch dates from the last part of the 8th century or the beginning of the 9th century and was found in the same area as the remains of a house, presumably dating from the 5th-7th century AD.[55]

Approximately 1-1.5 km east of Jelling, the eastern traces of a vast settlement area from the first half of the First Millennium, was registered in a trench. In the easternmost areas, parts of a settlement from the 8th-10th centuries were recognized. The extent of the settlement was not established.[56]

---

54 AMS Direct, 2021
55 Lindblom 2023
56 Christiansen 1999

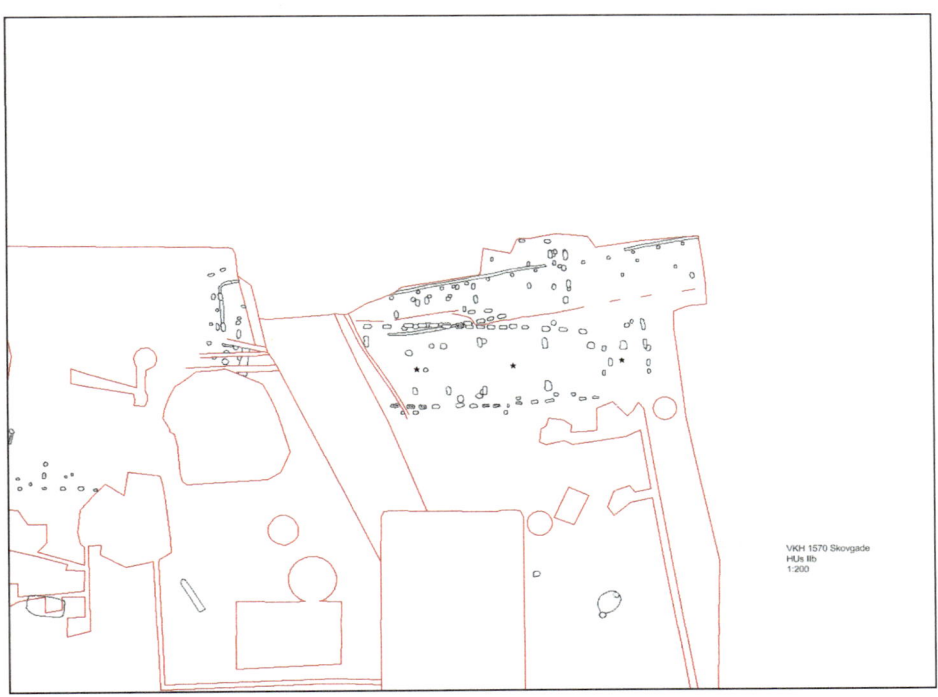

The youngest buildings from the settlement at Skovgade – dating from the middle of the 10th century. Graphics: Vejle Museum.

Fig. 10.

Furthermore, a longhouse with curved sides was excavated northeast of the monument area, interpreted as a single farmhouse from the 10th century.[57]

The best documented Viking Age settlement in the vicinity of the monument area is Skovgade, dating from the 7th-10th century and situated roughly 500 m southeast from the palisade and the monument area in Jelling. The excavated area revealed 10 houses, among those two longhouses from the middle of the 10th century. The early part of the settlement was built in the southern part of the area and has been interpreted as belonging to one farmstead, dating to the 7th-8th century. The dating of the house is based on a typological longhouse chronology as well as based on the pottery, which can be somewhat challenging as the results from Grangaard Allé have emphasised.

In the northernmost parts of the excavation area, two longhouses from the middle of the 10th century were found with one of the buildings succeeding the other stratigraphically. Unfortunately, both buildings were partly disturbed in modern times. Nevertheless, it was possible to document valuable details. The oldest longhouse was only partly preserved, with curved sides, consisting mostly of a foundation trench, but also of rectangular postholes. The later building consisted of well-preserved rectangular postholes, placed in evenly curved, long sides (Fig. 10). The excavation was carried out

57 Dengsø 2023

in 1992, i.e., 20 years before the discovery of the palisade and the buildings within it.[58] A comparison of the longhouses within the palisade, with the youngest longhouse from Skovgade, shows a resemblance in the construction details. Both are likely to be dated to the mid-10th century. The idea of these settlements being contemporary is fascinating as well as quite likely.

Taking nearby contemporary traces of settlements into consideration, it seems as if the monument area seems to stand rather by itself at the elevated area in the 10th century Jelling.

From a source critical point of view, such a statement is rather difficult to prove, as any possible contemporary settlement could be lying underneath present-day Jelling. Yet, it is important to keep in mind that vast areas around the centre of Jelling – with the monument area – have been excavated, in the search for traces of a settlement.[59]

Nevertheless, the 10th century Jelling does not appear very densely populated. This may be rather surprising, since an economic foundation, where a certain supply of for instance food and labour is included – would be expected at a royal site like Jelling and in the vicinity of it.

A different picture is seen in connection to the interaction between the magnate farm at Erritsø and the surroundings. Erritsø is situated southeast of Jelling, in the Elbo District. In the vicinity of Erritsø, at least 4 larger Viking Age settlements have been investigated within a fairly limited radius (2.5-3.5 km).[60] These may have been part of a local network, based upon mutual communication and functioned as a hinterland that also supplied resources to the magnate farm.[61] One may assume that the function of the monument area in Jelling, may have taken another form.

Dynamic societal changes

In Danish archaeology there has been an emphasis on longhouse chronology as well as state formation since the excavations of Vorbasse[62] followed by larger research projects such as From Tribe to State.[63]

Based on our chosen emphasis on dynamic societal changes the question is where to go now with the research of the late Iron Age and Viking Age Jelling? As archaeologists we always aim at peopling the past and to do so we would like to suggest an emphasis on societal changes and thus state formation. However, we need inspiration from other research fields than archaeology to fully understand state formation or state formations in the plural. Is it perhaps better to begin with a smaller place such as the Jelling site and area that has been very thoroughly investigated and then move on to the greater

58 Hvass 1992
59 Lindblom 2023
60 Ravn, Juel, Lindblom & Pedersen 2019
61 Lindblom 2023
62 Hvass 1993; 1989-1988
63 Mortensen & Rasmussen (eds.) 1991; 1988

Jelling area slowly.[64] Each new piece of the Jelling puzzle will add further knowledge and guide us towards a more holistic archaeology combining theories, methods, and data from excavations.

According to David Graeber & David Wengrow (2021) there has been a long search for the origins of the state which they find quite unfruitful, since the definitions of a state either ends up being too broad or too narrow, due to the many different types of states during the history of humankind. Today there is a tendency in social sciences to understand a state as very hierarchical with top-down structures and a desire to protect the elite within a complex society. In other words, traces of a complex society are often seen as traces of a state, which is challenging in relation to past societies.[65] Graeber and Wengrow defines this understanding as a circular argument stating that *"since states are complicated, any complicated social arrangement must therefore be a state"*.[66] This is relevant in relation to the archaeological definitions of a state and the processes from tribe to state that has been discussed within Danish archaeology since the 1980s.

Another relevant insight is defined as parallel societal developments by Mads Kähler Holst (2014), which is following the line of the critique on our understanding of a state put forward by the latter critique by Graeber and Wengrow which we agree upon. Seeing that Jelling is such a well-known archaeological site with numerous excavations and research investigations, Jelling of the First Millennium AD seems obvious to investigate to take our understanding of state development to a new level of insight. Furthermore, the status of Jelling as an archaeological core site makes it highly relevant to discuss the possible traces of state formation during the First Millennium AD. Yet, we find it very likely that the traces will be dynamic and changing over time as most traces of past human societies are. There is not just one specific pattern of a state or complex society but rather a need to investigate the parallel societal developments in times of state formation and social change. Once more, the holistic approach will be fruitful to compare traces of human settlements with traces of social organisation, state formation, identities and roles expressed by women and men of the past societies.

Although this has been an important research topic for many decades, we still discuss state formation as a single event setting aside the knowledge of parallel societal developments as put forward by Kähler Holst.[67] The formation of a state was by no means a simple or straightforward process. And the narrative of Jelling has been embraced by its simplicity and coherence.[68] We want to stress the likeliness that several state formations occurred at the same time within the current Danish area.

---

64 See Fig. 1 and 2
65 Graeber & Wengrow 2021, 360
66 Graeber & Wengrow 2021, 360f.
67 Kähler Holst 2014, 179ff.
68 Sindbæk 2005

From postholes to societies

When dealing with people of the Viking Age, some individuals such as Harold Bluetooth receive tremendous interest from archaeological research, whereas most of the population end up as a blurry mess of larger communities and groups.[69] At the Grangaard Allé settlement from AD 250-550 it is extremely difficult to find traces of individuals among 20,000 postholes. We must however explore settlement traces as the core of the archaeological research, leading to new knowledge about people of the past, when combined with a proper methodological and theoretical approach. One approach is to investigate their settlements and cultural landscape within the core site in relation to the periphery, in a more refined relative and absolute chronological setting. Then it is important to be able to combine multiple investigations and approaches of the same area. Finally, the greater regional area is to be investigated. In our opinion, Jelling is to be treated as a core site and area for this contextual approach due to the vast number of investigations conducted by scholars over the past centuries. There are many levels of knowledge moving from the actual use of the Jelling core site and area in AD 0-1000 to the widened archaeological knowledge and analysis of the wider Jelling site and area. The understanding of Jelling will be dynamic whether seen through the eyes of a dweller of the Grangaard Allé site of the 6th century AD, the eyes of Harold Bluetooth of the 10th century AD, or the eyes of an archaeological scholar of the 19th or 21st century AD.

One approach could be to investigate various traces of societal development. This approach is well-known in the archaeological research where some use burials as their primary material to reach knowledge of past societies.[70] This approach is also followed by Heiko Steuer (1982) dividing the societies of the past into quality groups based on status. Steuer also investigates roles in past societies leading to the creation of identities such as peasants, warriors, priests, and patroness/patron.[71] Others use an historical approach of investigating past societies emphasising changes and written sources, leading to a new understanding of the First Millennium (see for instance Wickham 2005: 41ff). As described above many use settlements to understand societal development leading to discussions of state formation.[72]

Another approach deals with the essence of settlement archaeology and postholes in terms of the Danish longhouse chronology leading to a deeper insight of continuity and change of the societies of AD 0-1000. In the latter years several suggestions of

---

69 Pedersen 2014
70 See for instance Balsgaard Juul 2019, 2017 and in particular Hedeager 1992; Hodder 2002, 1991; Binford 1972; Dickinson 2002; Symonds 2009; Effros 2003; Lucy 2000, 1998; Williams 2003; Sayer 2013
71 Steuer 1982, 46; Balsgaard Juul 2017, 91
72 See for instance Balsgaard Juul 2017 as well as Hedeager 1992; Hamerow 2002; Mortensen & Rasmussen 1991, 1988; Fabech & Ringtved 1991; Stidsing, Høilund Nielsen et al. 2014; Kähler Holst 2014, 2010, 2004; Sørensen 2011; Ethelberg 2003; Hambro Mikkelsen & Nørbach 2003; Egeberg Hansen, Hvass et al. 1991; Hvass 1989, 1988; Egeberg Hansen 1987

regional longhouse chronologies have been introduced in Danish archaeology.[73] With other classic sites such as Vorbasse[74] and Nørre Snede[75] within a distance of less than 40 kilometres from Jelling, we suggest that it is time to create a regional longhouse chronology for the greater Jelling area as well, combining the excavations of Jelling, Nørre Snede and Vorbasse leading to new knowledge of the regional longhouse chronology of south-eastern Jutland as well as testing the validity of the overall Danish longhouse chronology. The overall Danish longhouse chronology is mainly based on the results from Vorbasse emphasising the typological development but without combining these results with the C-14 datings.[76] Perhaps the longhouse chronology based on typology is still applicable today? However, it is necessary to test this assumption with further investigations combining the typological datings and C-14 datings.

For future research it will be necessary with more large-scale excavations comparing the longhouse chronology with the results of C-14 dating. The investigations of Grangaard Allé[77] have stressed the need to do so, seeing the challenges of combining these.

If we want to push forward with a more holistic approach aiming at combining theoretical and methodological knowledge with the data deriving from the numerous excavations, a core area such as Jelling in the First Millennium AD will be very well selected. A wider knowledge of Jelling is best understood with several approaches combining investigations of postholes, constructions, and other traces of settlements with landscape studies, settlements, place names, metal detecting finds, graves, runestones, hoards, communication etc. This approach has been followed by the Jelling Project[78] and we wish to continue with putting the Grangaard Allé site into this context. In our opinion, archaeological research gains a lot when combining all the accumulated knowledge of a site such as Jelling from AD 0-1000. However, the amount of accumulated knowledge has grown immensely since post-processual archaeology was introduced forcing us to reconsider our interpretative approaches. This is evident in general in Danish archaeology where each new excavation contributes to a towering amount of data and hereby also in relation to the core site and core area of Jelling.

Following the statement of Hodder (2002) describing how archaeologists of the 21st century mainly are theoreticians; we define our theoretical approach as holistic archaeology where we connect as many pieces of the puzzle of the First Millennium as possible. Due to the vast number of investigations of Jelling this is truly a core site and area to test the possibilities for researching and understanding the societies and people of the early mediaeval period. To complete this approach a large research project is necessary

---

73   Boye 2011, 1992; Ethelberg 2003; Hansen 2015; Vestergaard Laursen & Holst 2017; Vestergaard Laursen & Birch Iversen 2020
74   Hvass 1989, 1988
75   Egeberg 1987; Kähler Holst 2014, 2010, 2004
76   See Egeberg Hansen, Hvass & Mikkelsen 1991, 18; Hvass 1988
77   Balsgaard Juul (forthcoming), Balsgaard Juul & Lindblom 2022; Balsgaard Juul 2022; Lindblom & Balsgaard Juul 2018
78   Pedersen et al. eds. 2023

leading to new knowledge of the dynamic changes of society and settlements in the greater Jelling area in the First Millennium AD.

contact adress: balsgaardjuulkatrine@gmail.com and CHLIN@vejle.dk

Bibliography

AMS Direct, 2021: Report 2204-040170-040182.

Aggesøn: Sven Aggesøn, Kortfattet historie om Danmarks Konger. In: M. CL. Gertz (ed.), Sven Aggesøns Historiske Skrifter (København 1917).

Axboe, M. 2001: "Året 536", *Skalk*, 4, 28-32.

Axboe, M. 2022: "Guldskatten fra Vindelev", *Fund & Fortid*, nr. 4, 2021, 14-21.

Balsgaard Juul, K. 2017: *On the verge of a coastal culture. Dynamic identities in the North Sea areas, AD 400-700 expressed through gender, status and regionality.* Ph.D. thesis, Aarhus University.

Balsgaard Juul, K. 2019: "Static Dynamics of (Im)material Identities in an Emerging Coastal Culture", in *Early medieval waterscapes: Risks and opportunities for (im)material cultural exchange*, edited by Rica Annaert et al. (Neue Studien zur Sachsenforschung, Band 8). 139-152.

Balsgaard Juul, K. 2022: *Beretning VKH 7675, Grangaard Allé, Jelling Sogn, Tørrild Herred, tidl. Vejle Amt, Stednr. 170904, Sb.nr. 244*. Unpublished report, Vejlemuseerne, Vejle.

Balsgaard Juul, K (forthcoming): "Jelling før Jelling – byggeboom, udvikling og afvikling i jernalderens Jelling", in *Mellem orden og kaos i jernalderen*, edited by Karin Johannesen, Nanna Kirkeby & Katrine Balsgaard Juul.

Balsgaard Juul, K. & C. Lindblom. 2022: "Investigating new narratives of settlements in the greater Jelling area in the first millennium", *New Narratives for the First Millennium AD?: Alte und neue Perspektiven der archäologischen Forschung zum 1. Jahrtausend n. Chr.*, edited by Babette Ludowici & Heike Pöppelmann. Wendeburg: Uwe Krebs, 265-282.

Binford, L. 1972: *An Archaeological Perspective*. New York & London, Seminar Press.

Boye, L. 1992: "Huskronologi for sjællandske jernalderhuse? Fremlæggelse af metode med udgangspunkt i Bellingegårdbopladsen ved Ølby, Østsjælland", in *Sjællands jernalder*, edited by U.L. Hansen & S. Nielsen (Arkæologiske skrifter. Vol. 6). København: Arkæologisk Institut, Københavns Universitet, 159-166.

Boye, L. 2011: "Lots of postholes – but how do we progress?", in *The Iron Age on Zealand. Status and Perspectives*, edited by L. Boye. København, 9-16.

Brøndsted, J. 1940: *Danmarks Oldtid* III. *Jernalderen*. København 1940.

Büntgen, U., V.S. Myglan, F. Charpentier Ljungqvist, M. McCormick, N. Di Cosmo, M. Sigl, J. Jungclaus, S. Wagner, P.J. Krusic, J. Esper, J.O. Kaplan, M.A.C. de Vaan, J. Luterbacher, L. Wacker, W. Tegeland & A.V. Kirdyanov. 2016: "Cooling and societal change during the Late Antique Little Ice Age from 536 to around 660 AD", *Nature Geoscience* 9 (3), 231-236.

Christiansen, F. 1999: "Jelling. Bebyggelse fra jernalder og vikingetid", *KUML. Årbog for Jysk Arkæologisk Selskab* 1999, 181-226.

Dengsø, M. Jessen 2023: "The later settlement" In *Jelling – Monuments and Landscape*, I. (PNM. Publications from the National Museum Studies in Archaeology & History. Copenhagen. Studies in Archaeology and History, vol. 20.4, 1). 241-267.

Dengsø, M. Jessen. 2023: "The palisade houses of Jelling". In *Jelling – Monument and Landscape,* I. (Publications from the National Museum Studies in Archaeology & History. Jelling Series. Vol. 20:4 1). 193-241.

Dengsø, M. Jessen, M. Kähler Holst, C. Lindblom, N. Bonde & A. Pedersen. 2014: "A Palisade fit for a King – ideal architecture in King Harald Bluetooth's Jelling", *Norwegian Archaeological Review 47*, 2014, 42-64.

Dengsø, M. Jessen, Lindblom C. & A. Pedersen. 2023: "Jelling before Jelling" *In Jelling – Monuments and Landscape*, I. (PNM. Publications from the National Museum Studies in Archaeology & History, vol. 20.4. 1). Copenhagen, 365-385.

Dickinson, T. 2002: Review article: What's new in early medieval burial archaeology? *Early Medieval Europe,* 11(1), 71-87.

Dyggve, E. 1948: "The Royal Barrows at Jelling. Excavations made in 1941, 1942 and 1947, and finds and findings resulting therefrom", *Antiquity* 22, 1948, 190-197.

Dyggve, E. 1956: Jellingkongernes mindesmærker. Af et festskrift i anledning af Vejle Amts historiske Samfunds 50-års jubileum 6. jan. 1955. Kolding 1956.

Effros, B. 2003: *Merovingian Morturary Archaeology and the Making of the Early Middle Ages*. Berkeley, University of California Press.

Egeberg Hansen, T. 1987: "Die eisenzeitliches Siedlund bei Nørre Snede, Mitteljütland. Vorläufiger Bericht", *Acta archaeologica* 58 (1987), 171-200.

Egeberg Hansen, T., S. Hvass & D. Kaldal Mikkelsen. 1991: "Landbebyggelserne i 7. århundrede", in *Fra Stamme til Stat i Danmark 2. Høvdingesamfund og Kongemagt,* edited by P. Mortensen & B.M. Rasmussen (Jysk Arkæologisk Selskabs skrifter 22), 17-26.

Ethelberg, P. 2003: "Gården og landsbyen i jernalder og vikingetid (500 f. Kr. – 1000 e. Kr.)", in *Det Sønderjyske Landbrugs Historie. Jernalder, Vikingetid og Middelalder*, edited by L.S. Madsen & O. Madsen. Haderslev, 123-374.

Fabech, C. & J. Ringtved (eds.). 1991: *Samfundsorganisation og Regional Variation: Norden i romersk jernalder og folkevandringstid: Beretning fra 1. nordiske jernaldersymposion på Sandbjerg Slot, 11-15 april 1989*. Højbjerg, Jysk Arkæologisk Selskab.

Hambro Mikkelsen, P. & L.C. Nørbach. 2003: *Drengsted. Bebyggelse, jernproduktion og agerbrug i yngre romersk og ældre germansk jernalder*. Højbjerg.

Graeber, D. & D. Wengrow. 2021: *The Dawn of Everything. A New History of Humanity*. Farrar, Straus and Giraux. New York.

Gräslund, B. & N. Price. 2012: "Twilight of the gods? The 'dust veil event' of AD 536 in critical perspective", *Antiquity* 86 (332), 428-443.

Hansen, J. 2015: *Landsbydannelse og bebyggelsesstruktur i det 1. årtusinde – et bebyggelseshistorisk regionalstudie*. 1-3. (Tekst, Bilag & appendiks og Katalog). Ph.D. thesis. Institut for Historie, Kartografisk Dokumentationscenter, Syddansk Universitet.

Hedeager, L. 1992: *Iron Age Societies: From Tribe to State in Northern Europe, 500 BC to AD 700*. London, Basil Blackwell.

Hodder, I. 1991: *Reading the Past: Current approaches to interpretations in archaeology*. Second edition. Cambridge, Cambridge University Press.

Hodder, I. 2002: "Archaeological Theory", in *The Widening Debate*, edited by B. Cunliffe, W, Davies & C. Renfrew. Oxford, Oxford University Press, 77-90.

Hvass, S. 1988: "Jernalderens bebyggelse", in *Fra Stamme til Stat i Danmark 1. Jernalderens Stammesamfund*, edited by P. Mortensen & B.M. Rasmussen (Jysk Arkæologisk Selskabs Skrifter 22), 53-92.

Hvass, S. 1989: "Rural settlements in Denmark in the first millennium AD", in *The Birth of Europe: Archaeology and Social Development in the First Millennium AD (Roma 1989)*, edited by K. Randsborg, 91-99.

Hvass, S. 1992: Beretning for VKH 1570, Skovgade – Jelling: Bebyggelse fra germansk jernalder og vikingetid. Unpublished report, Vejlemuseerne, Vejle.

Hvass, S. 1993: "Bebyggelsen", in *Da Klinger i Muld … 25 års arkæologi i Danmark,* edited by S. Hvass & B. Storgaard, København, 187-194.

Hvass, S. 1998: "Schon in der Wikingerzeit eine tausenjährige Siedlung", in *Studien zur Archäologie des Ostseeraumes. Von der Eisenzeit zum Mittelalter. Festschrift für Michael Müller-Wille*, edited by A. Wesse. Neumünster, 161-176.

Juel, C. 2013a: Kulturhistorisk rapport om arkæologisk udgravning af gårde fra yngre romersk jernalder ved Rønnelunden, Jelling. Unpublished report, Vejlemuseerne.

Juel, C. 2013b: Udgravningsberetning. VKH 7372 Rønnelunden, Jelling Sogn, Tørrild herred, tidl. Vejle amt. Sted nr. 17.09.04. Sb. nr. 179. Unpublished report, Vejlemuseerne, Vejle.

Kaldal Mikkelsen, D. 1987: "Haughus (1314)", in *Danmarks længste udgravning. Arkæologi på naturgassens vej 1979-89*, edited by Rigsantikvarens Arkæologiske Sekretariat. København.

Kaldal Mikkelsen, D. 1988/89: "To ryttergrave fra ældre romersk jernalder – den ene med tilhørende bebyggelse", *KUML, Årbog for Jysk Arkæologisk Selskab*, 143-199.

Kornerup, J. 1875: *Kongehøiene i Jellinge og deres Undersøgelser efter Kong Frederik VII's Befaling i 1861*. Det Kongelige Nordiske Oldskriftselskab, Kjøbenhavn.

Krogh, K. og B. Leth-Larsen. 2007: *Hedensk og Kristent. Fundene fra den kongelige gravhøj i Jelling. Vikingekongernes monumenter i Jelling. Bind 2, København.*

Krogh, K. 1993: *Gåden om Kong Gorms Grav. Historien om Nordhøjen i Jelling. Vikingekongernes monumenter i Jelling. Bind 1, København.*

Kähler Holst, M. 2004: *The Syntax of the Iron Age Village: Transformations in an orderly community.* Ph. D thesis. Aarhus University.

Kähler Holst, M. 2010: "Inconsistancy and stability – Large and small farmsteads in the village of Nørre Snede (Central Jutland) in the first millennium AD", *Siedlungs- und Küstenforschung im südlichen Nordseegebiet* 33 (2010), 155-179.

Kähler Holst, M. 2014: "Warrior aristocracy and village community", in *Wealth and Complexity: Economically specialised sites in Late Iron Age Denmark*, ideated by E. Stidsing, K. Høilund Nielsen & R. Fiedel (Museum Østjylland, vol. 1). 179-198.

Kähler Holst, M., M. Dengsø Jessen, S. Wulff Andersen & A. Pedersen. 2012: "The Late Viking-Age Royal Constructions at Jelling, central Jutland, Denmark. Recent investigations and a suggestion for an interpretative revision", *Praehistorische Zeitschrift* 87 (2), 474-504.

Laursen, K.O. 2021: *Rapport for arkæologisk eftergravning og forundersøgelse. VKH 8206 Vindelev.* Vejlemuseerne. Unpublished report, Vejlemuseerne, Vejle.

Laursen, K.O. & M. Ravn. 2022: *Magt og Guld. Vikinger i øst. Power and Gold. Vikings in the East.* Edited by Mads Ravn og Charlotta Lindblom. 2022. Vejlemuseerne og Turbine.

Lindblom, C. 2023: "Jelling and its surroundings – the archaeological evidence". In *Jelling – Monument and Landscape,* II. (Publications from the National Museum Studies in Archaeology & History. Jelling Series. Vol. 20:4, 2). Copenhagen, 9-61.

Lindblom, C. 2020: The royal monuments in their regional setting. *In Viking Encounters "Proceedings of the Eighteenth Viking Congress.* 2020.

Lindblom, C. & K. Balsgaard Juul. 2018: "Jelling før Gorm", *Skalk* 3, 9-15.

Lindblom, C., M. Dengsø Jessen & A. Pedersen 2023: "Jelling before Jelling". In *Jelling – Monument and Landscape,* I. (Publications from the National Museum Studies in Archaeology & History. Jelling Series. Vol. 20:4, 1). Copenhagen, 365-385.

Lucy, S. 1998: *The Early Anglo-Saxon Cemeteries of East Yorkshire: An Analysis and Reinterpretation.* Oxford, J. & E. Hedges.

Lucy, S. 2000: *The Anglo-Saxon way of death: Burial rites in early England.* Stroud, Sutton.

Mortensen, B. & B. Rasmussen (eds.) 1988: *Fra Stamme til Stat i Danmark*, Bd. 1: *Jernalderens Stammesamfund.* Aarhus, Aarhus Universitetsforlag.

Mortensen, B. & B. Rasmussen (eds.) 1991: *Fra Stamme til Stat i Danmark,* Bd. 2: *Høvdingesamfund og Kongemagt.* Aarhus, Aarhus Universitetsforlag.

Müller, S. 1897: *Vor Oldtid: Danmarks forhistoriske Archæologi almenfattelig fremstillet*, København.

Måge, B. 2006a: Beretning. VKH 6676 Grangård, Jelling Sogn, Tørrild Herred, Vejle Amt, Stednr. 17.09.04. KUAS j.nr: 2003-2122-0716. Unpublished report, Vejlemuseerne, Vejle.

Måge, B. 2006b: Bygherrerapport. VKH 6676, Grangård, Jelling sogn, Tørrild sogn, Tørrild Herred, Vejle amt. Stednr. 17.09.04. Unpublished report, Vejlemuseerne, Vejle.

Pedersen, A. 2014: "The Jelling Monuments – A National Icon between Legend and Fact", In *Quo vadis? Status and Future Perspectives of Long-Term Excavations in Europe,* edited by C. von Carnap-Bornheim, (Schriften des archäologischen Landesmuseums Ergänzungsreihe 10). Neumünster, Hamburg, 249-263.

Pedersen A. et al. (eds.) 2023: *Jelling – Monuments and Landscapes.* (Publications from the National Museum. Studies in Archaeology and History, vol. 20.4, 1-2).

Randsborg K. 2008: "King's Jelling. Gorm & Thyra's palace – Harald's monument & grave – Svend's Cathedral", *Acta Archaeologica* 79, 1-23.

Randsborg K. 1980: *The Viking Age in Denmark: The Formation of a State*, London.

Ravn, M. et al. 2024: Arkæologisk Strategi. *2023-2028* Vejlemuseerne. https://www.vejlemuseerne.dk/media/63985/vejlemuseernes-arkaeologisk-stategi_2023-2028_webudgave.pdf [accessed 04.09.2024].

Ravn, M., C. Juel, C. Lindblom & A. Pedersen. 2019: "Erritsø – new investigations of an aristocratic, early Viking Age manor in Western Denmark c. 700-850 AD", in *Early medieval waterscapes. Risks and opportunities for (imm)aterial cultural exchange* (Neue Studien zur Sachsenforschung 8). Braunschweig.

Roesdahl, E. 2008: "The Emergence of Denmark and the Reign of Harald Bluetooth", in *The Viking World,* edited by S. Brink and N. Price, *London,* 652-664.

Roesdahl, E. 2011: "Scandinavia in the Melting-pot, 950-1000", in *Viking Settlements and Viking Society. Papers from the proceedings of the Sixteenth Viking Congress, Reykjavik and Reykholt, 16th-23rd August* 2009, edited by Sigmundsson et al. Reykjavik, 2011, 347-374.

Saxo: J. Olrik/H. Ræder (eds.), *Saxonis Gesta Danorum* (Haunis/København 1931).

Sayer, D. 2013: "Investigating the Social Aspects of Early Medieval Mortuary Practice", *History Compass,* 11(2), 147-162.

Sindbæk, S. 2005: "Popular myths and scholarly debate". *Perceptions of a Viking-Age Past. Norwegian Archaeological Review,* 38, 1, 113-114.

Staecker, J. 2005: "The Concepts of Imitatio and Translatio: Perceptions of a Viking-Age Past", *Norwegian Archaeological Review,* 38, 1, 3-121.

Steuer, H. 1982: *Frühgeschichtliche Sozialstrukturen in Mitteleuropa. Eine Analyse der Auswertungsmethoden des archäologischen Quellenmaterials.* Göttingen.

Stidsing, E, K. Høilund Nielsen & R. Fiedel (eds.). 2014: *Wealth and Complexity: Economically Specialised Sites in Late Iron Age Denmark.* Randers, East Jutland Museum.

Symonds, L. 2009: "Death as a Window to Life: Anthropological Approaches to Early Medieval Mortuary Ritual", *Reviews in Anthropology,* 38(1), 48-87.

Sørensen, A.B. 2011: *Østergård. Vikingetid og Middelalder.* Haderslev.

Vestergaard Laursen, S. & M. Kähler Holst. 2017: "Late Iron Age longhouse chronology. A study aimed at constructing a formal house chronology for the Late Iron Age, based on selected localities in central and eastern Jutland", *Danish Journal of Archaeology* 6, 1-20.

Vestergaard Laursen, S. & R. Birch Iversen. 2020: *Hummelure. Landsby, langhus og landbrug i Østjyllands yngre jernalder.* Jysk Arkæologisk Selskabs Skrifter, Højbjerg.

Wickham, C. 2005: *Framing the early Middle Ages: Europe and the Mediterranean, 400-800.* Oxford, Oxford University Press.

Williams, H. 2003: *Archaeologies of Remembrance: Death and Memory in Past Societies.* London, Kluwer Academic / Plenum Publishers.

PART 2.
POWER, WAR AND ARISTOCRATIC SITES IN NORTHERN EUROPE

BY CHRISTOPHER SCULL

Chapter 7

"Great Hall" and "Central Place": characterising power in the settlement geography of England in the fifth to eighth centuries

ABSTRACT

This article explores the archaeological evidence for elite residences in England during the fifth to eighth centuries. It examines the "Great Hall Complexes," which are monumental timber buildings arranged in structured layouts, typically associated with elite or royal power. The study highlights sites like Yeavering and Rendlesham, noting their roles in regional rulership, surplus extraction, and political power. It also discusses how recent findings, especially from metal-detecting and contract archaeology, are reshaping our understanding of these sites' significance and functions within broader social and economic networks.

This brief overview summarises aspects of archaeological evidence for elite or aristocratic residences in England in the fifth to eighth centuries, and examines how recent findings are prompting some revisions of received opinion. Much of what follows is covered in greater detail in two recent papers that Gabor Thomas and I have published jointly,[1] and also draws on analysis undertaken for the project *Lordship and Landscape in East Anglia CE 400-800* funded by the Leverhulme Trust.[2] I should like to acknowledge my debt to Dr Thomas, and to my colleagues on the Leverhulme-funded project.[3]

---

1   Scull & Thomas 2020; Thomas & Scull 2021
2   Funded by Research Project Grant RPG-2017-172 and based at University College London Institute of Archaeology between November 2017 and April 2021. A monograph is in preparation with publication anticipated in 2024.
3   Dr Martin Allen, Dr Eleanor Blakelock, Dr Stuart Brookes, Ms Faye Minter, Dr Tim Pestell, Ms Judith Plouviez, Dr. Eleanor Rye, Prof Tom Williamson, Dr Andrew Woods and Prof Barbara Yorke

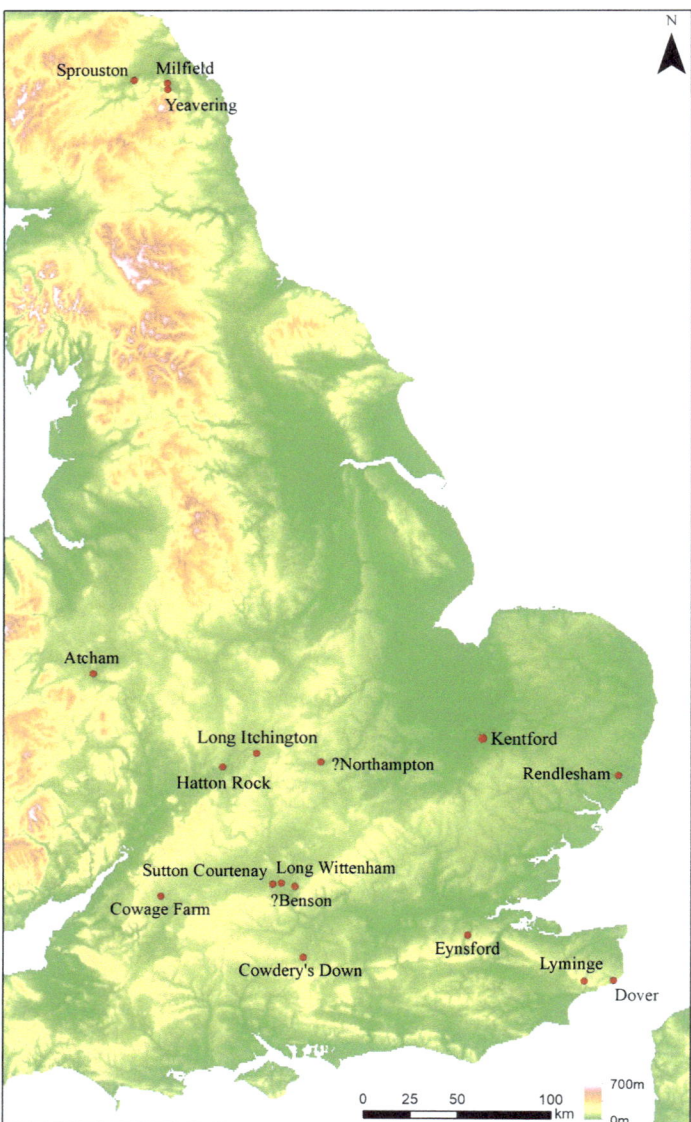

Fig. 1. *Location map of great hall sites in England (adapted from Austin, Anglo-Saxon Great Hall Complexes, Fig. 2.1).*

In the early post-Roman archaeology of England, the study of rulers' residences and centres of power has focused upon so-called "Great Hall Complexes".[4] These are arrays of monumental-scale rectangular timber buildings, known from their foundations and ground plans. They typically occur in structured linear and orthogonal configurations, within which individual buildings are often associated with enclosed spaces that suggest social restrictions on access. Where there has been excavation on a sufficient scale

---

4   Austin 2017; Blair 2018, 111-113; McBride 2020

to provide evidence for site sequence, the broad spatial layout typically persists across, or structures, episodes of rebuilding or renewal, indicating multi-generational recognition of, or adherence to, the spatial logic of the original layout. It has been argued that some individual buildings may have been barns, but the architectural complexity evident from construction details, which in some cases includes evidence for plastered walls and opus signinum floors, tells against this, as does their multiple co-occurrence in planned configurations.[5]

Between 15 and 20 such places, depending upon interpretation and definition,[6] are known in England (Fig. 1). Perhaps the best known is Yeavering in Northumberland, which was the first to be identified and excavated.[7] Cowdery's Down in Hampshire and Lyminge in Kent have also seen excavation on a large scale;[8] Sutton Courtenay and Long Wittenham in Oxfordshire, and Cowage Farm near Malmesbury in Wiltshire have all seen targeted excavation;[9] foundations of great halls are also known from excavation at Dover and Eynesford in Kent,[10] Northampton,[11] and Kentford in Suffolk.[12]

Around half of these sites are known only or primarily from aerial photography. Consequently, information on dating and chronology is limited or inferred, and there is little or no information about associated activities and functions. Before excavation at Lyminge, and recognition of the settlement at Rendlesham, it was widely accepted that one feature of such sites was that they were materially poor: excavation did not turn up the large material culture assemblages or status items that might be expected at elite centres.[13] Possible explanations include the scarcity on these sites of negative features such as pits and *Grubenhäuser*, in which rubbish and detritus might be deposited or accumulate, and refuse disposal regimes that saw rubbish deposited away from high-status dwellings.

Where there has been excavation, our evidence is that Great Hall Complexes are a phenomenon of the late sixth to early eighth centuries.[14] They are seen as elite residences and monumental arenas for the exercise of authority, and centres of surplus extraction and redeployment – and so as engines for the transformation of landed surplus into political power, underpinning the exercise of regional rulership and extensive lordship.[15] The identification of these as elite or royal places rests on two main grounds. A very few are identified as royal centres in seventh- or eighth-century documents: Yeavering and

---

5   Alcock 2003, 255-256; Reynolds 2021; Thomas et al. 2021, 76; Thomas 2018, 283-285
6   Austin 2017, 23-62; McBride 2020, 1-3
7   Hope-Taylor 1977
8   Millet & James 1983; Thomas 2018
9   Hamerow et al. 2007; Hamerow & Brennan 2015; McBride et al. 2020; Hincliffe 1986
10   Philip 2003; Thomas 2018, 274-288
11   Williams et al. 1985
12   Minter 2016, 627-628
13   Hope-Taylor 1977, 168, 170-203; Millet & James 1983, 249-250
14   Blair 2018, 111-131; Scull & Thomas 2020, 61-63
15   Hamerow 2012, 102-189; Walker 2010; Alcock 2003, 244-256; Thomas 2013

Milfield in Northumberland are mentioned in Bede's *Historia Ecclesiastica*,[16] and Lyminge in a Kentish royal charter.[17] Otherwise, the scale and sophistication of the buildings and layout imply a command of resources only available to elites. They have been accorded Central Place functions and interpreted as estate centres – although exactly what this might mean or entail at this time is an open question and subject to debate; it has also been argued that they are located in the "core" territories of early kingdoms or polities.[18]

Great Hall Complexes can therefore be seen as specific to the conditions of regional rulership from the late sixth to early eighth centuries. However, those known only from aerial photography are not dated except by the assumption that a broad equivalence of form and layout indicates contemporaneity. It seems unlikely that eighth- and ninth-century elite complexes wholly lacked equivalent structures, and we therefore have to entertain the possibility that some of the sites known only from aerial photography, if excavated, may prove to be later than currently assumed.

The main focus of archaeological attention has been the hall arrays, which typically cover an area of 4 ha–6 ha, rather than the wider areas in which they are situated. In the apparent scarcity of evidence for associated settlement, and in the absence of significant material culture assemblages, enquiry has concentrated on what the monumental buildings, individually and as complexes, can tell us about expressions and configurations of power. It is fair to say that three strands of discourse have become particularly influential in shaping current readings of these places. Proximity to prehistoric monuments is taken to indicate an emphasis on the legitimation of power though fictive association with the deep past, a perspective that – whatever its validity – tends to minimise association with immediately antecedent and contemporary early medieval activity.[19] The monumental scale of their built environment sees them evoked as theatres of power, with an emphasis on display, assembly and cult.[20] And they have been characterised as short-lived, mirroring the transience of personal secular rulership in contrast to the enduring institutions of the Christian church in England.[21]

As a consequence, this very specific archaeological phenomenon, interrogated in isolation, has come to stand for elite residence and royal power in the settlement record. The focus on specific site type and building form has yielded important insights, but it also risks divorcing halls and hall complexes from both their contemporary and longer-term contexts. At the same time there is an abundant and increasing body of archaeological data bearing on these contexts being generated by contract archaeology and metal-detecting. Excavation in advance of development has hugely increased the number of known settlement and burial sites of the period. Metal-detecting has also identified foci of settlement and exchange, the so-called "productive sites", and the

---

16   H.E. ii, 14
17   S. 1968, 12; Kelly 2006, 105, no. 8
18   Austin 2017, 282-285; Thomas 2013, 112-114; Welch 1992, 43-53; McBride 2020, 286-300
19   Hamerow 2012, 105-106; Semple 2013, 94-99, 207-209; Scull 2022, 134-136
20   McBride 2020, 139-155; Hamerow 2012, 106-109; Blair 2005, 54-57
21   Blair 2005, 247-286; Blair 2018, 122-124

aggregate of metal-detector finds reported through the Portable Antiquities Scheme[22] allows us to situate these places within local, regional and inter-regional geographies of production, consumption and exchange.

There has, though, been a tendency to see "productive sites" as a single site-type rather than understanding the term to refer to an archaeological metalwork signature that might arise from a range of activities at places of differing date and character. This has been compounded by an understandable numismatic focus on the early silver penny (sceat) assemblages which has led to an emphasis on "productive sites" as market centres of the eighth and ninth centuries.[23] It has always been clear, however, that some "productive site" assemblages, notably those from Coddenham and Barham in Suffolk, indicate centres of wealth and power of the sixth and seventh centuries.[24] Here was the elite material culture signature that was missing from the excavated Great Hall Complexes – did these metalwork assemblages from the ploughsoil indicate settlements of the same or equivalent status and complexity? Excavation at both Coddenham and Barham confirmed settlement features and deposits, but was not undertaken on a scale that might identify building arrays or site morphology.[25] More recently, however, the identification by metal-detecting of the site of the East Anglian royal centre at Rendlesham in Suffolk and the excavation of what turned out to be a great hall sequence at Lyminge in Kent have provided overlapping bodies of evidence that allow us to start addressing this question and to start refining and expanding upon previous models.

The early medieval settlement complex at Rendlesham, in the valley of the river Deben in south-east Suffolk, is known from a programme of systematic metal-detecting supplemented by geophysics and analysis of aerial photography, and trial excavation has demonstrated the presence of settlement features and deposits.[26] The extent of archaeological features and the distribution of metalwork in the ploughsoil indicate settlement and related activity over an area of *c.* 50 ha over the course of the fifth to eighth centuries (Fig. 2).

The finds assemblage, which includes gold and gold-and-garnet jewellery, Merovingian and English gold coinage, status items acquired through inter-regional exchange, and evidence for metalworking in copper-alloy and precious metals, indicates an elite presence from the later sixth to the early eighth centuries. This is the most extensive and materially the richest settlement known from fifth- to eighth-century England. It can be identified confidently as the East Anglian *vicus regius* or royal settlement recorded by Bede as a place of royal baptism in a context of the mid-seventh century.[27]

It is possible to identify two main areas of habitation within a broader zone of activity: an area of settlement and burial in use from the fifth century and, to its south-

---

22 https://finds.org.uk [accessed 20 June 2022]
23 Ulmschneider 2000
24 Newman 2003
25 Martin et al. 2004, 506; Newman 2003, 101-102
26 Scull et al. 2016
27 H.E. iii, 22

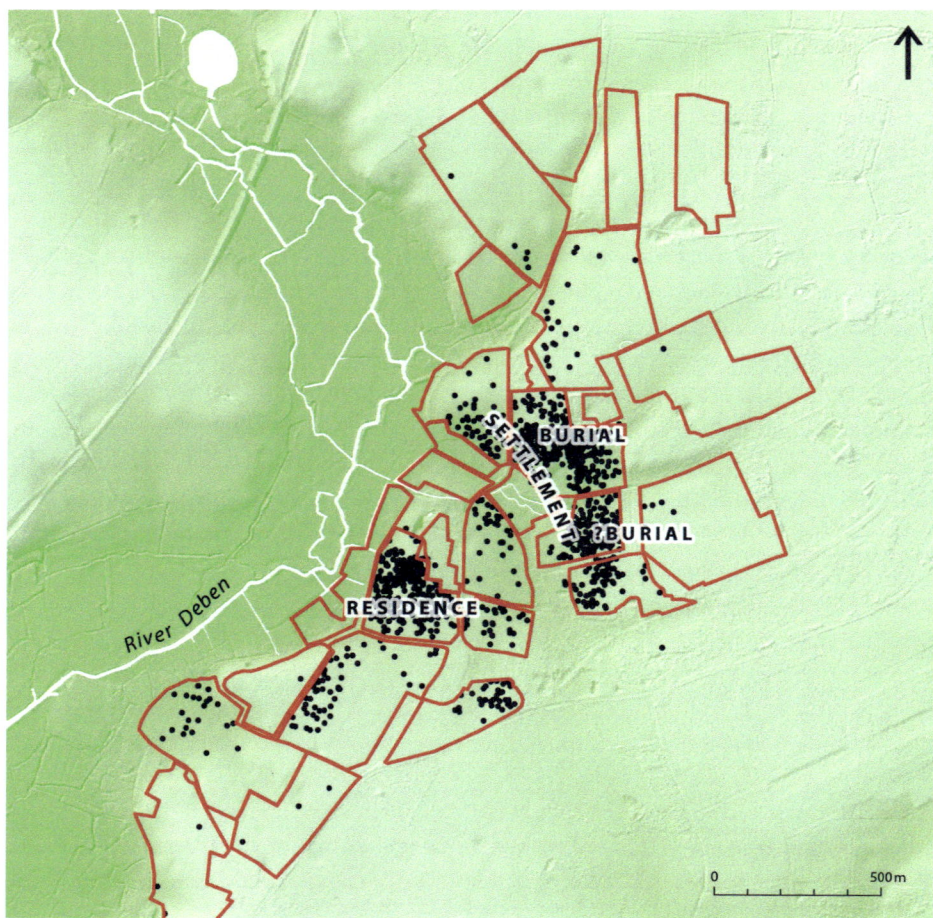

Fig. 2. *Plan of the Rendlesham survey area (outlined in red) showing the distribution of metal finds of the fifth to eighth centuries A.D. and principal functional zones (illustration by Stuart Brooks).*

west and separated from it by a small tributary valley, a high-status establishment on a promontory overlooking the river Deben where the cropmark of a probable timber great hall has been identified. The high-status establishment appears to have been founded in the later sixth century immediately adjacent to an existing settlement. As an elite centre it was a focus of inter-regional social and exchange contacts, and was an early centre of coin use and monetisation. The settlement complex as a whole can be seen as the focus of entangled social, jurisdictional and economic geographies at a range of scales.

The probable hall cropmark was not identified until *after* our interpretative model was formulated on the basis of the artefact assemblage and spatial distributions. Rendlesham is now routinely cited as a Great Hall Complex but this is misleading. Rather, it is a poly-focal settlement complex of which a great hall or halls were probably one component, and the current weight of evidence is that the elite residence was established here because it was already an important place and had been for over a century. It lost this special character and status in the second quarter of the eighth century.

The data from Rendlesham add significant new dimensions to the wider picture: we have the material culture signatures of a range of activities including the materialisation of elite identities, assemblies, conspicuous consumption, long-distance social and exchange contacts, early coin-use and monetisation, and skilled metal smithing. This was not short-term or transient: Rendlesham was an important place for 300 years and an elite centre for 120-150 years. These conclusions are complemented by the results of Gabor Thomas' excavations at Lyminge, where the halls sat within a wider zone of activity and were built at a place of pre-existing importance, and where there is also a rich material culture assemblage and evidence for conspicuous elite consumption.[28] Together, Lyminge and Rendlesham prompt a re-examination of the other English sites.

Settlement activity at Rendlesham covers a very much greater area than that of Great Hall Complexes at other places. However, when attention is paid to the immediate environs of other great hall sites there are indications that some, if not all, were in fact components of larger-scale and chronologically-deeper settlement aggregations. This is perhaps seen most clearly at Sutton Courtenay where there is evidence for a settlement with *Grubenhäuser*, and where metal-detected material suggests a similar range of activities to those identified at Rendlesham.[29] At Yeavering there is evidence for buildings and activity, including non-ferrous metalworking, beyond the boundaries of Brian Hope-Taylor's excavation, and evidence that the Great Hall Complex was laid out over the site of an existing settlement.[30] At Milfield, the halls sit within an extensive cropmark landscape, including possible *Grubenhäuser*,[31] and there are similar indications at Hatton Rock and Long Itchington in Warwickshire.[32] This all suggests that at these places the great halls were an element of larger settlement complexes, and that at some at least they represent a late phase of a longer occupation history.

This is not to dispute the importance of monumental elite residences as theatres for rulership and displays of power, their role in promoting and consolidating the social relations underpinning early royal power, or indeed the role of hall and building cultures in the transmission and negotiation of elite ideologies. However, these were very much more entangled in networks of landed production, surplus extraction and exchange, embedded in contemporary landscapes of settlement, and rooted in antecedent geographies of power, than has sometimes been acknowledged. It is worth noting that at Rendlesham our impression is that a significant proportion of the material recovered by metal-detecting had become incorporated in the ploughsoil after being dropped on the old ground surface rather than being ploughed-up from stratified settlement features. Either way, had the site been recognised by aerial photography, and investigated

---

28 Thomas 2013
29 Hamerow et al. 2007; Hamerow & Brennan 2015
30 Scull 1991; Tinniswood & Harding 1991
31 Gates & O'Brien 1988
32 Rahtz 1970, 118-119, Fig. 32

by excavation without prior metal-detecting, it is unlikely that the material wealth of the place would have been recognised, and this may go some way to explaining the perceived lack of material wealth at some other sites.

Turning to consider the centrality of these sites, both physically and conceptually, it is important to draw a distinction between central persons and central places. Networks of social and economic relationships might focus on elite individuals regardless of where they are at any one time, inherent to a person's social identity and roles. They might focus on elite individuals but in ways that are enacted only at specific places such as residences, assembly sites and cult sites; or they might focus on a specific place or places in ways which may or may not require the presence of the central person. These overlapping social geographies are further complicated by the fact that where the roles of central persons are linked to specific places these may or may not be at the same site, and that some central place functions, notably agrarian administration and the gathering of dues and renders, were likely the province of delegated authority. It is therefore possible to draw a further useful distinction between the practice and materialisation of rulership, and the social and economic infrastructures that supported it. To the former belong evidence for elite lifestyle, culture and contacts, patronage and conspicuous consumption, and for assemblies and the theatre of rulership; to the latter belong farming, the collection and processing of a landed surplus, and routine craft production and exchange.

There is little doubt that a range of social, economic, ideological, cultic and rulership actions and transactions were performed at Rendlesham. Its character and importance stem from the spatial coincidence of functions and actions that could be, and other times were, distributed between different places in the landscape. There is a strong case to be made that Rendlesham in the late sixth to early eighth centuries was the principal centre from which royal rulership was exercised over an extensive region – a territory broadly equivalent to the catchments of the rivers Deben and Alde.[33] It undoubtedly had its own farming territory or estate, but as a periodic residence and a tribute and administrative centre it had wider-reaching importance – sitting above and extracting from a nested hierarchy of social obligations and rights to landed resource, and integrating the regional landed economy with elite-focused inter-regional exchange. Such *regiones* were constituent building blocks of the seventh-century East Anglian kingdom.

It is worth emphasising that, when viewed in the longer-term in its immediate landscape, the Rendlesham complex represents a major episode of settlement agglomeration that replaces a dispersed pattern of Roman-period farms and reverts to a more dispersed pattern of rural settlement from the eighth century. The decline in Rendlesham's importance in the early eighth century can be explained with reference to the ways in which, over the course of the eighth and ninth centuries, the needs for royal residences and places of jurisdiction were met in different ways through new geographies of rulership

---

33   Scull & Williamson 2018; Thomas & Scull 2021, 18, Fig. 5

The hall sequence at Lyminge under excavation in 2013 (Photo by Hawkeye Elevated Photography; © University of Reading). Fig. 3.

linked to the transition from extensive to locally distributed systems of lordship.[34] This reinforces the point that there was no single simple pathway to settlement nucleation in early medieval England nor, necessarily, a link between administrative sophistication and nucleation in the settlement record.

The title of this workshop is *Aristocratic Residences in Northern Europe* but the places considered so far are either documented royal centres or, by analogy, have a good claim to be connected to paramount elites. That said, it is important to emphasise that such poly-valent, multifunctional centres would, as well as periodically hosting an elite household and retinue, and gatherings or assemblies, have a permanent retainer and service population with a considerable social range. It is possible, though, to identify places that are more likely to be the seats of local magnates than regional rulers. Adam

---

34   Faith 1997, 153-77; Pestell 2003; Scull & Thomas 2020, 61-64

Fig. 4. Sampling a 50 ha settlement complex: excavation at Rendlesham in 2021 (Photo by Tom Juggins; © Suffolk County Council).

McBride has identified a number of "second order" great hall sites,[35] and it is possible to see something equivalent in the material culture signature of some "productive sites".

A good example is provided by Coddenham and Barham, which lie close to each other 20 km west of Rendlesham in the Gipping valley in south-east Suffolk. The Coddenham settlement complex, which at its peak extended over *c.* 20 ha, was clearly at the apex of the social and settlement hierarchies. It has a very similar material culture signature to Rendlesham and, like Rendlesham, it was an early centre of coin-use and monetisation.[36] Though not as extensive as Rendlesham, which might be seen as *primus inter pares* in south-east Suffolk in the late sixth to early eighth centuries, the settlement complex at Coddenham can be considered the focal place of a region broadly equivalent to the catchment of the river Gipping which, like the Deben / Alde territory focused on Rendlesham, is plausibly interpreted as a jurisdictional constituent of the early East Anglian kingdom. Barham lies 4 km south of Coddenham. It is a smaller site, covering *c.* 6 ha, and although linked to the social and economic networks dominated by Coddenham and Rendlesham it has a narrower range of material, is less wealthy, and appears to have followed the material and monetary trends seen earlier at the two major elite centres. There is no strong high-status signature before the early to middle seventh century, and it is tempting to see Barham as a precursor of thegnly and proto-manorial centres, linked to the emergence and consolidation of a regional aristocracy amongst the

---

35   McBride 2020, 91-95
36   Woods 2021, 19-26

major client kindreds of the early East Anglian rulers. A similar relationship has been suggested between the sites at Sutton Courtenay and Long Wittenham in Oxfordshire.[37]

At the time of writing (June 2022) we are about to embark on the second of three seasons of excavation at Rendlesham as part of a community archaeology project funded by the National Lottery Heritage Fund.[38] Initial results from the first season (2021) of excavation and geoarchaeological sampling have already gone a long way to augment and refine our understanding of the character and spatial organisation of the place, its economy, and its environment. These are exciting times. Much of what we thought we knew about this aspect of the settlement record has been challenged or overturned by new discoveries over the past 10-15 years, and this poses a series of questions and opportunities that, as a discipline, we are still coming to terms with. Gabor Thomas and I have argued for a practice-led framework as a fruitful approach to understanding these places.[39] Among the other challenges we face are establishing a consistent understanding of the associated settlement topography and site sequence for known Great Hall Complexes – how many are elements of larger settlement complexes with significant antecedent activity? – and establishing their economic and environmental contexts. There is also a need to integrate the results of excavation with ploughsoil archaeology and surface finds at site-specific, local and regional scales in order to contextualise these places within wider geographies of power and rulership.

Abbreviations

H.E. = Colgrave, B and Mynors, R (eds): 1969. *Bede's Ecclesiastical History of the English People*. Oxford: Oxford University Press.
S = Sawyer, Peter. 1968. *Anglo-Saxon Charters: an Annotated List and Bibliography*. London: Royal Historical Society.

Digital sources:
Portable Antiquities Scheme: https://finds.org.uk [accessed 20 June 2022]
https://heritage.suffolk.gov.uk/rendlesham [accessed 20 June 2022]

Bibliography

Alcock, L. 2003: *Kings and Warriors, Craftsmen and Priests in Northern Britain AD 550-850*. Edinburgh: Society of Antiquaries of Scotland.
Austin, M. 2017: *Anglo-Saxon 'Great Hall Complexes': Elite Residences and Landscapes of Power in Early England, c. AD 550-700*. University of Reading, PhD Thesis.
Blackburn, M. 2003: "Productive' sites and the pattern of coin-loss in England, 600-1180', in *Markets in Early Medieval Europe: Trading and 'Productive' Sites, 650-850*, edited by Timothy Pestell and Katharina Ulmschneider. Macclesfield: Windgather, 20-36.
Blair, J. 2005: *The Church in Anglo-Saxon Society*. Oxford: Oxford University Press.

---

37 McBride et al. 2020, 41-43
38 https://heritage.suffolk.gov.uk/rendlesham [accessed 20 June 2022]
39 Thomas & Scull 2021, 21-22

Blair, J. 2018: *Building Anglo-Saxon England*. Princeton: Princeton University Press.
Faith, R. 1997: *The English Peasantry and the Growth of Lordship*. London: Leicester University Press.
Gates, T. & C. O'Brien. 1988: "Cropmarks at Milfield and New Bewick and the recognition of *Grubenhäuser* in Northumberland", *Archaeologia Aeliana*, 5th series 16, 1-9.
Hamerow, H. 2012: *Rural Settlements and Society in Anglo-Saxon England*. Oxford: Oxford University Press.
Hamerow, H. & N. Brennan. 2015: "An Anglo-Saxon great hall complex at Sutton Courtenay/Drayton, Oxfordshire: a royal centre of early Wessex?", *Archaeological Journal*, 172, 325-350.
Hamerow, H., C. Hayden & G. Hey. 2007: "Anglo-Saxon and earlier settlement near Drayton Road, Sutton Courtenay, Berkshire", *Archaeological Journal*, 164, 109-96.
Hinchliffe, J. 1986: "An early medieval settlement near Cowage Farm, Foxley, near Malmesbury". *Archaeological Journal*, 143, 240-259.
Hirst, S. & P. Rahtz. 1972: "Hatton Rock, 1970". *Transactions of the Birmingham and Warwickshire Archaeological Society*, 85, 160-77.
Hope-Taylor, B. 1977: *Yeavering: an Anglo-British Centre of Early Northumbria*. London: Her Majesty's Stationary Office.
Kelly, S. 2006: "Lyminge Minster and its early charters", in *Anglo-Saxons: Studies Presented to Cyril Hart*, edited by Simon Keynes and Alfred Smyth. Dublin: Four Courts Press, 98-113.
McBride, A. 2020: *The Role of Anglo-Saxon Great Hall Complexes in Kingdom Formation, in Comparison and in Context AD 500-750*. Oxford: Archaeopress.
McBride, A., H. Hamerow & J. Harrison. 2020: "A seventh-century high-status settlement at Long Wittenham, Oxfordshire". *Anglo-Saxon Studies in Archaeology and History*, 22, 23-49.
Martin, E., C. Pendleton & J. Plouviez. 2004: "Archaeology in Suffolk 2003", *Proceedings of the Suffolk Institute of Archaeology and History*, 40 (4), 485-521.
Millet, M. & S. James. 1983: "Excavations at Cowdery's Down, Basingstoke, Hampshire, 1978-81", *Archaeological Journal*, 140, 151-279.
Minter, F. 2016: "Archaeology in Suffolk in 2015", *Proceedings of the Suffolk Institute of Archaeology and History*, 43 (4), 611-640.
Newman, J. 2003: "Exceptional finds. Exceptional sites? Barham and Coddenham, Suffolk", in *Markets in Early Medieval Europe: Trading and 'Productive' Sites, 650-850*, edited by Timothy Pestell and Katharina Ulmschneider, Macclesfield: Windgather, 97-109.
Pestell, T. 2003: "The afterlife of 'productive' sites in East Anglia", in *Markets in Early Medieval Europe: Trading and 'Productive' Sites, 650-850*, edited by Timothy Pestell and Katharina Ulmschneider. Macclesfield: Windgather, 122-37.
Philp, B. 2003. *The Discovery and Excavation of Anglo-Saxon Dover*. Dover: Kent Archaeological Rescue Unit.
Philp, B. 2014: "A major Anglo-Saxon site at Eynsford", in *Discoveries and Excavations across Kent, 1970-2014*, edited by Brian Philp. Dover: Kent Archaeological Rescue Unit, 118-136.
Rahtz, P. 1970: "A possible Saxon palace near Stratford-upon-Avon", *Antiquity*, 44, 137-43.
Reynolds, A. 2021: "Commonalities, differences and lacunae: some comments on elite settlement in Britain and Ireland in the early middle ages", *Norwegian Archaeological Review*, 54:1-2, 56-59.
Scull, C. 1991: "Post-Roman phase 1 and Yeavering: a reconsideration", *Medieval Archaeology*, 35, 51-63.
Scull, C. 2022: "Periodisation and the language of transition: barriers to characterising and understanding change across the 4th to 7th centuries in Southern Britain", in *Transitions and Relationships over Land and Sea in the Early Middle Ages of Northern Europe*, edited by Andrew Richardson, Michael Bintley, John Hines, Andrew Seaman and Ellen Swift. Canterbury: Canterbury Archaeological Trust, 131-140.
Scull, C. & T. Williamson. 2018: "New light on Rendlesham: lordship and landscape in East Anglia 400-800", *The Historian*, 139, 6-11.
Scull, C. & G. Thomas. 2020: "Early Medieval great hall complexes in England: temporality and site biographies", *Anglo-Saxon Studies in Archaeology and History*, 22, 50 – 67.
Scull, C., F. Minter & J. Plouviez. 2016: "Social and economic complexity in early medieval England: a central place complex of the East Anglian Kingdom at Rendlesham, Suffolk", *Antiquity*, 90, 1594-1612.
Semple, S. 2013: *Perceptions of the Prehistoric in Anglo-Saxon England. Ritual, Religion and Rulership in the Landscape*. Oxford: Oxford University Press.

Tinniswood, A. & A. Harding. 1991: "Anglo-Saxon occupation and industrial features in the henge monument at Yeavering, Northumberland", *Durham Archaeological Journal*, 7, 93-108.

Thomas, G. 2013: "Life before the minster: the social dynamics of monastic foundation at Anglo-Saxon Lyminge, Kent", *Antiquaries Journal*, 93, 109-145.

Thomas, G. 2018: "Mead-halls of the *Oiscingas*: a new Kentish perspective on the Anglo-Saxon great hall complex phenomenon", *Medieval Archaeology*, 62/2, 262-303.

Thomas, G. & C. Scull. 2021: "Practice, power and place: southern British perspectives on the agency of early medieval rulers' residences", *Norwegian Archaeological Review*, 54:1-2, 1-28.

Thomas, G., C. Scull & P. Gleeson. 2021: "Halls of mirrors: reflections on the social meanings of early medieval rulers' residences", *Norwegian Archaeological Review*, 54:1-2, 75-79.

Ulmschneider, K. 2000: *Markets, Minster and Metal-Detectors. The Archaeology of Middle Saxon Lincolnshire and Hampshire Compared*. Oxford: British Archaeological Reports.

Walker, J. 2010: "In the hall", in *Signals of Belief in Early England*, edited by Martin Carver, Alex Sanmark and Sarah Semple. Oxford: Oxbow, 82-102.

Welch, M. 1992: *Anglo-Saxon England*. London: Batsford.

Williams, J., M. Shaw & V. Denham. 1985. *Middle Saxon Palaces at Northampton*. Northampton: Northampton Development Corporation.

Woods, A. 2021: "The production and use of coinage in East Anglia 500-800", *British Numismatic Journal*, 91, 13-59.

BY TERJE GANSUM

Chapter 8
Borre – A Royal Manor with Halls, Mounds, Harbour and Ship Graves

ABSTRACT

This article explores the archaeological site of Borre in Vestfold County, Norway. New investigations using methods like Lidar scans and ground-penetrating radar (GPR) have revealed complex monumental constructions, including four hall buildings and a new ship grave. The site also features a potential harbour and several mounds, indicating its significance as a royal manor comparable to Old Lejre in Denmark and Old Uppsala in Sweden. The findings suggest a rich historical context of ritual and elite activities from the 6th to the 10th centuries.

Borre in Vestfold County in Norway is situated on the west side, where the Oslo fjord narrows into a small strait and is an intriguing archaeological site. The big mounds have drawn people's attention ever since they were constructed. New investigations have revealed much information about the complexity of the site, which I will briefly present here.

The ship grave and the mounds were the focus of Bjørn Myhre's work and is published extensively.[1],[2] New investigations have been carried out within the partnership of *LBI ArchPro* where *Vestfold* and *Telemark County Council* was partner.

The new methods revealed a complex of monumental constructions, that makes it tempting to see Borre in combination with the *Old Lejre* in Denmark and *Old Uppsala* in Sweden, complexes which have been associated with and interpreted as royal manors.[3] Lidar scan added with geological expertise have additionally pointed out a possible harbour construction.[4] Additionally, ground-penetrating radar (GPR) has detected four hall buildings.[5] Also, a new ship grave was detected in 2017.

1 Myhre 1992
2 Myhre 2015
3 Ljungkvis 2013; Christensen 2016; Jörpeland & Seiler 2017
4 Draganits et al. 2015
5 Tonning et al. 2020

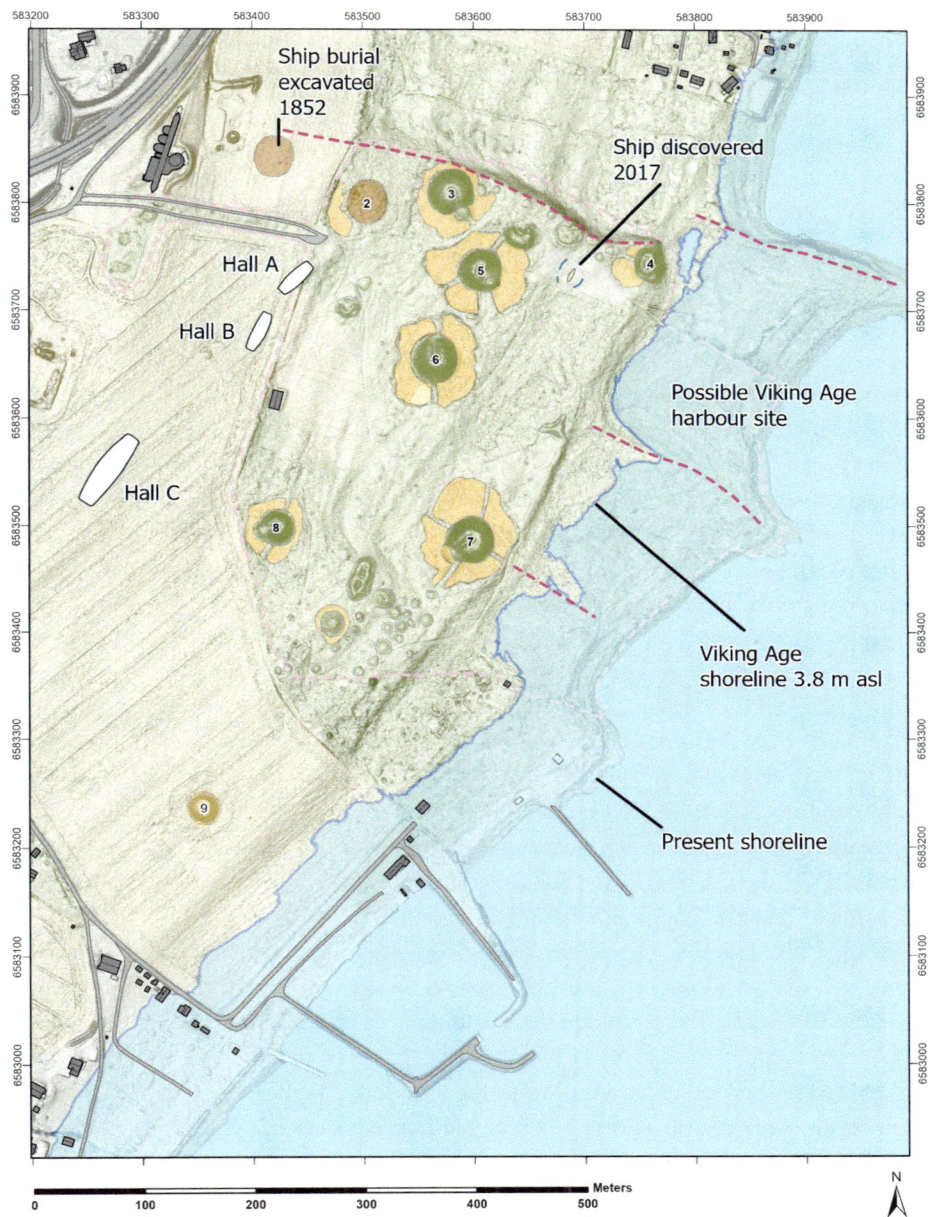

Map showing the Borre site where the halls, mounds and harbour is situated. The pink, dotted lines are marking out wave breakers that are man-made and can be dated to the late Iron Age. This endeavour is part of the monumentalisation of Borre. Illustration: Christer Tonning, Vestfold and Telemark Fylkeskommune (Vestfold and Telemark County Council).

Fig. 1.

A monitoring project is now in progress with the aim of understanding the relationship between temperature, water content and how those factors of local geology interplay with and provide information that may predict good conditions for implementing GPR. In other words, under which circumstances should we use GPR, and when is this method not favourable.[6] This basic source-critical approach is necessary to discuss, as is also other challenges with geophysical methods, such as dealing with the lack of chronology in general and the dating of structures in particular.

The ship graves

The early investigations at Borre were concluded in a publication by Prof. Bjørn Myhre in 2015. He summed up more than 150 years of investigations in his monography. Nicolaysen's rescue excavation revealed what was left of the ship grave. This was after the road authorities had used the mound as a quarry for sand and gravel.[7] Finds from the mound have been published several times with different interpretations.[8] This ship grave may have much in common with graves from Viking Age Valsgärde.[9] Twelve metres of the ship in the ship-mound was preserved. A qualified guess is that the ship measured approximately 16-19 metres.

The construction workers dug up many artefacts, and Nicolaysen was told that there were three horses and one dog buried on board the unburned ship. Also, an iron caldron filled with cremated bones was present. The bones were not collected. This mix of cremation and inhumation caused some uncertainty amongst archaeologists and Prof. A.W. Brøgger did not believe that the observations were right.[10] He argued that the burial must have been an inhumation. The re-excavation of the site in 1989 revealed ship nails with oak fragments attached, sherds of glass and burnt human bones. There is no reason to mistrust Nicolaysen's observations that there were burnt bones in an iron caldron and that the ship, animals, and other artifacts were not burnt.[11]

In the Ship Mound there were five stirrups and a harness bow that indicate high social status.[12],[13] A closer look at the stirrups shows ornament inlay with silver.[14] It measures 9.8 cm at the tread. It is not much if a horse rider wears leather shoes. Taking a closer look at the stirrup that may come from Mound 2, it is even tighter, just measuring 8.5 cm at the tread.[15] These observations prompt the question, whether they can be ascribed to a grown-up, male person or if they might indicate other users?

---

6   Schneidhofer et al. 2022
7   Nicolaysen 1854
8   Brøgger 1916; Blindheim 1954; Myhre 1992
9   Ljungkvist 2008; Andersson 2017
10 Brøgger 1916, 4
11 Myhre & Gansum 2003, 67-68
12 Braathen 1989
13 Pedersen 1997
14 Inventory number at University of Oslo's Museum of Cultural History: C1812c
15 Inventory number at University of Oslo's Museum of Cultural History: C12259

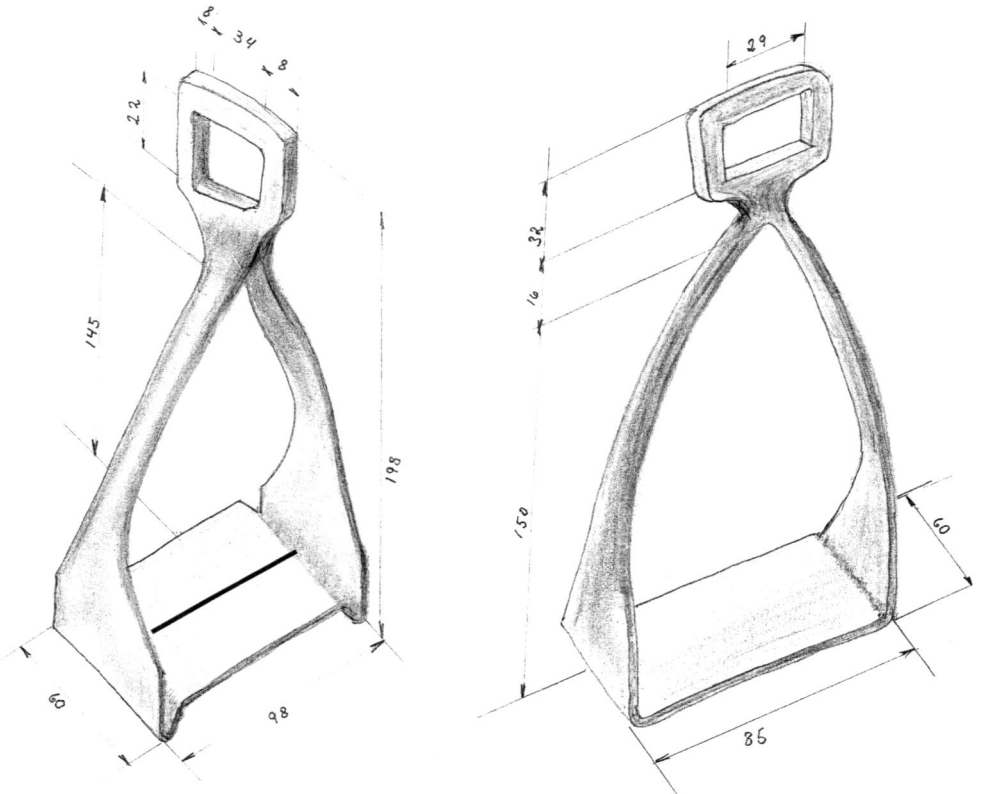

Drawings of two of the stirrups from the Ship Mound and possible Mound 2. The tread (Norwegian: footplate) is quite narrow. Drawing: Hans-Johnny Hansen 2007.

Fig. 2.

The harness bow has eastern parallels, mainly from Sweden.[16] Both the crystal bead and the enamelled metal fittings, belonging to a leather sheath indicate that a woman was present in the ship grave. The jewellery indicates an eastern connection.[17] Even though there are uncertainties, this ship burial represents a double grave with a man and a woman cremated elsewhere and brought to Borre to finish the sequence of death rituals.[18]

The recent scientific work conducted on the site includes the use of GPR. There are difficulties with GPS positioning between the huge trees. In addition, the archaeologist used a single channel GPR on minor fields within the cemetery. *Dyrskusletta* is one of the fields that has been investigated in this way. In 2017, Christer Tonning and his daughter prospected part of this field and picked up a boat-shaped anomaly. New tests the following year by the company, Leica confirmed the observations. In May 2022, new

---

16   Myhre 2015, 57
17   Myhre 2015, 193-197, Katalog 1
18   Myhre & Gansum 2003, 79

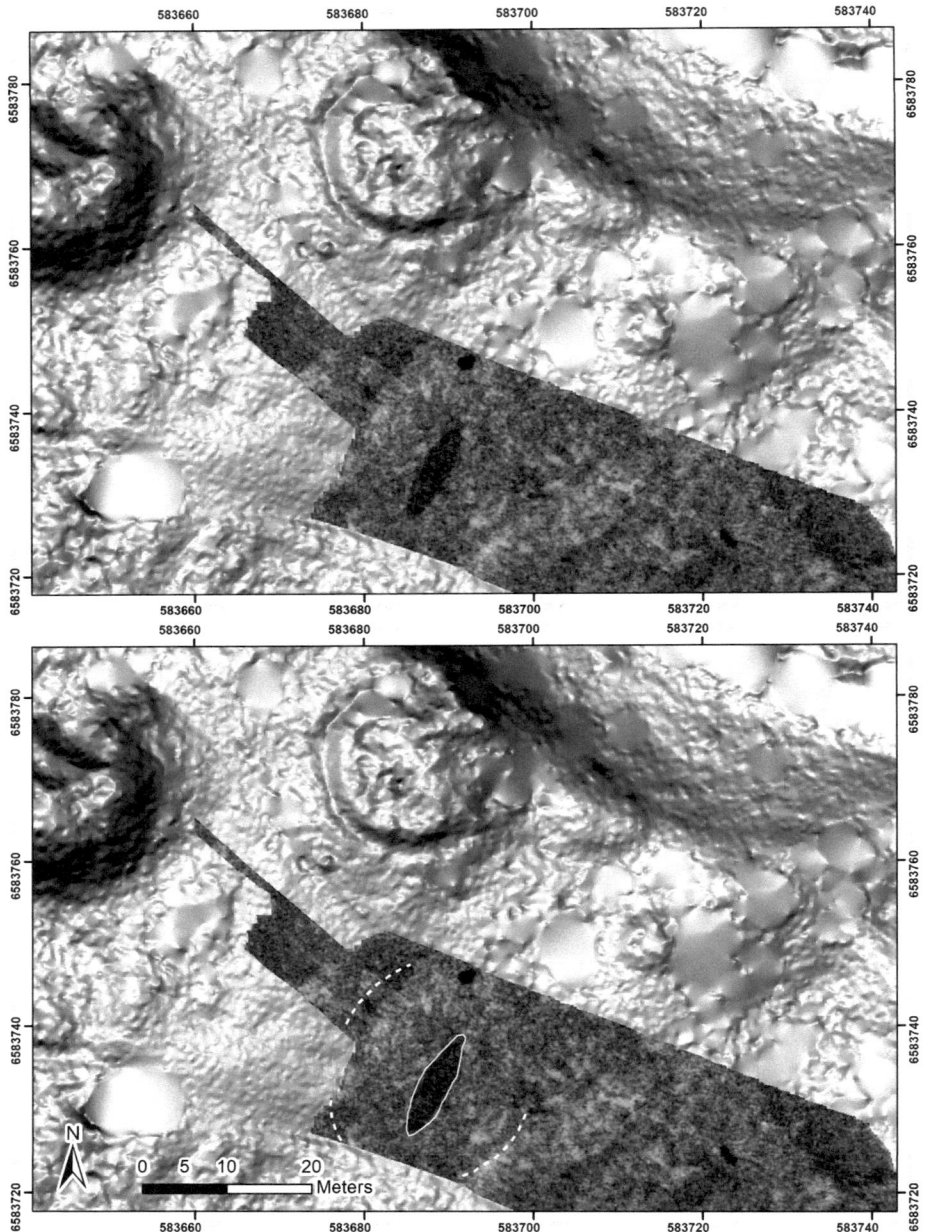

Fig. 3. The anomaly of a ship at Dyrskusletta inside the cemetery. Mound 33 is situated 20 metres north of the possible narrow ditch that surrounds the ship anomaly and may be a good analogy to the new discovered ship anomaly that partly has a narrow ditch marked with white stripes. Illustration: Christer Tonning, Vestfold and Telemark Fylkeskommune (Vestfold and Telemark County Council).

surveys were conducted and there is now strong evidence that the anomaly indicates another ship buried at the site. At this stage of investigation, the anomaly measured 13.6 meter in length, and 3.7 metres in width. If we take into account that at least 1.5 metres in the bow and aft may have rotted, the ship may have measured 17-18 metres in length. A narrow ditch surrounds the ship anomaly and gives the impression that a monument once was delimited by a surrounding construction.

There is no other historical evidence of mound constructions on this field. The oblong, narrow ditch structure measures 24 metre. The closest parallel to the newly discovered ship grave is situated some 20 metres to the north. Here a narrow ditch surrounds a cairn, measuring 23 metre in diameter. The cairn has been evaluated as a possible older feature dating to 550-900 AD. This date is, however, necessary to reconsider. If there has been a cairn covering the ship grave, and the stones were removed to clear the field, this would be in line with the observations made on site. If there are such similarities between these two constructions, we are facing a new understanding of the cairns at the Borre site.

A 45 meter long and 19-meter-wide stone ship is situated within the cemetery. This monumental ship has not previously been given much attention in the discussion of this site. As a vital symbol for the elite, it is tempting to draw parallels to Old Lejre ship settings in stone, and how the retrospective Jelling site is using the ship symbolism as a relation to old traditions.[19],[20],[21]

The hall buildings

In 2007 there was a pilot project with the aim of testing out new non-intrusive methods in Norway. The project was a cooperation between the *Norwegian National Heritage Board (NIKU, Riksantikvaren)* and *Vestfold County Council* (Vestfold Fylkeskommune). The Swedish Heritage Board was hired to conduct the initial investigation. In October 2007, two areas were prospected. One area inside the southern cemetery and a field measuring 25 × 100 metres outside the stone fence was prospected with GPR and within the field where B. Myhre and his team conducted minor excavations in 1991.

The GPR surveys (Fig. 4) resulted in the detection of four buildings. Two of the buildings were situated at the same location, Hall A1 and A2. The reinterpretation of the 1991 excavation revealed that one trench was dug inside a building, measuring 40 × 12 metre. Two postholes S1 and S10 were dated with radiocarbon dating: S 1 (phase A1) to 545-645 AD and 430-620 AD, S 10 (phase A2) to 662-778 AD and 430-780 AD.

The third building, Hall B, is 36 meter long. A pipeline runs through the building and was emptied during a minor investigation in 2017. Two radiocarbon dates were 532-638 AD and 428-598 AD.[22]

---

19   Pedersen 2014, 256
20   Hvass 2011, 32-39
21   Christensen 2016, 35
22   Gansum et al. 2018, 18

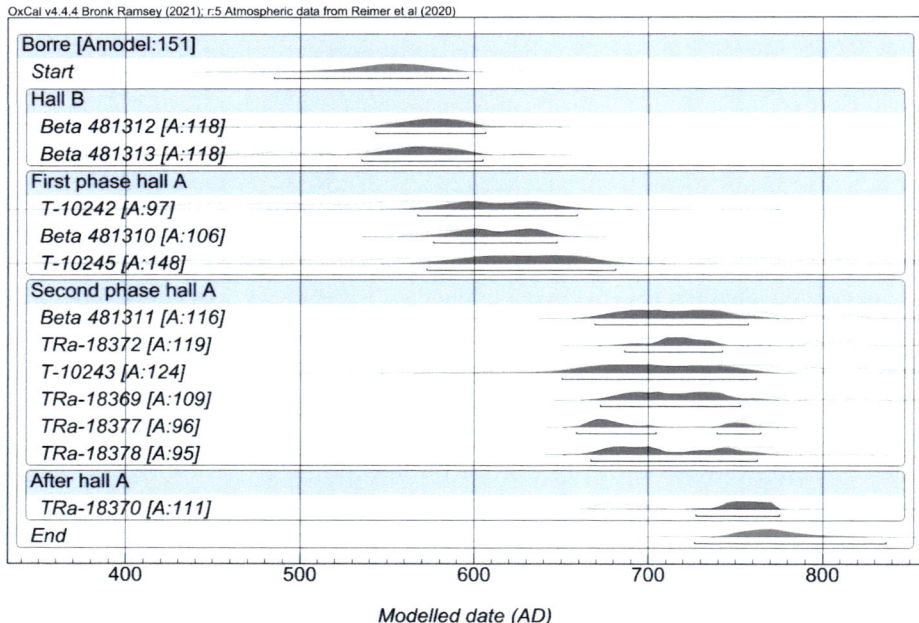

Fig. 4. The sequence of the ¹⁴C dating's from Hall A 1, A2 and Hall B show that Hall B is the oldest of the three. The dated material is oak and that may influence the dating's accuracy by being older that the actual building. Illustration: Bente Phillipsen, NTNU.

In reality, Borre has become a test site for GPR surveys in Norway. In March 2013, a survey was conducted with a GPR motorised by a skidoo. The data was very good, and a 63 metre-long building was detected. The four buildings are recognised as hall buildings.[23] There are still problems with data interpretation of the settlement structure at the Borre site. This is work in progress and will be published in the years to come.

The harbour

One of the main goals for the Borre-project (1988-1992) was to detect the harbour that ought to be located close to the mounds. Despite prospection in the field and examination of old maps, there were no results concerning where the inhabitants at Borre landed their ships. The waters are very shallow, as also the name *Langgrunn* indicates, with huge stones making it is difficult to manoeuvre and land a ship near these shores.

With active use of Lidar scan and cooperation within an international and multidisciplinary group of researchers there was progress in the search for the harbour.[24] The geologists identified from the contexts what was human-made, and which were from

---

23 Tonning et al. 2020, 157
24 Doneus et al. 2013

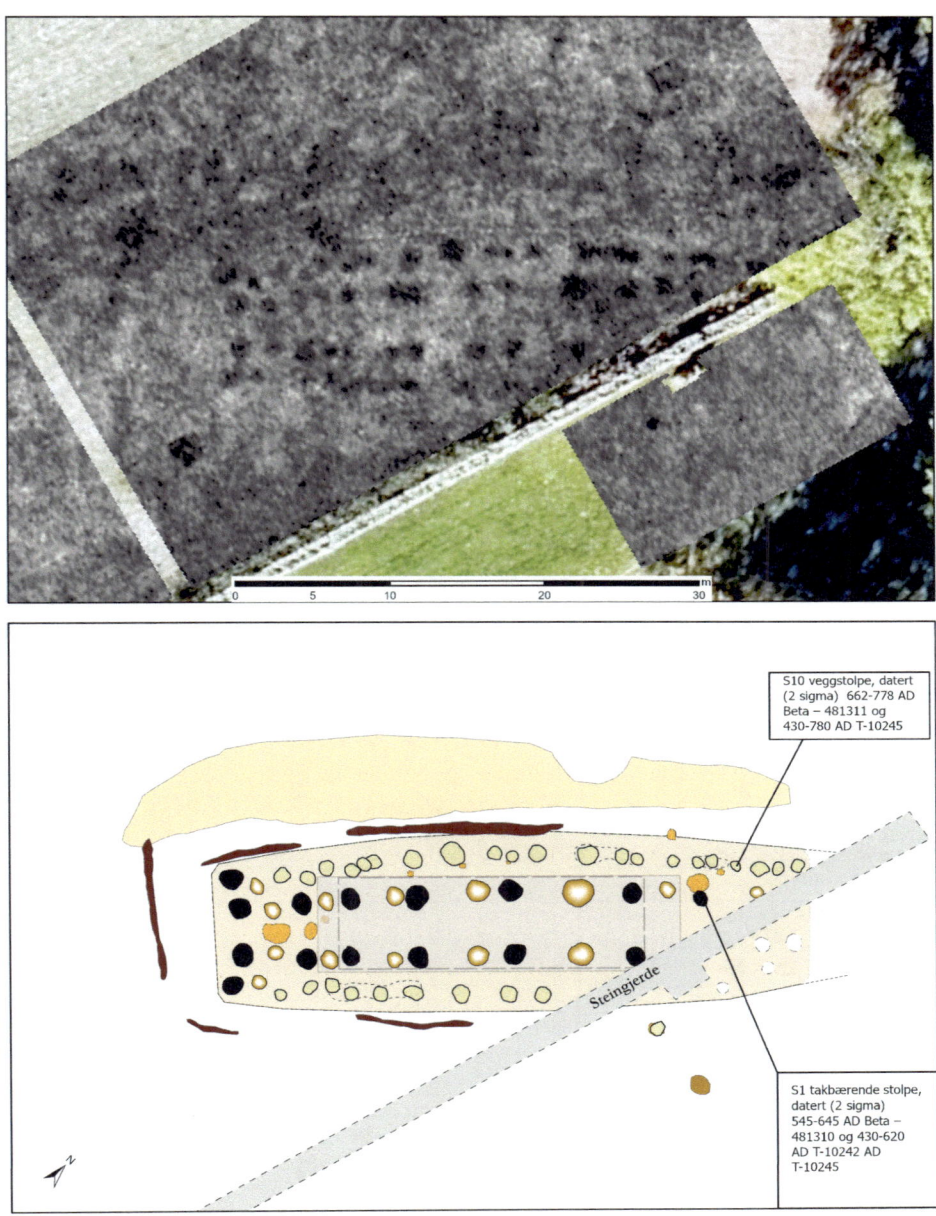

Hall A1 and A2 buildingsare situated in the same location. Illustration: Christer Tonning, Vestfold and Telemark Fylkeskommune (County Council).

Fig. 5.

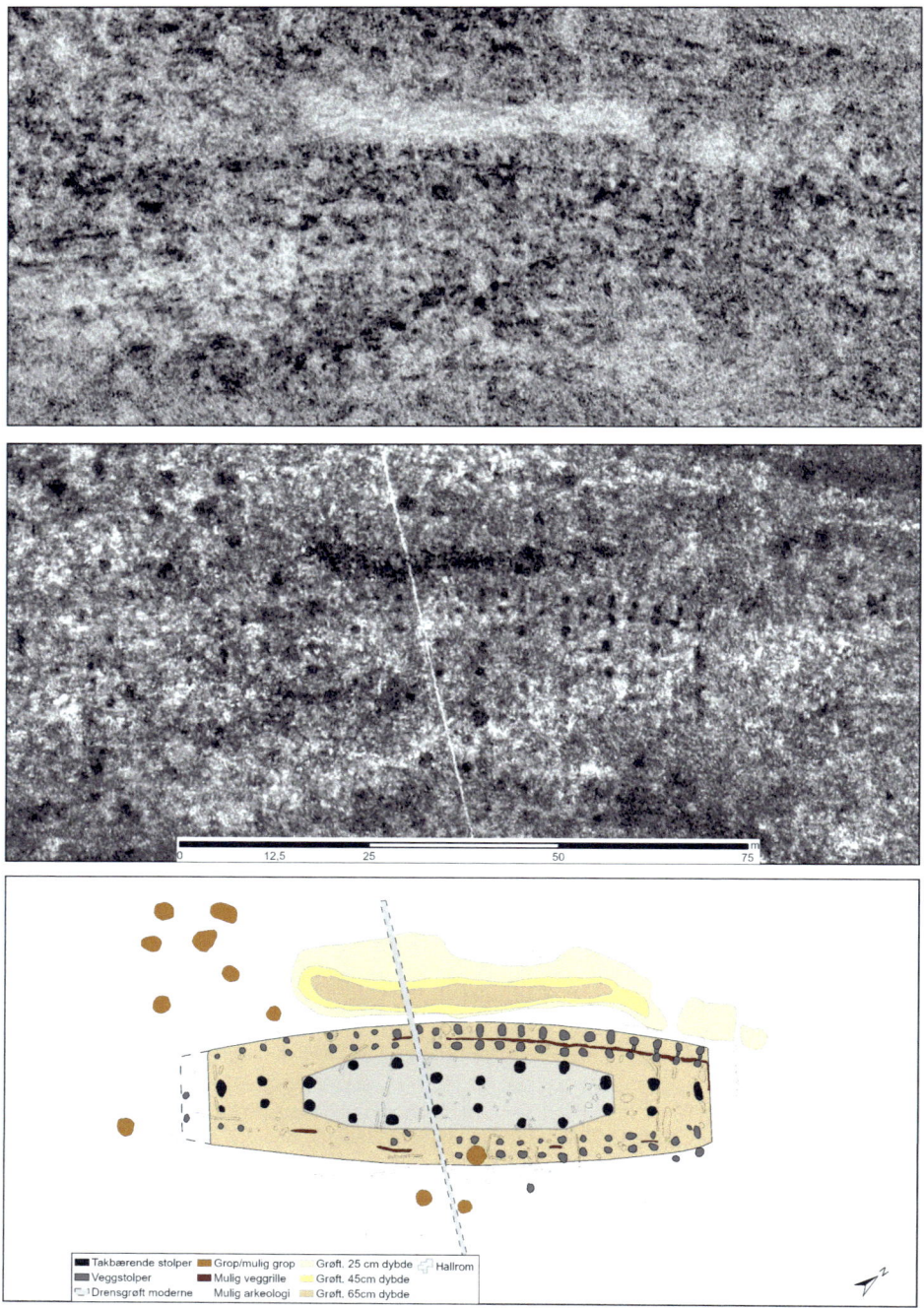

Fig. 6. *The Hall C building. Illustration: Christer Tonning, Vestfold and Telemark fylkeskommune.*

natural processes. Locations at *Klokkertangen* and *Prestetangen* were constructed from stone material from the geological moraine layer *Raet*, and they must have functioned as wave breakers. They are marked with pink, dotted lines in Figure 1. Beach ridges are visible features caused by upheaval of land, combined with waves washing on the shore, and they follow the shoreline. The beach ridges follow the human constructions, show that the wave breakers are old, and may be dated by the ongoing land upheaval in Norway. The wave breakers probably were built during the same period as the hall buildings and the mounds[25]. These big earth works into the fjord form part of the monumentalisation of Borre.

The mounds

In 1832, Johannes Flintoe made a drawing of the Borre site, and it is possible to detect the place he was standing, and from there reconstruct the various mounds. The Ship Mound and Mound 2 are drawn and seem to be well preserved. The Ship Mound was, however removed in 1851-1852 and revealed important archaeological finds, dating to 900-925 AD.[26]

Mound 2 was removed between 1852 and 1915.[27] Little is known about this enterprise, but a qualified guess about what happened could be the following. In 1885 there was delivered a stirrup, an iron bridle, a "rangle", a soapstone bowl and a minor soapstone cup to the museum in Oslo (C12256-60) with a notice that it was found 16 years ago, near the first train station south of *Horten*, which is Borre. The guess is that these finds may have come from the owner that removed the mound in 1869. Another possibility is that the mound was removed during the railway construction in the area in the 1870s. The train line with Borre station was opened in 1881. The finds are dated ca. 950 AD.[28],[29]

It was a huge challenge to find a strategy to date the mounds with minor damage. B. Myhre advocated the idea that sediments from the centre of the mound were thrown out and deposited in a reversed succession and that bones and charcoal then was accessible with minor efforts by digging test pits. It is from these test pits the dated charcoal were taken and dated.

Mound 3 has not been investigated, but Myhre excavated three test pits, where he found charcoal or bones from the reopened trench that is highly visible on the south side of the mound. The two ^{14}C dates from charcoal gave the result 690-890 and 700-900 AD within 1 sigma.[30]

Mound 4 was investigated by Nicolaysen in 1852. He dug a trench in the centre of the mound but concluded very briefly that there were "only a few unburnt horse bones

---

25   Draganits et al. 2015, 103
26   Myhre 2015, 59
27   Myhre 2015, 78-79
28   Braathen 1989, 29, 36
29   Myhre 2015, 78
30   Myhre 2015, 80

and dust from charcoal".[31] Myhre's test pit contained charcoal from spruce, and a ^{14}C was not prioritised.[32]

Mound 5 was treated the same way as Mounds 3 and 4 by excavating a test pit in the fill thrown out from the centre of the mound when it was reopened. The charcoal that was collected was dated, but the ^{14}C analysis turned out to be quite modern, dating to the 15-17th century.[33]

An archaeological 30-metre-long trench was dug into Mound 6 in 1989. The trench reached 5 metres into the mound construction[34]. Layer 13 that is interpreted as the ancient arable field that was in use before the mound was built contained charcoal and burned bones from sheep/goat, dog and humans. This may be remains from a cremation.[35] Two ^{14}C dates, one taken from Layer 13 on charcoal revealed a date to 560-720 AD. One from a layer underneath, Layer 14, also made on charcoal was dated to 640-860 AD.[36]

Mound 7 was also investigated by a 25 meter long trench. It was excavated across a circular ditch, approximately 5 metres into the mound construction.[37] Four ^{14}C dates taken from the upper and middle part of the mound construction were analysed and three of them gave the following results: 410-570 AD (Layer 13), 530-710 and 540-710 AD (Layer 2), but the charcoal from the lower layers were sadly ruined.[38] Some burned animal bones were detected, but as far as species are concerned, they were not possible to specify.

During the reopening of the mound, sand, earth and possibly remains from a cremation was replaced and superimposed in part of the ring-ditch that surrounds the mound. The accumulation of organic material in the ditch was sealed with sediments from the reopening process. The sealed organic layer was dated and indicates when the mound was reopened. The reopening of Mound 7 was ^{14}C dated to the period 860-1040 AD.[39]

Mound 8 has not been investigated but Myhre made a test pit where he expected to find charcoal or bones from a later reopening of the trench. He found charcoal and burned bones but ^{14}C dates were not prioritised.[40]

Mound 9, named *Spillemannshaugen*, is today situated some 125 metres south of the main mounds. A potato cellar was dug into the mound in the early 19th century and was expanded in 1927 without a proper archaeological excavation. Bjørn Hougen made excavations on some of the smaller mounds, south of the major mounds the same year, asking the workers if they had found anything. In this connection, he retrieved

---

31 Nicolaysen 1854, 30 [Gansum translation]
32 Myhre 2015, 80
33 Myhre 2015, 81
34 Myhre 2015, 68
35 Myhre 2015, 65
36 Myhre 2015, 67
37 Myhre 2015, 72
38 Myhre 2015, 72
39 Myhre 2015, 74
40 Myhre 2015, 82

two rings of iron, probably pieces of a "rangle" that Myhre guessed could be dated to the 8-9th century.[41] When the potato cellar was removed in 1979, an archaeological investigation was carried out, but unfortunately, there are only a few photographs, and no report explaining what they found. One ^{14}C date of charcoal from the mound collected in 1979 dates to 220-400 AD. The context is, however unclear.

In 1927 the students Bjørn Hougen and Eivind Engelstad investigated eight of the minor mounds in the southern part of the cemetery.[42] In Mound 10 they found iron rivets, probably from one or two cists and small bone fragments that were impossible to collect. In Mound 12, one rivet was found together with charcoal and bunt bones. In Mound 29, they detected a posthole in the centre of the mound, but no artefacts, charcoal or bones. The other mounds did not reveal artefacts but did show different elements that are usual in mound constructions, like circular stone rows delimiting inner- or outer part of the mounds and distinct layers with charcoal.

Artefacts and eastern connections

During the last ten years, there has been limited investigations with metal detector on the Borre site. From the minor archaeological excavations, we have experienced that there are few finds of old metal debris. This is confirmed by metal detectorist, but some of the most interesting finds are: two parts of a relief brooch from the 5th or 6th century (Style I), a pendant shaped as a duck foot from the 8th or 9th century, and a dirhem dated to 866-869 AD.[43] The pendant and brooch are probably grave goods from two mounds that were destroyed in 1921, some 100 metres north of the Ship Mound. The pendant and dirhem have eastern origins and together with artefacts from the Ship Mound and the fact that there are chamber graves detected at the Borre cemetery, it clearly shows that the deceased had eastern connections.[44]

Concluding remarks

The royal manor at Borre is still not fully understood, and we are struggling to interpret the role the possible kings at this site played in the interregional network of Scandinavia. As it stands now, we are looking at a centre established in the 6th century, expanding and playing a vital role into the 10th century. How climate change, plague, and comet incidents in years AD 536-543 are to be understood at Borre and in the region is still unknown.

The investigation at the Borre site will continue and there is still much work to be done regarding the geophysical surveys. The settlement structure will probably be bet-

---

41 Myhre 2015, 82
42 Hougen & Engelstad 1927
43 Lie 2019, 48, 52
44 Myhre & Gansum 2003: 35; Gansum & Kobro 2003; Gansum 2008, 58 and attachment; Lie 2019, 50

ter understood in the years to come. New ^{14}C dates from documented archaeological contexts will supply our current knowledge of the site. The prospection campaign will continue, and new methods will be applied.

Acknowledgements

Thanks to Ragnar Orten Lie and Christer Tonning for long time cooperation.

Bibliography

Andersson, K. 2017: *Krigerna från Valsgärde: glimtar från en guld- och granatskimrande forntid*. Atlantis.
Blindheim, C. 1954: "Borre i lys av Borre-funnet og Nasjonalparken", *Borre bygdebok*. Borre kommune, 1-26.
Brøgger, A.W. 1916: *Borrefundet og Vestfoldkongenes graver*, Videnskapsselskapets Skrifter.II. Hist. Filos. Klasse, No. 1.
Braathen, H. 1989: *Ryttergraver. Politiske strukturer i eldre rikssamlingstid*. Varia 19. Universitetets Oldsaksamling.
Christensen, T. 2016: *Lejre bag myten: De arkæologiske udgravninger* (Jysk Arkæologisk Selskab Skrifter 87). Moesgaard, Aarhus Universitet.
Doneus, M., E. Draganits & T. Gansum. 2013: "The Viking-Age royal burial site of Borre (Norway): Lidar-based landscape reconstruction and harbour location at an uplifting costal area", in *Archaeological Prospection. Proceedings of the 10th International Conference on Archaeological Prospection*, edited by Wolfgang Neubauer, Immo Trinks, Roderick. B. Salisbury & Christina Einwögerer. Vienna: Austrian Academy of Sciences Press, 36-38.
Draganits, E., M. Doneus, T. Gansum, Lars Gustavsen, Erich Nau, Christer Tonning, Immo Trinks & Wolfgang Naubauer. 2015: "The late Nordic Iron Age and Viking Age royal burial site of Borre in Norway: ALS- and GPR-based landscape reconstruction and harbour location at an uplifting costal area", *Quaternary International 367*, 96-110. https://doi.org/10.1016/j.quaint.2014.04.045
Gansum, T. 2007: Helhetsplan for Borreparken. Rapport og vedlegg til politisk sak mars 2008. Vestfold fylkeskommune.
Gansum, T. & L. Ueland Kobro. 2003: "Gullfunn på Borre", *Borreminne*, 8-15.
Gansum, T., C. Tonning & P. Schneidhofer. 2018: "Hallbygg og tidlig kirkearkitektur i tre", *Borreminne*, 9-26.
Hougen, B. & E. Engelstad. 1927: Innberetning om utgravinger på gravfeltet på Borre i Vestfold. 21. august – 16 september 1927. Innberetning KHM topografisk arkiv.
Hvass, S. 2011. *Jelling-monumenterne – deres historie og bevaring*. Kulturarvstyrelsen.
Jörpeland, L. Beronius & A. Seiler. 2017: "En annan slags monumentalisering – temasyntes", in *At Upsalum – människor och landskapande. Utbyggnad av Ostkustbanan genom Gamla Uppsala*, edited by Lena Beronius Jörpeland, Hans Göthberg, Anton Seiler & Jonas Wikborg (Rapport 2017: 1_1. Statens historiska museer), 441-453.
Lie, R.O. 2019: "Svømmefot fra vikingtiden", *Borreminne*, 43-66.
Ljungkvist, J. 2008: "Valsgärde – Development and change of a burial ground over 1300 years", in *Valsgärdet studies: the Place and its people, Past and Present*, edited by Svante Norr (OPIA 42), 13-55
Ljungkvist, J. 2013: "Monumentaliseringen av Gamla Uppsala", in *Gamla Uppsala i ny belysning*, edited by Olof Sundqvist & Per Vikstrand, 33-68.
Myhre, B. 1992: "Borre – et merovingertidssenter i Norge", in *Økonomiske og politiske sentra i Norden ca 400-1000 e. Kr.*, edited by Egil Mikkelsen & Jan Henning Larsen (*Universitetets Oldsaksamings Skrifter. Ny rekke*, nr. 13), 155-179.
Myhre, B. 2015: *Før Viken ble Norge. Borrefeltet som religiøs og politisk arena*. (Norske Oldfunn XXXI). Vestfold fylkeskommune.
Myhre, B. & T. Gansum. 2003: *Skipshaugen 900. E.kr. Borrefunnet 1852-2002*. Midgard Historisk senter.
Nicolaysen, N. 1854: "Om Borrefundet i 1852", *Foreningen til Norske Fortidsminnesmerkers Bevaring. Aarbog 1852*, 25-32.
Pedersen, A. 1997: "Weapons and riding gear in burials – evidence of military and social rank in 10th century Denmark?", in *Military Aspects of Scandinavian Society in a European Perspective, AD 1-1300*, edited by Anne Nørgård Jørgensen & Birthe. L. Clausen (PNM Studies in Archaeology and history 2). Nationalmuseet København, 123-136.

Pedersen, A. 2014: "The Jelling-monuments – a national Icon between Legend and Fact", *Quo vadis? Status and Future Perspectives of Long-Term Excavations in Europe*, edited by Claus von Carnap-Bornheim (Schriften des archäologischen Landesmuseums Ergänzungsreihe Bd. 10), 249-263.

Schneidhofer, P, C. Tonning, R.J.S Cannell, E. Nau, A. Hinterleitner, G.J. Verhoeven, L. Gustavsen, Knut Paasche, Wolfgang Neubauer & Terje Gansum. 2022: "The influence of Environmental Factors on the Quality of GPR Data: The Borre Monitoring Project", *Remote sensing 14*, 3289, 1-33. https://doi.org/10.3390/rs14143289

Tonning, C., P. Schneidhofer, E. Nau, T. Gansum, V. Lia, L. Gustavsen, R. Filzwiser, M. Wallner, M. Kristiansen, W. Neubauer, K. Paasche & I. Trinks. 2020: "Halls at Borre: discovery of three large buildings at a Late Iron and Viking Age royal burial site in Norway", *Antiquity* Vol. 94, 145-163. https://doi.org/10.15184/aqy.2019.211

BY ELNA SIV KRISTOFFERSEN & ALF TORE HOMMEDAL

Chapter 9
Iron Age Monuments and Finds from the Tinghaug Plateau – a Synthesis

ABSTRACT

This article discusses the rich archaeological heritage of the Tinghaug plateau in Rogaland, in Southwest Norway. The area is notable for its high density of monuments and rich grave finds, including local high-quality objects and imports. The synthesis draws on historical surveys, literature, and archived data to explore the aristocratic environment of the plateau. Key features include prominent grave mounds, court sites, and evidence of cult practices. The article also addresses the political and social significance of the area, highlighting its centrality in regional power structures during the Iron Age and early Medieval period.

The Tinghaug plateau in Klepp, county of Rogaland, Southwest Norway, stands out with a high density of varied monuments (Figure 1-2) and rich grave finds with local objects of high quality as well as imports. Finds have come to light through a long period, and few monuments are professionally excavated. The following synthesis is based on a survey aimed at reaching a research status for the plateau,[1] articles that accumulated and developed our knowledge of this highly interesting area. In addition, our synthesis includes a discussion on the written sources from the Medieval period.

Our data consist of information from literature and archives as well as an updated evaluation of old finds, objects, standing monuments and their relationship in the landscape, and not of results from recent excavation of house sites. By weaving together various pieces of knowledge, the article aims at a further understanding of the term 'aristocratic environment'.

Due to the prominent position of the monuments on the Tinghaug plateau, many historians and archaeologists have taken an interest in the area. In the 19th century Bendix Edv. Bendixen, Jens Kraft, Anders Lorange, Nicolay Nicolaysen and Gabriel

---

1 Kristoffersen et al. 2014

The Tinghaug plateau from Krosshaug towards the hight Tinghaug. Photo: Arne Johan Nærøy, Museum of Archaeology, University of Stavanger.

Fig. 1.

Gustafson studied the monuments.² In the early 20th century, the ones still preserved and visible at the farms Hauge and Tu were surveyed and mapped by Tor Helliesen.³ Since then various monuments, single objects from the rich grave assemblages as well as the role of the area in the political development through the Iron Age have attracted much attention.⁴ Bente Magnus' thesis from 1975 on the unique Krosshaug grave stands out as a major work.

---

2   Bendixen 1880; Gustafson 1900; Kraft: 1829; Lorange 1880; Nicolaysen 1870
3   Helliesen 1907
4   e.g., Axboe 2004; Bukkemoen 2014; Grimm 2010; Hauck 1985-86; Hauken 2005; Kristoffersen 2000, 2006, 2012; Magnus 1975, Meyer 1935; Myhre 1987; Møllerop 1963, 1989; Pesch 2007; Reiersen 2017; Shetelig 1914; Straume 1987; Særheim 1980; Watt 2019

The Tinghaug plateau in the Jæren Landscape

The plateau is situated in the low-lying Jæren region – a coastal rim covered by thick Quaternary deposits.[5] Throughout most of its history, Jæren was characterised by shallow lakes, wetlands and bogs, and a uniform, agrarian landscape, intensively cultivated and mainly treeless farmland.[6] The plateau, with the farms Hauge and Tu, makes out the southern end of the NNE-SSW aligned Tu Mountain ridge. The soil on the ridge is more fertile than the landscape below, well-drained, and rich in minerals.[7] As the highest point of Jæren, the Tinghaug height, with its steep, southern edge, rises 102 m above sea-level and offers an expansive view to the North Sea and the landscape below. The prominent ridge features an exceptional high density of ancient monuments of various types.[8]

The plateau is reached by the old post road that cut across the Tu ridge, from the south by a steep hill, a rare occurrence in the flat Jæren landscape. Coming from the north, the path towards the Tinghaug height today follows the boundary between the farms Hauge and Tu. Still, in the 19th century a line of five grave mounds, at least two of them among the largest at the plateau,[9] lined the way towards the height, where a cairn or a beacon was situated, a sight that did impress Nicolaysen in 1869 when the mounds were still intact.[10] They are all marked on the detailed map by Ingebrikt Anda from 1884 (Figure 2), continuing the curved line, an old road, from the historical farm Tu. Today only two mounds are preserved – Sadelhaugen in SSW and the one nearest Tinghaug, Grønhaug, both excavated and restored.

Based on the notion that routes and movement lines are important elements in the structuring of the landscape, Grete Bukkemoen regards the old routes traversing the area, lined with grave mounds, as a confirmation of the centrality of the plateau.[11] The impression of continuity through the Iron Age in mind, the line of mounds towards Tinghaug could well be perceived as an expression of genealogy and a hero- or ruler

---

5 Prøsch-Danielsen et al. 2018, with references.
6 Lillehammer 2014, 14-15
7 Magnus 1975, 143
8 According to Helliesen's inventory: Tu: 61 monuments; Hauge: 18 monuments, within an area of 4 km². Tu: 20 mounds larger than 10 m across or in length, 13 mounds larger than 20 m across, most more than 25 m, or in length, one 41,5 m long, one 36 m long. Hauge: 12 mounds larger than 10 m across or in length, 6 mounds larger than 20 m across or in length, one 40 long and one 34 m across. Håkon Reiersen ('Elite milieus', 167, Fig. 6.5) has counted 87 mounds larger than 20 m in Klepp kommune.
9 From the north, according to Helliesen a) a smaller mound with a Viking period female grave (cf. below); b) Sadelhaugen, according to test excavation by Bjørn Myhre 34 m across; c) the middle mound, according to Helliesen more than 19 m across; d) mound with equestrian burial from the Merovingian period; e) Grønhaug 21 m across, 2,8 m high with equestrian burial from the Viking period. According to Nicolaysen Sadelhaugen and Grønhaug were the largest mounds in the line.
10 Nicolaysen 1870, 141
11 Bukkemoen 2014, 40, 44-46

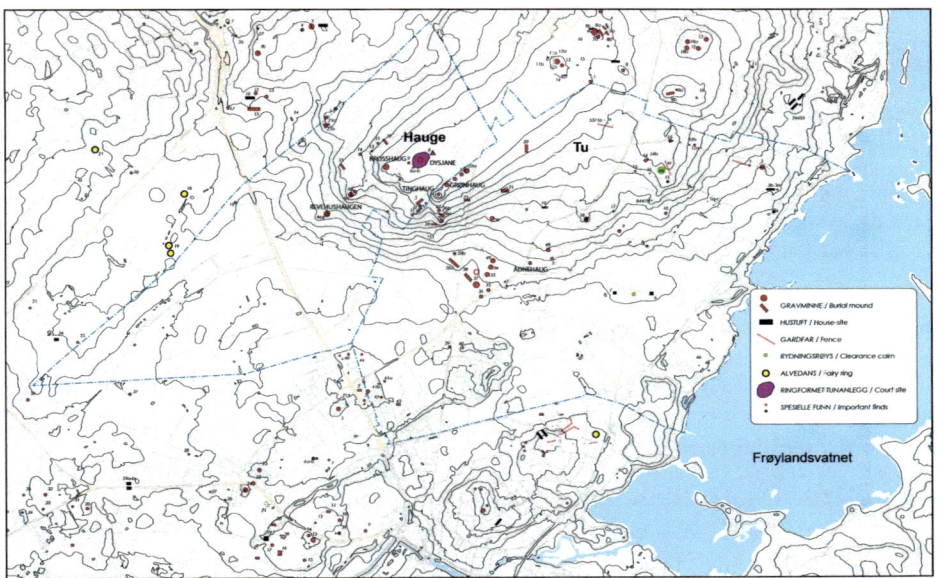

2a. Map showing the monuments on the farms Hauge and Tu. Map by Theo Gil Bell, Museum of Archaeology, University of Stavanger.

Fig. 2a.

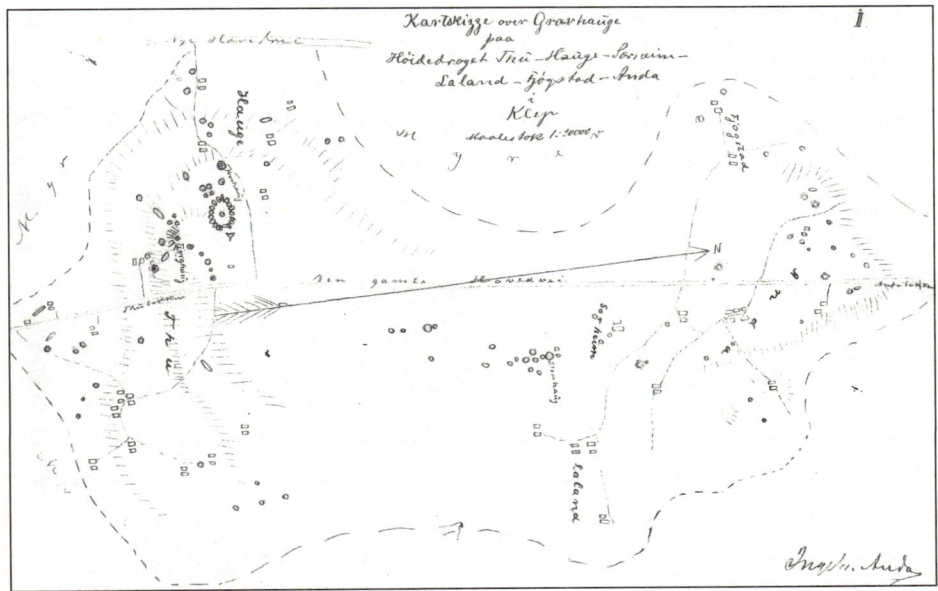

2b. Sketch showing monuments on the Tinghaug plateau. Drawing: Amtsagronom Ingebrigt Anda, 1884, Topographical Archive, Museum of Cultural History, University of Oslo.

Fig. 2b.

cult often ascribed to monumental grave mounds.[12] Helliesen mentions in all 14 grave mounds along the border between the two farms.[13] some of them still visible below Tinghaug, perhaps lining a path towards the height from the south. Bukkemoen distinguishes between grave mounds connected to the farmsteads and mounds placed centrally in the topographical structure, often in places where people came together, such as assemblies.[14] She sees the former as expressions of territorial relations and ancestral bounds and the latter as nodal points that 'tied people together through shared genealogies, history and landscape'. Many grave mounds are situated in, and thereby focussing on, the transition between Tinghaug and the landscape below, separating the height. Hence, the mounds are attributed a legitimating role, giving authority to the height and the activities taking place there.

Traditions and place names

Several place names connected to the farms Hauge, and Tu refer to various central functions.[15] *Tu* refers to *height* and is probably the original name of Tinghaug.[16] *Hauge*, because of its original definite form, refers to one of the large mounds as an assembly place for a larger area.[17] Inge Særheim presents a sacral interpretation of the name *Frøylandsvatnet*, the lake below the Tu farm, with reference to the goddess Frøya.[18] Several *Lunden*-names, probably referring to sacred groves, and traditionally connected to cult activity, are known, such as *Tulunden, Lundarsberget* and two *Lunden*. *Lundarkjelda* was a holy well, dedicated to St. Hans and visited at Midsummer. Fertility offerings in the spring and autumn are recorded in connection with the huge mound Tuhaugen once situated in the farmyard at Tu, a tradition that continued until the 18th century.[19] A stone called *Njåre* (the God Njord?) was involved, in the tradition identified as the Tu stone (cf., below).

Cultic practices

Magnus Olsen described the Tinghaug plateau as a place where the old gods were worshiped.[20] Based on the occurrence of gold foils, gold bracteates, a 'three-corn' cairn (*treudd*), a white phallic stone and the monumental grave mounds, Olof Sundqvist regards the area as an important cultic place during the Iron Age. He argues that the

---

12   Sundqvist 2014, 94-96, with references
13   Lillehammer 2014, 21
14   Bukkemoen 2007, 37-47
15   Særheim 2014, 49-62, Fig. 22
16   Rygh 1915, 128-129; Særheim 1980, 76, 2014, 53-54
17   Særheim 2014, 53
18   Særheim 2014, 54-55, with references
19   Særheim 2014, 55; Lillehammer 2014, 32; both with reference to Hauge, *Gamle Jæren*.
20   Olsen 1909, 27

women in the aristocratic burials in Krosshaug, Revehushaugen and Ådnehaugen may have played a central role in the cult activities.[21] Their role did not only involve the *Vanir* deities, but also the *Æsir* gods of the public cult, a cult known to be performed at important aristocratic central places in connection with the farm of the leading ruler.[22]

Monuments and finds

The catalogue in the 2014 publication[23] gives an overview of all archaeological objects found on the farms Hauge and Tu, an area covering approximately 4 km², and it offers a detailed description, including type references and illustrations. The following is a selection of this body of material.

Roman period
Two brooches testify to activity in the Early Roman period; a copper alloy brooch (AD 70-150) and a spindle whorl found in a destroyed mound somewhere on Hauge (B4420)[24] and a silver brooch with long catch plate (C4912) from the court site (cf., below).

A double-layered glass vessel (*Überfang*), *Tu-begeret* (Tu, S1494) (Figure 3), with a Greek inscription,[25] was found in 1882 in a large grave mound, 23 m across and 2 m high, together with an iron spear head, a wooden bucket with copper alloy fittings and gaming pieces, objects that are all lost.[26] The glass has an eastern origin, probably the Black Sea area.[27]

Court sites, found within the modern borders of Norway, many of them in Rogaland, consist of the remains of houses arranged side by side in a circular formation around an open space (Figure 1-2). The large court site Dysjane (Hauge) was partially excavated in the late 19th century by Nicolaysen and by Bendixen.[28] Object finds date Dysjane to the Roman period, and it has been interpreted as some sort of assembly place with military, judicial and cultic activities.[29] Grete Lillehammer regards the court site, erected in the old common outfield, as a place where people from the Tu ridge came together, and as an indication of a change in a process of concentration of power. A 'leader house' has been defined, based on the mentioned silver brooch and the position of the house.[30]

The three-corn cairn *(treudd)* at Hauge, is situated close to the court site, and was excavated in 1869 by Nicolaysen. Apart from a layer of coal, nothing was found. These

---

21 Sundqvist 2014, 89-105
22 cf. also Sundqvist 2003, 2005, 2012
23 Hauken 2014, 141-156
24 Hauken 2014, 141
25 Translated: Drink, and you shall live happily (Drikk og må du leve lykkelig!).
26 Hauken 2014, 63-64; 2014, 147
27 Näsman 1984, 62; Straume 1987, 100, nr. 44
28 Then assumed to be burial mounds, hence the name *Dysjane* which means *mounds*.
29 e.g., Grimm 2010, 30-44, 124-125, 138-139; Hauken 2014, 144-145; Lillehammer 2014, 30-32, 36
30 Reiersen 2019, 280

Fig. 3. *Glass beakers from the Tinghaug plateau. Above, from the left: Cut glass beaker (Überfang) with inscription in Greek from Tu (S1494). Photo: Annette G. Øvrelid, Museum of Archaeology, University of Stavanger; Trailed glass beakers from Hauge (Krosshaug) (B2272), photo: Svein Skare, University Museum of Bergen and below from Tu (Ådnehaugen) (S1479), photo Terje Tveit, Museum of Archaeology, University of Stavanger. Hights 16,5, 18,3 and 20,5 cm.*

cairns are common in Rogaland and often occur in connection with cultic activities.[31] They have been regarded as cosmic symbols and as a manifestation of the world tree *Yggdrasil*.[32] A possible three-corn cairn is also recorded from Tu.[33]

In the Roman period objects such as a gold berlock, a Hemmor bucket and Eastland cauldron are found on the farms at the northern part of Tu ridge, and Håkon Reiersen has suggested that these farms, the *Anda milieu*, might have controlled the court site, a situation that changed with the transition to the Migration Period, when Hauge and Tu became the central area, and the thing site was established on Tinghaug at the Tu farm.[34]

Migration Period

The assemblies from the female burials in Krosshaug, Revehushaugen and Ådnehaugen mounds stand out due to the elaborate dress equipment. All three also include so-called iron weaving battens, in Rogaland only found in connection with what seems to have been elite residences[35]. Remnants of other well-equipped female burials are preserved, such as a grave from a long mound[36] with four cruciform brooches, silver clasps, key ring, spindle whorls and ceramics (Tu, B2505-2517).[37]

The 5th century female burial in Krosshaug (Hauge, B2269-2289, 2288-2292, 2294-2299), originally 30-35 m wide and 5-6 m high, was brutally handled by the farmers who discovered the grave, but still counts as one of the richest Migration Period graves in Norway.[38] The deceased was put to rest on bearskin and birch bark in an oak coffin with a gabled lid. The grave contained, among other objects, a rare and several times repaired bronze hanging basin with anthropomorphic escutcheons, probably of central European origin, a trailed glass vessel, wooden bucket with copper alloy fittings, gilt silver relief brooch with a provincial roman type of ornamentation, two smaller silver brooches and a golden miniature shield (Figure 4). In the 2014-publication, Magnus has focussed on the close relationship with the rich female grave from Hol in Trøndelag.[39]

Revehushaugen (Hauge, B4000) measures 29 m across with a height of 3.5 m and was excavated by Lorange in 1882.[40] An exceptionally large and elaborate relief brooch, two gold bracteates (Figure 5), bronze brooches, iron weaving batten, spindle whorls, key

---

31 Myhre 2005; Sundqvist 2014, 94
32 Andren 2004; Zachrisson 2004
33 Lillehammer 2014, 24-26
34 Reiersen 2017, 282
35 Hauge, Tu, Lye and Erga; cf. e.g., Kristoffersen 2000
36 According to Helliesen there are nine long mounds recorded from Tu, with the following lengths: 16,5, 21, 23,5, 25, 25, 36, 41,5 m and one large mound covering a length from 'the schoolhouse to the nearest farm' (my translation).
37 Hauken 2014, 148
38 Magnus 1975, 16-18; 2014, 71-87; Hauken 2014, 65, 2014, 141; Straume 2014
39 Magnus 2014
40 Lorange 1883

Fig. 4. *Golden miniature shield from Hauge (Krosshaug) (B2299). Photo: Svein Skare, University Museum of Bergen. Size 3,3 cm across.*

ring, beads, and ceramics are preserved, dating the grave to AD 500-550.[41] Arrowheads, hone- and a girdle stone indicate an additional burial.

In Ådnehaugen (Tu) two inhumation burials in stone coffins, dated to the 5th century, were found on two different occasions, in 1882 and 1901[42]. The female grave (C21407) contained a silver relief brooch with runic inscription[43], golden ring, silver clasps, beads, cruciform brooch, spindle whorl, iron weaving batten and knife, pots, and a horse tooth. The male grave (S1476-1493), aligned with the female grave, contained sword, shield boss, lance, scissors, knife, two payment rings of gold, trailed glass vessel (Figure 3), Westland cauldron, pots, hone, and a horse tooth. Organic material was preserved, such as wood and leather from the scabbard, bone or antler covering the grip and a wooden scissor case.

41 Hauken 2014, 144; Kristoffersen 2000, 316
42 Hauken 2014, 150, 2014, 65-66; Kristoffersen 2000, 318; Shetelig 1917, 198-201
43 translated: '*denne handling*' (this act/action), Særheim 2009, 11

Fig. 5. The large relief brooch and two gold bracteates from Hauge (Revehushaugen) (B4000). Photo: Svein Skare, University Museum of Bergen (brooch) and Terje Tveit, Museum of Archaeology, University of Stavanger (bracteates). Preserved length relief brooch 16 cm.

Other objects[44] from the farm Tu are probably remnants of well-equipped grave finds or depositions, such as a wooden bucket (pine) with copper alloy fittings (S1843), a cremation grave with a gold ring and bear claws (B4644) as well as a payment ring of gold (S6475). A cairn built over an iron extraction site, contained a cremation grave from the older part of the Iron Age as well as a Viking period axe (S6847).

A phallic stone (*hellig hvit stein*) (Tu, S5681) is dated to the older part of the Iron Age (AD 150-550)[45]. Olof Sundqvist regards the stone in connection with phallos cult, calling attention to phallic figures recorded from hall buildings and cult houses connected to aristocratic farms elsewhere in Scandinavia.

Merovingian period
In 1899, 16 gold foils (Hauge, B5392) were found in the slope below the Tinghaug height, according to Gabriel Gustafson, within a house-like structure.[46] Most gold foil figures are dated to the midt-6th and 7th centuries, with a possible later date for some of the Hauge foils.[47] Metal detectorists, without further results, have searched the area. Gold foils are usually found in connection with hall buildings or cult houses, sanctifying the place where cult is performed.[48]

The graves dated to the Merovingian period, a rare occurrence in Rogaland, include one female burial from around AD 600 and two warrior graves dated to the 8th century, all three from Tu. One of the latter (S7299) is found in a destroyed mound and contained an axe and a celt.[49] The other grave (S2851), containing a bridle, was found by a farmer early in the 20th century in the mound situated next to Grønhaug (cf., below) in the mentioned line towards Tinghaug. The grave also contained a rare type of axe, a shield boss, arrow heads, iron fitting from a casket in addition to rivets and cremated bones.[50] Trond Meling relates graves with horse equipment and horses to families with important roles in the political development towards the end of the Merovingian period, marked by an increased centralisation of power. The female grave was found during the winter 1864-65 (C3614-3618).[51] It contained three equal-armed brooches of gilded copper alloy, beads, spindle whorls, iron scissors, fragments of a gaming piece of white glass and a sherd of a blue squat jar of Aylesford-type, a rare type with only one parallel in Norway,[52] but more frequent in England.[53]

---

44 Hauken 2014, 148-155
45 Solberg 1999; Myhre 2006; Sundqvist 2014, 92-93, with references
46 Gustafson 1900, 86; Hauken 2014, 145; Petersen 1955
47 Watt 2019, 38
48 Sundqvist 2014, 90-91
49 Meling 2014, 107-108; Hauken 2014, 150
50 Meling 2002 and 2014, 107-115; Hauken 2014, 150
51 Hougen 1968; Hauken 2014, 65, 2014, 150
52 C19362 Løland, Lindesnes, Agder
53 Näsman 1986, 75

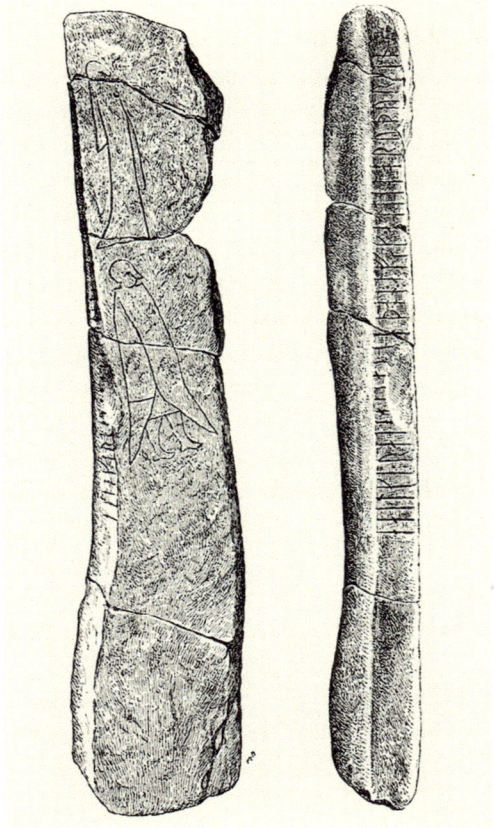
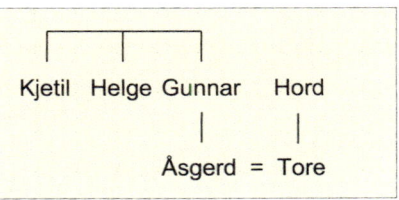

Left: The Tu stone with runic inscription and human figures. After Olsen and Shetelig 1909. Right: The family relationship recorded on the Tu and Klepp stones. After Hines 2014, Table 2.

Fig. 6.

Viking period
Viking period finds from Tu include the remnants of four grave finds[54] and a rune stone. In 1879, Lorange discovered a lower guard of a sword in a 'large' mound he excavated in that year (B3449). A single edged sword with a lower guard decorated with silver inlays is recorded to be found in a field (S5475). Helliesen excavated a 9th century cremation grave (S2852) in a smaller grave mound connected to mounds in the line towards Tinghaug, with oval brooches, copper alloy pin, spindle whorls, iron knife, iron weaving batten and two pots, covered by an iron frying pan. Grønhaug, 21 m across and 2,8 m high, situated in in the south-western end of the mentioned line of mounds, just below Tinghaug, was excavated by Lorange in 1879.[55] Scattered in the mound, which had been opened earlier, were the upper guard of a sword with silver inlay, a shield boss, a human skull and the skeleton of a horse (B3328). Based on the sword, the grave

---

54   Hauken 2014, 150-156
55   Lorange 1880, 156

is dated to AD 800-950. Viking period equestrian burials are associated with military organisation and related to high-ranked, royal followers.[56]

A concentration of runic inscriptions to Jæren, both on objects and stones, bear witness to an increasingly, widespread role of literacy during the time of change between the Viking period and the Christian Middle Ages.[57] The Tu stone (B13731), rune inscribed and decorated with two human figures, is dated to around AD 1000 (Fig. 6). Folk tradition connects it to Tuhaugen and tells us that the stone served as a focus for agrarian fertility rituals as late as the 18th century. John Hines has analysed the inscription anew and discussed the connection with a rune stone once situated by the church in Kleppe (B13735).[58] The Tu stone was commissioned by a man called Helgi of Kleppe who appears to be the uncle of the dead woman mentioned on the Kleppe stone (Fig. 6). Hines argues that the stones reflect the importance of a dominant kin-group in the Hauge-Tu area, highlighting 'the significance of the lateral relationships within the same generation – with brothers, or with created kindred, through marriage', as well as the renegotiating and reconstructing of their position in society, necessary for the social elite group represented by these rune stones.[59]

Settlement

Both Hauge and Tu are considered as old farm names, and remains of Iron Age farm structures are surveyed in the Tinghaug area, but none have been excavated, in contrast to the many well-known deserted farms from that period on Jæren.[60] None of the surveyed farm remains, which are visible on the surface, are of a size that would correspond to elite residences. According to Bente Magnus, at least such farms from the Migration Period, are located under the historic farms, at Hauge below the slope from Krosshaug, close to Revehushaugen, and at Tu with Tuhaugen centrally placed in the farmyard. It is mentioned that agrarian fertility rituals relate to the mound.

The Medieval period

When discussing the Tinghaug plateau in the dawn of and during the Scandinavian Middle Ages, the stone cross at Hauge is essential, indicating a marker of Christianity (Fig. 7), and perhaps an indication of 'cult place continuity'. The c. 118 cm high[61] and 60 cm wide (across arms) stone cross is heavily damaged and creatively as well as rather poorly restored (1935) after the cross broke down into several pieces c. 1855. However, from drawings and descriptions we have an impression of the cross' condition and location in the 19th century. The oldest reference was published in 1745, when the cross is

---

56 Meling 2014 107-115, with references
57 Hines 2014, 117-125
58 cf. also Olsen & Shetelig 1909
59 Hines 2014, 125
60 Magnus 1975, 135-143; Lillehammer 2014, 19-20
61 In early 19th century it seems to have been c. 188 cm high, see Gabrielsen 2002, 91.

The stone cross on Krosshaug. Photo: Museum of Archaeology, University of Stavanger. Fig. 7.

mentioned as standing in its present and assumed original position.[62] The cross is in its typology possible of Iris Crouwers type A.1.1.7 with V-shaped armpits, wedge-shaped terminals and with side-arms significantly smaller than the upper arm. Crouwers dates it to late 10th to 12th century.[63]

With the central position of Hauge-Tu in previous centuries and the early Christian cross, one may ask why no indication of a church can be traced at the site. Most churches in Norway are in the narratives documented from the 13th and 14th centuries onwards. It is only from then on, we have an impression of the church landscape with

---

62 De Fine, *Stavanger amptes udførlige beskrivelse*, 301. However, we do not know if the present orientation of the cross was the original one. See also Gabrielsen 2002, 90-92; Crouwers 2019, 488-489 with literature.

63 Crouwers 2019, 163-164, 489; Gabrielsen 2002, 91, 41-42 suggests the earliest possible dating of the cross (her type E) to the 7th or 8th centuries, even though she stresses that this is not certain – and doubtful. Nordeide 2010 opens also for a later dating of the crosses.

its public church organisation, also on Jæren.⁶⁴ The narrative does not mention a church at Hauge, but both at Time to the southeast of the farm and Klepp to the northwest churches are documented.⁶⁵

These churches, most certainly wooden stave churches, followed the c. 13th century establishment of the general ecclesiastical organisation units with parishes. However, we must assume that the churches' locations to Time and Kleppe are older. Thus, the locations must have been part of an early public church organisation that seems based on civil subdivisions closely connected to the various levels of judicial districts ('*skipsreide*') with assemblies, the *þing*.⁶⁶ The local assembly for the Klepp district is in the 14th century documented to Kleppe and thus with a concurrent location and name to the parish's church. The assembly place for Haug district is in the 15th century documented to Hauge and thus <u>not</u> with a concurrent location to the (parish) church at Time.⁶⁷ The border between the two adjoining assemblies runs across the middle of the Tinghaug plateau.⁶⁸ Even though the farms Hauge and Kleppe most probably both were central political arenas in Mid-Jæren, an interesting observation here is that the *þing* at Hauge was located to the farm and site with an early Christian free-standing cross. The *þing* at Hauge may also have had a higher position ('*fjerdingsting*') than the assembly at Kleppe.⁶⁹

It seems then as the stone cross was located at, or close to, an assembly place, a known combination from other West-Norwegian stone crosses such as the West-Norwegian main-assembly (*Gulaþing*), founded before the 930s.⁷⁰ We cannot exclude that a church was located in Hauge in the early Christian period, and if so, most likely built as a private church ('*høgendeskirke*') at the farm and in a combination with a function as public church for the assembly. However, if so, the church later was abandoned, and the public-church-function transferred to Time. It seems then just as likely that the more public church from the beginning was located at Time and the free-standing cross solely marked the new religion close to the assembly site. With the cross' location, there would from the site also be a magnificent view across the landscape in all directions except to the southeast, where the proper Tinghaug would "obstruct" the view. From Hauge and the cross, the churches' locations both at Time and Kleppe would be visible.

---

64 Hommedal 2023, 53-56; Skeiseid 2007; Inntjore 2018, 56-60
65 A priest at Time (*præstr á Thimini*) is mentioned in 1329 indicating a church, and in 1395 Time church (*Thyminæs kirkiu*) is directly mentioned (*Diplomatarium Norvegicum*, vol. IV, 189; vol. IV, 650). The church at Klepp (*Klæps kirkiu*) is mentioned in an undated letter from c. 1280. However, a runic inscription from the wooden church building, now lost with the church but documented in the 17th century, indicates that the church at Klepp already was standing there in the 12th century (Olsen, *Norges innskrifter*, 153-156, N227).
66 Iversen and Brendalsmo 2021, 147
67 Iversen and Brendalsmo 2021, 147; Crouwers 2019, 163-164, 489, 164, seems to think that both assemblies were located at Hauge.
68 The border between Hauge skipreide and Kleppe skipreider divided the Tu ridge. See Lillehammer 2014, 33
69 Iversen and Brendalsmo 2021, 147
70 Helle 2021, 23-30

The cross' grand location would likewise give it a long-range visibility with its religious and profane messages.[71] Related to the cross, divine offices then may have been said and masses may have been celebrated at portable alters, e.g., in periods with assembly meetings. One may also ask if the cross was raised because there was no intention of a church at Hauge, and the cross thus was raised to take on the Christian marking at the assembly site.

Kristine Holme Gabrielsen finds it most likely that the farmer at Hauge, a magnate, erected the cross.[72] Based on 17th century real estate sources, she finds Hauge to be a farm larger than average in Haug judicial districts ('*skipreider*'), on the other hand a more medium farm among the farms with known stone crosses in Rogaland.[73] However, we do know that the farm during the Middle Ages came into the ownership of the church of All Saints in Bergen[74] and thus was in royal ownership. The church and hospital of All Saints became in 1308 a part of the Norwegian king's exclusive Royal Chapel organisation, but the hospital was also earlier under royal patronage.[75] It was probably founded in the 13th century by King Håkon IV Håkonsson (reigning 1217-1263), and from the narratives we are told that King Håkon gave a considerable grant of estate to the hospital's church "when he laid ill".[76] It seems then most likely that Hauge was a part of this 13th century grant. It is also interesting to see that the church of All Saints seems to have owned the *complete* Hauge farm and not only parts of it. The farm seems thus *not* to have been spitted between many owners. This may indicate that the farm had been in royal ownership for a long period, and likewise it seems to indicate that the king had taken over the ownership from an older estate.

Function and development through time

The overview of monuments on and objects from the prominent Tinghaug plateau is here attempted to fill out the term 'aristocratic environment' with a meaning in archaeological terms. We have highlighted the unique number (cf., note 8) of monumental grave mounds and their position in the landscape, and put forward the notion that the mounds confirm the centrality of the plateau, separating and legitimating the authority of the height. The well-equipped Migration Period female burials support the impression of prominence. Hauge is one of two farms in Norway with two generations of females buried with high quality relief brooches.[77] Tu is one of few farms in south-western

---

71 Gabrielsen 2002, 92; Skeiseid 2007, 27, 57-59
72 Gabrielsen 2002, 118-124
73 Gabrielsen 2002, 119-121
74 Lindanger 1990, 68
75 The farm Nordre Braut was also a part of the Royal Chapel organisation, but the Nordre Braut was divided between the Church of All Saints and the Church of the Apostles, the most distinguished of the churches in the organisation and the *Capella Regis* in the royal *palatium* in Bergen. See Lindanger 1990, 68; Hommedal 2020, 471-472, 484-487.
76 Hommedal (in print)
77 The other farm is Kvåle in Sogndal, a prominent farm in Sogn.

Norway with graves from the various phases of the Merovingian period, including an equestrian grave[78] as well as a rare 7th century female burial. There is another equestrian grave from the Viking period, and both are situated in the line of monumental mounds towards the height. Objects relating to the idea of 'aristocratic environment' include in all eight gold objects such as rings, bracteates and a miniature shield, in addition to 16 gold foil figures, two large and elaborate relief brooches and one smaller with a runic inscription, all three in gold covered silver. Imports are four glass vessels, including a cut-glass beaker of *Überfang* type with Greek inscription and a sherd of a blue squat jar of Aylesford-type, in addition to one large copper alloy hanging basin and two Westland cauldrons. The Viking period swords with silver inlays can be added to this list. All monuments and objects are found within an area of 4 km².

Based on this body of material, the farms Hauge and Tu can be defined as elite or magnate farms, and the Tinghaug plateau, shared by the two farms, as an assembly place for a larger area. The Roman-period court site is interpreted as a military or juridical centre. Based on three-corn cairns, the phallic stone, gold bracteates, gold foil figures, the monumental grave mounds and a stone cross, supported by place names such as *Hauge*, *Frøylandsvatnet* and the several *Lunden*-names, the Tinghaug plateau appears to be an important centre for cult practice through the Iron Age. The hero cult expressed in the line of mounds towards the Tinghaug height seems to substantiate this. The aforementioned female graves are argued to represent cult leaders within the official cult. Runic inscriptions suggest that literary culture and knowledge of writing was present already in the 5th century and in the later part of the Iron Age. Representatives of a family with important roles in political development are argued to be buried in the equestrian graves from the Merovingian and Viking periods, in a time of increased centralisation of power and military organisation. Some of their names are probably revealed on the Tu stone. The existence of a dominant kin-group in the area is substantiated by the relationship between the stones from Tu and Kleppe.

Although lacking direct evidence, such as workshop finds, the Tinghaug plateau has been discussed as a centre of innovation and craft production during the Migration Period, according to the many occurrences and specific similarities, from the farms and in the vicinity, of pottery and fine metal art.[79]

In the Medieval period the Hauge farm seems to have been a central political arena in Mid-Jæren, as centre in Haug *skipreide* and as an assembly place with '*fjerdingsting*'. The *þing* at Hauge was located at the farm in connection with an early Christian free-standing cross, maybe as a substitute for a church at the assembly place? The Hauge farm itself, however, seems rather early in the Middle period to have come into the ownership of the King, and the farm was probably in the 13th century a royal grant to the church and hospital of All Saints, as later documented in the narratives.

---

78 Meling 2014, 115
79 Axboe, 2004; Kristoffersen 2000, 150-171; Kristoffersen & Pedersen 2020, 48; Kristoffersen & Magnus 2010, 60; Pesch 2007, 357

Two farms – one unit?
The way we regard the Tinghaug plateau is also dependent on the relationship between Hauge and Tu. Their names suggest that they are both old farms,[80] although today's border between the farms can have changed.[81] Tu is the larger farm, concerning outcome[82] and surface area.[83] Bente Magnus has suggested that Hauge might have been a part of Tu, perhaps within a complex farm structure organised by extended families or a kin-group,[84] where people from farms in the vicinity erected their grave mounds. Bjørn Myhre regarded the area as an inner centre in a political unit that stretched along the waterways towards the farm Orre as a coastal centre.[85] Håkon Reiersen argues for a close connection between the plateau and elite milieus in the northern part of Jæren as well as Erga, a farm on the plain below, 7 km towards the coast.[86] Søren Diinhof has, based on excavations in Sogn and Nordfjord along the western coast of Norway, shown that large Migration Period farms with hall buildings seem to have existed as neighbouring farms.[87] An organisation with the two farms cooperating on equal terms would fit with the notion of power centralisation, and it would also constitute a basis for the stability through the Iron Age, indicated by monuments and finds, enhanced by the judicial and cultic importance of the elevated area of both farms – the plateau.

During the Medieval period the Hauge farm stands out as a central political arena in Mid-Jæren. Early in the Middle Ages the farm seems to have come into the ownership of the crown.

The change
This prominent position is attested by monuments and finds from the various periods through the Iron Age. Whether these occurrences bear witness of continuity, however, is another question. In any case, the position of the plateau seems to have changed by the end of the Late Iron Age, due to conflicts during the formation of a kingdom and the establishment of the Christian church.[88] Early in the 10th century, the political centre seems to have moved to the northern part of Jæren.[89] We might ask whether the names on the rune stones from Tu and Kleppe belonged to the old kin-group that ruled from the plateau, or rather named a new one, perhaps among the King's men after the battle in Hafrsfjord (AD 872-900). The old seat of power might well have been considered a threat for the King and his project and therefore transferred to Kleppe.[90] We know

---

80   Særheim 2014, 53
81   Magnus 1975, 136
82   Cf., Lillehammer 2014, 16
83   Tu covers an area of 2.57 km², while Hauge covers 1.57 km².
84   Cf., Myhre 1982, 213-214
85   Myhre 2022
86   Reiersen 2017, 283
87   Diinhoff 2010, 84-86
88   Lillehammer 2014, 36
89   Møllerop 1989, 212
90   Lindanger 1990, 47; Møllerop 1963, 21

that the official cult was moved there, where the medieval Church was erected.[91] Masses may also have been celebrated at the cross or portable alters, but no medieval church is attested at the Tinghaug-plateau. On the other hand, we know from written sources from the 15th century that Hauge might have continued as an administrative centre. The *fjerdingsting* was held here and the farm was the centre in the *skipreide*. The border between Hauge and Kleppe *skipreider* divided the Tu ridge in two parts,[92] perhaps as a consequence of the establishment of the *skipreide* organisation in the 10th century.[93]

We have seen that the Hauge farm during the Middle Ages came to be in the ownership of the Church and Hospital of the Apostles in Bergen and thus that Hauge then was a part of the estate within the exclusive Royal Chapel organisation. We have likewise argued that Hauge was granted to the hospital church by King Håkon IV in the 13th century, and we have suggested that the Hauge farm then already for a long period had been in royal ownership.

The question will then be: How and when did the King get hold of Hauge? Was the Hauge farm a royal confiscation from one of the fallen chieftains at the 9th century battle of Hafrsfjord?

Aristocratic?

We have defined Hauge and Tu as elite or magnate farms through the Iron Age. Whether the monuments and objects are elements of an 'aristocratic environment', however, depends on the definition of the concept. It would perhaps fit a general definition of 'aristocratic', which, according to Britannica online is: 'government by a relatively small privileged class or by a minority consisting of those presumed to be best qualified to rule … the term *aristocracy* often is used to mean the ruling upper layer of a stratified group'.[94] On the other hand, it depends on how we understand this concept in the context of Iron Age Scandinavia and within the local frame of southwestern Norway. Håkon Reiersen has discussed centre indicators in various Scandinavian contexts.[95] He lists a set of indicators for the Roman and Migration periods in western Norway[96], and according to these he establishes Tinghaug/Tu ridge as a centre with two elite milieus: Anda (Roman period) and Hauge-Tu (Migration Period).[97] He regards the Tinghaug/Tu ridge as the centre, at least in western Norway, that 'most clearly reflects the wealth and continuity associated with the major southern Scandinavian central places', including the assumed production of status objects on the ridge and in the vicinity in his arguments.[98]

---

91 Sundqvist 2014, 97
92 Lillehammer 2014, 33
93 Lindanger 1990, 52
94 https://www.britannica.com/topic/aristocracy
95 Reiersen 2017, 71-87. Cf. Stylegar and Grimm 2005
96 Reiersen 2017, 87, Table 4.4
97 Reiersen 2017, 298, Table 7.1
98 Reiersen 2017, 329

Our conception of an elite environment is not based on traces of settlement. The body of material from the Tinghaug plateau fills the concept with material manifestations of social and political actions through a long period of time, early expressions of power as well as democracy, cult practice, literary culture, contacts with and knowledge about faraway places, knowledge of craft and shared ideas of aesthetics. Concerning the term *aristocratic*, in the Medieval period it certainly fits the Hauge farm – as the ownership of the King.

Bibliography

Andrén, A. 2004: "I skuggan av Yggdrasil. Trädet mellan idé och realitet i nordisk tradition", in *Ordning mot kaos. Studier av nordisk förkristen kosmologi*, edited by Anders Andrén, Kristina Jennbert & Catharina Raudvere (Vägar till Midgård 4). Lund: Nordic Academic Press, 389-430.

Axboe, M. 2004: *Die Goldbrakteaten der Völkerwanderungszeit. Herstellungsprobleme und Chronologie*. Ergänzungsbände zum Reallexikon der Germanischen Altertumskunde 38. Berlin: De Gruyter.

Bendixen, B.E. 1880: "Udgravninger og undersøgelser i 1879. Jæderen". *Foreningen til Norske Fortidsmindesmerkers Bevaring. Aarsberetning for 1879* (1880), 60-138.

Bukkemoen, G.B. 2007: "Alt har sin plass. Stedsidentitet og sosial diskurs på Jæren i eldre jernalder", in *Sjøreiser og stedsidentitet. Jæren/Lista i bronsealder og eldre jernalder*, edited by Lotte Hedeager (OAS 8). Universitetet i Oslo, 135-302.

Bukkemoen, G.B. 2014: "Sosiale strukturers romlige manifestasjon. Gravanlegg og landskap som kilde til mentalitet og sosiale inndelinger", in *Et Akropolis på Jæren? Tinghaugplatået gjennom jernalderen*, edited by Elna Siv Kristoffersen, Marianne Nitter & Einar Solheim Pedersen. AmS-Varia 55, Stavanger, 37-47.

Crouwers, I. 2019: Late Viking-age and medieval stone crosses and cross-decorated stones in Western Norway. Forms, uses and perceptions in a Northwest-European context and long-term perspective. PhD-thesis, University of Bergen.

De Fine, B.C. 1745: *Stavanger amptes udførlige beskrivelse*. Rogaland historie- og ættesogelag, Stavanger: Dreyer, 1987 [1745].

Diinhoff, S. 2010: "Store gårde og storgårde på Vestlandet fra yngre romersk jernalder og folkevandringstid", in *På sporet av romersk jernalder*, edited by Ingar M. Gundersen & Marianne Hem Eriksen (Nicolay skrifter 9). Oslo, 79-89.

Diplomatarium Norvegicum, ed. by Christian C.A. Lange and others, 23 vols. (Kristiania/Oslo, 1847-2011).

Gabrielsen, K.H. 2002: Vestlandets steinkors. Monumentalisme i brytningen mellom hedendom og kristendom. Master thesis, University of Bergen.

Grimm, O. 2010: *Roman Period court sites in south-western Norway. A social organisation in an international perspective* (AmS-Skrifter 22). Stavanger.

Gustafson, G. 1900: "Et fund af figurerede guldplader", *Foreningen til norske fortidsminnesmærkers bevaring. Aarsberetning for 1899* (1900), 86-95.

Hauck, K. 1985-86: *Die Goldbrakteaten der Völkerwanderungszeit*. Münstersche Mittelalterschriften 24:1-3. München: Wilhelm Fink.

Hauge, Alfred. 1986: *Gamle Jæren. Andre boka om tradisjon og folkeminne etter Lars A. Tjøtta*. Stavanger: Universitetsforlaget.

Hauken, Å. Dahlin. 2005: *The Westland cauldrons in Norway* (AmS–Skrifter 19). Stavanger.

Hauken, Å.D. 2014: "Katalog over jernalderfunnene fra Hauge gnr. 19 og Tu gnr. 17, Klepp kommune", in *Et Akropolis på Jæren? Tinghaugplatået gjennom jernalderen*, edited by Elna Siv Kristoffersen, Marianne Nitter & Einar Solheim Pedersen (AmS-Varia 55). Stavanger, 141-156.

Hauken, Å.D. 2014: "Jæren og verden. Bronsekar og glass fra Hauge og Tu", in *Et Akropolis på Jæren? Tinghaugplatået gjennom jernalderen*, edited by Elna Siv Kristoffersen, Marianne Nitter & Einar Solheim Pedersen (AmS-Varia 55). Stavanger, 63-70.

Helle, K. 2021: *Gulatinget og Gulatingslova*. Skald: Oslo.

Helliesen, T. 1907: "Oldtidslevninger i Stavanger amt". *Stavanger Museums Aarshefte 1906* (1907), 33-118.

Hines, J. 2014: "På terskelen til historisk tid. Runesteinene fra Tu og Kleppe", in *Et Akropolis på Jæren? Tinghaugplatået gjennom jernalderen*, edited by Elna Siv Kristoffersen, Marianne Nitter & Einar Solheim Pedersen (AmS-Varia 55). Stavanger, 117-125.

Hommedal, A.T. 2020: "The Royal Edifice at Avaldsnes. A Palatium for the King or a Residence for his Canons?", in *Rulership in 1st to 14th century Scandinavia. Royal graves and sites at Avaldsnes and beyond*, edited by Dagfinn Skre. Berlin: Walter de Gruyter, 465-516.

Hommedal, A.T. 2023. Ogna kyrkje på Jæren: Eit blikk på ei arkeologisk utgraving. In *Primitive Tider*, Sivs Festskrift. 45-57. DOI: https://doi.org/10.5617/pt.10683

Hommedal, A.T. (in print). "*For at dei der kan bli friske eller døy*. Om etableringa av nokre hospital i norsk høgmellomalder", in *Sjukdom og helse i Norden i vikingtid og mellomalder*, edited by Else Mundal.

Hougen, E.K. 1968: "Glassbegre i Norge fra sjette til tiende århundre". *Viking* 32. 85-109.

Inntjore, H. 2018: "Kirkeorganisasjonen i Stavanger bispedømme ca. 1250-1500". PhD-thesis, University of Bergen.

Iversen, F. & J. Brendalsmo. 2021: "Den tidlige kirkeorganisasjonen i Stavanger stift". *Collegium Medievale* 34, 115-166.

Kraft, J. 1829: *Topographisk-statistisk Beskrivelse over Kongeriget Norge. Det vestenfjeldske Norge*. Kristiania.

Kristoffersen, S. 2000: *Sverd og spenne. Dyreornamentikk og sosial kontekst*. Studia Humanitatis Bergensia 13. Kristiansand: Høyskoleforlaget.

Kristoffersen, S. 2006: "Tu". *Reallexikon der Germanischen Altertumskunde* 31. Berlin: De Gruyter, 307-309.

Kristoffersen, S. 2012: "Brooches, bracteates and a goldsmith's grave", in *Goldsmith Mysteries Archaeological, pictorial and documentary evidence from the 1st millennium AD in northern* Europe, edited by Alexandra Pesch and Ruth Blankenfeldt. Neumünster: Wachholtz, 169-176.

Kristoffersen, S. & B. Magnus. 2010: *Spannformete kar. Utvikling og variasjon* (AmS-Varia 50). Stavanger.

Kristoffersen, E.S., M. Nitter & E. Solheim Pedersen. 2014: *Et Akropolis på Jæren? Tinghaugplatået gjennom jernalderen*. (AmS-Varia 55). Stavanger.

Kristoffersen, E.S. & U. Pedersen. 2020: "Changing perspectives in southwest Norwegian Style I", in *Barbaric Splendour. The Use of Image Before and After Rome*, edited by Toby F. Martin & Wendy Morrison, 47-69. Access Archaeology, Cambridge: Archaeopress. https://doi.org/10.2307/j.ctv1zcm0nn.7

Lillehammer, G. 2014: "Jærens Akropolis. Landskap og fornminner på Anda/Tuhøyden", in *Et Akropolis på Jæren? Tinghaugplatået gjennom jernalderen*, edited by Elna Siv Kristoffersen, Marianne Nitter & Einar Solheim Pedersen (AmS-Varia 55). Stavanger, 13-36.

Lindanger, B. & I. Klepp. 1990: *Bygdesoge fram til 1837*. Klepp: Klepp kommune.

Lorange, A. 1880: "Reiseindberetning til direktionen for den bergenske filialafdeling". *Foreningen til Norske Fortidsmindesmerkers Bevaring. Aarsberetning for 1879*. Kristiania, 139-159.

Lorange, A. 1883: "Antikvariske undersøgelser i 1882. 1. Jæderen". *Foreningen til Norske Fortidsmindesmerkers Bevaring. Aarsberetning for 1882*. Kristiania, 81-94.

Magnus, B. 1975: *Krosshaugfunnet. Et forsøk på kronologisk og stilhistorisk plassering i 5. årh.* (Stavanger Museums Skrifter 9). Stavanger.

Magnus, B. 2014: "Kvinnene fra Krosshaug i Klepp og Hol på Inderøya", in *Et Akropolis på Jæren? Tinghaugplatået gjennom jernalderen*, edited by Elna Siv Kristoffersen, Marianne Nitter & Einar Solheim Pedersen (AmS-Varia 55). Stavanger, 71-87.

Meling, T. 2002: "Graver med hest og hesteutstyr. Eit uttrykk for makt og alliansar på Sørvestlandet mot slutten av merovingartida". *Arkeologiske Skrifter* 11, Universitetet i Bergen, 119-130.

Meling, T. 2014: "To graver med hest og hesteutstyr fra Tu. Maktpolitiske forhold på Sørvestlandet i yngre jernalder", in *Et Akropolis på Jæren? Tinghaugplatået gjennom jernalderen*, edited by Elna Siv Kristoffersen, Marianne Nitter & Einar Solheim Pedersen (AmS-Varia 55). Stavanger, 107-115.

Meyer, E. Nissen. 1935. *Relieffspenner i Norden*. Bergens Museums Årbok. Bind 4. Bergen.

Myhre, B. 1982: "Settlement of SW Norway during the Roman and Migration Periods". *Offa* 39, 197-215.

Myhre, B. 1987: "Chieftain"s graves and chiefdom territories in South Norway in the Migration Period". *Studien zur Sachsenforschung* 6, 169-188.

Myhre, B. 2005: "Krossane på Ullandhaug, døds-sjødno på Sele og fem dårlige jomfruer på Norheim. Symboler for Yggdrasil – livets tre?", *Frå haug ok heiðni* 3, 3-10.

Myhre, B. 2006: "Fra fallos til kors – fra horg og hov til kirke?", *Viking* 69, 215-250.

Myhre, B. 2022: "Lye i Time på Jæren i Sørvest-Norge – et glemt sentralsted fra eldre jernalder", in *Jenny-Rita.org. Et utradisjonelt skrivested i Jenny-Ritas ånd*, edited by Grete Lillehammer & Lotte Selsing (AM-Profil 9), Stavanger, 2017, last modified October 16, 2022.
https://www.uis.no/sites/default/files/2020-10/Amprofil 9.pdf

Møllerop, O. 1963: "Fra de forhistoriske tider i Klepp", *Klepp gards- og ættesoga gjenom 400 år. 1519-1900*, edited by Erling Brunes. Klepp kommune, 9-22.

Møllerop, O. 1989: "Fra forhistorien i Klepp". *Frå haug ok heiðni* 2, 201-212.

Nicolaysen, N. *Norske fornlevninger. En oplysende fortegnelse over Norges fortidslevninger, ældre en reformationen og henførte til hver sit sted.* Foreningen til norske fortidsminnesmerkers bevaring 1862-1866, Kristiania.

Nicolaysen, N. 1870: "Tillæg til Norske fornlevninger". *Foreningen til norske fortidsminnesmerkers bevaring. Aarsberetning for 1869.* Kristiania, 117-169.

Nordeide, S. Walaker. 2010: "Cross monuments in north-western Europe". *Zeitschrift für Archäeologie des Mittelalters* 37, 163-178.

Näsman, U. 1984: *Glas och handel i senromersk tid och folkvandringstid. En studie kring glas från Eketorp-II, Öland, Sverige* (Aun 5). Uppsala university.

Näsman, U. 1986: "Vendel Period glass from Eketorp – II, Öland, Sweden. On glass and trade from the late 6th to the late 8th centuries A.D.", *Acta Archaeologica* 55, 55-116.

Olsen, M. 1909: "Fra gammalnorsk myte og kulthus". *Maal og minne* 1, 17-36.

Olsen, M. 1954: *Norges innskrifter med de yngre runer.* Tredje bind. Oslo: Kjeldeskriftfondet.

Olsen, M & H. Shetelig. 1909: "De to runestener fra Tu og Klepp paa Jærderen". *Bergens Museums Aarbog, Historisk–Antikvarisk rekke* 11, 3-29.

Pesch, A. 2007: *Die Goldbrakteaten der Völkerwanderungszeit. Thema und Variation.* (Ergänzungsbände zum Reallexikon der Germanischen Altertumskunde 36). Berlin: De Gruyter.

Petersen, J. 1955: "Reise fra Hauge og Tu i Klepp 15/5-1955". Innberetning i top.ark, Arkeologisk museum, Universitetet i Stavanger.

Prøsch-Danielsen, L., C. Prescott & M. Kähler Holst. 2018: "Economic and social zones during the Late Neolithic/Early Bronze Age in Jæren, Southwest Norway. Reconstructing large-scale land-use patterns". *Praehistorische Zeitschrift* 93,1 (2018) 48-88
https://doi.org/10.1515/pz-2018-0002

Reiersen, H. 2017: "Elite milieus and centres in Western Norway 200-550 AD". PhD-thesis, University of Bergen.

Reiersen, H. 2019: "From Eketorp to Jæren. "leader houses" in the court sites of south-western Norway". *Archäologisches Korrespondenzblatt* 49, 2 (2019), 245-257.

Rygh, O. 1915: *Norske Gaardnavne 10. Stavanger amt*, Kristiania.

Shetelig, H. 1917: Universitetets oldsaksamlings tilvekst 1904-1915. *Oldtiden VI* (1917), 191-314.

Shetelig, H. 1914: *Arkeologiske tidsbestemmelser av ældre norske runeindskrifter.* Særtrykk av Norges Indskrifter med de ældre Runer III, Kristiania.

Skeiseid, A. 2007: "Seks kyrkjestader i Rogaland. Ein arkeologisk analyse av kyrkjestader i ytre og indre delar av Rogaland". Master thesis, University of Bergen.

Solberg, B. 1999: "'Holy white stones'. Remains of fertility cult in Norway", in *Völker an Nord- und Ostsee und die Franken*, edited by Uta von Freeden, Ursula Koch & Alfried Wieczorek, 99-106. Bonn: Habelt.

Straume, E. 1987: *Gläser mit Facettenschliff aus Skandinavischen Gräbern des 4. und 5. Jahrhunderts n. Chr.* Instituttet for sammenlignende kulturforskning B:73, Oslo: Universitetsforlaget.

Straume, E. 2014: "Gläser mit Fadenauflage aus norwegischen Gräbern des 5. und 6. Jahrhunderts n. Chr", *Bericht der Römisch-Germanischen Kommission* 92, 2011, 381-498.

Stylegar, F.-A. & O. Grimm. 2005: "Das südnorwegische Spangereid. Ein Beitrag zur Diskussion archäologischer Zentralplätze und norwegischer ringförmiger Anlagen". *Offa* 59/60, 81-124.

Sundqvist, O. 2003. "Priester und Priesterinnen". *Reallexikon der Germanischen Altertumskunde* 23. Berlin: De Gruyter, 424-435.

Sundqvist, O. 2005: "Kvinnliga kultledares religiösa och sociala position i forntida Skandinavien". *Chaos. Dansk-Norsk tidskrift for religionshistoriske studier* 43, 9-29.

Sundqvist, O. 2012: "Religious ruler ideology in pre-Christian Scandinavia. A contextual perspective", in *More than Mythology. Narratives, ritual practices and regional distribution in pre-Christian Scandinavian religions*, edited by Catharina Raudvere & Jens Peder Schjødt. Lund: Nordic Academic Press, 225-262.

Sundqvist, O. 2014: "Gårdarna Hauge och Tu i Klepp. En kultplass med kvinnelige ledare?", in *Et Akropolis på Jæren? Tinghaugplatået gjennom jernalderen*, edited by Elna Siv Kristoffersen, Marianne Nitter & Einar Solheim Pedersen (AmS-Varia 55). Stavanger, 89-105.

Særheim, I. 1980: *Stadnamn i Klepp. Om namngjeving av busetnad og hagar i ei Jær-bygd i endring* (Rogalandsforskning, Rapport, S 7). Stavanger.

Særheim, I. 2009: *Ryger ristar runer* (AmS-Småtrykk 81). Stavanger.

Særheim, I. 2014. "Stadnamn og sentralitet i eit jærsk jordbrukssamfunn frå jernalderen", in *Et Akropolis på Jæren? Tinghaugplatået gjennom jernalderen*, edited by Elna Siv Kristoffersen, Marianne Nitter & Einar Solheim Pedersen (AmS-Varia 55). Stavanger, 49-62.

Unimusportalen https://www.unimus.no/portal/#/ last modified October 16, 2022.

Watt, M. 2019: "Gold foil figures – fact and fiction", in *Gold foil figures in focus. A Scandinavian find group and related objects and images from ancient and medieval Europe*, edited by Alexandra Pesch & Michela Helmbrect (Advances studies in ancient iconography I). München: Verlag Dr. Friedrich Pfeil, 35-71.

Zachrisson, T. 2004: "Det heliga på Helgö och dess kosmiska referenser", in *Ordning mot kaos. Studier av nordisk förkristen kosmologi*, edited by Anders Andrén, Kristina Jennbert & Catharina Raudvere (Vägar till Midgård 4). Lund: Nordic Academic Press, 343-388.

BY MALENE REFSHAUGE BECK

Chapter 10
On Top of the World
An Aristocratic Settlement from the 7th-10th Century on Munkebo Bakke, Funen

ABSTRACT

In this preliminary study the archaeological evidence from a recently discovered aristocratic settlement on Munkebo Bakke, North East Funen (Denmark) is presented. In 2015, a detectorist discovered a treasure of hack silver and dirhams on Munkebo Bakke. The detector find led to three archaeological campaigns and further detector surveys. The excavations have so far demonstrated the existence of a large hall-building surrounded by a palisade from the 7th-8th century, and Trelleborg-type houses from the early 10th century. In addition, sunken featured, so-called grubenhauser, post-built houses, a culture layer and fences have been excavated. The detector finds support the ^{14}C datings of the buildings and indicate, that the site was founded around 550 AD and abandoned no later than 1050 AD, probably because of the town of Odense some 14 kilometres to the southwest emerged as a new centre of royal attention on Funen. Munkebo Bakke has a topographic and strategically excellent position dominating the landscape of North East Funen. The hilltop overlooks both Odense Fjord, Storebælt and Kerteminde Fjord including a barrage and the Ladby ship grave. Munkebo Bakke has similarities with other aristocratic settlements such as Lejre, Tissø and Erritsø in regard to the find picture, monumental buildings, chronology, topography and the intended use of landscape and older grave monuments, supposedly demonstrating a symbolic language underlining a manifestation of power. It is suggested that the site belongs to a network of magnate or royal estates, covering the eastern part of Denmark.

Munkebo Bakke and its surroundings

Munkebo Bakke is situated on the narrow strip of land that separates Kerteminde Fjord to the south from Odense Fjord to the north. Storebælt lies approximately six km to the east, as the crow flies. From the hilltop, there is an excellent view over large parts of

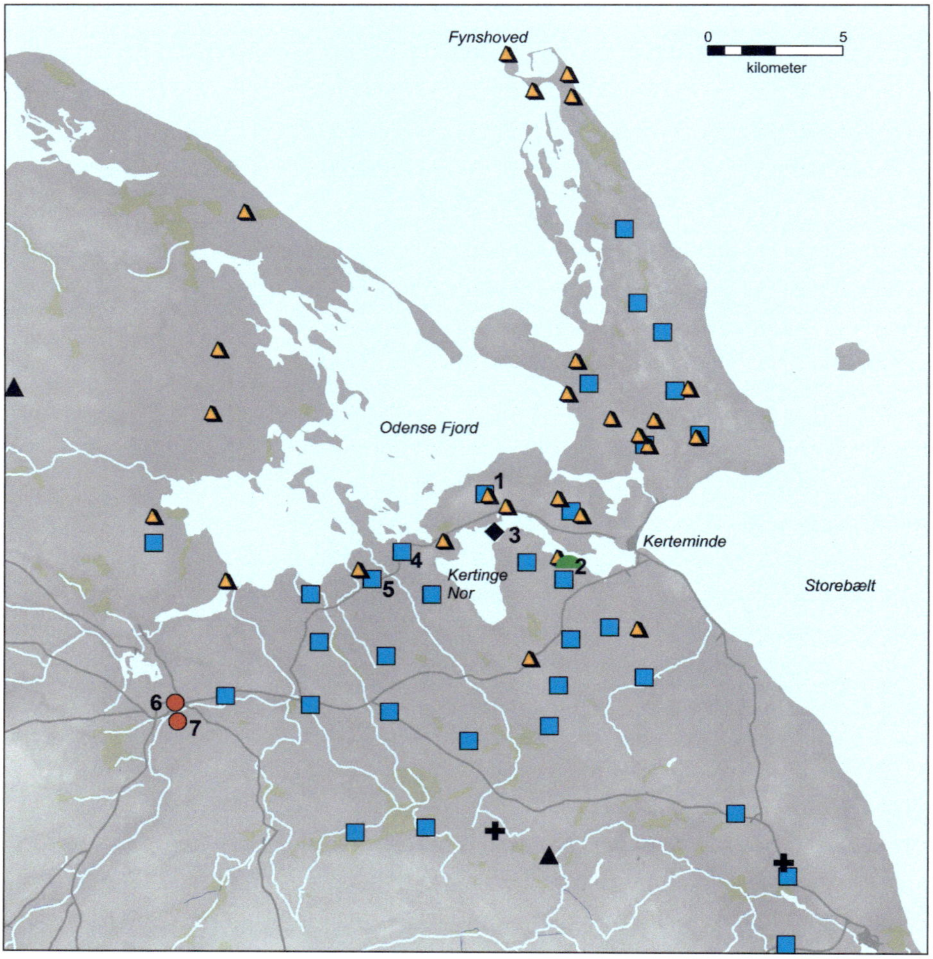

Fig. 1. Munkebo Bakke and surrounding area of North East Funen. 1) Munkebo Bakke. 2) Ladby ship grave. 3) Barrage at Kertinge Nor. 4) Dræby. 5) Vester Kærby. 6) Odense. 7) Nonnebakken ring fortress. Blue squares: Metal rich sites 6th – 12th century. Yellow triangles: Beacon related place names. Black triangles: Runic stones. Black cross: Warrior graves. Coastline based on the first cadastral map. Graphic: Malene R. Beck.

North East Funen and surrounding waters not least the entrances to both Odense and Kerteminde Fjords. Munkebo Bakke is the most prominent morainic hill in the area and the highest point in the landscape within a distance of more than 25 km, reaching 54 metres above sea level – or 58 metres, including the Bronze Age barrow Loddenhøj on the hilltop. In a Danish landscape perspective, it is a position literally, on the top of the world.

Within the larger area of Munkebo Bakke several extraordinary archaeological finds in combination with place names indicating the presence of a central place, point to the existence of a central area or gateway community in the late Iron Age and the Viking Age.[1] The most famous find is without comparison the *Ladby* ship grave, situated at the southern coast of Kerteminde Fjord 3.5 km east of Munkebo Bakke. Since the finding and excavation of the Ladby grave in 1934 and 1935,[2] several attempts have been made to name the person who was buried here in the first decades of the 10th century, so far, without success. But it is generally agreed that this is the grave of a person belonging to the aristocracy – possibly even a member of a royal dynasty.[3] Until the beginning of this century, the Ladby ship grave was in a sort of spatial vacuum, regarding finds from the Germanic Iron Age and the Viking Age in the area.[4] The picture of a sparsely inhabited landscape has changed dramatically since 2010, when systematic and large scale detector surveys in collaboration with local detectorists was initiated, in order to understand the background and context of the Ladby grave, but also in a search for a contemporary rich settlement.[5] By 2022, more than 30 metal-rich sites have been discovered in North East Funen. The sites are situated with a distance of one to three kilometres. With a few exceptions, every metal-rich site contains detector finds from the 6th to the 12th century but in varying percentages, indicating changes in activity through the centuries.[6]

It is difficult to observe significant differences between the metal-rich sites in the area. Almost every site contains a wide range of fibulas, weaponry, weights, silver coins and hack silver, various examples of import, melting lumps and scrap metal and in that way they resemble the majority of the metal-rich sites in areas, where systematic surveys have been conducted.[7] The density of metal-rich sites indicates, that North Eastern Funen was a region with a lot of activity, external contacts, central functions and socially high-ranking persons during the late Iron Age. In that sense the background and context of the Ladby ship grave can now be better understood.

---

1   Baastrup 2012, 54; Beck et al. 2021, 123; Christensen 2016
2   Thorvildsen 1957
3   Andersen 1985
4   Sørensen 2001, 152
5   Feveile 2016a, 5; Feveile 2016b
6   Beck et al. 2021a; Beck et al. 2021b, 118
7   Beck et al. 2021a; Beck et al. 2021b; Borake 2019; Christiansen 2017; Nielsen 2014

Fig. 2. *Munkebo Bakke excavation plan. The numbers refer to buildings and structures mentioned in the text. Dark grey: Bronze Age fire pits. Light grey: Modern disturbances. Background map © Danish Geodata Agency.*

Find discovery and excavations

In the spring of 2015, a detectorist found a small treasure of dirhams and hack silver, after trees had been cut down on the hilltop.[8] In search for the remaining parts of the treasure and the original place of deposition, an archaeological survey was conducted, and traces of two houses of Trelleborg-type were discovered on the top of the hill. Presently 4500 m² have been excavated during three campaigns in 2015, 2017 and 2018.[9]

The excavated areas cover only a small percentage of the settlement. Earlier finds from the Viking Age on the western slope of the hill as well as detector surveys north

---

8   Beck 2016
9   Journal no. ØFM 732, Munkebo Bakke. Sites and Monuments no. 080109-155. Excavation reports from the three campaigns can be found at https://www.kulturarv.dk/fundogfortidsminder/Lokalitet/218488/
    Two earth and stone built dykes run east-west and north-south across the hilltop and is the reason why there's unexcavated areas between the three excavation campaigns.

and north west of the excavated areas indicate, that the settlement probably covers at least 140.000 m². [10]

The excavated areas are situated between two Bronze Age barrows on the hilltop. Only the scheduled Loddenhøj survives today. The eastern barrow, excavated in 1926, contained a grave from the early Bronze Age.[11] Between the two barrows, systems and rows of cooking pits dating to period III and IV of the Bronze Age indicate, that the hilltop played a role in terms of rituals and social gatherings centuries before the Late Iron Age settlement.

Houses of Trelleborg-type and culture layer

Three post-built houses of Trelleborg-type have been excavated, all of them oriented east-west. Between the houses, a culture layer has been partly investigated.

The largest house (K10) was 26 metres long, 7.7 metres wide, and 6 metres at the gables. The house had a wall-trench and supporting outer posts, three pairs of inner roof bearing posts and a single post, where the fourth pair should have been in the west-end of the house. The roof bearing posts were up to 56 cm in diameter and supported by stone packing. No traces of inner walls or separate rooms were observed. The lack of a wall trench combined with two centrally placed posts indicate that there was a gate or door in the western gable of the longhouse. No door opening was observed in the long walls. In the wall-trench and in some of the outer supporting wall posts several pieces of iron slags were found, as well as two small iron bars, iron rivets and an iron wedge. This indicates that the house functioned as a smithy. In further support of the existence of a smithy is the culture layer partly investigated north of the house. The culture layer was up to 50 cm thick and covered the Bronze Age cooking pit system. The lower part of the layer held no finds, but in the uppermost 20 cm, several finds of iron slags, and pieces of a bellows stone of clay, iron tools, iron rivets and different kinds of iron fittings indicate the presence of a blacksmith or weapon smith. Also, an iron sword pommel of Petersen's type H with inlays of copper alloy was found in the culture layer.[12]

To smaller houses of Trelleborg-type (K1 and K2) were situated 49 metres north of the large Trelleborg house K10 and north of the culture layer. They measured 19-20 metres in length and 5.3 metres in width at the gable, and 7.2 metres wide at the middle. The western house K2 was better preserved with wall trenches, outer roof-supporting posts, inner partition wall and a central structure of four smaller posts that could perhaps be connected to a long, central fireplace. The eastern house K1 was in general badly preserved and only partly investigated. The size and construction was similar to K2. The two Trelleborg houses could have been standing at the same time, or they could be two phases of the same building. The possible existence of a long fireplace indicates that the

---

10   Sites and Monuments no. 080109-58, 080109-107 and 080109-120
11   Sites and Monuments no. 080109-41, Aner & Kersten 1977, 101 no. 1726
12   Petersen 1919, 91

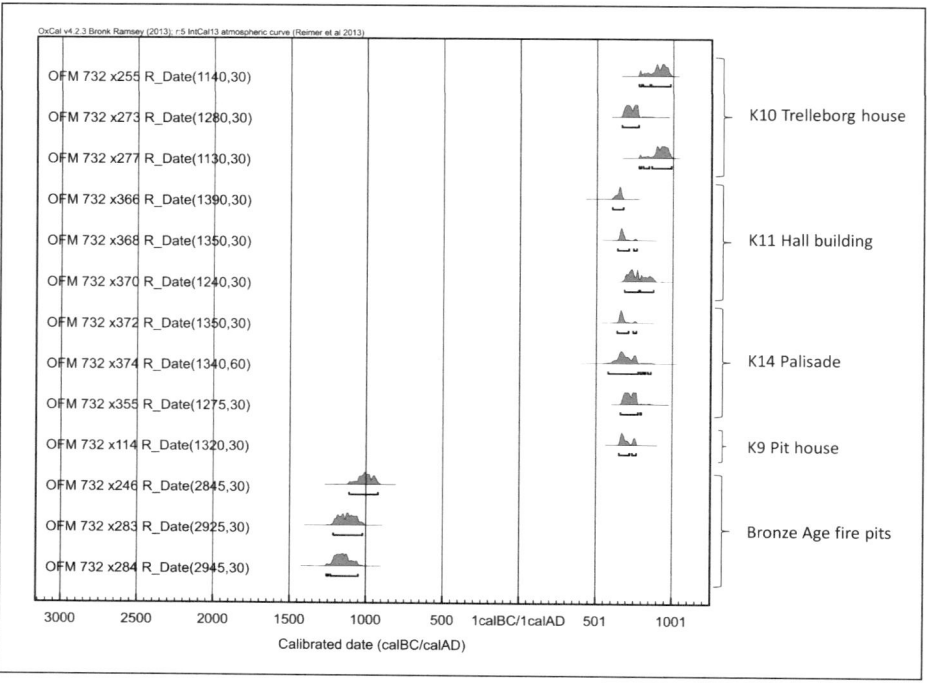

Fig. 3. ¹⁴C datings, Poznan Radiocarbon Laboratory. All dates are calibrated in OxCal v. 4.2.4 Bronk Ramsey (2013).

houses' central focus was on the living quarters. Based on building typology and orientation it seems most likely, that they are contemporary with the large Trelleborg house.

The large Trelleborg house K10 had a prominent position just south of the highest point of the hilltop, and right between the two Bronze Age barrows. The building thus faces *Kertinge Nor*, the inner part of Kerteminde Fjord and a barrage founded in the late 10th century.[13] Judging from a view-shed analysis and the present day white-washed buildings that were torn down prior to one of the excavations on Munkebo Bakke, the building would have been visible from a vast distance, for example from Ladby. The ¹⁴C datings of K10 falls within the 10th century, but no later than 980 AD.[14] This means, that the longhouse could be coeval with the construction of the Ladby-grave, but probably did not exist, when Harold Bluetooth built his ring fortress *Nonnebakken* in Odense.[15]

---

13   Jørgensen 2002, 129
14   ¹⁴C datings performed at Poznan Radiocarbon Laboratory, unless otherwise stated, all AMS dates are cited at two σ (95,4 % probability).
15   Runge 2021

Sunken featured buildings

During the first excavation campaign in 2015 a sunken featured building (hereafter called *Grubenhaus*) (K9/A206) was investigated. The oval pit, or sunken feature measured 4 × 3.3 meter and had a depth of 22 cm. 40 cm deep posts were placed at the east and west end. Following the outline of the pit, 20 small stake holes from a wall construction were observed. At the eastern end, traces of the entrance in the shape of two steps were recorded. At the bottom layer of the pit an area with unburnt clay indicates the existence of loom weights. Also a sewing needle and a spindle weight was found. The finds indicate that the original use of the Grubenhaus was connected to different sorts of textile work.[16] The sunken feature was filled with rubbish in the shape of animal bones.[17] Five glass beads were also found and more surprisingly in the top layer an iron key and a spur.[18] The spur can be dated typologically to the 8th-9th century.[19] The Grubenhaus has been AMS dated to the late 7th-early 8th century. Another less well-preserved Grubenhaus (K13) was excavated in 2018. Apart from animal bones, small pieces of metal slag were found in the filling of the pit. This indicates that metalwork of some kind was performed at the site. The Grubenhaus K13 has not been dated. Most likely it also belongs in the 7th or 8th century.

Hall building

In 2018, the farm buildings dating to the late 19th century on Munkebo Bakke were demolished. Below the modern-day buildings traces of a hall building (K11) was discovered. It was not possible to uncover the hall in its full length.

The building is oriented NNE-SSW. The walls are curved. An assessment, based on the uncovered parts of the building and the curving of the long walls, indicates a full length around 35-40 metres. The width ranges from 8.7 metres at the southern gable to 10.70 meter. The hall building thus covered an area between 350 and 400 m². The curved walls were constructed of large, paired posts placed within two to three metres. The wall posts were between 35 and 60 cm in diameter, placed in up to one meter broad and 62 cm deep pits and supported by stones. Traces of a wall ditch was observed along the northern part of the west wall. An entrance, marked by two posts on the inner side of the wall, was found in the west wall. Next to the entrance, a partition wall created a separate room in the southern end of the building. No inner roof-bearing posts were found – unless the not very sturdy posts in the partition wall had this function. In what must have been the central room of the hall building, traces of an inner ditch following the overall shape of the building could be observed. The exact function of the ditch could not be determined, but it must belong to some kind of inner construction in the hall.

No archaeological finds were made in relation to the building, even though the

---

16 Sarauw 2021
17 Kveiborg 2016
18 Beck 2016, 53
19 Pedersen 2017: 102f

area was thoroughly searched by detectorists during the excavation. ^{14}C dates the hall to the 7th century. Regarding size, construction details and date, the hall building has no parallels on Funen. The closest parallels would be the hall buildings from *Lejre, Tissø or Erritsø*.[20] The orientation of the building is unusual. Because very little of the settlement complex has been uncovered, the hall could relate to other buildings or structures we do not know of yet. Important is that the orientation probably ensured that the hall building was visible from both Odense Fjord and Kerteminde Fjord, having a monumental setting on the hilltop between the two ancient barrows. Seen from the water or the lower-lying landscapes around Munkebo Bakke, it must have been even more impressive, the whole setting accentuating the importance and role of the person living there.[21]

Other post-built structures

Several other post-built houses have been uncovered on Munkebo Bakke. So far, they can only be broadly dated typologically. Two small economic buildings (K6 and K7) and two, partly excavated post-built longhouses (K5 and K16), probably dates in the late Iron Age. A small building (K12) found 12 metres west of the large hall is important, because of the north-south orientation. The dimensions of the building are very modest with a length of maximum seven metres. In several cases smaller buildings seems to relate to the magnate halls of the late Iron Age playing a role in ritual acts[22] and that could be the case here as well.

Fences and palisades

Traces of several fences, visible as ditches with traces of closely set cleaved tree trunks, and sturdier palisade-like structures have been excavated. Because of the limited size of the investigated area, it is, however, difficult to estimate with certainty the function and context of the different structures. In this paper, only the palisade-like structure K14 close to the hall building will be touched upon, as it differs markedly in its construction from the other fence-structures at the site. Very close to the western wall of the hall building and following the same orientation was a palisade structure in two phases (K14 and K15).

The palisade closest to the hall building (K14) was constructed of uniformly worked posts, placed approximately two metres apart in 65 cm deep, stone-packed postholes. In-between, them were traces of 10-15 cm thick and up to almost one-meter-wide planks set vertically in a ditch. The depth of the worked posts indicates that the structure had a substantial height. An opening is seen in the palisade, facing the estimated middle of the hall building. Along the eastern side of the palisade – towards the hall – was a

20 Bican 2010; Christensen 2015, 59f; Jørgensen 2002; Ravn et al. 2019
21 Ulriksen 2018, 375
22 Jørgensen 2002, 237

further row of postholes, perhaps constituting extra reinforcement or the foundation for a gallery. The palisade is AMS dated to the 7th-8th century and it is probably coeval with the K11 hall building.

The other phase of the palisade (K15) had a slightly different orientation and a lighter construction in the shape of an up to 18 cm deep trench without traces of posts. It was not possible to determine stratigraphically which phase was younger, but based on AMS datings and orientation, it seems most likely, that the sturdy palisade-structure K14 belongs to the hall building, while the more lightly constructed phase K15 belongs to a building or structure not yet uncovered.

In several ways, the structure resembles the palisades in Jelling[23] and it is possible, that it represents a sort of military fortification. However, in this context the palisade more likely marks a fenced area in relation to a hall building with special functions, like the fenced areas at Lejre and Tissø.[24]

Detector finds

The area was surveyed with detector before and during excavations. There is a marked difference in the dispersion of detector finds. In the area of the hall-building K11 there were no detector finds in the plough soil, apart from modern waste. Likewise, no metal finds were discovered in the archaeological structures. A single Carolingian coin and a bipolar weight was found in the plough soil in connection with the excavation of the Trelleborg-type house (K10) in 2017 as well as some iron tools and rivets. As mentioned earlier, several finds of iron were made during the excavation in relation to the house and cultural layer. During the first excavation campaign in 2015 more than 50 detector finds were uncovered within the excavated area of 1419 m², mainly in the plough soil. Apart from the hack silver treasure consisting primarily of dirhams,[25] weights, pieces of jewellery, silver coins used as pendants,[26] weaponry, scrap metal and iron rivets were discovered in the area.

The differences in the dispersion of finds probably reflects different zones of use within the settlement. The empty area around the hall building and to some degree the Trelleborg-type house finds its parallel in Tissø, where there are markedly fewer finds in connection to the hall building.[27] This probably reflects an area with special functions.

Detector surveys conducted on the field north of the excavated area have so far revealed 121 finds. The finds cover an area of approximately 400 × 200 metres or 80.000 m², indicating that the settlement covers a substantially larger area. The main part of the

---

23 Dengsø Jessen et al. 2014, 5f.
24 Christensen 2015, 275; Jørgensen 2002, 231
25 The dirhams have been identified by the Royal Collection of Coins and Medals, National Museum of Denmark. The dirhams belong in the 9th and 10th century, 19/00131 / FP 15525.
26 Beck 2016; Moesgaard 2018
27 Jørgensen 2002, 240

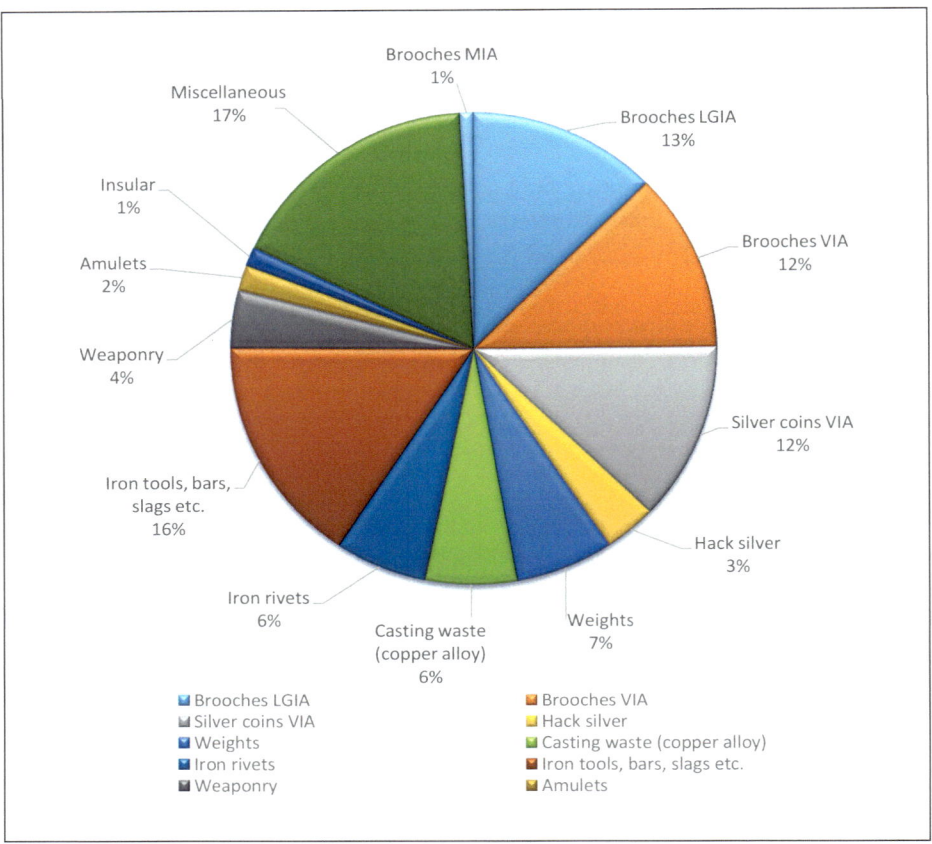

Fig. 4. *Categories and percentages of detector finds from Munkebo Bakke. Total number 229.*

finds is securely dated to the 6th-10th century, only two fibulas can be dated to the early 11th century.

Compared to the other metal-rich sites in North East Funen, the metal finds from Munkebo Bakke do not stand out in regards of find types, number or quality.[28] The only exception is a relatively high amount of small amulets in the shape of spearheads, a wheel-shaped pendant and a helmed figure, indicating that the settlement could have held special religious functions.[29]

---

28   Beck et al. 2019; Beck et al. 2021b, 127
29   Gardela 2022: 409; Jørgensen 2002, 236f

To see or be seen

At Munkebo Bakke there is a very clear and intentional use of the landscape comparable to other aristocratic residences of the late Iron Age. Like at Lejre, the hall building erected in the 6th-7th century takes full advantage of the natural settings as well as the existing monuments in the cultural landscape.[30]

The two Bronze Age grave mounds on the hilltop created a monumental stage for the hall building and the fenced sacred area in connection to it. This was probably a way to underline a connection with ancestral traditions, powers or rights all though there most certainly was no direct link to the persons buried in the barrows. The same intentional use of (older) grave barrows in connection with central places and hall buildings can, among others, be observed at Lejre[31] and Uppsala.[32] The scheme was obviously an integrated part of what was needed to be a place of importance or power, since Harold Bluetooth meticulously copied it in his planning of the Jelling complex.[33] In a greater landscape context, the grave mound at Ladby on the southern side of the fjord reflects the Bronze Age barrows at Munkebo Bakke. The mounds are guarding important points in a sea-route from Storebælt to Kertinge Nor, leaving no ship travelling the waters of Kerteminde Fjord in doubt of who was in power.

Today Munkebo Bakke and the landscape surrounding it is somewhat blurred because of the expansion of the town of Munkebo with new settlement areas covering the southern and western side of the hill slope, and a growing harbour area at Lindø northwest of the hill. But even so, Munkebo Bakke is still a highly visible landmark in the area around Kerteminde Fjord and Hindsholm. An essential aspect of the site is that the buildings were visible from a great distance. The now demolished white-washed modern buildings, the dimensions of which correspond precisely to the Trelleborg-type house, could be seen without difficulty from Ladby and Vester Kærby. View-shed analyses support and underline the high visibility of the buildings of the Late Iron Age in the in the surrounding landscape. A major degree of visibility is also associated with several other royal or magnates residences of the period.[34]

The settlement on Munkebo Bakke was highly visible and conspicuous due to the size of the buildings and the extraordinary palisade construction. The visibility was an important aspect. It demonstrated control of the area because the ruling power was physically present in the landscape. The location also enabled the inhabitants of the site to overlook and control the landscapes or perhaps more importantly the waterways in a strategic way, like Füsing at the Schlei or Erritsø at Lillebælt.[35] Munkebo Bakke has an ideal position. From here it was possible to monitor the fjords on both sides as well as maintaining an overview of Storebælt to the east and the waters north of Funen. The

---

30 Christensen, 2016, 224
31 Christensen 2015, 221
32 Ljungkvist & Frölund 2015
33 Pedersen 2017, 12
34 Bican 2018, 95; Christensen, 2016, 221f.
35 Dobat 2022, 2f.; Ravn et al. 2019, 41

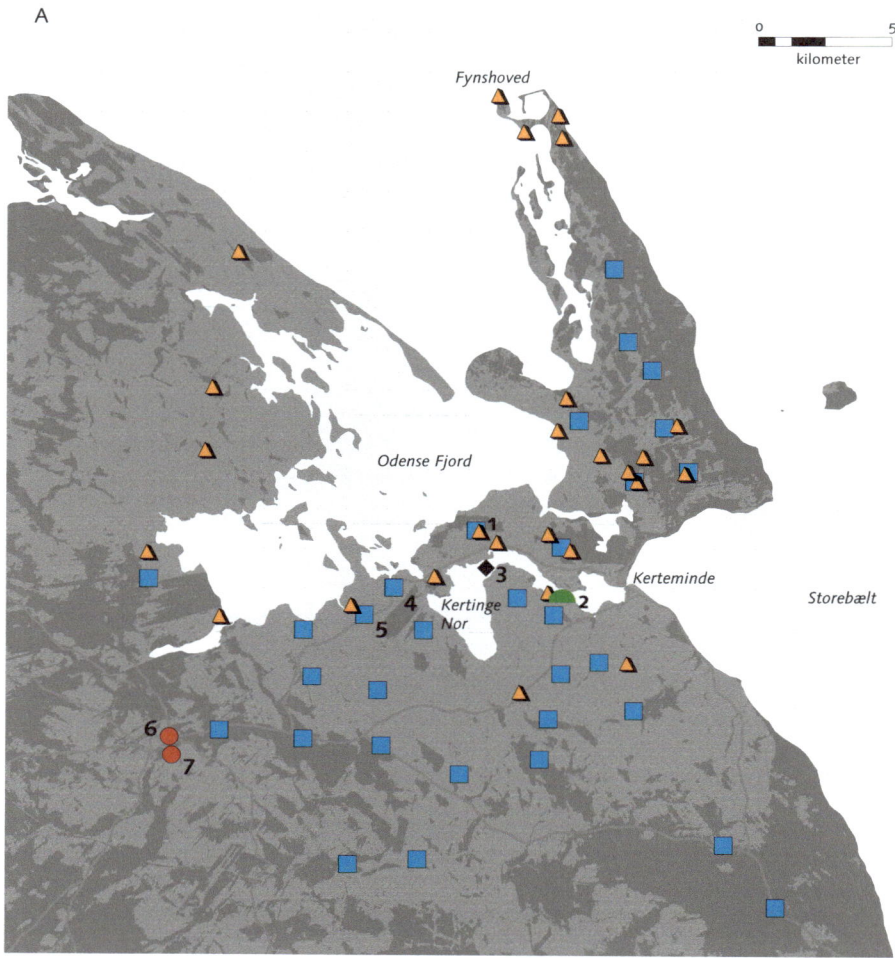

Fig. 5. a) View shed analysis of the Munkebo settlement based on the 2015 LIDAR scan. Visibility of the great hall (K11) in the landscapes surrounding Munkebo Bakke, line of sight 1.7 m above ground surface. In a landscape wihout trees, the hall building was visible from large areas around Kerteminde Fjord and Odense Fjord, as well as from the seaside. View-shed analysis by Casper Skaaning Andersen, IT Department of Moesgaard Museum and Aarhus University. Graphics: Malene R. Beck

b) View shed analysis based on a line of sight 1.7 m above the top of Loddenhøj. The analysis demonstrates that the entrances and waterways into both fjords, the barrage in Kerteminde fjord and beacons all the way from Fyns hoved and along the coast of Odense Fjord could easily be monitored from the hilltop. 1) Munkebo Bakke. 2) Ladby ship grave. 3) Barrage at Kertinge Nor. 4) Dræby. 5) Vester Kærby. 6) Odense. 7) Nonnebakken ring fortress. Blue squares: Metal rich sites 6th – 12th century. Yellow triangles: Beacon related place names. Coastline based on the first cadastral map. View-shed analysis by Casper Skaaning Andersen, IT Department of Moesgaard Museum and Aarhus University. Graphics: Malene R. Beck

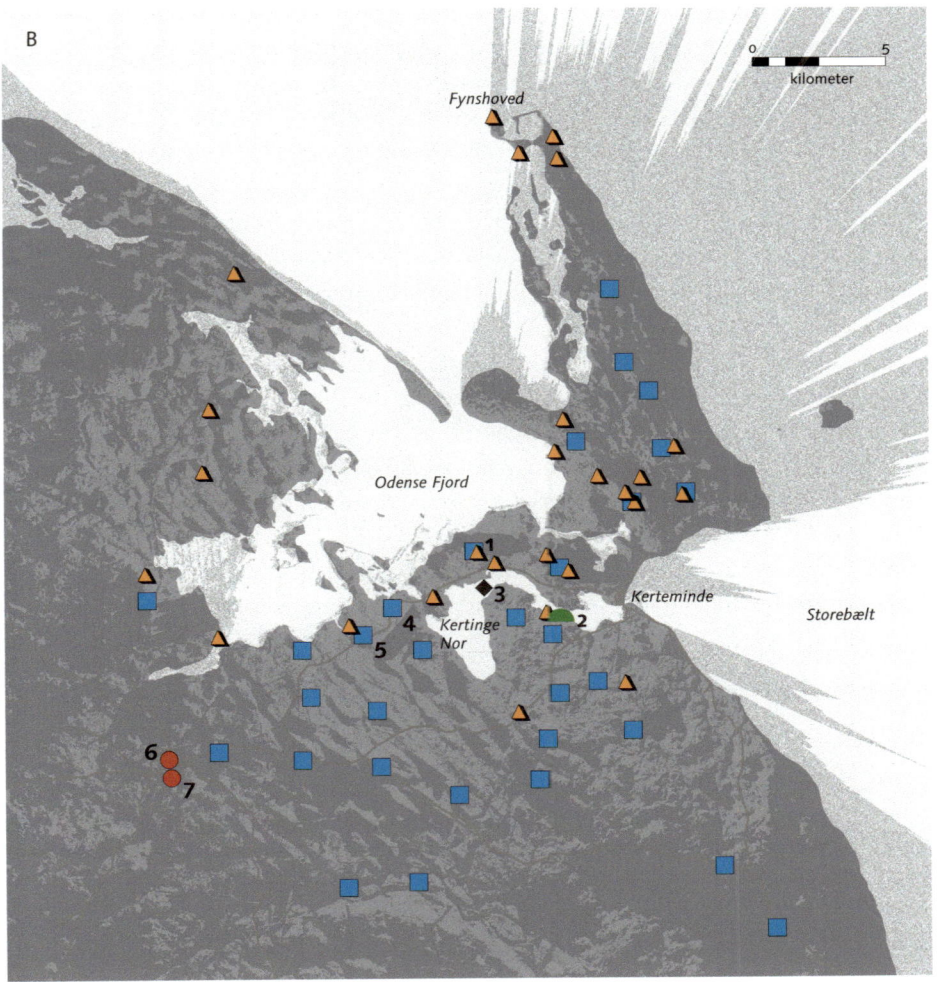

site is part of a possible early-warning system based on place names, indicating beacon hills or warning points.[36] The barrage in Kerteminde Fjord just below Munkebo Bakke, where the fjord turns into Kertinge Nor underlines the supposed strategic position as well. The barrage is ^{14}C dated to the late 10th century with possible repair works in the 12th century,[37] and as such, it must belong to the later phase of the Munkebo Bakke settlement. A possible hauling site at Dræby west of Munkebo must also be mentioned, although it is only indicated by the place name.

The barrage at Munkebo was possibly aimed at protecting a harbour or landing area in Kertinge Nor. Written sources testify that Munkebo was the harbour of Odense from the onset of the Middle Ages. Kerteminde Fjord is deep and easily navigable all the way

36   Beck et al. 2021, 220
37   Jørgensen 2002, 129

Chapter 10 • On Top of the World   **169**

into present day Munkebo. This is in contrast to at least the inner part of Odense Fjord where sedimentation is heavy and there is a constant need of excavating for keeping the current sail routes.[38] The bay at Munkebo was an anchorage for larger ships, that could dock at the small island Galgeholm, and for smaller vessels which could be hauled ashore at the berths. Most likely, the easily accessible stretches of coast along the bay at Galgeholm, where there are also abundant supplies of fresh water from a number of springs, functioned as a landing place for the onward transport of goods to the interior of Funen and the earliest Odense. Kertinge Nor was also an obvious choice as a naval base for gathering a *leding* fleet for example in relation to maritime defences associated with the ring fortress Nonnebakken.[39]

Munkebo Bakke is the geographical centre of the old juridistiction of Bjerge *hundred*, that was originally known as Bjerg hundred: the Bjerg referred to was most likely Munkebo Bakke. Munkebo is mentioned in the *Danish Census Book* as patrimonies,[40] and it was the main town in the area, prior to the emergence of Kerteminde, with its own *birketing*. Whether there is a direct connection between these circumstances and the archaeological discoveries at Munkebo Bakke is too early to say, but the medieval written sources suggest that the area around Munkebo Bakke had special functions rooted in prehistory and possibly was of particular interest to a central power controlling the area.

A web of aristocratic residences

The ^{14}C dates for the monumental hall and the coeval palisade on Munkebo Bakke, as well as the large number of metal-rich sites in the area, indicate the presence of an economic and military elite on North Eastern Funen from the 6th century and onwards, setting a more detailed background for the Ladby grave. The archaeological discoveries and finds raise the possibility that the settlement on Munkebo Bakke should be seen in combination with the Ladby ship burial and its elite expression. So far, no other settlement of a similar character is known from Funen, and the area stands out on Funen between the 6th and 11th century in regard to the density of metal-rich sites, and monumentality of the Munkebo Bakke settlement, the Ladby ship burial and the barrage in Kerteminde Fjord. Looking at the site in a South Scandinavian perspective it fits nicely into a web of aristocratic residences, regarding structures, functions and symbols at the site and in regard to topographical location. There seems to be an almost fixed distance between the late Iron Age, aristocratic settlements in Eastern Denmark.[41] This could be a result of their function as religious and aristocratic or perhaps royal estates. Their even distribution is most likely connected to the exercise of power, either by local magnates, presiding over uniform areas of land or by royalty constantly travelling between their estates throughout the realm, as a way of exercising and staying in power.

38 Beck et al. 2021a, 26f.
39 Beck et al. 2021, 217; Jørgensen 2002
40 Andrén 1983, 38f.
41 Ulriksen et al. 2020.

A change of focus

The archaeological finds on Munkebo Bakke together with the landscape context indicate a settlement with an important role or function in relation to the exercise of power, religious matters, control of trade as well as military organisation of North East Funen in the late Iron Age and Viking Age.

So far, the excavated structures point towards two main phases of use. In the 7th-8th century and late 9th-10th century. The detector finds implicate, that there was a continuous use of the site from the 6th to the early 11th century, although the decreasing number of finds from the 10th and 11th century indicate that the activities or importance of the place around 1000 AD were not the same as earlier.

Looking at the present data it seems as if there is a change of function through the centuries. The earlier finds indicate the existence of a central place incorporating religious functions, production and trade, while the later phase seems to have a more pronounced military and strategic function.

For now, the archaeological evidence indicates that the settlement ended around 1000 – 1050 AD or more likely, it was moved down the hill to the area around the Romanesque church in present day Munkebo. This could very well be a result of changes in society and a new power structure, where Odense was the new centre of royal attention on Funen.[42] This corresponds to changes seen in other magnate or royal settlements in the late 10th century. These former settlements seem to loose importance or at least change in function, probably as a result of a new royal power where, among other things, Harold Bluetooth's ring fortresses deliberately moved the centre of attention from the old central places to his new symbols of power.[43]

Future research

Further excavations are needed to get a better and more detailed understanding of the Munkebo Bakke complex, and a lot of questions remain unanswered as regards to foundation, functions, local and regional context just to mention a few. Is Munkebo Bakke the successor of the Gudme/Lundeborg complex some 50 km further to the south? Gudme/Lundeborg was still active but at a significantly lower level during the Late Germanic Iron Age and the Viking Age, and so far, no monumental buildings of the same kind from the period have been discovered. There seems to be a displacement of central functions from the Gudme area towards the Odense area during the 6th century.[44] The major increase in activity levels at metal-rich sites of North East Funen can be seen as an expression of a growth centre or central environment in the Late Germanic Iron Age and Viking Age. It is possible, that the concentration of metal-rich sites around Odense and Kerteminde Fjords in connection with the elite expressions at Munkebo Bakke and the Ladby ship burial is a redefinition of the central functions

---

42 Runge 2021, 307; Runge & Henriksen 2018
43 Ulriksen et al. 2020
44 Henriksen 2010

formerly held by the centre in Gudme, but why and when exactly did this change and relocation happen?

What is the relation to the other coeval aristocratic settlements of South Scandinavia? Munkebo Bakke and in general East Funen resembles the opposite coast of Storebælt with the *Tissø* site and surrounding metal-rich sites.[45] The mouth of Halleby å is opposite Kerteminde Fjord, and the travelling distance between the two aristocratic estates (approximately 18 sea miles from coast to coast) could be covered in less than one day.[46] The settlement and hall on Munkebo Bakke in combinations with the metal finds from North East Funen indicate close contacts or associations with Tissø, and possibly other central places in eastern Denmark. This reflects a high degree of interaction, personal contacts and trading networks and it could indicate that both sides of Storebælt were controlled by the same power. Future research will hopefully clarify the position and context of Munkebo Bakke in the aristocratic network of the late Iron Age and Viking Age.

Bibliography

Andersen, H.H. 1985: "Hedenske danske kongegrave og deres historiske baggrund", *KUML* 1985, 11-34.

Aner, E. & K. Kersten. 1977: *Die Funde der älteren Bronzezeit des Nordischen Kreises in Dänemark, Schleswig-Holstein und Niedersachsen. Band III. Bornholms, Maribo und Svendborg Amter.* Verlag Nationalmuseum København, Karls wachholtz Verlag Neumünster.

Andrén, A. 1983: "Städer och kungamakt – en studie i Danmarks politiska geografi före 1230", *Scandia* 49:1, 31-76.

Baastrup, M.P. 2012: *Kommunikation, kulturmøde og kulturel identitet – tingenes rejse i Skandinaviens vikingetid.* Unpublished PhD thesis. University of Copenhagen.

Beck, M.R. 2016: "Vikinger på Munkebo Bakke", *Cartha 2016 Årsskrift for Østfyns Museer* 2015/16, 39-58.

Beck, M.R. 2021: "Specialisation of metal crafts", in *From Central Space to Urban Place. Urbanisation processes in Viking Age and Medieval Odense and Aalborg, Denmark,* edited by M. Runge, M.R. Beck, M.M. Bjerregaard & T.B. Sarauw (Archaeological & Historical Studies in Centrality, vol. 5). Research Centre Centrum – Odense City Museums, University Press of Southern Denmark, 157-166.

Beck, M.R., T.T. Christiansen & M.B. Henriksen. 2019: *Fynske og nordjyske lokaliteter med metalfund 400-1100 e. Kr. Katalog, From Central Space to Urban Place. CENTRUM.* Rapport nr. 7. Odense.

Beck, M.R., Christiansen, T.T. & Henriksen, M.B. 2021a: "Topography. Landscape and seascape in the hinterland of Aalborg and Odense", in *From Central Space to Urban Place. Urbanisation processes in Viking Age and Medieval Odense and Aalborg, Denmark,* edited by M. Runge, M.R. Beck, M.M. Bjerregaard & T.B. Sarauw (Archaeological & Historical Studies in Centrality, vol. 5). Research Centre Centrum – Odense City Museums, University Press of Southern Denmark, 23-36.

Beck, M.R., T.T. Christiansen & M.B. Henriksen. 2021b: "Metal-rich sites in the hinterlands of Odense and Aalborg", in *From Central Space to Urban Place. Urbanisation processes in Viking Age and Medieval Odense and Aalborg, Denmark,* edited by M. Runge, M.R. Beck, M.M. Bjerregaard & T.B. Sarauw (Archaeological & Historical Studies in Centrality, vol. 5). Research Centre Centrum – Odense City Museums, University Press of Southern Denmark, 69-128.

Beck, M.R, Jensen, C.V. & Runge, M 2021: "The military expression and organisation of power", in *From Central Space to Urban Place. Urbanisation processes in Viking Age and Medieval Odense and Aalborg, Denmark,* edited by M. Runge, M.R. Beck, M.M. Bjerregaard & T.B. Sarauw (Archaeological & Historical Studies in Centrality, vol. 5). Research Centre Centrum – Odense City Museums, University Press of Southern Denmark, 199-240.

---

45 Beck 2021, 162; Borake 2019; Henriksen 2010, 13.
46 Englert 2015, 59

Bican, J. 2010: "Bulbrogård, the first aristocratic complex at Tissø – and a new approach to the aristocratic sites", in *Gedächtnis-Kolloquium Werner Harnagel, 1907-1984: Herrenhöfe und die Hierarchie der Macht und Raum südlich und östlich der Nordsee von der Vorrömischen Eisenzeit bis zum frühen Mittelalter und zur Wikingerzeit: 11.13. Oktober 2007*, edited by Strahl (Siedlungs- und Küstenforschung im südlichen Nordseegebiet 33). Burg Bederkesa in Bederkesa, 147-154.

Bican, J.F. 2018: "Hvide Haller – Store haller på kongsgårdene i yngre germansk jernalder og vikingetid, konstruktion og farver", in *Farverige vikinger*, edited by H. Lyngstrøm (Studier i teknologi og Kultur 4), 87-98

Borake, T. 2019: No man is an island. Anarchism and social complexity in Western Zealand 550-1350. PhD thesis. Department of Achaeology and Heritage Studies, Aarhus University, Museum of Western Zealand.

Christensen, L.E. 2016: "Centralpladsrelevante stednavne og centrale pladser på Fyn – Nye fund og mulige strukturer", in *Navn og navnebærer. Rapport fra NORNAs 45. symposium i Skagen 1.-4. oktober 2014*, edited by M.S. Danielsen, B. Eggert & J.G.G. Jakobsen, Uppsala, 7-33.

Christensen, T. 2015: *Lejre bag myten. De arkæologiske udgravninger.* Højbjerg.

Christiansen, T.T. 2017: *The Productive Limfjord Region in perspective. A Study of Metal Detecting Sites and Socioeconomic Development in Denmark, AD 400-1150.* Unpublished PhD thesis. Aarhus University.

Dengsø Jessen, M., M.K. Holst, C. Lindblom, N. Bonde & A. Pedersen, 2014: *A palisade fit for a King: Ideal Architecture in King Harald Bluetooth's Jelling.* Norwegian Archaeological Review, 2014.

Dobat, A.S. 2022: "Finding Sliesthorp? The Viking Age settlement at Fusing", *Danish Journal of Archaeology* 2022, Vol. 11, 1-22.

Englert, A. 2015: "Forbundet af havet – vilkår for sejlads og kommunikation over Skagerrak og Kattegat", in *Et fælles hav – Skagerrak og Kattegat i vikingetiden. Artikler fra et seminar på Nationalmuseet København, 19. – 20. september 2012*, edited by A. Pedersen & S. Sindbæk, 52-71

Feveile, C. 2016a: "Nordøstfyn – fra ingen til mange metalrige pladser på få år", in *Viele Funde – große Bedeutung? Potenzial und Aussagewert von Metalldetektorfunden für die siedlungsarchäologische Forschung der Wikingerzeit. Schriften des Museums für Archäologie Schloss Gottorf, Ergänzungsreihe, Band 12, Bericht des 33. Tværfaglige Vikingesymposiums 9. Mai 2014*, edited by T. Lemm and V. Hilberg. Kiel, 29-48.

Feveile, C. 2016b: "Understanding the Hinterland of the Ladby Ship Grave", in *Shetland and the Viking World. Papers from the Proceedings of the Seventeenth Viking Congress, Lerwick*, edited by V.E. Turner, O.A. Owen & D.J. Waugh. Glasgow, 229-235.

Gardela, L. 2022: "Miniature Spears in the Viking Age. Small Symbols of Óðinn?", RvT 74 (2022), 396-430.

Henriksen, M.B. 2004: "På vejen til Nyborg – nye fund af vikingetidsbopladser ved Vindinge og Avnslev", *Nyborg Før & Nu* 2003, 7-26.

Henriksen, M.B. 2010: "Gold deposits in the Late Roman and Migration Period landscape – a case study from the island of Funen (Fyn), Denmark", in *Worlds Apart? Contacts across the Baltic Sea in the Iron Age. Network Denmark-Poland, 2005-2008*, edited by U.L. Hansen & A. Bitner-Wróblewska (Nordiske Fortidsminder Serie C, volume 7). Copenhagen & Warsaw, 389-432.

Jørgensen, A.N. 2002: "Naval Bases in Southern Scandinavia from the 7th to the 12th Century", in *Maritime Warfare in Northern Europe. Technology, organisation, logistics and administration 500 BC-1500 AD*, edited by A.N. Jørgensen et al. (Publications from The National Museum. Studies in Archaeology & History 6). Copenhagen, 125-152.

Jørgensen, L. 2002: "Kongsgård – kultsted – marked. Overvejelser omkring Tissøkompleksets struktur og funktion", in *Plats och praxis*, edited by K. Jennbert, A. Andrén & C. Raudvere (Vägar til Midgård 2). Lund, 217-249.

Kveiborg, J. 2016: Zooarkæologisk analyse af dyreknogler fra ØFM 732, Munkebo Bakke. FHM 4296/2290

Ljungkvist, J. & P. Frölund 2015: "Gamla Uppsala – the emergence of a centre and a magnate complex", *Journal of Archaeology and Ancient History* 16, 2-29.

Moesgaard, J.C. 2018: "Den fremadskuende hjort. En hidtil uerkendt fase i Ribes udmøntning i 800-tallet?", *By, marsk og geest* 30, 17-27.

Nielsen, K.H. 2014: "Key issues concerning 'central places'", in *Wealth and Complexity. Economical specialized sites in Late Iron Age Denmark*, edited by E. Stidsing, K.H. Nielsen & R. Fiedel (East Jutland Museum Publications 1). Aarhus, 11-50.

Pedersen, A. 2014: *Dead Warriors in Living Memory. A Study of Weapon and Equestrian Burials in Viking-Age Denmark, AD 800-1000*. Publications from the National Museum. Studies in Archaeology & History 20:1. Jelling Series. Viborg.

Pedersen, A. 2017: "Monumenterne i Jelling. Fornyet tradition på tærsklen til en ny tid", in *At være i centrum. Magt og minde – højstatusbegravelser i udvalgte centre 950-1450,* edited by M.M. Bjerregaard & M. Runge (Kulturhistoriske studier i centralitet vol. 1). Odense, 44-61.

Petersen, J. 1919: *De Norske Vikingesverd. En typologisk-kronologisk studie over vikingetidens vaaben*. Videnskapsselskapets Skrifter II, Klasse 1919 No. I. Ravn, M., C. Juel, C. Lindblom & A. Pedersen. 2019: "Erritsø – new investigations of an aristocratic, early Viking Age manor in Western Denmark c. 700-850 AD. Early medieval waterscapes. Risks and opportunities for (im)material cultural exchange", Neue Studien zur Sachsenforschung 8, 37-44.

Runge, M. 2021: "From central place to town – dynamics and drivers in the early urbanisation process", in *From Central Space to Urban Place. Urbanisation processes in Viking Age and Medieval Odense and Aalborg, Denmark*, edited by M. Runge, M.R. Beck, M.M. Bjerregaard & T.B. Sarauw (Archaeological & Historical Studies in Centrality, vol. 5 2021). Research Centre Centrum – Odense City Museums, University Press of Southern Denmark, 290-317.

Runge, M. & M.B. Henriksen 2018: "The origins of Odense – New aspects of early urbanisation in southern Scandinavia", *Danish Journal of Archaeology* 2018, 2-68.

Sarauw, T.B. 2021: "Large-scale production? Pithouses and urbanization", in *From Central Space to Urban Place. Urbanisation processes in Viking Age and Medieval Odense and Aalborg, Denmark*, edited by M. Runge, M.R. Beck, M.M. Bjerregaard & T.B. Sarauw (Archaeological & Historical Studies in Centrality, vol. 5 2021). Research Centre Centrum – Odense City Museums, University Press of Southern Denmark, 148-156

Sørensen, A.C. 2001: *Ladby. A Danish ship-grave from the Viking Age* (Ships and Boats of the North 3). Roskilde.

Thorvildsen, K. 1957: *Ladby-Skibet* (Nordiske Fortidsminder VI:1). Copenhagen.

Ulriksen, J. 2018: *Vester Egesborg. En anløbs- og togtsamlingsplads fra yngre germansk jernalder og vikingetid på Sydsjælland* I. Aarhus.

Ulriksen, J., M.K. Schultz & M.F. Mortensen 2020: "Dominating the Landscape – the emblematic Setting of Borgring and the Viking Age Ring Fortresses of Denmark", *Danish Journal of Archaeology* 9, 1-22.

Wamers, E. 1995: "The Symbolic Significance of the Ship-graves at Haidaby and Ladby", in *The Ship as Symbol in Prehistoric and Medieval Scandinavia. Papers from an International Research Seminar at the Danish National Museum, Copenhagen 5th-7th May 1994,* edited by O. Crumlin-Pedersen & B.M. Thye (Publications from the National Museum. Studies in Archaeology and History I). Copenhagen, 149-159.

BY SVEN KALMRING & JOHAN RUNER

Chapter 11
A "Tissø Complex" at Birka
Birka-Korshamn and the Origins of the Viking Town

ABSTRACT

Viking-age towns seem generally to be characterised by 'close-by' situations of both administrative and ecclesiastical functions. Where known, manorial halls and churches are only to be found at the vicinities of the maritime trading towns themsleves. For Birka, for a long time it has been assumed that Hovgården on the neighbouring island of Adelsö was the site of the Viking-age manor, whereas the location of Saint Ansgar's church is still being debated. The identification of a 'Tissø-complex' at Birka-Korshamn, however, challenges earlier assumptions: The hitherto unexcavated site seems to be the whereabouts of the town's bailiff Herigar, his manorial hall with a so-called 'fenced special area' and possibly even the location Ansgar's first church. Seeing that the Vendel-period roots of the Korshamn-complex as a significant administrative and religious centre, the origins of the Viking town needs to be reassessed.

Birka is situated on the island of Björkö in Lake Mälaren some 30 kilometres inland from present-day Stockholm in Eastern Central Sweden. Next to Ribe, Hedeby and Kaupang, it was one of the few proto-urban centres in Viking Age Scandinavia. The Viking Age activities in Birka are dated to the period between c. CE 750-975, even though there are indications for a predating, late Vendel Period horizon.[1] During the Early Birka Period (*c.* CE 750-860) long-distance trading contacts with Western Europe prevailed, while in the Late Birka Period (*c.* CE 860-975) they shifted eastwards towards the Rus', Byzantium and the Arabic World. According to written sources Birka was frequented by Friesians (Rimbert cap. 20), Danes, Norwegians, Slavs, Sambians (a Prussian tribe) and "Scythians"[2] and, according to Rimbert (cap. 19), "contained many rich merchants

---

1 Cf. Arrhenius, 1976
2 Adam of Bremen 2002, lib. I, cap. 60

and a large amount of goods and money". Urban life in Central Sweden shifted from Birka to Sigtuna in the late Viking period, c. CE 975-1050.

Today, the site of Birka is to be counted among the prime monuments in Swedish archaeology, which is also reflected in its status as a UNESCO world heritage site which it was awarded – together with the royal manor of Hovgården on the island just opposite of Adelsö – in the year 1993.[3] In the past, Hovgården – not least due to the existence of several large barrows, a 11th century runestone (U 11) mentioning the king's bailiff (*bryte*) and the location of the later 13th century palace of Alsnö Hus of King Magnus Ladulås (1275-1290) – has been assessed to be the royal estate controlling the Viking town across the sound of Björkfjärden. Based on the archaeological record, it has been interpreted that a royal estate was established at the site in the 8th century, simultaneously with Birka.[4]

The few historic accounts on Birka are connected to Saint Ansgar and the missionary efforts of the archdiocese of Hamburg-Bremen. The fact that we know the name of Birka at all is due to the later archbishop, and Rimbert's account of his life and work. Rimbert himself was Ansgar's disciple, and as such probably had good personal knowledge of Birka. Rimbert's book about Ansgar, *Vita Ansgarii*, tells of when Ansgar and his companion Witmar first came to Birka around CE 830, and how the king's bailiff there, a man named Herigar, was Christianised:

> "*With great difficulty they* [Ansgar and Witmar] *accomplished their long journey (…) and eventually arrived at the Swedish port called Birka. They were kindly received here by the king, who was called Biörn (…). (…)* [H]*e granted them permission to remain there and to preach the gospel of Christ, and offered liberty to any who desired it to accept their teaching. (…)* [S]*ome of them desired earnestly to receive the grace of baptism. These included the prefect of this town named Herigar, who was a counsellor of the king and much beloved by him. He received the gift of holy baptism and was strengthened in the Catholic faith. A little later he built a church on his own ancestral property and served God with the utmost devotion*".[5]

Scholars have long wondered where Herigar had his manor and thus where the church from CE 830, the first one in all Scandinavia, was built. A variety of different locations have been proposed, with Helgö as a prime candidate.[6] Here, however, it is argued that the bailiff's manor controlling Birka was situated much closer, in fact on the island of Björkö itself[7]: After identifying a couple of conspicuous settlement remains at the southern end of Korshamn, which is on the north side of the island of Björkö, an obvious conclusion was that there could be traces of a large manor such as the likes where

3   Cf. Kalmring, et al. 2020, 7-9
4   Carlsson, 1997, 84; cf. Brundstedt 1996; Ambrosiani 2016
5   Rimbert 1921, chap. 11
6   Staecker, 2009, 320-322
7   Kalmring, et al. 2017, 18

Birka-Korshamn. In the foreground the Korshamn bay with the adjacent burial ground of Hemlanden, in the background the ridge with the fortress "Borg". In between the so-called "Black Earth" urban settlement area (photo: J. Norrman, Riksantikvarieämbetet/Kulturmiljöbild).

Fig. 1.

one would expect someone like Birka's bailiff to have lived: The remains are made up of two large terraces lying in close vicinity to each other, both with metre-high edges facing the former harbour bay of Korshamn to the north. The house foundations, one raised plateau and another one-sided terrace, had an appearance that suggested that they were built to accommodate large buildings. The location directly on the shore of Korshamn supported the idea that this was an indeed something extraordinary. Adding to this, Korshamn is still one of the best harbour locations on the whole of Björkö, with a well-protected harbour bay – much better than the harbour directly next to the town of Birka, for example.[8] (Fig. 1). Even the place name 'Korshamn' (eng: *Cross-harbour*) might indicate a maritime connection, since this group of names is generally being associated with navigation marks often found at the inlet to harbours.[9]

The area where the terraces are located is on the edge of Björkö's largest burial ground,

---

8   Arrhenius, 1976, 191
9   Westerdahl 1989, 107, 169-170: However, as being argued in this paper, there is even a possibility that the 'cross' in the place name in this specific case may have a different derivation.

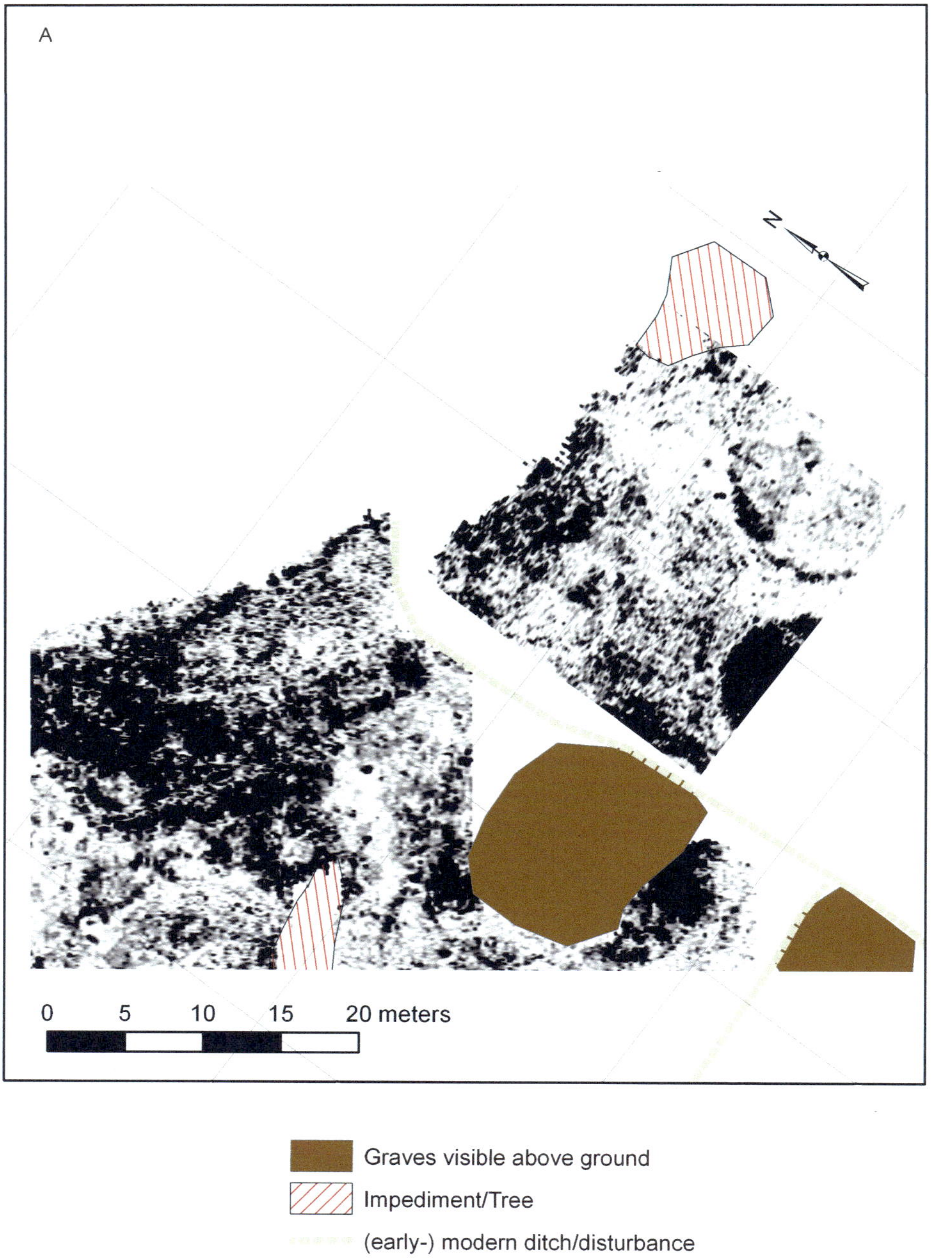

A
N
0 5 10 15 20 meters
Graves visible above ground
Impediment/Tree
(early-) modern ditch/disturbance

Hemlanden, which stretches from the town of Birka's northern rampart to the sea to the north. There are around 1,600 visible graves here. Today, the graves in Hemlanden enclose both Korshamn and the terraces. Previously, there was only one known trace of a dwelling at Korshamn: Inside the graves of Hemlanden on the eastern side of Korshamn ("Erik Steffanson's home-field") there is a since long noted artificial plateau, which,

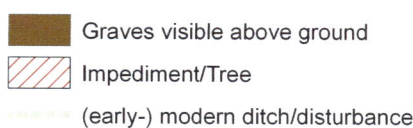

Birka-Korshamn, Viking-age hall. Results of the georadar survey of September 2016 by A. Viberg (left) and the suggested interpretation (right) (adapted after Ka1mring et al. 2017, fig. 6-7). Fig. 2.

however, has never been investigated more closely. The raised plateau is elevated about one metre, and its flat crest measures about 27 × 10 metres. It appears to be a typical building plateau of a house from the Late Germanic Iron Age, i.e. the Vendel Period.

To verify whether the terraces really were house foundations, a geophysical survey with ground penetrating radar was conducted in September of 2016. At the one-sided plateau, the survey also included the associated meadow behind it, in order to determine what a possible settlement here might have looked like.[10] The georadar survey estab-

---

10   Kalmring et al. 2017, 4-7

Fig. 3. *Birka-Korshamn, parallel stone rows. Upper left: northern row of stones, recent situation. In the background the bay of Korshamn (photo: the authors), lower left: original documentation by N.H. Sjöborg (1830) from 1821. Right: detail of Hemlanden map from H. Arbman (1940/43, pl. I), parallel stone rows marked out.*

lished that a three-aisled hall was located on the newly discovered one-sided terrace, fronting Korshamn to the north. The postholes appeared very large, and the hall can be determined to have been almost 40 metres long and 12 metres wide. The terrace itself, today cut in two by an early modern drainage ditch, was over 50 metres in length. The slightly higher eastern part seems to be the result of the easternmost section of the large Viking Age hall having a foundation consisting of large amounts of stone.[11] During

---

11   That the foundation of the eastern gable was given such manifest design might have had a special meaning. Several previously excavated Iron Age houses on terraces have had gables made in a similar fashion. One of the best preserved and most thoroughly examined cult-places in middle Sweden, the Vendel Period site of Lilla Ullevi in Bro parish, Uppland, had a core consisting of a massive stone platform that clearly mimicked such gables (e.g. Bäck et al. 2009, 33; et al. 2012, 29-38; cf. Zachrisson, 2010, 85).

B

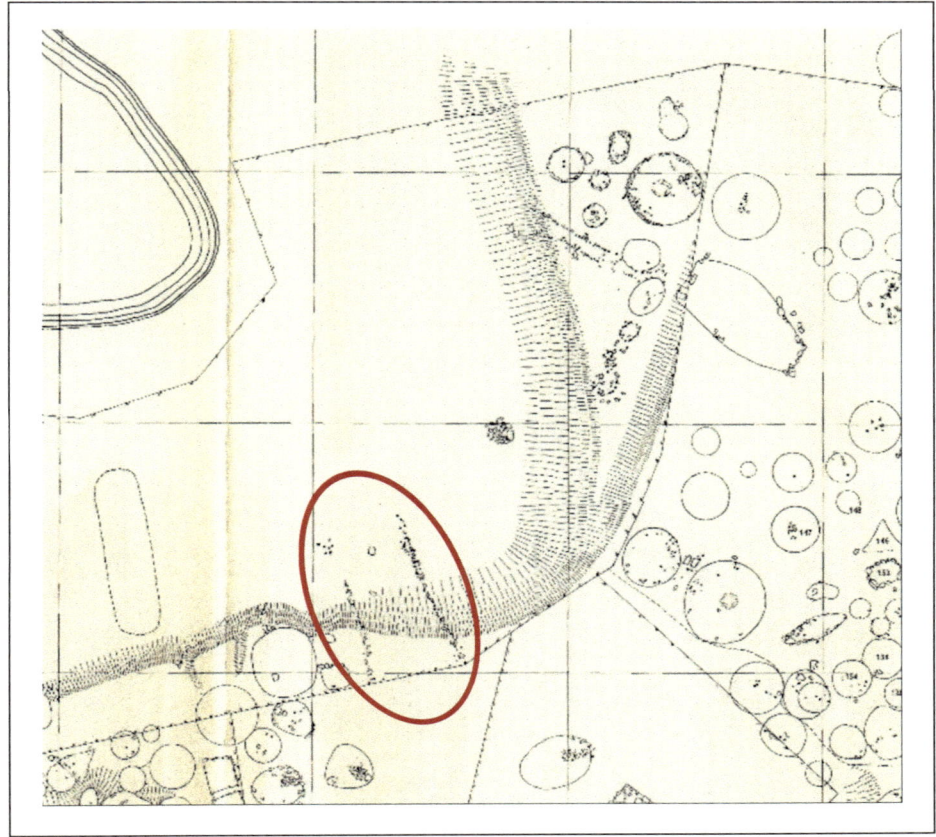

later cultivation on the site, long after the hall disappeared, all the underlying stone meant that the soil ploughed out over the ground surface here ended up higher (Fig. 2).

A part of the manorial complex is still visible above ground as two long, parallel rows of stones. These rows run from the hall on the terrace for more than 30 metres in a straight line down the slope towards the harbour bay to the north. The stone rows have been known for a very long time.[12] (Fig. 3), but it is only now, after establishing how they connect to the western part of the hall building, that the rows can be understood as the base of a rectangular enclosure. The presence of the enclosure means that the manor house on Björkö belongs to an exclusive category of aristocratic manor houses from the Late Iron Age. Large halls connected to rectangular fenced-in areas have previously only been known of in a few places in southern Scandinavia. In present-day Sweden, only one such complex is previously known; i.e. the manor of Järrestad in Scania.[13] All additional examples from Southern Scandinavia are to be found in present-day

---

12   Sjöborg 1830, 16 pl. 34
13   Söderberg 2003

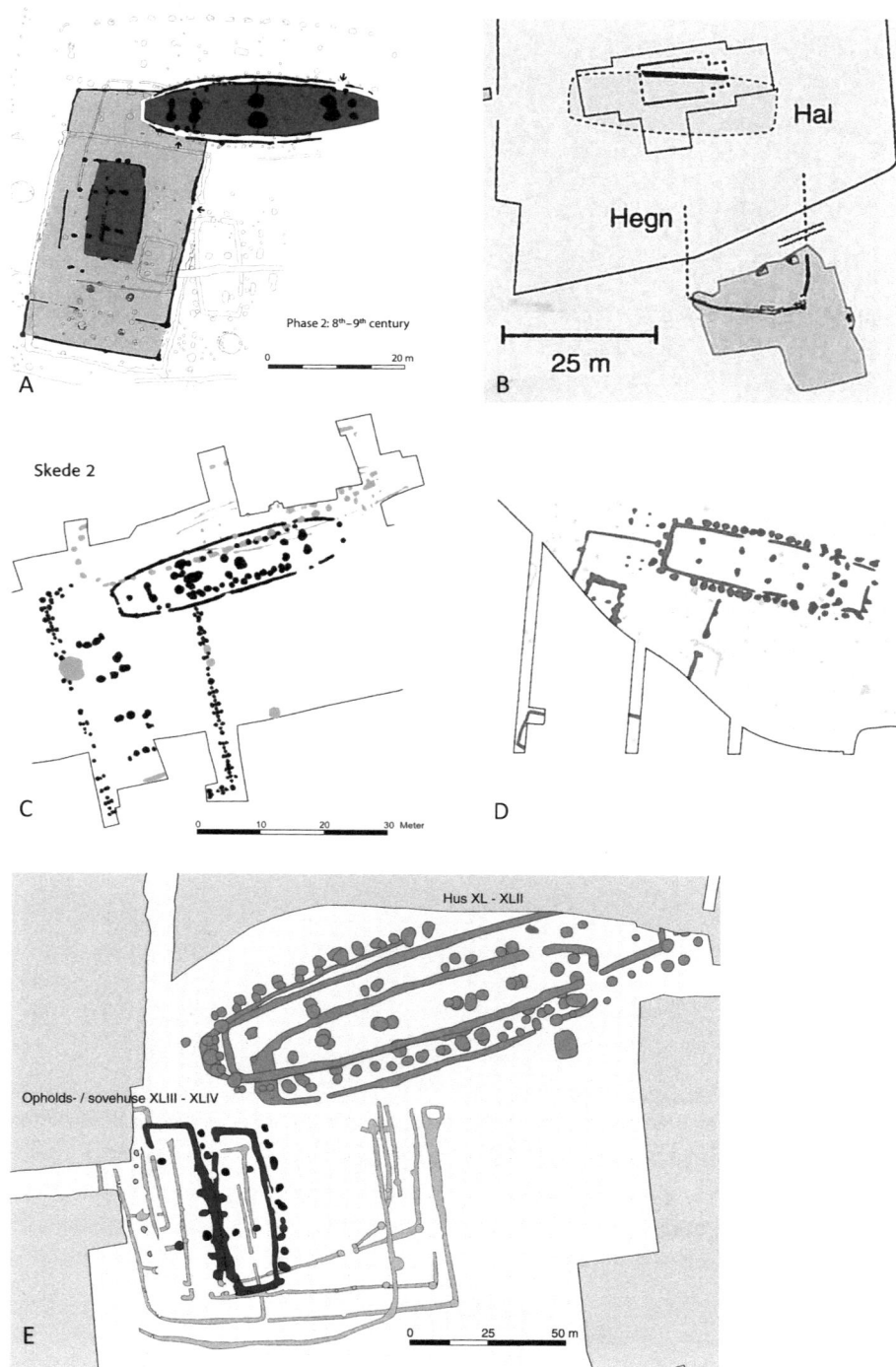

Fig. 4. *Tissø-complexes from Southern Scandinavia. A – Tissø, B – Lisbjerg, C – Järrestad, D – Erritsø, E – Gammel Lejre (after Kalmring et al. 2017, fig. 11, with ref. therein).*

	Viking-Period Hall	Fenced Special Area	In-fenced Building
Birka Korshamn	c. 37 x 11.5 m	33.5 x 17.5 m	?
Tissø (phase 2)	36 x 10 m	37 x 17 m	20 x 6 m
Lisbjerg	?	27.5 x 19 m	?
Erritsø (phase 2)	39 x 13 m	? x 28 m	? x 6 m
Järrestad (phase 2)	37 x 8.5-9 m	37 x 20-22 m	21 x 7 m
Gammel Lejre (phase 2)	61 x 12 m	c. 30 x 40 m	20 x 6.5 m

Table 1.

Comparison of Tissø-complexes by size. Viking-period halls, fenced special areas and in-fenced building with their accordant dimensions (after Kalmring et al. 2017, tab. 1).

Denmark, such as Gammel Lejre, Lisbjerg and Erritsø as the latest addition.[14] (Fig. 4). Next to Tissø as the *locus classicus*, the by far largest one is the royal estate at Lejre on Zealand, which is thought to be linked to the Danish royal Skjǫldungar dynasty.[15] The royal estate included a monumental, over 60-metre long, hall building with an attached large enclosure.[16] The manor at Korshamn is by far the northernmost example known to have an enclosure of this type. A manor that in its second phase appears to be very similar to the hall at Korshamn, in terms of the lay-out of the hall and the dimensions of the hall and the enclosure, has been found at Tissø-Fuglegård on Zealand in Denmark; it has been dated to the 8th-9th century CE.[17]

When the fenced areas of the known southern Scandinavian manor houses of this type were examined, it was found that they all enclosed smaller buildings (Tab. 1). Based on the manor at Tissø, Lars Jørgensen has interpreted these manorial complexes with fenced special areas as a Scandinavian version of the royal palaces (Ger. *Pfalzen*) of the Frankish kingdom[18]: The enclosure with its cult building corresponds to the palace chapel with its connection to the royal hall via an atrium, i.e., a building element with an open roof. The Scandinavian enclosures with their cult buildings were generally dedicated to pre-Christian worship. Yet, when Tissø was Christianised, the older pagan cult building was replaced by what has been cautiously interpreted as a Christian church building with – at least in some of the published reconstructions – a cruciform plan.[19]

The structure enclosed by the rows of stones in Korshamn, for the time being, can be dated indirectly on the basis of the land upheaval.[20] Towards Lake Mälaren, both stone

14 E.g. Jørgensen 2009; Jeppesen 2005; Mohr Christensen 2009
15 Christensen 2015, 15-29
16 Ibid., 71-74, 459-461
17 Jørgensen 2003, 191-200
18 Jørgensen 2002, 246-247; 2003, 204-207
19 Jørgensen 2002, 240; 2003, 197-199
20 Cf. Risberg 2016

rows reach an elevation of 5.75 metres above sea level. This elevation has been interpolated to correspond to, the post-glacial land upheaval, where the waterline was about 810 CE.[21] Since the water level was even higher in previous times, the corresponding stone rows were probably at the earliest built in the early 9th century CE. This supports the dating of the fenced area to the early Viking Age. It is possible that the shoreline of the time wholly coincided with the enclosure's northern limits. That the shoreline in itself could be considered as a significant religious boundary is evident from Norse law as well as from the saga material.[22]

On the raised plateau mentioned above, the georadar survey showed traces of at least one house, which can be determined to have been about 26 metres long and with curved long walls. The traces were not entirely clear, but it seems that the house had a fireplace in the central northern part. There are still visible ramps up to the top of the plateau from both the east and west sides, where the house probably had its entrances. On the western side of the plateau, the ramps connect to a built-up road bank. Towards the south, the road bank makes a westward turn towards the area of the house terrace. If a road continued here, it must have been abandoned early on. The area is completely covered by the graves of the Hemlanden. To the northwest, the road bank runs straight towards a pair of stone jetty foundations, located at the edge of the older harbour bay about 20 metres from the plateau. The harbour facilities must therefore have been used at the same time as the house on the plateau. The ground level where the stone foundations are located is about 7.75 metres above sea level, a height which has been interpolated to correspond to the level of the waterfront 430 CE.[23] Although the foundations were land-based, they were built close to the water. The height thus indicates the jetties predate the Viking Age, a dating that also is valid for the connected raised plateau with the house.

Returning to the one-sided terrace, the georadar survey of the one-sided terrace also showed traces of an older house under the Viking Age Hall at Korshamn (cf. Fig. 2). The appearance of this house has not been fully determined. The house should have been a direct predecessor to the Viking Age Hall and was probably built during the Vendel Period. A qualified assumption is that the older house under the Viking Age Hall and the house on the plateau might have been contemporary and thus parts of one and the same large manor complex, which was built in the Vendel Period, before Birka existed. Both in the design of the houses and in the larger structure of this manor, there are similarities with the Danish manors at Fredshøj and Bulbrogård from the 5th-6th centuries CE that respectively preceded the halls with enclosures in Lejre and Tissø. The plateau house and the buildings' locations near the harbour also resemble the appearance of the Vendel Period complex in Fornsigtuna. The presence of a Vendel Period manor gives a new picture of Björkö before Birka emerged and provides important information about

---

21 Risberg/Alm 2016, 10-18
22 Cf. Toplak 2016: 291
23 Risberg, J. /Alm 2016, 10-18

Birka-Korshamn. Reconstruction of the Viking-age manor at Korshamn. Towards the left the raised plateau of the Vendel period predecessor, in the background to the right the Viking-age town of Birka (after Kalmring & Runer 2017, 18; illustration Jacques Vincent).

Fig. 5.

the background to the development of urban society. The relationship with the known royal estate on Adelsö must also be re-examined.

The appearance, location and preliminary dating of the later Viking Age manor house strongly support that this may indeed have been the seat for the bailiff of Birka (Fig. 5). Similar manors, of the same time, from southern Scandinavia suggest that the cultic enclosure connected to the hall may primarily have been used for pre-Christian worship. Perhaps an original pagan cult may have been replaced by a Christian cult when Herigar was baptised? One person who very early on drew attention to the rows of stones at Korshamn as possibly connected to the earliest missionary activities was the antiquarian Nils Henrik Sjöborg (1767-1838), who visited Björkö in 1821: "The place between the stones is about 100 cubits long and the width about 40. Who knows if it was not here that Christianity in Sweden was first preached, and the cross was erected? I find it quite probable."[24] In accordance with the new results, and until full archaeologi-

---

24 Sjöborg 1830, 16; transl.: the authors

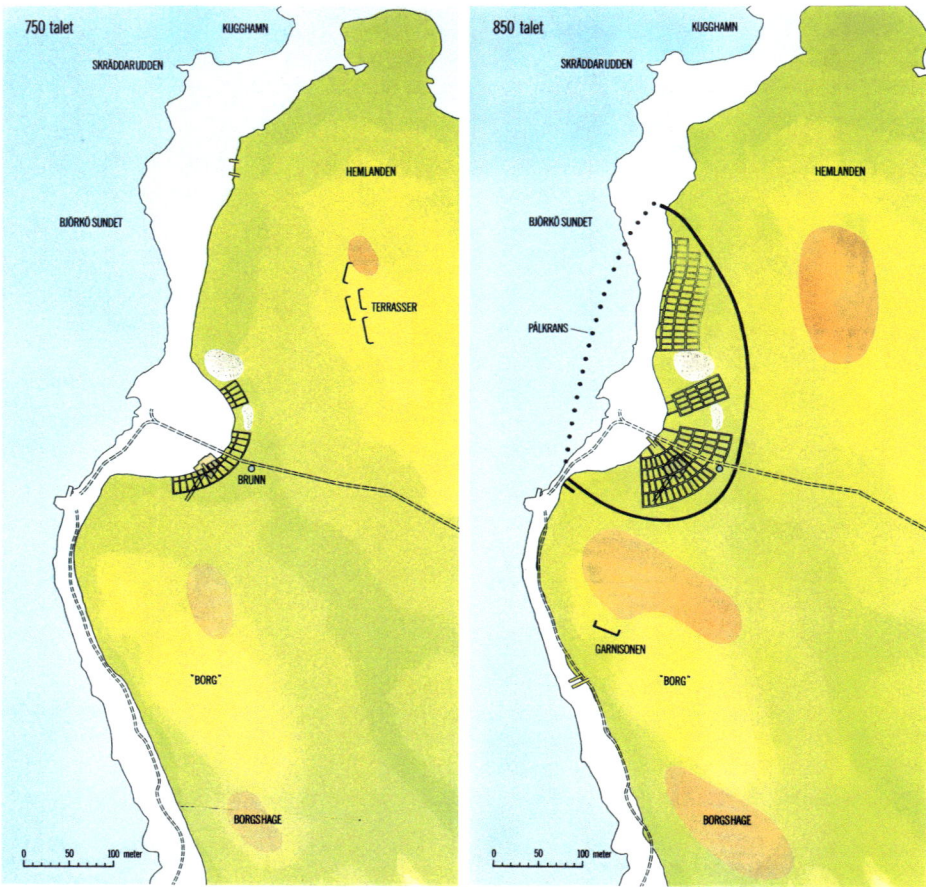

cal excavation, it is fully possible that Sjöborg indeed was right, and that the remnants of Herigar's church really are to be found at this site.

The identification of the "Tissø Complex" of Birka-Korshamn even challenges earlier, largely evolutionary, models based on a gradually expanding settlement centred around the Black Earth harbour. Here, it had been suggested that Birka's earliest roots originated in a couple of "merchant farmsteads" in the late Vendel Period/Early Viking Age[25], deduced from a series of particularly early burials that predate the otherwise largely Early and Middle Viking Age graves on the island of Björkö. From these humble origins in the late Vendel Period, a rather linear, evolutionary model of Birka's urban development was suggested, with an expanding radial building-plot system centred around the bay of the Black Earth harbour, which was slowly silting up.[26] (Fig. 6). Based on the results of the Black Earth settlement excavation carried out between 1990 and 1995, the excavator

25 Arrhenius 1976, 178-184; Kyhlberg 198, 62-63
26 Ambrosian & Erikson 1996, 38-40

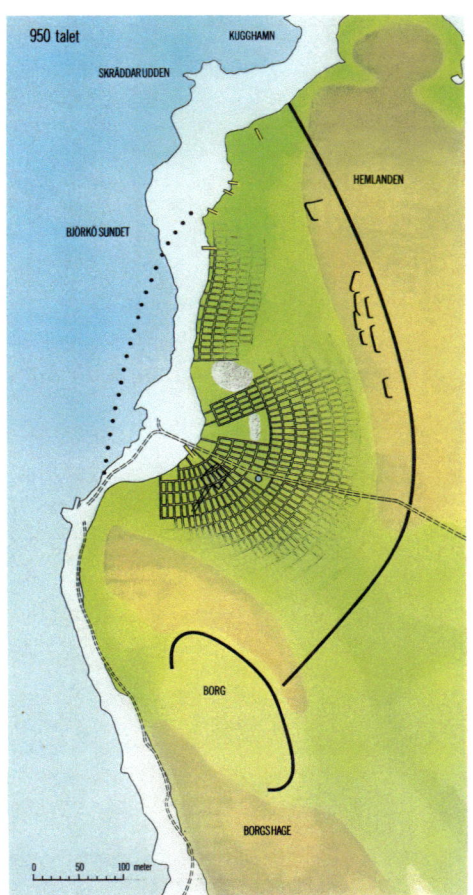

Birka. Earlier evolutionary model of a radial urban development around the silting Black Earth harbour, in three time slices (after Ambrosiani & Erikson 1996: 38-40).

Fig. 6.

reasoned that "The original plots from the foundation of Birka during the first half of the 8th century were laid out in a fan-shaped pattern with boundary ditches at right angles to the shore".[27]

As mentioned above, today, seen from the Black Earth settlement area, Korshamn is in a rather peripheral location on the far edge of the extensive burial ground at Hemlanden and clearly situated outside the town rampart *stadsvallen*. Concerning the latter, most of the many openings in the town rampart are likely to be of early modern origin only. However, the one opening between rampart segments 4 and 5 might be a genuine Viking Age gateway. From there runs what was probably an ancient track that forked immediately behind the town rampart, with the main path leading straight to Korshamn and to the rear of the Viking Age manorial hall.[28] The existence of a once-

---

27 Ambrosiani 2013, 210
28 Kalmring 2020

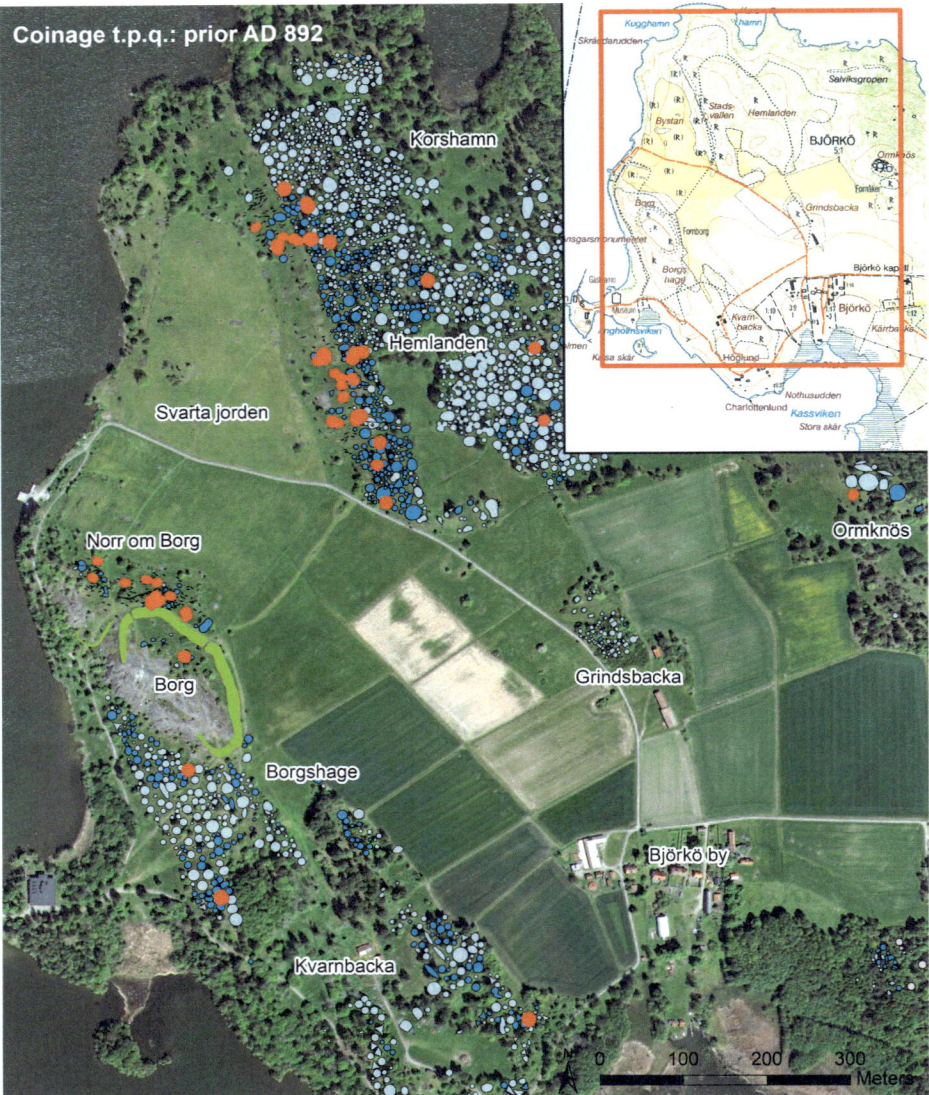

Fig. 7. *Birka, burial grounds. Excavated (dark blue) and unexcavated graves (light blue). Marked in red: Burials with coins, dated prior to CE 892. Note the gap along the course of the later town rampart, i.e. between Svarta Jorden and Hemlanden (after Kalmring 2020, fig. 2).*

important line of communication between Korshamn and the Black Earth settlement area therefore seems more than likely.

In an unpublished manuscript of a master's thesis on "The Coins in Birka's Burials"[29], E. Jonsson maps the coin-dated burials by means of a basic GIS. In doing so, she does

---

29   Swed. *Mynten i Birkas gravar*

not refer to the established categories of the Early and Late Birka Periods, but divides the coin-dated burials into two basic categories: before and after Samanid issues begin to dominate the Islamic coinage, i.e. before and after CE 892.[30] For the earlier period, prior to CE 892, she observes: "The empty section along the rampart at Hemlanden is striking: it could be seen to a certain degree on previous maps but emerges more clearly here (pathway? dwelling?)".[31] (Fig. 7). In the later period, after CE 892, this gap in the burials along the town rampart is no longer discernible and is now occupied by the later coin-dated burials. This eye-catching burial-free stretch prior to CE 892 coincides with rampart segments 3-5 and thus with the location of the gateway identified between rampart segments 4 and 5 as well as that of the ancient pathway towards the manorial estate at Korshamn.

An axis between Korshamn and the main Black Earth settlement area can already be recognised in the phosphate survey undertaken by the Swedish National Heritage Board *Riksantikvarieämbetet* in 1968.[32] The results of this survey were first published by B. Ambrosiani (1974), who briefly pointed out that the high concentrations measured in the Black Earth settlement area do not end at the town rampart but, instead, continue towards Korshamn. In the figure caption, he adds that the phosphate survey also reveals the fact that "the latter [concentration in the Black Earth settlement area] almost reaches Korshamn and is partially covered by the Hemlanden burials".[33] This assessment is consistent with later discussed settlement debris deriving from the fillings of the burial mounds themselves.[34] B. Arrhenius, too, discusses the by far highest phosphate values of P_i 240 "stretching far beyond the eastern rampart as far as Korshamn".[35] She also draws the attention to that one extraordinarily high phosphate value of P_i 630 derives from a plateau in the western part of Korshamn, which would strongly speak for the existence of a dwelling at the location commonly called "the church".[36]

Indeed, this older early settlement layer underneath the later Hemlanden burial ground even could become observed by transects through the thus younger town rampart: In H. Arbman's southern transect (*södra schaktet* or *Ausgrabung 1932 II*) towards the southern end of rampart segment 1 from 1932, immediately above the glacial clay, a thin cultural layer beneath the town rampart suggested some degree of settlement activity prior to the erection of the town rampart.[37] In L. Holmquist's transect through rampart segment 4 from 1987, too, a thin cultural layer plus some additional postholes, dated to cal. CE 531-612 (feature A7) and cal. CE 578-692 (feature A14) were recorded.[38]

---

30 Jonsson 2007, 19-22
31 Jonsson 2007, 19; transl.: the authors
32 Cf. Kalmring et al. 2017, 133
33 Ambrosiani 1974, Fig. 2; transl.: the authors
34 Holmquist Olausson 1993, 40-41 Tab. 5.1
35 Arrhenius 1976, 191 Fig. 13; transl.: the authors
36 Arrhenius 1976, 191 note 60
37 Cf. Arbman 1940-43, 484-485 Fig. 459
38 Holmquist Olausson 1993, 80, 92-95 Fig. 6.7

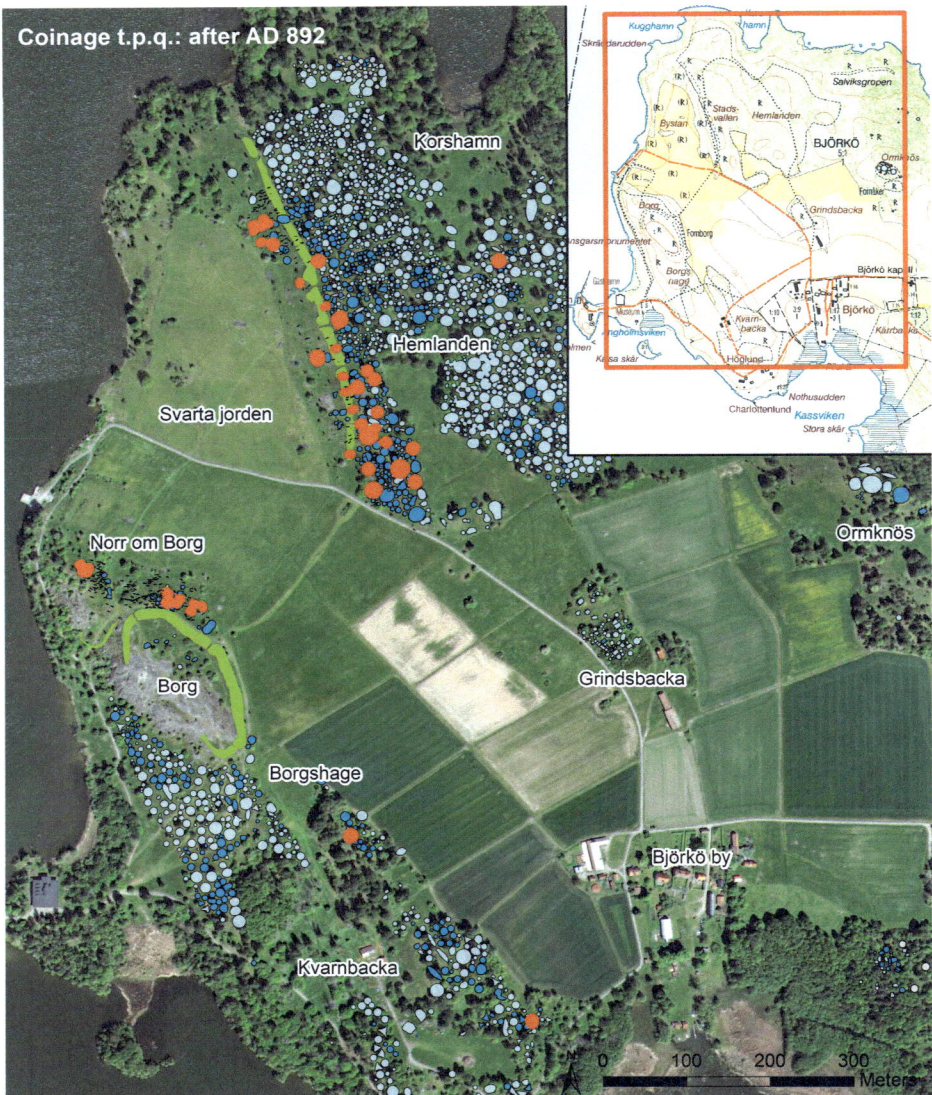

Fig. 8. *Birka, burial grounds. Excavated* (dark blue) *and unexcavated graves* (light blue). *Marked in red: Burials with coins, dated after CE 892. Note the even distribution and the filled gap along the course of the rampart* stadsvallen *(after Kalmring 2020, fig. 3).*

Thus, as early as from the 6th/7th century CE onwards Korshamn and its Vendel Period plateau house clearly seems to relate to the later Black Earth settlement area as one single coherent settlement area. The interconnected, extraordinarily high phosphate values at the succeeding Viking Age manorial hall mentioned above suggest, that this axis even prevailed through the shift from the raised plateau of the Vendel Period "Erik Steffanson's home-field" to the one-sided terrace and "Tissø-Complex" at Kalvhagen.

However, at a certain point in time this formerly all-important axis in the settlement development had evidently ceased to exist and the focus of settlement shifted towards the inside of a semi-circular line of defence. On the closer point in time the erection of the latter, which indisputably lead to its ultimate truncation, can give further insights: Settlement debris from a henceforth abandoned settlement area beyond Black Earth could become observed in the filling of the rampart dated to CE 886-890.[39] This dating chronologically corresponds remarkably well with the burials filling the observed former void as extrapolated from the numismatic evidence after CE 892.[40] (Fig. 8). On Björkö, henceforth all that remained as a reminder of the former significance of the "Tissø Complex" at Korshamn was a gateway between rampart segments 4 and 5.

Based on the evidence presented above, it is proposed that there had been a whole former northern settlement linked to the manorial complex at Birka-Korshamn.[41] In the Early Birka Period, it constituted a vital part of the early emporium in the form of a so-called "one-street shoreside complex"[42], which only became transformed around CE 880/90. Therewith, Birka's early urban fabric developed in parallel with other Viking towns such as Ribe, Hedeby and Kaupang.

Bibliography

Primary Sources
Adam of Bremen: History of the Archbishops of Hamburg-Bremen. Transl. F.J. Tschan (2002). New York.
Rimbert: Anskar. The Apostle of the North, 801-865. Transl. Ch.H. Robinson (1921). London.

Secondary Sources
Ambrosiani, B. 2013: *Stratigraphy 1. Part One: The Site and the Shore. Part Two: The Bronze Caster's Workshop. Excavations in the Black Earth 1990-1995.* (Birka Studies 9). Stockholm.
Ambrosiani, B. 1974: Neue Ausgrabungen in Birka. In: H. Jankuhn/W. Schlesinger/H. Steuer (eds.), Vor- und Frühformen der europäischen Stadt im Mittelalter. Bericht über ein Symposium in Reinhausen bei Göttingen in der Zeit vom 18. bis 24. April 1972 Vol. 2 (Göttingen) 58-63.
Ambrosiani, B. 2016: Alsnöhus och den vikingatida hallen på Alsnö – rekonstruktionsförslag. Meta Historisk arkeologisk tidskrift, 7-24.
Ambrosiani, B. & B.G. Erikson. 1996: *Vikingastaden lever upp igen i TV:s modell av 800-talets Birka!* Birka Vikinga-Staden 5 (Stockholm).
Arbman, H. 1940-43: *Birka I. Die Gräber.* Kungl. Vitterhets Historie och Antikvitets Akademien. (Uppsala).
Arrhenius, B. 1976: "Die ältesten Funde von Birka", *Prähistorische Zeitschrift* 51, 178-195.
Brundstedt, S. 1996. Alsnu Kungsgård. Forskningsprojekt Hovgården. Uppland, Adelsö socken, RAÄ 46 m fl. Arkeologisk undersökning. UV Stockholm, Rapport 1996:71/1. Riksantikvarieämbetet, Stockholm.
Bäck, M., A.-M. Hållans Stenholm, J.Å. Ljung & Lilla Ullevi. 2009: Historien om det fridlysta rummet. Vendeltida helgedom, medeltida by och 1600-talsgård. Uppland, Bro socken, Klöv och Lilla Ullevi 1:5, Jursta 3:3, RAÄ 145.

---

39 Holmquist Olausson 1993
40 Jonsson 2007
41 Kalmring 2020
42 Cf. Ellmers 1984, 184, 216, 268; Søvsø 2018, 80 Fig. 5

Arkeologisk undersökning. UV Mitt, Avdelningen för arkeologiska undersökningar. Riksantikvarieämbetet, Hägersten.

Bäck, M. & A.-M. Hållans Stenholm. 2012: (with a contribution of M. Pettersson), *Lilla Ullevi – den heliga platsens geografi*. Riksantikvarieämbetet (Hägersten).

Carlsson, A. 1997: "Birkas Kungsgård på Adelsö och Svearnas Fornsigtuna – två aristokratiska miljöer i Mälardalen. "-gick Grendel att söka det höga huset-"", in *Arkeologiska källor till aristokratiska miljöer i Skandinavien under yngre järnålder. Rapport från ett seminarium i Falkenberg 16-17 november*, edited by J. Callmer & E. Rosengren. Halmstad, 83-88.

Christensen, T. 2015: *Lejre bag myten – de arkæologiske udgravninger*. Roskilde: Roskilde Museum/Romu.

Ellmers, D. 1984: *Frühmittelalterliche Handelsschiffahrt in Mittel- und Nordeuropa*. (Offa-Bücher 28). Neumünster.

Holmquist Olausson, L. 1993: *Aspects on Birka. Investigations and Surveys 1976-1989* (Theses and Papers in Archaeology B:3). Stockholm: Stockholm university.

Jeppesen, J. 2004. Stormandsgården ved Lisbjerg kirke –Nye undersøgelser. *Kuml*, 53(53), 161-180. https://doi.org/10.7146/kuml.v53i53.97497

Jonsson, E. Mynten i Birkas gravar. Magisteruppsats i arkeologi vt -07. Stockholm Numismatic Institute [unfinished manuscript, 27 pages].

Jørgensen, L. 2002: "Kongsgård – kultsted – marked. Overvejelser omkring Tissøkompleksets struktur og funktion", in *Plats och praxis. Studier av nordisk förkristen ritual*, edited by K. Jennbert, A. Andrén & C. Raudvere. Lund, 215-247.

Jørgensen, L. 2003: "Manor and Market at Lake Tissø in the Sixth to Eleventh Centuries: The Danish "Productive" Sites", in *Markets in Early Medieval Europe. Trading and "Productive" Sites, 650-850*, edited by T. Pestell / K. Ulmschneider. London, 175-207.

Jørgensen, L. 2009: "Pre-Christian cult at aristocratic residences and settlement complexes in southern Scandinavia in the 3rd-10th centuries AD", in *Glaube, Kult und Herrschaft. Phänomene des Religiösen im 1. Jahrtausend n. Chr. Akten des 59. Internationalen Sachsensymposions und der Grundprobleme der Frühgeschichtlichen Entwicklung im Mitteldonauraum*, edited by U. von Freeden / H. Friesinger / E. Wamers (Kolloquien zur Vor- und Frühgeschichte, 12). Bonn, 329-354.

Kalmring, S. 2020: "A different Birka. Emergence of the First Urban Fabric in the Early Birka Period (AD 750-860)", *Zeitschrift für Archäologie des Mittelalters* 48, 1-23.

Kalmring, S., L. Holmquist & A. Wendt. 2021: *Birka's Black Earth Harbour. Archaeological Investigations 2015-2016. Uppland, Adelsö Parish, Björkö, L2017:1568, RAÄ 199:1*. (Theses and Papers in Archaeology B:16). Stockholm.

Kalmring, S., J. Runer & A. Viberg. 2017: "At Home with Herigar: A Magnate's Residence from the Vendel- to Viking Period at Korshamn, Birka (Uppland/S)", *Archäologisches Korrespondenzblatt* 47, 117-140.

Kalmring, S., J. Runer & A. Viberg. 2017: "Hemma hos Hergeir", *Populär Arkeologi* 1, 18-21.

Kyhlberg, O. 1980: *Helgö & Birka. Kronologisk-topografisk analys av grav- och boplatser*. (Arkeologiska rapporter och meddelanden 6). Stockholm: Stockholms universitet.

Mohr Christensen, P. 2009: "Erritsø", *Skalk* 4, 9-15.

Risberg, J. 2016: "Från istid till sluss. Landskapets utveckling före staden", in *Stockholm före Stockholm. Från äldsta tid fram till 1300*, edited by S. Thedéen / T. Zachrisson (Monografier utgivna av Stockholms stad 247). Stockholm, 229-239.

Sjöborg, N.H. 1830: *Samlingar för Nordens fornälskare* 3. Stockholm.

Staecker, J. 2009: "The 9th-century Christian mission to the North", in *Wulfstan's Voyage. The Baltic Sea region in the early Viking Age as seen from shipboard*, edited by A. Englert & A. Trakadas (Maritime Culture of the North, 2). Roskilde, 309-329.

Söderberg, B. 2003: "Integrating Power. Some Aspects of a Magnate's Farm and Presumed Central Place in Järrestad, South-East Scania", in *Centrality – Regionality. The Social Structure of Southern Sweden during the Iron Age*, edited by L.-O. Larsson & B. Hårdh (Uppåkrastudier 7 = Acta Archaeologica Lundensia Series in 8°, 40). Stockholm, 283-310.

Søvsø, M. 2018: "Emporia, sceattas and kingship in 8th c. 'Denmark'", in *The Fortified Viking Age. 36th Interdisciplinary Viking Symposium (Kulturhistoriske studier i centralitet)*, edited by J. Hansen & M. Bruns (Archaeological & Historical Studies in Centrality, 3). Odense, 75-86.

Toplak, M. 2016: Das wikingerzeitliche Gräberfeld von Kopparsvik auf Gotland. Studien zu neuen Konzepten sozialer Identitäten am Übergang zum christlichen Mittelalter, Dissertation. Eberhard Karls Universität, Tübingen.

Westerdahl, Chr. 1989: *Norrlandsleden I. Källor till det maritima kulturlandskapet. En handbok i marinarkeologisk inventering* (Arkiv för Norrländsk hembyggdsforskning, 24). Härnösand.

Zachrisson, T. 2010: "Helgö. Mer än ett *vi*", in *Makt, kult och plats: högstatusmiljöer under äldre järnåldern & kultplatser. Två seminarier arrangerade av Stockholms läns museum under 2009 och 2010*, edited by P. Bratt & R. Grönwall (Arkeologi i Stockholms län, 5). Stockholm: Stockholms läns museum, 79-88.

Personal communication

Risberg/Alm 2016-10-18 = J. Risberg & G. Alm, Department of Physical Geography, Stockholm University.

PART 3.
ATTACKS AND COMMUNICATION BY LAND AND SEA

BY KASPER H. ANDERSEN

Chapter 12
Failure or success?
The Frankish Invasion of Jutland in AD 815

ABSTRACT

This article investigates the Frankish invasion of Jutland in 815 ordered by Emperor Louis the Pious the previous year, when the potential king of the Danes, Harald Klak, subordinated himself to the new Emperor, who in return supported Harald Klak military in his struggle for power amongst the Danes. The invasion is unfolded in a relatively long passage of the entry corresponding to the year 815 in Annales Regni Francorum (the Royal Frankish Annals) and focusing on this specific description this study unfolds the course of the invasion from the preparations prior to the attack to the army leaders returned to the emperor later that same year. The article argues, that despite not achieving a decisive military victory the emperor must have been satisfied with the imminent outcome of the event as he obtained a peace agreement with the Danes and Harald Klak a few years later became co-ruler of the Danes.

Shortly after his farther Charlemagne's dead in 814 the new emperor Louis the Pious ordered an invasion of Jutland. This military campaign into the Danish realm, which took place the following year, has intrigued researchers for a long time. The historian Timothy Reuter described the invasion as a 'half-hearted' Frankish military campaign, and others consider this remarkable event as either rather unsuccessfully or even as a failure for the new emperor.[1] This article, however, will argue that the invasion was a military campaign of a considerable scale, and that Louis the Pious must have been satisfied with the imminent political outcome of the attack. The course of the invasion is unfolded in a relatively long passage of the entry corresponding to the year 815 in *Annales Regni Francorum* (the Royal Frankish Annals) and focusing on this specific description this study investigates the invasion of Jutland. The goal is to illuminate Danish-Frankish political relations in the early 9th century and to unfold the course of the invasion. Due

1   Reuter 1998, 133; Lund 1989

to its central role in the following discussions, it seems relevant to present the Royal Frankish Annals' account of the invasion. The relevant part of the entry is quoted in its entirety in an English translation by Bernhard Walter Scholz, while the Latin text in the reference is from Reinhold Rau's edition of the Annals:

> The emperor commanded that Saxons and Obodrites should prepare for this campaign, and twice in that winter the attempt was made to cross the Elbe. But since the weather suddenly turned warm and made the ice on the river melt, the campaign was held up. Finally, when the winter was over, about the middle of May, the proper time to begin the march arrived. Then all Saxon counts and all troops of the Obodrites under the orders to bring help to Heriold, marched with the imperial emissary Baldrich across the River Eider into the land of the Norsemen called Silendi. From Silendi they went on and, finally on the seventh day, pitched camp on the coast at …. There they halted for three days. But the sons of Godofrid, who had raised against them a large army and a fleet of two hundred ships, remained on an island three miles off the shore and did not dare to engage them. Therefore, after everywhere laying waste the neighboring districts and receiving hostages from the people, they returned to the emperor in Saxony, who at this time was holding a general assembly of his people at Paderborn.[2]

The study below follows the structure of the entry, beginning with the preparation of the invasion and finishing with the Frankish army returning to Saxony. Firstly, however, it seems relevant to touch upon questions related to the Royal Frankish Annals as a historical source.

Annales Regni Francorum

Although the Royal Frankish Annals has been the subject of much scholarly attention for well over a century, numerous inquiries remain unsolved. We do not know, for example, who around the year 790 took the initiative to begin the Annals, or where this

---

[2] Scholz 1990, 99; Annales Regni Francorum 1977, 106: "Iussum est ab imperatore, ut Saxones et Abodriti ad hanc expeditionem praepararentur, temptatumque in illa hieme duabus vicibus, si Albia transiri posset, sed mutatione subita aeris emolliti glacie fluminis resoluta negotium remansit inperfectum, donec tandem hieme transacta circa medium fere Maium mensem oportunum proficiscendi tempus adrisit. Tunc omnes Saxonici comites omnesque Abodritorum copiae cum legato imperatoris Baldrico, sicut iussum erat, ad auxilium Harioldo ferendum trans Egidoram fluvium in terram Nordmannorum vocabulo Sinlendi perveniunt et inde profecti septimo tandem die in loco, qui dicitur …, in litore oceani castra ponunt. Ibique stativis triduo habitis, cum filii Godofridi, qui contra eos magnis copiis et ducentarum navium classe conparata in insula quadam tribus milibus a continenti separata residebant, cum eis congredi non auderent, vastatis circumquaque vicinis pagis et acceptis popularium obsidibus XL ad imperatorem in Saxoniam reversi sunt. Ipse enim tunc temporis in loco, qui dicitur Padrebrunno, generalem populi sui conventum habebat"

first version was produced. If we turn to the final part of the Annals, the responsibility of the annual registration of events of relevance to the Carolingians seems to have been placed in the hands of Abbot Hildvin of Saint Denis from the year 818 until 829, when Hildvin fell into disfavour with the emperor. Hildvin's fall from grace appears to be the explanation way the Annals ends in a interrupted manner in 829.

In this light, the original initiative must have sprung from learned and politically influential men, who were based either at Charlamagne's court or with very close ties to his court. That this was the case, is mirrored in the Annals tendentious character: the Royal Frankish Annals are clearly partisan in relation to the Franks and their rulers, the Carolingians. Thus, when the Annals are used as a historical source, one gets a glimpse of the history of Europe in the late 8th and early 9th century through the eyes of the Carolingians. On the other hand, the credibility of information founded in the Annals is supported by the fact, that they were written down by scribes, who had close ties to the emperor and therefore had direct access to knowledge about current politics and warfare. Therefore, the learned men behind the annals were often well informed on the political situation in territories surrounding the empire, for example amongst the Danes.[3]

The Royal Frankish Annals immediately became popular in learned milieus across Europe. Something which is revealed in the relative high number of preserved manuscripts from the 9th and 10th centuries. One of the oldest, *Codex Vindobonensis 473*, is located at the Austrian National Library. This manuscript was probably produced as part of the coronation celebration of Charles the Bald in 869, most likely in Saint Amand monastery.[4] The manuscript's copy of *Annales Regni Francorum* is separated in two parts: the period until Charlemagne's death in 814 and the period between 815 and 829. The two parts are separated by a copy of a section of Einhard's *Vita Karoli Magni*, a biographical work about Charlemagne originally written *c.* 817.[5] The first version of the Royal Frankish Annals has not been preserved, but *Codex Vindobonensis 473* is believed to be close to the original version.[6]

An imperial vassal

According to both the Royal Frankish Annals and Einhard, King Godfred was sole ruler of the Danes in the first decade of the 9th century. The sources report, that the Danish king controlled a large fleet as well as a well-organised army, which consisted of mounted warriors and advanced military installations such as the fortification Danevirke. Benefiting from this military force, Godfred was able to attack regions, which Charlemagne considered part of his geo-political sphere of interest. The two sources clearly

---

3 The introduction to the Royal Frankish Annales is based on: McKitterick 2004, 16-22; McKitterick 2008, 31-39; Helten 2011.
4 Reimitz 2000; McKitterick 2004, 216
5 Noble 2009, 7-21
6 *Codex Vindobonensis 473* has been digitised by the Austrian National Library: https://digital.onb.ac.at/RepViewer/viewer.faces?doc=DTL_8933188&order=1&view=SINGLE [visited 07.12.22]

leave us with the impression, that King Godfred and his power was taken seriously by the Carolingians. Actually, the Annals informs that the emperor launched a military campaign against the Danes in 810, his last major campaign according to Einhard, but it never came to military confrontation, as Godfred was murdered by his own people.[7] The motives behind the murder of Godfred are unknown, but it is probably not far from the truth if we assume that Danish magnates were not interested in a war with the Carolingians.[8] Hemming succeeded Godfred as King of Danes, and he secured the peace with Charlemagne in 811, but died the following year.

The sudden deaths of Godfred and Hemming resulted in a power vacuum amongst the Danes, in which two different parties aimed for the throne. One contender was Sigfred, a nephew of Godfred, another was Anula, who was the nephew of an else unknown King Harald. Both Sigfred and Anula was killed during the war that followed, and therefore power went to Harald (Klak) and Reginfred, whom were brothers of Anula. In 813, while Harald and Reginfred were still in the process of consolidating their power, the sons of Godfred returned from exile in Sweden and reached out for the throne. Godfred's sons, amongst others the later King Horik I, defeated Harald and Reginfred in both 813 and 814, when Reginfred was killed. After the death of his brother, Harald Klak turned to Louis the Pious for support.[9]

Following the chronology of the Royal Frankish Annals, Harald Klak arrived at Louis' court in the second part of 814. The fugitive king was received well by Louis, who agreed to support Harald, and told him to stay in Saxony until the emperor was ready to help him. In his biography on Louis (*Anonymi Vita Hludowici Imperatoris*) from around 840 an anonymous author, commonly known as "The Astronomer", used the Royal Frankish Annals in his description of these events,[10] but also supplements the Annals with information about how Harald arrived at the imperial court in Aachen, and that it was in this Carolingian center of power, that he submitted himself to Louis according to "Frankish custom" (*morem Francorum*).[11] The latter illustrates the character of the political relationship between Harald and the emperor after the meeting in Aachen. From this point onwards Harald became a subordinated allied of Louis. That this was the case, has also been pointed out by Niels Lund, who stressed how the Latin concept used to describe the political relationship in the Annals (*commendatio*) was normally labelled on political agents, who submitted themselves to the emperor, and hereby accepted him as their lord.[12] In other words: Harald Klak became the vassal of Louis the Pious – if one is to use this disputed concept.

This vassal-lord system was essential to the military and political success of the Franks. The typical model was, that the king or emperor granted each vassal a domain,

---

7   *Einhardi Vita Karoli Magni*, 1977, 182, 96
8   Lund 2020, 51
9   Coupland 1998
10 Noble 2009, 219-226
11 *Anonymi Vita Hludowici Imperatoris* 1977, 294
12 Lund 2020, 54

which enabled the vassal to fulfil his military obligations to his lord, that is the king or emperor. In the case of Harald Klak, the emperor seems to have granted him a domain in Saxony, at least this was the case after the year 826, when the political circumstances had changed dramatically, and Harald together with his wife and allied were baptized in Mainz/Ingelheim.[13] In return for political and military support to the emperor, Harald could also expect to be supported by the emperor. Although the exact character of the relationship between Harald and Louis is unclear, it seems to follow this typical model in this matter. Harald's case was, however, also different from the typical process: When other lords in the periphery of the empire subjected themselves to the emperor, baptism was a central part of the process.[14] In Harald's case, he did not become a Christian until twelve years later.

The alliance with Louis sprung from a political and military context in which Harald was forced to look for potential allies, and the emperor saw a possibility to place a subordinate allied as king of the Danes. Thus, Harald's submission must have been seen as a significant achievement for the new emperor by members of the Frankish elite. Furthermore, if the alliance did succeed, the Franks could expect a more stable situation north of the empire. In Harald's perspective the alliance strengthened his position towards the sons of Godfred. Backed up by the emperor, Harald could continue his struggle for the Danish throne, and he could also expect to be supported by the emperor in the future. Therefore, both parties could benefit from their vassal-lord relationship, which was essential to the invasion of Jutland in 815.

The commander-in-chief

The emperor was supreme commander of the Frankish army, but neither the entry in focus nor any other sources suggest in any way, that Louis personally took part in the invasion of Jutland. Instead, he appointed the nobleman Balderic as the leader of the campaign. Harald was, obviously, a central and decisive agent, but it is very unlikely that he as a pagan and new allied of the emperor, would have been given the authority as commander-in-chief of a campaign of this scale.[15] That Baldric had a leading role in the attack is underlined by 'The Anonymous', who described how Louis ordered Baldric to assemble and organize the Saxon counts and troops from the Obotrites, who were going to take part in the invasion.[16]

Balderic was a member of the Frankish nobility, else it was unlikely that he would have played any leading role in any military campaign.[17] As a nobleman Balderic was a warrior with knowledge of Frankish military traditions and tactics, and as all other

---

13   *Annales Regni Francorum* 1977, 144
14   McKitterick 2008, 278-279
15   Melleno 2017
16   *Anonymi Vita Hludowici Imperatoris* 1977, 294
17   On the organization and structure of the Frankish army, see Coupland 1990, 58-61

noblemen he was obliged to serve in the emperor's army.[18] That Balderic was considered as a skilled warrior and capable leader is reflected in the fact, that he in 819 was appointed Duke of Friuli in the southeastern corner of the empire near the Adriatic Sea.[19] Here Balderic replaced the former duke, who had died earlier that same year, following a campaign against the Pannonian Slavs on the Balkans and their rebellious leader Ljudevit Posavski.[20] The year after he became Duke of Fruili, Balderic waged war against Ljudevit, and soon the Franks and their allies gained the upper hand,[21] and in 823 Ljudevit was murdered.[22] Following this victory, Balderic had to protect the empirie against the Bulgarians as well as other Slavic enimies.[23] In 828, however, Baldric was unable to resist ongoing attacks, and therefore he fell into disfavour with the emperor.[24] Thus, from the invasion of Jutland in 815 up until 828 Baldric was a key political and military figure among the Franks with close ties to the imperial court. One example of the latter is, that he took part in the general assembly in 826, when Harald Klak was baptized.[25]

The planning and launch of the invasion

Frankish military campaigns were in general well-planned.[26] Therefore, preparations for the invasion of Jutland must have begun shortly after Harald submitted to the emperor. Perhaps, Louis could benefit from earlier plans of an attack on the Danes, developed during the final years of Charlemagne's reign. In contrast to potential earlier plans, the emperor now had the advantage of experienced warriors (Harald and his men) with profound local knowledge of both the enemy and the territory they were planning to invade. The entry in focus gives us a glimpse of the planning with the description of how Louis ordered his allied among the Obotrites and Saxons to prepare themselves for the invasion.[27] These groups must have been joined by a number of Haralds allies of Danish origin.[28] Finally, a certain number of Franks also took part in the attack, as Baldric was a Frankish nobleman, and therefore was required to provide troops for the emperor's military campaigns.[29] Because neither the entry in focus nor any other of the relevant sources mention the size of this multi-ethnic army it is not possible to determine the exact size of the invading force. It is, however, beyond any doubt, that

---

18   Coupland 1998
19   *Annales Regni Francorum* 1977, 118
20   Curta 2006, 135-137
21   *Annales Regni Francorum* 1977, 122
22   *Annales Regni Francorum* 1977, 113
23   Borri 2018; Curta 2006, 137
24   *Anonymi Vita Hludowici Imperatoris* 1977, 328
25   *Annales Regni Francorum* 1977, 144; *Anonymi Vita Hludowici Imperatoris* 1977, 324
26   Bachrach 2001, 202-207
27   On Louis' complicated relationship to the Saxons see Cragle, *Converting the Saxons.*
28   Lund 2020, 54
29   Bachrach 2001, 51-65

Charlemagne and later Louis the Pious were able to raise armies of several thousand well-equipped troops, both mounted troops as well as foot soldiers. It was, however, rare, that a Frankish army counted more than 10,000 troops, and during the first half of the 9th century, most imperial armies numbered only some thousand troops.[30] It is, therefore reasonable to assume, that the invading force was of this scale.

After the army had crossed the Elbe in May, it had to march north through Nordalbingia territory. It is likely that the newly established fort at Esesfelth near Itzehoe, which had been established by Charlemagne in 810 as a Frankish bridgehead north of the Elbe, played a central strategic role in this part of the campaign. The fortress was placed near the so-called Hærvejen/Ochsenweg, the main route between Jutland and Northern Germany, and was therefore the obvious place to gather and organize the army before it began its march further north.[31]

The crossing into Jutland

On its way through Nordalbingia the Frankish army had to cross the river Eider. The river was considered by both parties as a natural boarder between the Frankish parts of Saxony and the Danish king's domains,[32] and therefore the river was an important symbolic line to cross. The river could also function as a defensive line for the forces of sons of Godfred, who must also have had a deep understanding of the best ways to cross the river and how to protect these places. However, the scribe behind the entry did not mention any fighting when the army crossed the river. Likely because Godfred's sons had decided to withdraw their forces from the border region. This strategic move may have been motivated by the fact, that this must have been one of the situations, where the Frankish army benefited from the alliance with Harald and his Danish allies, who also had profound knowledge of the border region, for example how and where to cross the Eider.

After crossing the Eider, the army had to pass the Danevirke fortification a bit further to the north. This impressive defensive structure is, however, not mentioned in the entry, something which seems odd, as Danevirke is mentioned in the Annals in 808. Here the scribe unfolded how Godfred ordered the construction of a *vallum*, not only to protect his kingdom from invasion, but also to control the traffic in and out of the kingdom, as the fortification only had one gate.[33] According to the last decades intensive archaeological excavations at Danevirke, the *vallum* mentioned in the annals may very well be identical with a construction phase built of boulders, which was 3 meters high, 3 meters wide and 4 km long.[34] Indeed a significant military defensive structure in 9th

---

30 For further discussions of the sizes of Frankish and early medieval armies in general see: Coupland 1990, 56-58; Halsall 2003, 123-133; Bachrach 2001, 57-59.
31 Lemm 2021
32 *Annales Regni Francorum* 1977, 98
33 *Annales Regni Francorum* 1977, 88
34 Witte and Tummuscheit 2018

century Europe. It is undoubtable that the scribe, who wrote down the description of the invasion of Jutland in 815, knew about the Danish king's great defensive structure, which was a political and symbolic manifestation of Danish royal power. Therefore, it must have been a conscious decision not to include the fortification. Another royal Danish site in the region was *Sliesthorp*, which is mentioned twice in the Annals: First in the year 804 when the Annals described how Godfred arrived to *Sliesthorp* with his fleet, and then again as part of the events in 808 when he attacked the Reric and reinforced Danevirke.[35] The character and locality of this place has been much debated. Recently, Andreas Dobat has argued, that *Sliesthorp* may be identical with the Viking Age settlement at Füsing, just north of the Schlei Fjord, which functioned as a royal Danish naval base, and as a part of the Danevirke defensive structure.[36]

The Danish defensive system of Danevirke and *Sliesthorp* was an important part of different Danish king's strategy against attacks from the south. But the reality is, that the scribe behind the entry did not mention any kind of fighting at either *Sliesthorp*, Danevirke or anywhere else in this region. One cannot, of course, rule out the possibility, that a battle did take place, and that the scribe behind the entry in focus simply decided to omit this from his description of the invasion. However, as the invading army must have been victorious in such a battle, it seems unlikely that the scribe would have deliberately decided to ignore such an event. Therefore, a likely scenario may very well be, that the sons of Godfred simply left the gate of Danevirke open and decided to retreat from their strongholds in the region and instead rely on their naval superiority further north. Godfred's sons understood that they were facing a strong enemy, who could rely on allies (Harald Klak and his men) with detailed local knowledge of the region. In this light a strategic retreat seems the reasonable thing to do. Another possibility, which has been suggested by H. Helmuth Andersen, is that the Carolingian army never came any further north than Danevirke and the Schlei Fjord, and that it was here, that the two armies were separated from water.[37] But this does not seem to fit with the annals' description of how the Frankish army continued onwards from the region of *Silendi*.

According to the entry in focus the invading army entered *Silendi* in "the land of Norsemen" when it had crossed the Eider. The meaning of the ethnonym *Nortmanni* is complicated,[38] but in this context, however, there can be no doubt, that it must be understood as a synonym for the Danes. In the same manner the character and geographical scope of the place name *Silendi* has intrigued scholars for a long time, and although it remains uncertain, *Silendi* may have been another name for the region of Angel.[39] In the context of this article, it is, however, only relevant to notice how the scribe, who wrote this part of the Royal Frankish Annals, makes it clear, how the army continued further north from *Silendi*, that is into Jutland.

---

35 *Annales Regni Francorum* 1977, 78-80, 88
36 Dobat 2022
37 Andersen et al. 1976, 79
38 Garipzanov 2008; Andersen 2015
39 Laur 1985; Garipzanov 2008, 129; Gazolli 2011, 32

The campaign in Jutland and a missing link

The obvious route through Nordalbingia and into went along Hærvejen/Ochsenweg, which led to the gate in Danevirke, and this was also the most likely route of the invading army. Another possibility is that Harald and his men with their knowledge of the geographical and topographical character of the landscape, may have guided the army through the wetland areas to the west or across Danevirke at a weak part of the fortification. Considering the size and character of the Frankish army, none of these alternative options seem rather likely. The entry is more informative concerning the timespan of the invasion, as it describes how the army was on the move for seven days, before it set up camp at a place, which is not mentioned in the text. Apparently, the scribe behind the entry did not know the name of this locality where the army camped for three days, and therefore he left an empty place in his text, which could be filled out later, if it would be possible to find accurate information about the place of the camp. A method also used elsewhere in the Royal Frankish Annals.[40] But where exactly was this place, where the two armies was only separated by a narrow body of water? Obviously, we will never be able to answer this intriguing question with certainty. However, one way to try to reflect upon the question and hereby to fill out the missing link in the Annals is to look at the mobility and speed of early medieval armies, and to consider the total time span of the invasion of Jutland. Obviously, any indication of military travel times in premodern periods can only be an estimate, as the mobility and speed of an army is very difficult to determine. A broad variety of factors such as weather conditions, size and character of the army and the topographical character of landscapes must be considered.[41]

According to the entry, the Frankish army crossed the Elbe in the middle of May, and it is also clear that the army's leaders had returned to the emperor around early July (see below). Therefore, the campaign covered a period of approximately six weeks. As mentioned above, the fort at Esesfelth was the obvious place to gather and organize the army before it began its march. The route from Esesfelth to Danevirke went for about 75 kilometers along Hærvejen/Ochsenweg, a distance which a person traveling by foot could do in roughly two days.[42] However, an army on the move, would spend longer time to move the same distance. According to some scholars, a 9th century Frankish army could travel around 25 kilometers per day, according to others the distance was around 15 kilometer per day.[43] If the army average daily speed it set to 20 kilometers per day the distance from Esesfelth to Danevirke could be done in three or roughly four days. Furthermore, the army also needed at least one or two days to organize its forces at Esesfelth. Therefore, the army would need at least five or six days to move from the Elbe to Danevirke. Taking all these factors into account, the army needed at

---

40   *Annales Regni Francorum* 1977, 98
41   Holterman et al. 2022
42   Holterman et al. (ed.) 2022: https://www.viabundus.eu. (Visited 10.11.22)
43   Lund 2020, 54; Halsall 2003, 131

least a week to reach Danevirke, and therefore it probably did not arrive at Danevirke before the end of May or more likely early June.

It is difficult to determine the correct understanding of the entry's information about how the army marched for seven days before it set up camp for three days near the coast, as neither the point of departure for the army's march or the name of the location of the camp are explained. However, the seven days march must have begun either when the army had crossed the Eider and hereby entered enemy territory or when it left the region of *Silendi*. From the newly archeological located gate in Danevirke to the town of Fredericia north of Kolding Fjord the distance is roughly 145 kilometers. And if the speed of the army is set to 20 kilometers per day, the army could have reached this region. In this perspective, the manor at Erritsø cannot be ruled out as the unnamed place near the coast where the Frankish army set up camp for three days. Another, and perhaps more realistic possibility is, that the campsite was located a bit further south. If this was the case, Erritsø, was an obvious target for the attacks in the region, which is mentioned in both the Annals and by "The Astronomer", who described how the invading forces "… plundered and burned everything they encountered …"[44] At least the invading forces through Harald Klak and his men knew where to find the enemy's important sites such as Erritsø, which may very well have been an easy target as the place probably was deserted by Godfred's sons as part of their strategical retreat to Funen.

In contrast to the lack of information about the size of the imperial army, the entry mentions that the sons of Godfred commanded a fleet of 200 ships. Here, it is relevant to emphasize, how accounts of sizes of military forces in medieval sources represent a methodological problem, as the sources tends to exaggerate the size of armies as well as fleets. As with the size of Frankish armies the size of Viking fleets has been a much-debated subject at least since Peter Sawyer's *Age of the Vikings* (1962), who concluded that 9th century Viking armies and fleets were small and only counting a few hundred men.[45] In contrast to Sawyers assessment Rikke Malmros argued that Danish kings could rise a fleet of 600-800 ships, so that if a warship carried 40 warriors, a fleet of 600 ships would make an army of 24,000 men.[46] This is not the place to go into a detailed discussion of the accurate size of Viking armies and fleets.[47] It is only relevant to notice, that the estimates of both Sawyer and Malmros have been questioned, and that it may very well be an overstatement by a tendentious scribe when the size of Godfred's son's fleet was set to 200 ships. The scribe may have wanted to underline the strength of the enemy, which the Frankish army was unable to defeat in battle. Still, if the sons of Godfred were able to raise a fleet half the size of the one described in the Annals, it would have consisted of 100 ships, and if a ship in advantage carried 30 men, they would have commanded force of 3000 men. No matter the exact size of the fleet, the sons of Godfred commanded a huge and strong military force of probably approximately the

---

44 *Anonymi Vita Hludowici Imperatoris* 1977, 296
45 Sawyer 1962
46 Malmros 1988
47 For a thorough discussion of the size of Viking armies and fleets see Spejlborg 2016, 120-133.

same size as the invading Frankish army. Thus, two strong military parties stood face to face only separated by a narrow body of water, the strait of Lillebælt, which the invading army was not able to cross. The two forces could probably glance at each other from each side of the strait, but there is no sign in the entry whatsoever, that the Frankish army tried to cross Lillebælt. To do so, the invading army must have been supported by a naval force, and there is no reason to believe that this was the case.

Returning to the emperor

According to the last part of the entry in focus the invading army began its journey back to Saxony after only three days. Presumably, Baldric soon realized that it would not be possible to defeat Godfred's sons on the battlefield, as his opponents where both keen on and able to avoid this kind of warfare. The Frankish army must have used around seven days to march back south through Jutland, that is the timespan the army spend on its march into Jutland. This means, that the Frankish army did not spend more than a little more than two weeks within the Danish realm. Here it was, however, exposed to potential surprise attacks from the sons of Godfred. With a fleet of Viking ships only a few miles from the Frankish army, it was a relatively easy task to carry out both minor as well as larger attacks on both the army as well as the supply lines, a kind of maritime warfare very well-known to Godfred's sons. This gave the sons of Godfred a strategic advance, and seriously weakened the invading army's position.

The entry describes how the Frankish army was given hostages from the Danes. Scholtz's English translation does not mention the number of hostages, but according to *Codex Vindobonensis 473* as well as other manuscripts the invading army was given 40 hostages. To exchange hostages was an integrated part of medieval warfare, and the phenomenon was commonly used by both the Vikings and by the Franks, and also played a central role in the diplomatic relations between Danish kings and the Carolingians. In this particular case the invealing army could kill the hostages if it was attached as it was moving back south. That the Frankish army received a relatively high number of hostages reveals how negotiations took place between Godfred's sons and the invading army during its few days in Jutland.

Conclusion: Failure or success?

The sources are silence about how Louis the Pious received the news about the course of the invasion when it was delivered to him in Paderborn in early July 815. If the ambition was a total victory over the sons of Godfred, and to install Harald Klak as sole ruler of the Danes, the immediate result of the invasion of Jutland must have been seen as a failure by the emperor. However, political developments in the following period illustrates that Louis must have been quite satisfied with the results of the campaign. This assumption is supported by the contemporary chronicler Thegan,[48] who mentioned

---

48   Noble 2009, 187-194

negotiations between Danish diplomats and the emperor. In his biographical work on Louis from the late 830s Thegan described how "… a legation of Danes came to him seeking peace …", in Paderborn, where the emperor also "… confirmed the boundaries of his realm in those regions …".[49] The Danish legates cannot have been representatives of Harald Klak, who as the emperor's allied had no reason to negotiate peace, but envoys sent by Godfred's sons shortly after the invading army had left Jutland.

The Danish delegation must have had a mandate to negotiate a peace agreement with the emperor, which also considered the future role of Harald Klak. Harald was not accepted as Danish king at this point, but the emperor's focus on the boundaries must have been related to both Louis' own as well as Harald's position towards Godfred's sons, who during the following years unsuccessfully struggled to resist Harald's ongoing attempts to reclaim his role as King of the Danes. Under the protection of the emperor, Harald was able to keep a military pressure on the sons of Godfred, who only two years later in 817 once again sent an embassy to Louis suggesting him peace if the emperor stopped Harald's attacks.[50] Louis had no intention of doing so. Instead, he seems to have strengthened his alliance with Harald, and in 819 the Annals reports how Godfred's sons were divided into two parties. One party left the Danish realm, another entered an alliance with Harald Klak. The emperor then ordered the Obotrites to sail Harald back to his homeland to claim power, although he had to share it with two of Godfred's sons.[51]

Four years after the invasion of Jutland in 815 a vassal of the emperor was partly ruler of the Danes, something which must have been considered as a success in the eyes of the Franks. Furthermore, during the following years the Annals inform us in a strange, almost astonished tone about a peace settlement with the Danes,[52] and Archbishop Ebbo of Reims began the first official mission among the Danes, which was supported by the emperor and approved by the pope in Rome.[53] The effort to convert the Danes was continued by the Frankish monk Ansgar in 826, when Harald and his Danish family and allied was baptized in Mainz, and hereby strengthened his alliance with the emperor.[54]

Another argument supporting that the emperor did not look at the campaign in 815 as a failure, is the fact that Balderic was made duke of the Friuli only a few years after he had been in charge of the invasion. This campaign had given him experience with unfriendly boarder regions, and therefore Balderic was an obvious candidate to defeat the rebellious Ljudevit and secure the boarders in these parts of the empire. If Louis the Pious had considered the attack on Jutland a failure, he would probably not have selected Balderic to solve this task. Furthermore, the invasion of Jutland positioned the new emperor as a powerful ruler. In the eyes of the Frankish elite the invasion of Jutland

---

49 *Thegani vita Hludowici* 1977, 224
50 *Annales Regni Francorum* 1977, 110
51 *Annales Regni Francorum* 1977, 120
52 *Annales Regni Francorum* 1977, 126
53 *Annales Regni Francorum* 1977, 136
54 Knibbs 2011

made it clear, that Louis was able to realize a campaign against a feared enemy in an unstable boarder region, which his famous farther had struggled to handle.

If we turn to the perspective of the sons of Godfred, it is more complicated to discuss the result of the invasion. Their strategic retreat secured their rule and was therefore successful as the invading army only spent a couple of weeks within their realm. In the following years, however Harald's alliance with the emperor weakened their rule, and Godfred's sons had to negotiate peace with the emperor. Despite these negotiations, Harald managed to weaken and finally divide the brothers and place himself as co-ruler of the Danes – at least for a decade. Thus, during the years immediately after the invasion in 815 and up until Horik I in 826-827 was able to push Harald out of Denmark once again, the invasion of Jutland turned out to be a political setback for the sons of Godfred. Their alliance fell apart and some of them lost their position as Kings of the Danes, and those who remained had to share power with Harald. However, in the eyes of later 9th century Danish kings such as Horik I and later Horik II, who seem to have ruled the Danes from around 830 to around 870, a positive long-term outcome of the invasion may very well have been that the Franks realized that an invasion of the Danish realm was a very different strategic task than other military expansions around Europe. The topographical character of the lands of the Danes, with its many rivers, streams, and wetlands, fjords and straits, made it extremely difficult to conquer for a Carolingian army specialized in land-based warfare.

Bibliography

Andersen, H.H., H.J. Madsen & O. Voss. 1976: *Danevirke*. Jysk Arkæologisk Selskabs Skrifter XII.

Andersen, K.H. 2015: "Glimt af Nordens etnografi i de frankiske kilder fra det 9. århundrede", in *Et fælles hav – Skagerrak og Kattegat i vikingetiden*, edited by Anne Pedersen & Søren Sindbæk. Nationalmuseet, 37-51.

Annales Regni Francorum. Die Reichsannalen. Quellen zur Karolingischen Reichsgeschichte I. *Ausgewählte Quellen zur Deutschen Geschichte des Mittelalters* V. Edited and translated by Reinhold Rau et al. Wissenschaftliche Buchgesellschaft Darmstadt, 1977, 9-155.

Anonymi Vita Hludowici Imperatoris. Das Leben Kaiser Ludwigs von. sog. Astronomus. Quellen zur Karolingischen Reichsgeschichte I. *Ausgewählte Quellen zur Deutschen Geschichte des Mittelalters* V. Edited and translated by Reinhold Rau et al. Wissenschaftliche Buchgesellschaft Darmstadt, 1977, 257-381.

Bachrach, B.S. 2001: *Early Carolingian Warfare. Prelude to Empire*. University of Pennsylvania Press.

Borri, F. 2018: "Dalmatian Romans and their Adriatic friends: Some further remarks", in *Transformations of Romanness. Early Medieval Regions and Identities*, edited by Walter Pohl, Clemens Gantner, Cinzia Grifoni & Marianne Pollheimer-Mohaupt. De Gruyter, 241-252.

Christensen, A.E. 1977: *Vikingetidens Danmark. Paa Oldnordisk baggrund*. Akademisk Forlag.

Coupland, S. 1998: "From poachers to gamekeepers: Scandinavian warlords and Carolingian kings". *Early Medieval Europe*, no. 7, 85-114.

Coupland, S. 1990: "Carolingian Arms and Armor in the Ninth Century". *Viator*, vol. 21, (1990), 29-50.

Cragle, J.M. 2023: *Converting the Saxons. A Study of Violence and Religion in Early Medieval Germany*. Routledge.

Curta, F. 2006: *Southeastern Europe in the Middle Ages, 500-1250*. Cambridge University Press.

Dobat, A.S. 2022: "Finding Sliesthorp? The Viking Age settlement at Füsing". *Danish Journal of Archaeology*, no. 22, 1-22.

Einhardi Vita Karoli Magni. Einhard, Das Leben Kaiser Ludwigs. Quellen zur Karolingischen Reichsgeschichte I. *Ausgewählte Quellen zur Deutschen Geschichte des Mittelalters* V. Edited and translated by Reinhold Rau et al. Wissenschaftliche Buchgesellschaft Darmstadt, 1977, 163-211.

Garipzanov, I. 2008: "Frontier Identities: Carolingian Frontier and the Gens Danorum", in *Franks, Northmen and Slavs. Identities and State Formation in Early Medieval Europe*, edited by Ildar H. Garipzanov, Patrick J. Geary & Przemysław Urbanczyk. Brepols Publishers, 113-145.

Gazolli, L. 2011: "Denemearc. Tanmaurk Ala, and Confinia Nordmannorum: The Annales Regni Francorum and the Origins of Denmark", *Viking and Medieval Scandinavia*, vol. 7, 29-43.

Halsall, G. 2003: *Warfare and Society in the Barbarian West, 450-900*. Routledge.

Helten, V. 2011. *Zwischen Kooperation und Konfrontation: Dänemark und das Frankenreich im 9. Jahrhundert*. Kölner Wissenschaftsverlag.

Holterman, B., A.B. Maartje & K.H. Andersen et. al. 2022: "Viabundus: Map of Premodern European Transport and Mobility", in *Research Data Journal for the Humanities and Social Sciences*, no. 7(1), 1-13.

Knibbs, E. 2011: *Ansgar, Rimbert and the Forged Foundations of Hamburg-Bremen*. Ashgate.

Laur, W. 1985: "Det gamle landskabsnavn Sinlendi eller Sillende". *Sønderjyske Årbøger*, 5-13.

Lemm, T. 2021: "The Fight for Nordalbingia: Reconstruction and Simulation of the Danish-Obodrite Attack on the Frankish Fortress of Esesfelth in AD 817", in *Viking Special Volume 1 – Viking Wars*, edited by Frode Iversen and Karoline Kjesrud, 63-84.

Lund, N. 1989: "Allies of God or Man? The Viking Expansion in a European Perspective", in *Viator*, vol. 20, 45-59.

Lund, N. 2020: *Jellingkongerne og deres forgængere*. Vikingeskibsmuseet i Roskilde.

Malmros, R. 1988. "Den danske ledingsflådes størrelse", in *Kongemagt og samfund i middelalderen. Festskrift til Erik Ulsig*, edited by Poul Enemark, Per Ingesman & Jens Villiam Jensen, 19-40. Aarhus University Press.

McKitterick, R. 2004: *History and Memory in the Carolingian World*. Cambridge University Press.

McKitterick, R. 2008: *Charlemagne. The formation of a European Identity*. Cambridge University Press.

Melleno, D. 2017: "Between borders: Franks, Danes, and Abodrites in the trans-Elben world up to 827", in: *Early Medieval Europe*, vol. 25:3, 359-385.

Noble, T.F.X. 2009: *Charlemagne and Louis the Pious. Lives by Einhard, Notker, Ermoldus, Thegan, and the Astronomer*, Penn State University Press.

Ravn, M., C. Juel, C. Lindblom & A. Pedersen. 2019: 'Erritsø – new investigations of an aristocratic, early Viking Age manor in Western Denmark c. 700-850 AD", in *Early medieval waterscapes Risks and opportunities for (im)material cultural exchange. Neue Studien zur Sachsenforschung* Band 8, edited by Rica Annaert, 37-46.

Reimitz, H. 2000: "Ein fränkisches Geschichtsbuch aus St. Amand: der Cvp 473", in *Text, Schrift und Codex. Quellenkundliche Arbeiten aus dem Institut für Österreichische Geschichtsforschung*, edited by Christoph Egger and Herwig Weigl. Mitteilungen des Instituts für Österreichische Geschichtsforschung: Ergänzungsbänd, 34-90.

Reuter, T. 1990: "The End of Carolingian Military Expansion", in *Charlemagne's Heir. New Perspectives on the Reign of Louis the Pious*, edited by Peter Godman and Roger Collins. Oxford University Press, 391-405.

Reuter, T. 1998: *Germany in the Early Middle Ages 800-1056*. Longman Group.

Saywer, P. 1962: *The Age of the Vikings*. St. Martin's Press.

Scholz, B.W. 1970: *Carolingian Chronicles. Royal Frankish Annals and Nithard's Histories*. Translated by Bernhard Walter Scholz. The University of Michigan Press.

Spejlborg, M.B. 2016: *There and back again. English connections in early medieval Denmark, c. 991-1086*. Aarhus University (PhD dissertation).

Thegani Vita Hludowici Imperatoris. Thegan, Das Leben Kaiser Ludwigs. Quellen zur Karolingischen Reichsgeschichte I. Ausgewählte Quellen zur Deutschen Geschichte des Mittelalters V. Edited and translated by Reinhold Rau et al. Wissenschaftlische Buchgesellschaft Darmstadt, 1977, 215-253.

Witte, F. & A. Tummuscheit. 2018: "The Danewerk in light of recent excavations", in *The Fortified Viking Age. 36th Interdisciplinary Viking Symposium,* edited by Jesper Hansen and Mette Buus. University Press of Southern Denmark, 69-74.

BY THORSTEN LEMM

Chapter 13
From Esesfelth to Echeho
– Continuity and change in a Nordalbingian landscape of power

ABSTRACT

This article examines the development of power structures in central and western Holstein, from chieftain-led settlements in the younger Germanic Iron Age to a royal landscape managed by counts in the Frankish period, and eventually to a private county under noble authority. It discusses the strategic importance of this region, marked by significant archaeological finds such as fortifications, rich graves, and elite residences. The study highlights the transformation from Saxon chieftaincies to Frankish-controlled domains, emphasizing key sites like the fortress of Esesfelth and later developments like the Kaaksburg and Itzehoe fortresses. The analysis provides insights into the socio-political shifts over nearly 400 years, illustrating the region's enduring significance and evolving power dynamics.

A major aspect of the workshop that gave rise to this publication was the presentation of sites in Northern Europe that are described in research, for example, as 'elite residence' or 'king's manor' or are assigned to an 'aristocratic environment'. Following on from this, this paper will trace archaeological and historical evidence for the presence of members of different elites and outline a certain meso-region's development from a settlement district led by chieftaincy, through a royal landscape administered by a count, to a private county under noble authority. Seen from the perspective of the inhabitants of Erritsø – the potentially royal farm at the centre of this book – this paper will focus on their southern neighbours' settlement area in central and western Holstein in the very south of the Jutish peninsula.

In the younger Germanic Iron Age and the Viking Age (7th-11th centuries), Saxon people populated this area, and due to its geographic position, it was always very significant for the history of Denmark. In the Royal Frankish Annals this Saxon territory is denoted as *trans Albia*,[1] which means 'across the Elbe' and is referred to in research as

---

1   Annales Regni Francorum 1987, 804

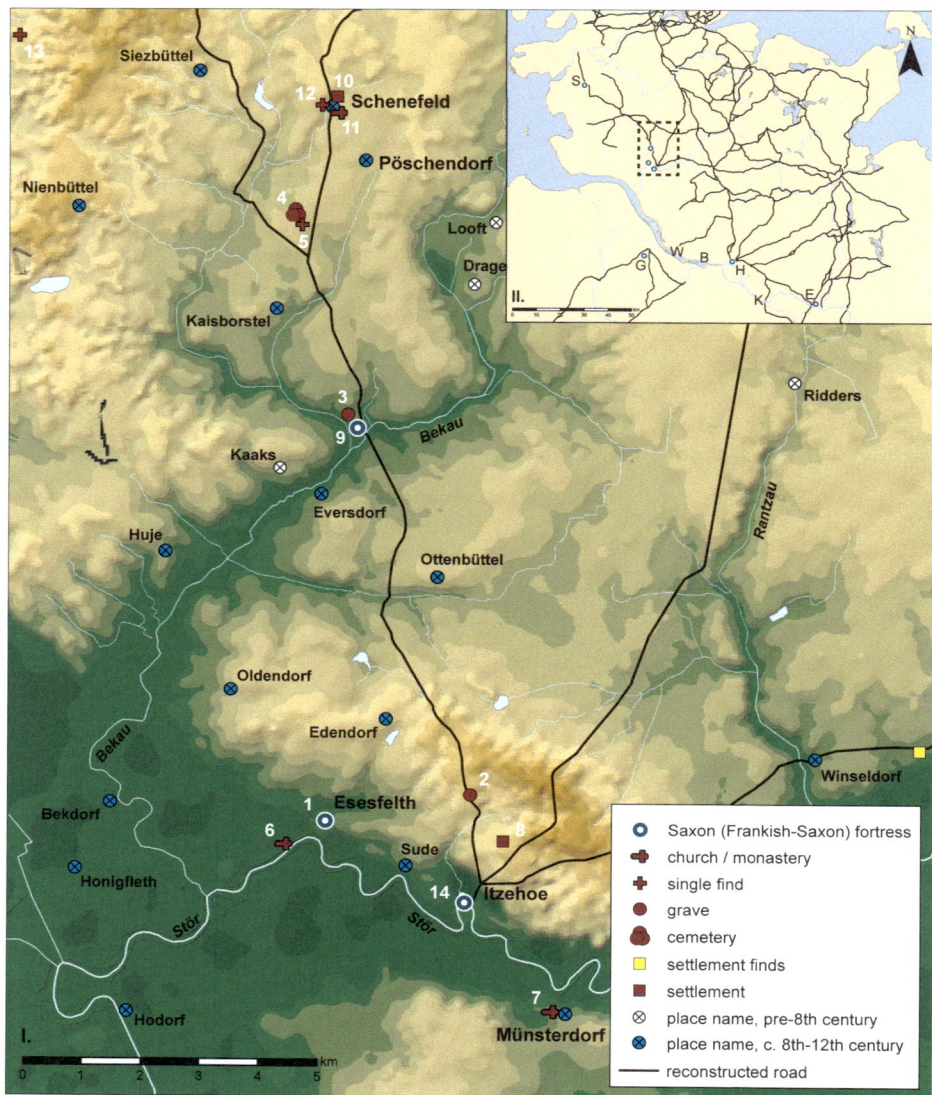

Fig. 1. *I. map of the meso-region Heiligenstedten–Itzehoe–Schenefeld. 1 Oldenburg I-II; 2 urn grave at Lehmwold, Itzehoe; 3 urn grave, Kaaks; 4-5 Krinkberg cemetery and hoard find, Pöschendorf; 6 Heiligenstedten church; 7 Welanao monastery; 8 pit-house, Itzehoe; 9 Kaaksburg; 10-12 Viking Age settlement, church and late 10th/early 11th century coin find, Schenefeld; 13 silver armring, Bokhorst; 14 Itzehoe fortress. II. map of Nordalbingia and parts of Wigmodia with reconstructed roads, Elbe river crossings and selected sites mentioned in the text such as Groß Thun (G), Stellerburg (S) and Ham(ma)burg (H). There seems to have been an ancient and a younger Iron Age/Viking Age fording situation near modern-day Wedel (W) and since the High/Late Medieval Period a ferry crossing at Blankenese (B) both west of Hamburg as well as fords close to Kirchwerder (K) and at the so-called Ertheneburg (E) both south-east of Hamburg.*

Nordalbingia. It was the northernmost part of the Old Saxon tribal area, which besides central and western *Holstein* spread over *Lower Saxony* and parts of *North Rhine-Westphalia* and *Saxony-Anhalt*. During Charlemagne's so-called Saxon wars from 772 until 804 AD the Saxon settlement areas were gradually conquered and incorporated into the Frankish kingdom with Nordalbingia being the last of them six years later.[2] In AD 843, the Frankish kingdom was divided amongst the sons of Emperor Louis the Pious. Henceforth Nordalbingia was the northernmost part of the East-Frankish kingdom, which in the following 200 years grew significantly in size on its way to become the Holy Roman Empire.[3]

When thinking about power structures and fortresses, it is of utmost importance to know the contemporaneous communication routes. The ancient road network in Nordalbingia has been reconstructed largely since the 1930s and gradually supplemented in recent years.[4] Nordalbingia was connected with the area south of the Elbe via a few far-distance roads that crossed the river at different locations (Fig. 1.II).[5] However, the most important connection between the areas north and south of the Elbe appears to have been the waterway between the modern-day towns of *Itzehoe* and *Stade*, because at Itzehoe also three important long-distance roads converged on the river *Stör*. One of these led to the inner Dithmarschen area, one led towards eastern Nordalbingia and the Slavic settlement area and one was connected with the so-called Ox Road or Army Road, which led further to the North of Jutland and eventually into the Danish territory.[6] Hence, within this particular region lay the key to control of the whole Nordalbingian area. It is therefore not surprising that the region between present-day *Heiligenstedten*, Itzehoe and *Schenefeld* is particularly suitable in order to present and discuss different 'rich' archaeological sites against the changing socio-political background of the whole Nordalbingian territory (Fig. 1.I).

The pre-Frankish period – 7th century

A first indication of the presence of members of elite circles in the meso-region focussed on in this paper during the younger Germanic Iron Age can be found about 2.5 km west of the aforementioned strategic nodal point of communication routes in present-day Itzehoe (Fig. 1.I.1). On the tip of a promontory, a fortification was excavated featuring two crescent-shaped rows of trough-shaped ditches, which were 5-6 m from each other and closed off an area of c. 100 × 50 m at the outermost point of the spur (Fig. 2). This double-ditch complex – referred to as *Oldenburg I* – can be dated to the 7th century based on ceramic finds from the deepest fill layers and the

---

2   Springer 2004
3   Brühl 2001, 115-119, 229
4   Kersten 1939, 145-155; Lemm 2013, 307-321; 2022, 255-259 with further references.
5   Cf. Holtermann et al. 2021
6   Struve 1965, 36

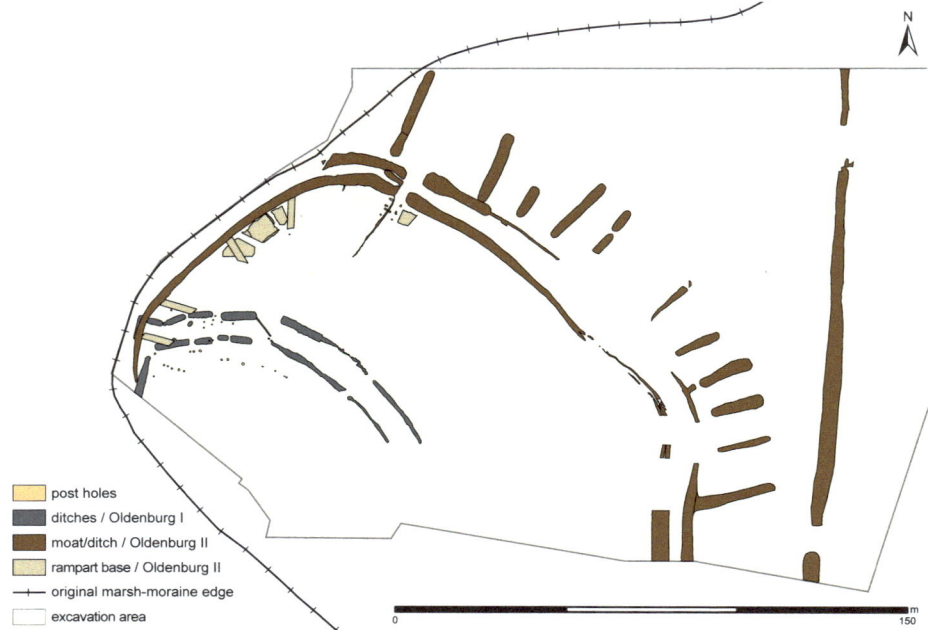

Fig. 2. *Oldenburg I (Saxon double-ditch complex) and Oldenburg II (the Fortress of Esesfelth) on the moraine spur 'Camp up der Oldenburg', east of Heiligenstedten. The original edge of the spur, i.e. the border between the moraine and the marsh, was also documented during the excavations.*

bottoms of a few ditches.[7] [14]C datings confirm this estimate and suggest use in the second half of the 7th century.[8] Due to its relatively small size, the fortification would not have been able to hold many people and is therefore unlikely to have served as a 'refuge fortress' (German: *Fluchtburg*) for the entire population of a certain region. If this function came into play at all, then the fortress probably only offered refuge to members of an elite upper class.[9] However, the fortification was not conceived as hide-out, but was built in a strategic and visible position on the north bank of the Stör. Therefore, it should rather be understood in the context of controlling the waterway.

Unfortunately, our knowledge of 7th century archaeological finds and sites in Holstein is still very sparse. To compensate somewhat for this lack of knowledge, research has for some time made use of Old Saxon place names.[10] The oldest place name stratum, which, according to Laur,[11] may already be of Roman Iron Age or older Germanic

---

7   Information on the archaeological find material from Oldenburg I: Lemm 2013a, 147-152, Fig. 65, 186-188, 474, 696 pl. 108.1-2, 697 pl. 109.1-2.
8   Information on the ^{14}C dates: Lemm 2013, 188-189, 657-662 pl. 69-74.
9   Cf. Struve 1965, 57; Brachmann 1993, 163
10 Kersten 1939; Ramm 1952; Jankuhn 1952, 1957
11 Laur 1957, 25

Iron Age origin, is assigned to the so-called 'short names' (Germ. 'Kurznamen'), which contain linguistic material that is no longer known in the languages concerned. Within the meso-region dealt with here, these are the places Looft, Drage, Ridders and perhaps Kaaks (Fig. 1.I). Names ending in -ing are also thought to have originated in this early period[12] – e.g., Peissen and Silzen northeast of Ridders. Place-name researchers consider the name endings in -stedt to be of younger Germanic Iron Age origin (5th-7th century), which spread partly at the expense of the -ing names or merged with them to form -ingstedt.[13]

Judging by the distribution of archaeological sites and Old Saxon place names, the Saxon settlement area north of the Elbe was sparsely settled over a relatively large area at that time, with some regions displaying a higher population density.[14] From the wider surroundings of Oldenburg I, an urn grave is known from Lehmwohld in Itzehoe (about 2 km to the east; Fig. 1.I.2), which Herbert Jankuhn dates to the period of the 6th/7th centuries.[15] Another urn grave from Kaaks (7 km north; Fig. 1.I.3), which contained a bead of rock crystal, may also date from the 7th century.[16] Based on these few finds it is not possible to make any substantial statements regarding the archaeological background of the fortification Oldenburg I. However, the short names Looft, Drage, Ridders and Kaaks at least indicate a certain settlement at that time in the northern part of the meso-region dealt with here. These old settlement nuclei, which can probably be traced back to the older Roman Iron Age, were each surrounded by wooded areas.[17]

If we take a look at the southern end of the mentioned waterway in Lower Saxony, we will find a fortress near the village of *Groß Thun* south of Stade (Fig. 1.II.G), which is directly located on the *Schwinge* river; it was built at the end of the 7th century and remained in use for c. 250 years.[18] Find sites in the vicinity of the so-called 'Schwedenschanze' seem to indicate central place functions in connection with the fortress. Andreas Schäfer therefore considers that the fortress served as residence of a Saxon chieftain until the Frankish conquest.[19] Perhaps a comparable background may be assumed for the Oldenburg I fortress. In any case, it seems rather likely that at the end of the 7th century starting point and endpoint of the waterway Schwinge–Elbe–Stör were controlled with the help of fortifications.

---

12 Laur 1957, 24
13 Laur 1957, 25f.
14 Lemm 2013, 208, 209 Fig. 73, 235 Fig. 89
15 Jankuhn 1957, 35
16 Lemm 2013, 559-560
17 Ramm 1952
18 Schäfer 2011, 344, 348
19 Schäfer 2011, 355

The pre-Frankish period – 8th and early 9th centuries

In the following period a cemetery was in use at *Pöschendorf* only c. 10 km north of the double-ditch complex (Fig. 1.I.4). It is one of only three cemeteries of this period so far known from the Nordalbingian region; the other two were located at *Immenstedt* and *Bendorf*. All three were investigated already at the end of the 19th century.[20] At Pöschendorf a Bronze Age burial mound had been used for a secondary grave in the early 8th century, of which a gilded sword pommel fragment, iron knifes and a sceatta coin of Wodan/Monster type were discovered in 1885.[21] The mound is known as *Krinkberg*, which translates as "circle mound" and refers to the circular earth embarkment surrounding it.[22] Intentional deep ploughing at the end of the 19th century in between the mound and the circular embarkment and minor excavations in the 1980s brought to light various and mostly fragmented artefacts. Among other things these include swords, seaxes, lance heads, axes, knifes and folding knifes, a stirrup, an arrowhead and three sceattas – two of the Wodan/Monster type and one of the Porcupine type.[23] Moreover, a lump of corroded iron is of special interest, as an x-ray image revealed that it represents a piece of chain mail (Fig. 3.A-B). It is highly likely that these objects represent the remains of once richly furnished burials.[24] Comparable graves were also discovered at *Bendorf* and *Immenstedt* as well as in the form of single graves across the Nordalbingian area[25] and in a much larger number in the Saxon settlement area south of the Elbe.[26]

In the Saxon cemeteries, certain individual burials stand out, because of their furnishing with weapons and riding equipment. In relation to the entirety of burials from the 8th and early 9th centuries, this type of grave is documented rather seldomly. This salient mismatch has led to the conclusion that the equestrian graves represent a high social standing of the deceased, which is especially true for Frauke Stein,[27] whose controversial interpretation of the graves as 'burials of the nobility' ('Adelsgräber') has met criticism.[28] Nevertheless, taken all archaeological evidence together, such grave complexes indicate clear social differentiation within the Old Saxon territory. On the one hand, this is based on the frequent absence and rare presence of rich grave goods, where the latter may lead to the interpretation as burials belonging to the local/regional elite.[29] On the other hand, differences within the group of richly furnished burials are visible in certain types of grave goods and elaborate grave constructions. Hence, in accordance with Babette Ludowici,[30] it may be assumed that those deceased, who were buried in

---

20 Lemm 2013, 209, 210 Fig. 74 with further references
21 La Baume 1957, 46-47, 48 Fig. 2.1-5
22 La Baume 1957, 46
23 Stein 1967, pl. 60.2-6; Lemm 2013, 214, Fig. 76, 560-563 with further references
24 Struve 1965, 49; Lemm 2013, 216
25 Lemm 2013, 216-219 with further references
26 Stein 1967; Kleemann 2002
27 Stein 1967
28 Cf. Steuer 1978, 481
29 Lemm 2013, 223
30 Ludowici 2019, 297

A lump of corroded iron from the Krinkberg cemetery (A), of which the x-ray image (B) shows that it represents a piece of chain mail. Photos: Stiftung Schleswig-Holsteinische Landesmuseen Schloss Gottorf.

Fig. 3.

wooden chambers and covered by mounds and were furnished not only with weapons and riding equipment, but also with horses, dogs and stags as well as with mail coats most likely belonged to the small group of socially privileged persons from which the Saxon leaders emerged.[31] Hence, judging from the grave goods, also at the Krinkberg cemetery members of an elite family – possibly that of a Saxon chieftain – were buried until the early 9th century.[32]

As mentioned in the beginning, Charlemagne's Saxon wars ended in AD 804. A Frankish army campaign into Nordalbingia marked the final point of this conflict.[33] Around this time, a silver treasure was deposited in a vessel of Badorf ware (Fig. 1.I.5), which consisted of 17 pieces of hacksilver and originally more than 95 silver coins – original Frisian denarii of the CAROLUS/DORSTAT type and a few Nordic imitations – that had been minted between 781/785 and 790/794.[34] Very likely, a member of the elite family may have deposited the silver hoard at the Krinkberg during the politically unstable times at the end of the 8th and the beginning of the 9th century.[35]

From the 8th century until the time of the German colonisation of eastern Holstein in the 12th century, place names ending in -dorf, -büttel, -husen and -borstel were in use.[36] As the examples of Esesfelth and Schenefeld ('Scanaveld'; see below) as well as 'Badenfliot'[37] show, place names with endings in -feld as well as -fleth also existed from the 9th century at the latest. Moreover, the appellative term *hûde* indicating a landing site was most likely established as place name during that time (cf. *Huje* and *Sude* in

---

31 Lemm 2013, 282-286; Lemm 2021b, 282-286
32 Kersten 1939, 185; Struve 1965, 51; Lemm 2013, 219
33 Annales Regni Francorum 1987, 804
34 Wiechmann 1996, 409-414
35 Cf. Wiechmann 1996, 125-127 with further references; Lemm 2013, 246
36 Ramm 1952; Laur 1957, 26
37 Annales Regni Francorum 1987, 809

Fig. 1.I).³⁸ Starting from the oldest settlement nuclei in the meso-region mentioned above, the land was developed, which can be seen in the somewhat younger place names. For example, Kaisborstel is thought to have been developed from Drage and Pöschendorf from Looft.³⁹ Heinz Ramm's results can be confirmed by Jankuhn through archaeological find material.⁴⁰ He assumes that Pöschendorf was created in the course of this land development around 700 or somewhat later. Although so far not proven archaeologically, Pöschendorf is presumed to be the dwelling site of the elite family that buried their dead at the Krinkberg.⁴¹

The Frankish annexation of Nordalbingia – early 9th century

While *Wihmuodi/Wigmodia* south of the Elbe was integrated into the Frankish kingdom in 804 and became a Frankish royal domain administered by counts,⁴² Charlemagne initially handed over Nordalbingia to his ally and dependent, the Obodrite Prince Thrasko,⁴³ making it a buffer zone between the Frankish and the Danish kingdoms.⁴⁴ After events in 808, however, the Danish King Gudfred threatened to appropriate the area, and forced Charlemagne to intervene in the events north of the Elbe.⁴⁵ Consequently, at the behest of his king, the Frankish Count Egbert together with some Saxon counts crossed the Elbe, occupied a site named 'Esesfelth' and began to fortify it in March 810.⁴⁶ According to the source, Esesfelth – of which the name is lost – was located on the river 'Sturia', which we know as *Stör*, today. It is highly likely that the historically known fortress of Esesfelth may be identified as the archaeologically excavated early 9th century rampart-ditch complex (Oldenburg II) on the above-mentioned moraine spur west of Itzehoe, which Saxons had already fortified in the 7th century (Fig. 1.I.1).⁴⁷

It may be generally formulated that during all eras two main factors were decisive for the choice of a site for the construction of a fortress: the course of contemporaneous communication routes and the protective position in the natural landscape.⁴⁸ Both factors apply to the fortification complex, which is interpreted as Esesfelth. Firstly, as already explained, c. 2.5 km to the east three far-distance roads coming from Dithmarschen, Jutland and the area of today's Ostholstein converged on the waterway providing the fortress with a key position for controlling the entire Nordalbingian area (cf. Fig. 1.II).⁴⁹

---

38 Udolph 1994, 460f., 473; Lemm 2013, 323-326 with further references
39 Ramm 1952
40 Jankuhn 1957; cf. Lemm 2013, 257 Fig. 106
41 Struve 1965, 51
42 Weidemann 1976, 166-168
43 Annales Regni Francorum 1987, 804
44 Struve 1957, 15; Kühn 1995, 17
45 Annales Regni Francorum 1987, 808
46 Annales Regni Francorum 1987, 809
47 Lemm 2013, 22, 37 fn 7, 138-139, 192-194
48 Lemm 2022, 264
49 Lemm 2021a, 67

Secondly, on the basis of a reconstruction of the historical topography it becomes clear that the chosen shallow spur, which was protected at three sides by the wetland area of the river Stör, provided the best strategic pre-conditions for a fortification.[50]

Prior to the field investigations there were no visible remains of the fortifications. Moreover, during the excavations extensive disturbances were discovered that can be attributed to gravel and sand extraction, as well as the construction of the West Holstein Marsh Railway, whose tracks ran across the site from 1878 to 1920. Conversely, diverse forms of deeply built rampart and ditch foundations had withstood the various ground disturbances. Today almost the entire outline of the fortification is known. Judging by the excavated archaeological features, the layout of the Frankish fortress of Esesfelth (Oldenburg II) was extraordinary (cf. Fig. 2). It consisted of a 10 m wide semi-circular rampart built from grass sods, which enclosed an area of c. 150 × 120 m. The side facing the Stör probably lacked a fortification. A 6 × 3 m stone paved box gate (German: 'Kastentor') was built into the northwestern part of the rampart. In front of the rampart, there were two moats, and connected with the outer moat at roughly right angles were eleven – presumably twelve originally – ditches of considerable sizes. In addition, a massive outer moat, which originally led from the moraine-wetland-slope in the north to that in the south, cordoned off the whole tip of the promontory.[51] Hence, by the order of Charlemagne in 810 AD Count Egbert had built a mighty stronghold that was conceived to withstand attacks of the strongest forces and served both as residence for the Frankish commander in Nordalbingia, his military and domestic household, and as garrison for soldiers.

Due to the intense cultivation of the archaeological site, building structures near the surface and occupation layers had been destroyed. Hence, unfortunately, the only traces of an assumed internal structure were a few postholes, and find material was for the largest part only preserved in the moats and ditches. Nevertheless, the latter can provide an insight into everyday life at the fortress. The artefacts consist almost exclusively of pottery sherds of locally made soft grey ware ('weiche Grauware'). Many sherds have cross- or rosette-stamp ornamentations and a few bear a decoration characteristic of early Slavic ware. Three sherds identified as Badorf ware from the Frankish Rhineland region were also found. The remaining find material includes fragments of basalt quern stones, slate whetstones, small iron and bronze fragments, as well as whorls and loom weights, which suggest that textiles were produced on site. There are no finds apart from one, a mouthpiece of a bridle from the outer moat, that may potentially provide archaeological evidence for the presence of Egbert or Saxon counts at the site ('*Egberto et comitibus Saxonicis*').[52]

The overarching strategic military purpose of the fortress of Esesfelth was to control the still unoccupied territory of Nordalbingia and prevent the Danish King Gudfred

---

50 Kühn 1995, 19; Lemm 2021a, 67
51 Kühn 1995, 18-19; Lemm 2013, 466-473
52 Annales Regni Francorum 1987, 809

from invading it.[53] An active influence in the territory was facilitated through the long-distance communication routes that enabled the Franks to respond quickly when the region was under severe threat. At the same time, the construction of Esesfelth can be seen as the initial step towards an integration of Nordalbingia into the Frankish realm. According to the Royal Frankish Annals Emperor Charlemagne ordered the establishment of a *civitas*[54] – a term describing much more than just a military base and indicating an administrative centre encompassing the surrounding area with the *castellum*, the actual fortress, representing only one element.[55] Further elements of the *civitas* of Esesfelth were the church at *Heiligenstedten*, 800 m to the west (Fig. 1.I.6). It was presumably built at the same time or shortly after the fortress, but definitely before AD 831.[56] Also a small monastery named '*Welanao*' c. 5 km to the south-east (Fig. 1.I.7) donated by Emperor Louis 'the Pious' to Bishop Ebo of Reims in AD 822/3, has been located.[57] Additionally, a settlement or commercial area, which we have to assume was beneath modern day Itzehoe (Fig. 1.I.8), where so far only a single sunken-featured building, a so-called Grubenhaus, from the 9th or 10th century has been discovered.[58]

The consequences of the incorporation of Nordalbingia into the Frankish kingdom were drastic and most probably the same as for any other territory occupied by the Franks, before. We have to assume that the whole of Nordalbingia, as Wigmodia had six years earlier,[59] became a royal domain,[60] that comital titles, land grants and privileges were introduced ('fränkische Grafschaftsverfassung') and that the Frankish legislation for Saxony (*Lex Saxonum*) and the forced Christianisation – both established years earlier in the South Elbian part of Saxony[61] – were now implemented north of the Elbe, as well. The effects of the latter are clearly indicated by the abandonment of traditional burial practises in the Nordalbingian ancestral cemeteries, during the first half of the 9th century.[62]

Having succeeded his father as Emperor in 814 Louis the Pious interfered in Danish affairs by supporting one pretender to the throne, known as Harald Klak.[63] In AD 817, it even came to the point that in order to push back Frankish control, Danes and Obodrites launched a combined attack on Esesfelth as the Frankish administrative centre and military stronghold north of the Elbe. It was probably not only the 'violent resistance' that the Franks and Saxons offered according to the Royal Frankish Annals,[64] but also

---

53   Lemm 2013, 367-368; 2021a, 68-69
54   Annales Regni Francorum 1987, 809
55   Cf. Schlesinger 1981, 119; Kühn 1995, 21; Lemm 2021a, 64, 69
56   Adam von Bremen 1961, I, ch. 20; Jankuhn 1957, 229; Struve 1965, 32
57   Rimbert 1961, ch. 13; Jankuhn, 233
58   Kersten, 307-308
59   Weidemann, 168
60   Lemm, 2014, 361
61   Springer, 56
62   Kleemann, 372-379
63   Annales Regni Francorum 1987, 814, 815
64   Annales Regni Francorum 1987, 817

the ingeniously built fortifications, which made the Obodrites and Danes give up the siege and depart.[65] The siege of 817 is the last time Esesfelth is mentioned in written sources, yet nothing is said about its actual abandonment. However, judging from the archaeological find material, it seems that the fortress was in use longer than until 817 – at least a few more decades.[66] In order to gain more control over Nordalbingia more fortresses were built on the initiative of the Franks; first in the south, at strategic nodal points, where roads connected with waterways and probably just a little later oriented towards the Slavic area, where similar fortresses existed.[67] In 834 AD, the so-called Hammaburg (Fig. 1.II.H) most probably became the successor of Esesfelth as the royal administrative and economic centre of Nordalbingia.[68] As such it became the target of a Danish attack in 845 AD, when King Horik I supposedly sent a fleet of allegedly 600 ships to plunder and destroy the town.[69]

Private fortress building – 9th/10th centuries

During the course of the first half of the 9th century, the feudal system and vassalage had become comprehensively established, and this led to profound social changes in the Frankish kingdom. Moreover, a weakening kingship and a strengthening of local powers had the effect that counts regarded conferred titles as hereditary and began to build fortresses on their own account. As an inevitable concomitant of the advancing social polarisation, the aristocratic manors were gradually moved into the fortresses.[70] Possibly, as a result of the division of the Frankish kingdom in 843, apparently a re-organisation happened in Nordalbingia and in the late 840s the fortresses known as *Kaaksburg* (Fig. 1.I.9) and *Stellerburg* (Fig. 1.II.S) were built, which remained in use for about 150 years.[71] A subsequent fortress of the destroyed Hammaburg, however, was not built before the early 10th century.[72] While the archaeological insights into the Hammaburg are very limited due to its location in the city centre of modern-day Hamburg, the excavation results for the Stellerburg and the Kaaksburg allow further conclusions to be drawn. In many cases, the fortresses in the East-Frankish kingdom from the 9th century onwards can be attributed to a 'manorial-aristocratic milieu',[73] and this is also true for the latter two.

---

65 An attempt has been made to reconstruct parts of this attack on the basis of the excavation results: Thorsten Lemm 2021a, 71-77.
66 Lemm 2013, 154; 2021a, 67-68. Information on archaeological find material from Oldenburg II: Lemm 2013, 152-155, 188, 474-476, 697 pl. 109.3-5, 698-709 pl. 110-121, 733 pl. 145.1-3, 735 pl. 147.3, 739 pl. 151. 3-5, 743 pl. 155. 2a-b.
67 Lemm 2013, 370-374; 2022, 260-261
68 Janson 2014, 273; Lemm 2014, 364; 2021a, 79, 80 end note 2, 81 end note 7
69 Lemm 2014, 364; 2021a, 79
70 Brachmann 1993, 80, 210-211
71 Lemm 2013, 195-197
72 Kablitz 2014, 75-79
73 Brachmann 1993, 210

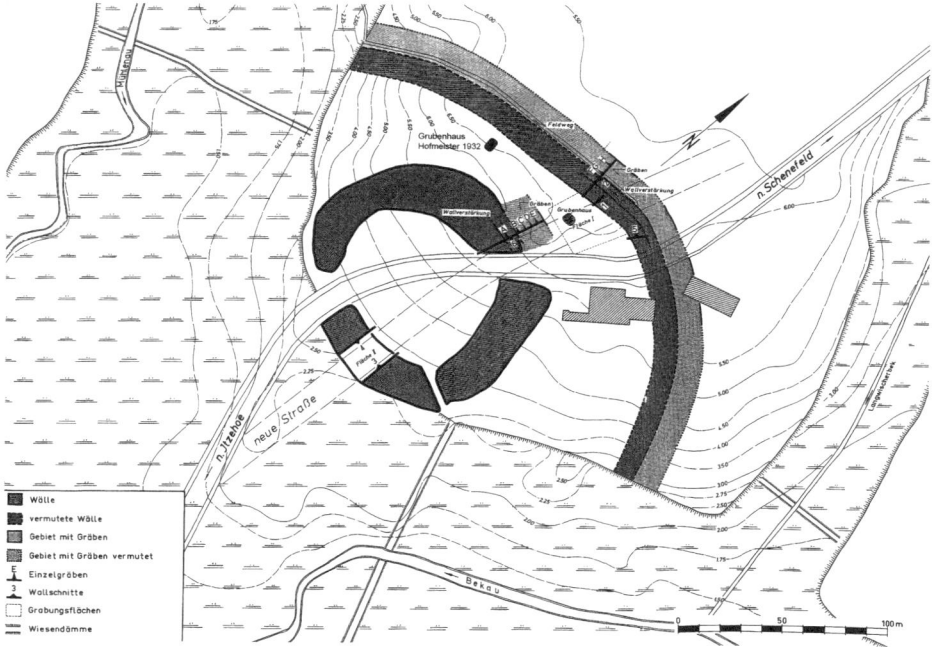

Fig. 4. *Layout of the Kaaksburg fortress consisting of a circular and a section rampart, both with one or more contemporary moats in front of them. At the outer bailey two pit houses and several settlement pits were excavated. After Lemm 2013, Ringwälle, 81 Fig. 30.*

Being placed 7 km north of the fortress of Esesfelth, the Kaaksburg is situated roughly in the centre of the meso-region discussed here. The fortress featured a section rampart sealing off the promontory and a circular rampart behind it, both with one or more contemporary moats in front of them (Fig. 4).[74] Based on the archaeological features it seems clear that the interior of the circular fortification was densely built-up.[75] Unfortunately, however, the original documentation is lost, and it is not possible to reconstruct any buildings within the ringfort based on the published excavation plan.[76] In between the circular and the section ramparts – at the outer bailey – two sunken-featured houses were excavated.[77] The separation between the living quarters at the inner and the ancillary buildings at the outer bailey may be due to the increasing social polarisation in the East-Frankish kingdom between the nobility on the one hand and their retinue and servants as well as the peasant population on the other.[78]

Besides more than 7,700 ceramic sherds – comprising the locally produced 'weiche

---

74 Section drawing through the ramparts: Lemm 2013, 53 Fig. 11
75 Lemm 2013, 92-94
76 Hofmeister 1932, plan 2; Lemm 2013, 94 Fig. 36
77 Hofmeister 1932, 53 Fig. 20; Lemm 2013, 94-95 Fig. 37, 669 pl. 81.1, 671 pl. 84
78 Cf. Brachmann 1993, 210

Fig. 5.

Hoard find deposited in the Kaaksburg, perhaps worn as a necklace: original dirhams decorated with silver wires, silver-plated beads with filigree granulation decoration, different types of carnelian and rock crystal beads. Photo: Stiftung Schleswig-Holsteinische Landesmuseen Schloss Gottorf.

Grauware', the shell-tempered 'Muschelgrusware' and Slavic ware – as well as spindle whorls, loom weights, slate whetstones and basalt querns also more than 200 metal objects have been found.[79] Axes, knives, keys, a ploughshare, shears, scale weights, fishing hooks, an ankle shackle, fire steels, an oval brooch and chest fittings reflect everyday life at the fortress. Weapons such as lance heads, arrowheads, a seax and a sword (fragment) point to the military household or even to the count himself. Pieces of riding equipment – different types of bridle bits, several prick-spurs and horseshoes – clearly indicate the presence of persons of higher social rank, probably the nobility. The same may be true for a hoard deposited within the ringfort around 925 AD,[80] the components of which have been interpreted as a necklace (Fig. 5).[81]

Judging from the significant culture-historical monuments and archaeological sites in the vicinity, one would expect that the Kaaksburg as elite residence would have been built further north.[82] 5.7 km north of the fortress, and 2 km north of the aforemen-

---

79 Information on the archaeological find material from the Kaaksburg: Lemm 2013, 487-497, 712-732 pl. 124-144, 733 pl. 145.6-8, 734 pl. 146.1,4-6,9,14-16,21, 735 pl. 147.1,7,9, 737 pl. 149.2-3, 738 pl. 150.3, 739 pl. 6-9, 744-752 pl. 156-164.
80 Wiechmann 1996, 130
81 Hofmeister 1932, 77, Fig on p. II
82 Cf. Struve 1965, 51

tioned Krinkberg with the elite burial ground and the silver hoard, in today's village of *Schenefeld*, a settlement began to emerge in the years around 800 AD, of which two large rectangular sunken featured houses or Grubenhäuser (5.2 × 3 m and c. 5.3 × 4 m) were excavated in 2007 (Fig. 1.I.10).[83] Only 150 m south of the settlement, according to written sources,[84] a church was built before 848 AD (Fig. 1.I.11).[85] Apparently this happened by detaching a part of the farmland from the old, originally larger area of Pöschendorf for the foundation of the church. Hence, the act of founding the Schenefeld church took place through corresponding land endowment from Pöschendorf, which Karl Wilhelm Struve[86] would most likely see as an act of will by a lord who had significant landholdings. Following from Adam von Bremen's narrative,[87] '*Scanaveld*' (Schenefeld) was the central place of the so-called Holstengau, the settlement district surrounding the river Stör.[88] From a macro perspective, the primary aim of the construction of the fortress seems to have been the establishment of a fortified residence of a count in the heart of the Holstengau. From a military point of view at the meso level, however, the closest defensible position for a fortress existed in the immediate vicinity of Schenefeld only 5.5 km to the south, at the site where the Kaaksburg was actually built – on the moraine spur, which protruded into the fluvial valley of the Bekau stream. In theory, it is at least possible that the Kaaksburg could also have been the temporary administrative centre for Nordalbingia after the destruction of Hammaburg. In any case, it was a fortress of some significance, being apparently one of only two fortresses in the Nordalbingian area in the second half of the 9th century and one of three in the 10th century. Judging from the find material the Kaaksburg may have been in use until the late 10th or early 11th century.[89]

Private fortress building – late 10th/11th centuries

In 1974/75 Hans Hellmuth Andersen investigated a fortress within present-day Itzehoe that was built on a former peninsula in the Stör river bend (Fig. 1.I.14).[90] He concluded that it originally was a ring-shaped earth-and-wood-rampart built in two phases. The

---

83   Tummuscheit 2008, 48-49
84   Rimbert, ch. 22; Adam von Bremen, II, ch. 17
85   Jankuhn 1957, 230; Struve 1965, 45-46. Approximately 70 m west of the church, furthermore, also High Medieval pit-houses were discovered (Fig. 1.I.12). The excavation also yielded a significantly older silver coin minted in Lüneburg under Duke Bernhard I of Saxony (973-1011); Lemm 2013, 571.
86   Struve 1965, 47
87   Adam von Bremen 1961, II, ch. 17
88   Just recently, a silver armring was discovered 5.5 km west of the village (Fig. 1.I.13); Tummuscheit, 2012, 58f. While the find may be seen as a further indication of the special significance of this meso-region, it should not necessarily be understood in the context of Schenefeld due to the relatively large distance.
89   Lemm 2013, 196-197
90   Andersen 1980, 12, 15-16

rampart of the first phase was almost 25 m wide with an estimated height of 6 m and surrounded an inner surface with a diameter of approximately 50 m.[91] On top of a c. 1 m high sub-construction of wood, earth and stone packing the turf core of the rampart was built, and on top of that a 1.5 m high wooden framework in sections of different lengths was erected. After its completion, this block construction was filled with a series of layers, mainly marine clay. Finally, a front embankment was constructed from heather sods.[92] Around 1180 AD, a second rampart phase was built on top.[93] The location on the marsh in a river bend and consequently also the elaborate multi-layered construction of the fortress in Itzehoe can be compared very well with the so-called 'Neue Burg' in Hamburg that was built by the Duke of Saxony, Bernhard II of the House of Billung, in the years 1021-1023. There, recent excavations were able to show that several sequential building steps had taken place in order to build the rampart. These included wooden sub-constructions, wooden racks filled with marine clay as well as sods of marine clay and a wooden framework built on top of that.[94]

Due to the fact that attempted dendrochronological dating approaches did not succeed, the dating of the first phase of the fortress in Itzehoe is still based on ceramic sherds. During the excavations, 124 pottery sherds from at least 12 different vessels, some of them in connection with a fireplace, were discovered in the front area of the fortification on top of the sub-construction of wood, earth and stone packing that was established prior to the building of the turf core of the rampart. These sherds stem from the workers who built the fortification and can probably be dated to around 1000 AD. Sherds found on the original inner surface appear to be slightly younger and may be dated to the 11th century.[95] Andersen refers to a note by the historiographer Caspar Danckwerth from the 17th century, according to which a certain 'Count Lüder Billung' is said to have fortified the new town of Itzehoe.[96] Assuming that there is a kernel of truth in Danckwerth's tradition, Andersen would like to identify this person with Count Liudger of the House of Billung, who was the brother of the reigning duke, Bernhard I, and died in 1011.[97] If Andersen's conclusion were correct, this would be a clue to the construction of the fortress before 1011. Helmold von Bosau in the 1160s mentions a Slavic siege of the 'Veste Echeho' (fortress Echeho),[98] which is usually assumed to have happened sometime around 1028.[99] A construction of the fortress of Echeho/Itzehoe around 1000 and a use until at least the 1030s is thus probable. This way it might also

---

91   Andersen 1980, 23
92   Andersen 1980, 23, 31-33 Fig. 12
93   Andersen 1980, 58, 79
94   Suchowa 2021, 230-241
95   Lemm 2013, 159-161, 199, 710-711 pl. 122-123
96   Andersen 1980, 78
97   Adam von Bremen 1961, II, ch. 44
98   Helmold von Bosau 1963, I, ch. 19
99   Brachmann 1993, 162

have served as a blueprint for the construction of the twice as large and slightly younger Neue Burg in Hamburg.

Conclusions

Judging from archaeological sites, culture-historical monuments, place names and written sources, there are various indications of power structures over a period of almost 400 years on a narrow strip of land of about 13 × 2 km. In this area of Heiligenstedten, Itzehoe and Schenefeld rich graves, hoard finds, churches and especially fortresses clearly indicate the presence of members of different elites, who were in charge based on different types of authority. The common denominator throughout time – and hence the continuity factor with regard to the title of this paper – was the three important long-distance routes that converged upon the river Stör and gave this meso-region its importance. Apart from that, the overall power-political significance of the region endured, but the actual power structures seem to have changed repeatedly over time. The latter can be observed particularly well in the shift of fortresses from the south to the north and back to the south. However, such changes are not only visible in the meso-region discussed here. As part of the Old Saxon tribal area, the Frankish and later East-Frankish kingdoms, the interpretation of these different elites and authorities in Nordalbingia can only be made in comparison with corresponding monuments and sites as well as conditions south of the Elbe and against a historical background that concerns the entire area.

Besides the fortifications at Heiligenstedten (Oldenburg I), at Aukrug-Bünzen and at Hamburg (Hammaburg I) north of the Elbe, fortresses of the 7th and/or 8th centuries have also been identified in recent years in the Old Saxon settlement area south of the Elbe, which date back to the time before the Frankish occupation.[100] As of yet, such sites are still low in number and the mostly small-scale excavations have not yielded significant archaeological material in order to interpret them satisfactorily. Hence, it is currently only possible to speculate about the function(s) of these early fortresses. Nevertheless, it is obvious that several of them were built in strategic positions, which may be seen in connection with control and protection of communication routes. Moreover, the fortifications in southwestern regions could theoretically have played a role in Frankish-Saxon conflicts prior to Charlemagne's Saxon Wars, such as those referred to in Frankish sources from the early 8th century onwards.[101] This would not contradict the assumption that the fortresses should tentatively be associated with members of elite circles of society.

The latter may also be true for the burials at the Krinkberg, of which a few were furnished with weapons, riding equipment and, to all appearances, even chain mail. According to such objects, these graves are very well comparable with burials of the 8th to early 9th century in the entire Saxon tribal area, which, on the basis of equip-

---

100 Ludowici 2019, 182-187
101 Springer 2004, 55-56; Ludowici 2019, 187 with further references

ment and grave construction, may be associated with the elite at the level of chieftain families in larger or smaller settlement districts. Conceivably, the interpretation of the graves at the Krinkberg as belonging to a chieftain family might also allow conclusions regarding the presence of 'elite' persons in the settlement district as early as the late 7th century and support the association of the double-ditch complex with this social background. This applies in particular to the secondary burial from the grave mound dated to the early 8th century, which, to all appearances, should not be too distant in time from the fortification complex. Should this assessment be correct, the Oldenburg I fortress on the Stör and the graves discovered at the Krinkberg could suggest that the meso-region dealt with here was dominated by a chieftain family – possibly even by one and the same – from about the second half of the 7th until the beginning of the 9th century. If Oldenburg I was built to control the river, the distance of c. 12 km between the fortress and the presumed elite residence in Pöschendorf need not speak against this interpretation.

With the Frankish annexation of Nordalbingia in 810 AD, the existing power structures came to an end. It must be assumed that the whole territory became a Frankish royal domain administered by counts, and so to speak, a new world order was implemented for the Saxon inhabitants, as profound changes in socio-political, judicial and religious respects took place. It is furthermore very likely, although not backed by written sources, that Egbert, the builder of Esesfelth and right-hand of Charlemagne in Saxony, was in charge of Nordalbingia in the next years and was himself bestowed with estates and landed property in the surroundings of the *civitas* Esesfelth. In contrast to Wigmodia, where the family of the Ekbertiner – descendants of Count Egbert – can be identified as landowners with named estates,[102] the land holdings of Count Cobbo – son of Egbert – 'on the northern side of the river, which is called Albia',[103] can unfortunately not be located more precisely.

The general development in the Frankish kingdom in the following decades, in which counts regarded conferred titles as hereditary and began to build fortresses on their own account, did not stop at the river Elbe. On the contrary, it can be assumed that the meso-region dealt with here gradually passed from a conquered royal domain, which had been granted as a fief, to the status of private property of a noble family. This was the socio-political background of the Kaaksburg. The first count using the fortress as residence could have been of Frankish origin – possibly even a descendant of Count Egbert – or a Saxon supporting the Frankish cause who had come from the south. On the other hand, given the short distance to the sites and monuments of traditional power structures a little further north, it cannot be ruled out that a local Saxon appointed count resided here, whose ancestors had still been buried in the cemetery at the Krinkberg. From the second half of the 10th century onwards the Billung family held the position as dukes of Saxony. The origins of this important family are obscure,

---

102 Weidemann 1976, 168
103 Traditiones Corbeienses 1843, § 349

but there are indications that the Billunger may have been related to the Ekbertiner.[104] Based on the male personal names preferred in the family ('Leitnamen') – Bernhard, Wichmann and Ekbert – individual mentions in the written sources before the 930s also allow us to trace at least presumed ancestors back to the early 9th century.[105] In view of their influence and extensive landholdings even north of the Elbe, which can now be reconstructed to a certain extent from the possessions of their descendants,[106] it is most likely that the (later?) lords of the Kaaksburg had ties to the House of Billung.[107]

It is possible, even if it cannot be decided beyond doubt based on the archaeological material, that the end of the Kaaksburg around the year 1000 was directly associated with the construction of a new fortress within present-day Itzehoe. In any case, the centre of power within the Holstengau now shifted south again, straight to the point where the above-mentioned far-distance roads converged on the river Stör. The fortress of Echeho/Itzehoe was in use in the 11th century and, along with the Neue Burg in Hamburg, was one of a series of fortresses that can be linked to noble families with ancestral homes south of the Elbe – the Billunger and the Udonen, the latter also known as the Counts of Stade.[108]

The supra-regional significance of the meso-region also persisted beyond the period dealt with here. Around 1180 AD, the Counts of Schauenburg – successors of the Billunger in Nordalbingia – converted the fortress of Itzehoe into a stone castle. Comparable to the Esesfelth fortress in the early 9th century, the castle of Itzehoe also played a role in the disputes with a Danish king – even if not the sole and decisive one. In 1227, Valdemar II unsuccessfully laid siege to Itzehoe Castle before suffering a defeat at the Battle of Bornhöved at the hands of Count Adolf IV of Schauenburg, which marked the end of the Danish hegemonic position in the area between the Elbe and Eider rivers.[109] It was not until the 14th century that the castle of Itzehoe, and thus also the meso-region, lost its importance, when the centre of power in this part of Nordalbingia was transferred to Steinburg, about 10 km further south, and hence moved out of the meso-region for the first time after about 700 years.

Bibliography

Primary sources

Adam von Bremen. 1961: *Gesta Hammaburgensis Ecclesiae Pontificum*, edited by Bernhard Schmeidler, Monumenta Germaniae Historica SS rer. Germ. 2, Hahnsche Buchhandlung, 1917. German translation: Adam von Bremen, 'Bischofsgeschichte der Hamburger Kirche', in *Quellen des 9. und 11. Jahrhunderts zur Geschichte der Hamburgischen Kirche und des Reiches*, Ausgewählte Quellen zur deutschen Geschichte des Mittelalters, Freiherr

---

104 Wenskus 1976, 276-277
105 Lemm 2014, 368-374
106 Bock 2018, 211-257, Figs. on p. 243, 272-273; Lemm 2014, 373 Fig. 18
107 Lemm 2014, 372-374
108 Bock 2018, 213-281; Lemm 2013, 199, 273-284, 286-288; 2014, 372-374
109 Andersen 1980, 79-81

vom Stein-Gedächtnisausgabe Band 11, edited by Werner Trillmich and Rudolf Buchner. Wissenschaftliche Buchgesellschaft, 137-499.

Annales Regni Francorum. 1987: *Carolingian Chronicles. Royal Frankish Annals and Nithard's Histories*. Translated by Bernhard Walter Scholz and Barbara Rogers, The University of Michigan Press.

Helmold von Bosau. 1963: *Chronica Slavorum*, edited by Bernhard Schmeidler, Monumenta Germaniae Historica SS rer. Germ. 32, Hahnsche Buchhandlung, 1937. German translation: Helmold von Bosau, 'Slawenchronik', Ausgewählte Quellen zur deutschen Geschichte des Mittelalters, Freiherr vom Stein-Gedächtnisausgabe Band 19, edited by Heinz Stoob, Wissenschaftliche Buchgesellschaft.

Rimbert, Vita Anskarii, edited by Georg Waitz. 1961: Monumenta Germaniae Historica SS rer. Germ. 55, Hahnsche Buchhandlung, 1884. German translation: Rimbert, 'Vita Anskarii', in *Quellen des 9. und 11. Jahrhunderts zur Geschichte der Hamburgischen Kirche und des Reiches*, Ausgewählte Quellen zur deutschen Geschichte des Mittelalters, Freiherr vom Stein-Gedächtnisausgabe Band 11, edited by Werner Trillmich and Rudolf Buchner. Wissenschaftliche Buchgesellschaft, 16-133.

Traditiones Corbeienses, edited by Paul Wigand. 1843. *Traditiones Corbeienses*, Brockhaus.

Secondary sources

Andersen, H.H. 1980: *Die Burg in Itzehoe*. Wachholtz.

Bock, G. 2018. *Adel, Kirche und Herrschaft. Die Unterelbe als Kontaktraum im europäischen Kontext des 10. bis 13. Jahrhunderts*. Aschendorff.

Brachmann, H. 1993: *Der frühmittelalterliche Befestigungsbau in Mitteleuropa. Untersuchungen zu seiner Entwicklung und Funktion im germanisch-deutschen Bereich*. Schriften zur Ur- und Frühgeschichte 45. Akademie-Verlag.

Brühl, C. 2001: *Deutschland-Frankreich. Die Geburt zweier Völker*. 2nd edition. Böhlau.

Hofmeister, H. 1932: *Urholstein*. Altsachsenforschung Band 1. Augustin.

Holtermann, Bart et al. ed. 2021: Viabundus Pre-modern Street Map 1.1. https://www.viabundus.eu, (released 6-12-2021).

Jankuhn, H. 1952: "Methoden und Probleme siedlungsarchäologischer Forschung", *Archaeologia Geographica*, no. 2.

Jankuhn, H. 1957: *Die Frühgeschichte. Vom Ausgang der Völkerwanderung bis zum Ende der Wikingerzeit*. Geschichte Schleswig-Holsteins 3. Wachholtz.

Janson, H. 2014: "Ansgar und die frühe Geschichte des Erzbistums Hammaburg", in *Mythos Hammaburg. Archäologische Entdeckungen zu den Anfängen Hamburgs*, edited by Rainer-Maria Weiss & Anne Klammt. Archäologisches Museum Hamburg, 262-279.

Kablitz, K. 2014: "Die Ergebnisse der Ausgrabungen 2005-2006' in *Mythos Hammaburg. Archäologische Entdeckungen zu den Anfängen Hamburgs*, edited by Rainer-Maria Weiss & Anne Klammt. Archäologisches Museum Hamburg, 67-85.

Kersten, K. 1939: *Vorgeschichte des Kreises Steinburg. Die vor- und frühgeschichtlichen Denkmäler und Funde in Schleswig-Holstein* 1. Wachholtz.

Kleemann, J. 2002: *Sachsen und Friesen im 8. und 9. Jahrhundert. Eine archäologisch-historische Analyse der Grabfunde*. Veröffentlichungen der urgeschichtlichen Sammlungen des Landesmuseums zu Hannover 50. Isensee.

Kühn, H.J. 1995: "Die Esesfeldburg' in *Heiligenstedten – Ein historisches Kleinod an der Stör*, edited by Erwin Papke. Gemeinde Heiligenstedten, 17-21.

La Baume, P. 1957: "Ein münzdatierter Grabfund der Merowingerzeit", *Offa*, no. 10 (1952).

Laur, W. 1957: "Die sächsischen Ortsnamen in Schleswig-Holstein", in *Die Frühgeschichte. Vom Ausgang der Völkerwanderung bis zum Ende der Wikingerzeit*, edited by Herbert Jankuhn (Geschichte Schleswig-Holsteins 3). Wachholtz, 22-26.

Lemm, T. 2013: *Die frühmittelalterlichen Ringwälle im westlichen und mittleren Holstein*. Schriften des Archäologischen Landesmuseums 11. Wachholtz.

Lemm, T. 2014: "Esesfelth und der Burgenbau des 9. bis 10. Jahrhunderts in Nordelbien' in *Mythos Hammaburg. Archäologische Entdeckungen zu den Anfängen Hamburgs*, edited by Rainer-Maria Weiss and Anne Klammt, 357-376. Archäologisches Museum Hamburg.

Lemm, T. 2021a: "The fight for Nordalbingia: Reconstruction and Simulation of the Danish-Obodrite Attack on the Frankish Fortress of Esesfelth in AD 817", in *Viking Wars*. VIKING LXXXIV Special Volume 1, edited by Frode Iversen and Karoline Kjesrud. Norwegian Archaeological Society, 63-84.

Lemm, T. 2021b: "Saxon Warriors, Carolingian and Ottonian Cavalry and a Southern Perspective on the Danish Equestrian Graves", in *Horse and Rider in the Late Viking Age. Equestrian Burial in Perspective,* edited by Anne Pedersen & Merethe Schifter Bagge, 281-297.

Lemm, T. 2022: "Fortifications and communication routes: The Nordalbingian fortresses from the micro, meso and macro perspectives", in *Fortifications in their Natural and Cultural Landscape: From Organising Space to the Creation of Power,* edited by Timo Ibsen, Kristin Ilves, Birgit Maixner, Sebastian Messal & Jens Schneeweiß (Schriften des Museums für Archäologie Schloss Gottorf, Ergänzungsreihe 14). Verlag Ludwig: Kiel, 249-266.

Ludowici, B. 2014: "Hamburg, Magdeburg und die Suche nach den spätsächsischen Befestigungen: Bemerkungen zu einem Forschungsproblem", in *Mythos Hammaburg. Archäologische Entdeckungen zu den Anfängen Hamburgs,* edited by Rainer-Maria Weiss and Anne Klammt. Archäologisches Museum Hamburg, 182-187.

Ludowici, B. 2019: "Schwer zu fassen. Die sächsischen Gegner der Karolinger", in *Saxones. Niedersächsische Landesausstellung 2019,* edited by Babette Ludowici (Neue Studien zur Sachsenforschung 7). Wissenschaftliche Buchgesellschaft, 294-299.

Ramm, H. 1952: Zur älteren Besiedlungsgeschichte Holsteins, *Archaeologia Geographica,* no. 2.

Schäfer, A. 2011: "Die Schwedenschanze – Ein frühmittelalterliches Zentrum an der Schwinge?", in *Flüsse als Kommunikations- und Handelswege,* edited by Felix Bittmann, Hauke Jöns, Peter Schmid, Matthias D. Schön & Wolf Haio Zimmermann (Siedlungs- und Küstenforschungen im südlichen Nordseegebiet 34). Rahden: Verlag Marie Leidorf, 343-357.

Schlesinger, W. 1981: "Burg II. §2", *Reallexikon der Germanischen Altertumskunde²* 4. De Gruyter, 118-122.

Springer, M. 2004: "Sachsenkriege", *Reallexikon der Germanischen Altertumskunde²* 26. De Gruyter, 53-60.

Stein, F. 1967: *Adelsgräber des achten Jahrhunderts in Deutschland.* De Gruyter.

Steuer, H. 1978: "Adelsgräber der Sachsen", in *Sachsen und Angelsachsen,* edited by Claus Ahrens. Veröffentlichungen des Helms-Museums, 471-482.

Struve, K.W. 1965: *Probleme der Burgenforschung im frühgeschichtlichen Holstengau.* (Sonderdruck aus 'Urkirchspiel im Holstengau'. Schenefelder Geschichtsbeiträge zum Ansgarjahr 1965). Wilhelm Constabel.

Suchowa, K.-P. 2021: "Die Neue Burg – Der Stolz der Billunger", in *Burgen in Hamburg. Eine Spurensuche,* edited by Rainer-Maria Weiss. Wachholtz, 226-243.

Tummuscheit, A. 2008: "Die Erforschung frühmittelalterlicher Grubenhäuser in Schenefeld, Kreis Steinburg", *Archäologische Nachrichten aus Schleswig-Holstein,* no. 14.

Tummuscheit, A. 2012: "Ein skandinavischer Armring der Wikingerzeit aus Bokhorst, Kr. Steinburg", *Archäologische Nachrichten aus Schleswig-Holstein,* no. 18.

Udolph, J. 1994: "hude", *Reallexikon der Germanischen Altertumskunde²* 9. De Gruyter, 460-473.

Weidemann, K. 1976: "Frühmittelalterliche Burgen im Land zwischen Elbe- und Wesermündung". *Führer zu vor- und frühgeschichtlichen Denkmälern* 30. Philipp von Zabern, 165-211.

Wenskus, R. 1976: *Sächsischer Stammesadel und fränkischer Reichsadel.* Vandenhoeck & Ruprecht.

Wiechmann, R. 1996: *Edelmetalldepots der Wikingerzeit in Schleswig-Holstein* (Offa-Bücher 77). Wachholtz.

BY MORTEN RAVN

Chapter 14
Unlocking the Mysteries of Erritsø Manor – the Maritime Aspects

ABSTRACT
Boat- and ship-finds show that different types of watercrafts were built in the early Viking Age, and that these types were built in diverse sizes. Log-boats, expanded boats and plank-built boats and ships were crafted. The watercrafts were use differently. Some types were primarily used in inland waters such as lakes, streams, fjords and bays, others for seafaring along the coast or at open sea. Bearing in mind the discussion of the navigability of the waters surrounding Erritsø manor, this chapter will discuss the manoeuvrability and seaworthiness of different early Viking Age vessels, mainly based on experimental archaeological results gained through test-sailings and trial voyages with reconstructed Viking Age boats and ships. The chapter concludes with a discussion about ships being moveable signs of power ascribing their splendour to the ports they visited.

In its heyday (AD 700-850), the waters surrounding Erritsø manor would have been buzzing with activities. Different types and sizes of watercrafts would have navigated the waters. Some used inland, in the sheltered waters of the Elbo Valley, in Eltang and Gudsø Vig and Kolding Fjord. Others used for seafaring along the coast or on the open sea passing through Lillebælt – perhaps en route to Hedeby in the south or north to Kaupang, or maybe stopping at Erritsø for a short or long stay.

As already stated by Ravn, Juel, Lindblom and Pedersen, the topographical location of the site, enabling monitoring and control of maritime traffic through Little Belt, is likely to be the key to unlocking some of the mysteries of the fortified manor.[1] Hence, an investigation of the maritime aspects of the site, such as the diversity in regard to the early Viking Age watercrafts and the building and use of these boats and ships, is fundamental for understanding Erritsø manor's function in late Germanic Iron Age and early Viking Age (650-900 AD).

---

1   Ravn, Mads et al. 2019, c. 700-850 AD'

Thus, the first aim of this chapter is to provide examples of southern Scandinavian vessel-finds dated between AD 700-950. Following this overview, I will discuss how the vessel-types, exemplified in the ship-finds, were built and used, mainly based on experimental archaeological insights gained through building and testing boat- and ship-reconstructions. Finally, I will discuss the role of large and impressively built ships as moveable signs of power for their owners, but also as mediators, transferring their splendour to the ports and other sites they visited.

Early Viking Age vessel-finds

The vessel-finds from the early part of Viking Age south Scandinavia (AD 750-900) demonstrate that many different types of watercrafts were built and used. Iron and Viking Age boat- and ship-finds from southern Scandinavia can be counted in hundreds. Especially rich in number are boat- and ship-burials.[2] However, many of the vessel-finds are only dated broadly to historical eras such as "Viking period", making it difficult to include them in the here conducted survey that focus on the early part of the Viking Age. Furthermore, bearing in mind the aim of this chapter, namely to conduct a survey of the maritime aspects of the Erritsø Manor, it will mainly be vessel-finds from Danish waters that will be presented.

However, exceptions from this spatial limit will be made. Especially with regard to the medium-sized and large plank-built ship-finds. Longer voyages were conducted in such ships, and it is therefore possible that some ships departing from ports located in all of Scandinavia and around the Baltic Sea could have navigated the waters surrounding the Erritsø manor.

The main types built were logboats, expanded boats, and plank-built boats and ships. In this chapter boats are defined as vessels smaller than 10 m and ships larger than 10 m. First, some of the logboat-finds will be presented, followed by a few cases of finds of expanded boats, and finally the chapter will put forward examples of plank-built boats and ships.

Logboats

The list of logboat-finds from the early part of the Viking Age presented here is not complete. In fact, most of the logboats found in Danish waters and wetlands are undated, making it impossible to assign them to a specific time period. However, based on construction details, choice of wooden raw material and the find-context, some of undated logboats have been dated typologically. Some of these typologically based dates are debated, and contents of Table 1 refer only the Danish-found logboats (including the two logboats from Hedeby in Northern Germany) which have been dated by either C-14-dating or dendrochronological analysis. However, judging from previous detailed studies of Danish logboat-finds from the Viking Age to modern times, it is highly likely

---

2   Müller-Wille 1974

that logboats were the most common vessel-type built and used in the Viking Age.[3] Hence, the list presented in Table 1 should only be viewed as a few examples of the once enormous fleet of logboats operating in Danish waters during the Viking Age. It is interesting to note that the early Viking Age vessel-finds from southern Norway apparently display a different situation. Here the plank-built vessels are the most common type used.[4]

Oak was by far the preferred wood species for constructing logboats. In a few cases, beech was chosen instead, but these are clearly exceptions to the rule. The length of the boats is between c. 3-6 m and all boats have a width measuring less than 1 m. They are all small vessels, and the Bronze and Iron Age traditions for building impressively long logboats, seems to have been completely abandoned in the Viking Age.

The logboats show no signs of rowlock attachments, oar ports or evidence for a mast being fixed in the boats. Hence, they were powered by paddling or punting. The overall design of the boats is quite diverse, but with regard to details, several common features can be found, such as bulkheads and transverse ridges hewn out of the log. Furthermore, two of the logboats appear to be unfinished, which allows for observations in regard to the building process of early Viking Age logboats. The building of logboats will be discussed in greater detail below.

Expanded boats

The key element in an expanded boat is the bottom component. This component is crafted from a tree trunk that is first hollowed-out and subsequently heated in order to expand the trunk beyond its own natural dimensions. To prevent the sides of the now expanded trunk from bending inwards, transverse frames are inserted and if spaced correctly in the boat, the hull form will hold its expanded shape. The expanded bottom component can serve as a boat as is or stems, keel and strakes can be added to the bottom component, transforming the boat into a more complex and seaworthy vessel.

The boat-type was first recognised in the archaeological record in the late 1960s during the excavation of the Iron-Age grave-field at Slusegård on Bornholm, Denmark. Here, some of the deceased were buried in small boats, which were interpreted as expanded boats due to evidence of collapsed boat-sides caused from the removal of frames before reuse as coffins.[5] However, this interpretation, proposed by Ole Crumlin-Pedersen, was first questioned by Sean McGrail[6] and later by Ole Thirup Kastholm.[7] They are not convinced by the evidence presented and both stress that more detailed wood fibre analysis is required before concluding that the boat-type was in use before the Middle Ages.

---

3 Bork-Pedersen 2011
4 Müller-Wille 1974
5 Crumlin-Pedersen 1991
6 McGrail 2001, 179 & 207
7 Kastholm 2018

In an experimental archaeological project conducted by the Viking Ship Museum in Roskilde from 2005-2007, three reconstructions of Iron and Viking Age expanded boats were built. Before building the reconstructions, the two best preserved boat-finds, the Björke Boat and the Tuna in Badelunda 75, were re-examined by both archaeologists and boatbuilders. Having seen the boat-finds themselves, they were convinced that the boat's bottom components were indeed expanded.[8] However, one has to admit that we still lack detailed wood fibre analysis of the presumed expanded bottom components, leaving us with some degree of uncertainty. Acknowledging this caveat, and based on the evidence known to date, I find the evidence supporting the existence of expanded boats from the Iron and Viking Ages convincing, but the reader should bear in mind the scholarly opponents' objections to this assumption.

Table 2 lists the expanded boats from Scandinavia and the West-Baltic Sea region dated to AD 700-950. They are few in number, and it is only Boat 75 from Tuna in Badelunda that has been subject to thorough investigation.

Plank-built boats and ships

The plank-built vessel-finds from the early Viking Age are truly diverse. Table 3 lists examples of both small boats and large ships. The smallest of the three boats found on board the Gokstad Ship are only 6.5 m long, while the largest plank-built vessel from this period, the Gokstad Ship, is approximately 23 m long. Only a small number of the vessel-finds listed on table 3 were powered exclusively by oars. All other examples were multi-powered vessels that could either be propelled by oars or sail. Whether or not this is a general feature with regard to the South-Scandinavian plank-built vessels from the early Viking Age cannot be concluded based on the investigation conducted in this chapter. However, it seems reasonable to assume that many of the small plank-built boats were powered exclusively by oars, whereas the larger boats and ships often were powered with a possibility to use either oars or sail.

The early Viking Age ship-finds were mostly multi-purpose watercrafts used for transport of both people and cargo. However, judging from the ship-finds, a new ship-type, with a long and narrow hull, began to be built around AD 900. This ship-type, the earliest example of which is the Ladby Ship, were designed to conduct the speedy transport of an armed crew. Later, around AD 1000, specialised cargo ships were built as well. The cargo ships were designed to transport a large amount of cargo and could be operated by a small crew. The specialised cargo ships were propelled by sail only, and some of these ships were ocean-going, designed to navigate the North Atlantic Sea.[9]

The best-known ship-finds from the Viking Age are without doubt the two burial-ships from Oseberg (21.5 m long) and Gokstad (23 m long) in Norway. These two exceptionally well-preserved ships are built with a degree of splendour not seen in any

---

8   Crumlin-Pedersen & Jensen 2018
9   Ravn (forthcoming), 15

other ship-finds from the Viking Age.[10] However, the Oseberg and Gokstad Ships are not the only burial-ships dated to the early part of the Viking Age. In Norway, near the Norwegian town of Sarpsborg, another burial mound contained an 18.5 m long ship, the Tune Ship, and more burial-ships are found in Norway, for example the Grønhaug Ship (c. 15 m long) and the recently discovered Gjellestad Ship (c. 23 m long).[11]

In Denmark and northern Germany, only two ship-finds can be dated to the early part of the Viking Age. Both are burial-ships, one found in a large mound at Ladby on Funen and the other found in a mound erected just outside one of the most important towns of the Viking Age, Hedeby.[12] In the eastern Baltic Sea Region, there are two ship-finds dated to the late Germanic Iron Age or early Viking Age found near the Estonian village of Salme on the island Saaremaa. Both ships were powered by oars, but it is debated whether or not Salme 2 also carried a sail.[13]

Finally, there is the three plank-built boats found on board the large Gokstad Ship. The boats measure 6.5, 8.0 and 9.75 m in length. All boats were equipped with rowlocks and powered by oars, and the two largest boats also carried a mast and sail.[14]

The chapter moves on now to consider how the different vessel types and sizes were built. It is, however, not possible to analyse the building of all the individual watercrafts stated above in this chapter, but the general steps in the building sequence, and the techniques and methods utilised, will be presented.

Building boats and ships in the early Viking Age

Judging from their design, and the tool marks found on early Viking Age logboats, the building sequence appears similar to how logboats were crafted in modern times (18th-19th-century) in Scandinavia:

"[…] a suitable tree was felled and transported out of the forest. Then the rough trimming took place and the log was stored for some years in a humid environment close to the beach, where the semi-manufactured boat was buried in the ground or loaded down with stones. Then after 2, 10 or even 18 years the unfinished boat was lifted out to be trimmed down to the final finish. It has been claimed that the long storage made it easier to complete the woodworking, but also that it prevented the formation of cracks and prolonged the lifetime of the wood. The final treatment of the hull was done with the use of various sizes of adzes and other tools, even in some cases with a controlled use of fire"[15]

Storing a semi-manufactured boat for 10 years or more seems like an awfully long time to wait for finishing a logboat, and we do not know if the early Viking Age boat-

---

10 Bischoff 2020
11 Bill 2020; Paasche 2020
12 Crumlin-Pedersen 1991, 252-254; Sørensen 2001
13 Price 2016
14 Planke & Eldar Heide 2022
15 Hirte 1997, 154

builders had the same patience. However, two logboats presented in Table 1 appear uncompleted/semi-manufactured. The inner surface of Boat 2 from Haddeby has several deep cuts and a much 'rougher' surface appearance compared to the other logboats. It seems as if the work was abandoned just before conducting the final finishing of the vessel. Perhaps the boat was never lifted out of the water after the above-mentioned process of storing?[16] In another case, the Mødbjerg boat, the process of hollowing-out the tree trunk was stopped, probably because of unsuitable features discovered in the trunk while conducting the initial work building the boat.[17]

The expanded boats from the early Viking Age are few in number, and it is only in one case, namely the boat in grave 75 from Tuna in Badelunda, that a detailed investigation of the boat has been conducted. In 2005, the Viking Ship Museum initiated a project aimed at presenting the archaeological evidence of Iron and Viking Age expanded boats in Scandinavia and to reconstruct three examples of the boat type: The boat from grave 1131 at Slusegård on Bornholm, dated to 1st-2nd centuries AD, the boat-find from Bjørke in Sweden, dated to 3th-6th centuries AD, and the boat in grave 75 from Tuna in Badelunda, Sweden, dated to the 9^{th}century AD. In the following, I will briefly present how the boat from Tuna in Badelunda was probably built, based on the details and insights that boatbuilder Hanus Jensen gained while reconstructing the boat-find.[18]

For building the 7 m long and 1.2 m wide boat, two large and straight grown pine trees were required, each with a trunk diameter of approximately 50 cm. One trunk was used for the bottom component, and the other was used for crafting the planks for the boat. Furthermore, thick pine branches were needed for the stems, and curved roots of spruce for crafting the frames.

After procuring the raw materials needed, the trunk for the bottom component was first cut and then hollowed out, followed by the process of expanding the log using heat. The expanding process prove to be a very challenging endeavour with several pitfalls, but finally the bottom component research the desired form and thickness, and the fore and aft stems could be attached with treenails and wedges (Fig. 1). The boat was also fitted with a keel, and with the keel and stems in place, a 30 cm wide plank of pine was lashed to the bottom component and the stems on both sides. Finally, the frames were inserted and fastened to the hull with treenails and wedges, and the boat was equipped with the possibility to mount rowlocks on the gunwale. It is presumed that the boat was powered by both rowing and paddling and maybe also by punting.

The building sequences for the plank-built vessels crafted in the Viking Age are fundamentally alike – from the smallest boats to the largest ships. The dimensions of the components and details differ, but the basic principles and the constructional concepts are highly similar.

16 Hirte 1997
17 Bork-Pedersen 2011, 50
18 Crumlin-Pedersen & Jensen 2018, 72-95

Expanding the bottom component for the reconstruction of the boat from Tuna in Badelunda. Photo: Werner Karrasch, Viking Ship Museum in Roskilde.

Fig. 1.

First, an appropriate building site was chosen and all the necessary raw materials procured. Then, the keel was laid and the aft and fore stems were raised. The keel and stems were nailed, spiked and riveted together. The next step was to fasten the planks of the first strake to the keel using rivets and spikes, followed by the rest of the planking up to the turn of the bilge. The planking seams were sealed with inlaid caulking material and fixed together with rivets and roves. Then the floor timbers were installed and held together with the planking using treenails locked with wedges. The next step was to install further strakes of planking before reinforcing the hull with stringers, beams and knees. If the vessel was built to carry a mast and sail, the keelson was installed before the beams. Spikes and treenails were used to hold the vessel components together, and finally, after the last planks and extra reinforcements of the hull were laid in the ship, the vessel was equipped with steering and propulsive components and other equipment, depending on the use of the vessel.[19]

Until now, no shipbuilding sites have been found near Erritsø manor. But if war fleets really did assembly in Gudsø Vig, as suggested by Anne Nørgård-Jørgensen[20], or if large ships passing through Lillebælt would occasionally have stopped to visit the manor, it is highly likely that repairs would have been conducted somewhere near the Erritsø manor complex. Judging from the many maritime trading endeavours and large

---

19 Ravn (forthcoming) 29-31
20 Nørgård Jørgensen 2002

seaborne military operations conducted by the Vikings, there must have been hundreds of boat and ship repair sites in Scandinavia, and many dedicated shipbuilding sites too. The traces of such activities are, however, easily perishable. Hence, today only a handful of sites have been assigned as having shipbuilding-related activities, but it is safe to say that we have only found a fraction of the Vikings' formerly operational shipbuilding sites – the rest are waiting to be discovered.[21] In the next section, I will welcome all on board the vessels of the Vikings to investigate how they were used.

Voyaging in different waters – usage, manoeuvrability, seaworthiness and travel speed

Some of the vessel-finds presented in Tables 1-3 have been reconstructed, but most of them have not. It is possible to extract estimated sailing capabilities based on the dimensions and hull structure of a vessel-find. However, a reconstruction – digital and physical – is a precondition for conducting a more detailed investigation of a vessel-find's usage, manoeuvrability, seaworthiness and travel speed, and since none of the logboat-finds listed in Table 1 have been reconstructed, the crew size and cargo capacity stated are only estimates. Nevertheless, ethnographic and historical accounts of paddling and punting logboats of similar sizes and hull structures indicate that lakes, streams and rivers most be considered as their main areas of use, and under favourable conditions even fjords, bays and coastal waters can be navigated in logboats (table 4).[22]

Only one of the four early Viking Age expanded boats has been reconstructed: the boat in grave 75 from Tuna in Badelunda, Sweden. This reconstruction had room for a crew of maximum 4 persons and was powered by punting, paddling or rowing.[23] However, only very few punting, paddling and rowing tests have been conducted with the reconstruction, and no cargo capacity experiments have been performed. This leaves us with only an estimate of the original boat's operational ability for carrying cargo.[24]

It is, however, possible to shed more light on the sailing capabilities of this boat-type, due to a recently conducted experimental voyage on Ukrainian and Russian rivers. In August 2021, Thomas Frank embarked on an expedition paddling 1,936 km from Staraja Ladoga to Astrakhan in a traditionally-built expanded boat comparable to the early Viking Age expanded boats. Using the rivers Volkov, Sjas, Tikhvinka, Sominka, Goryn, Tjagoda, Tjagodosja, Mologa and Volga, the voyage lasted 38 days. This equates to an average daily distance made good of 51 km, underlining how efficient and fast river transport can be. The voyage conducted by Thomas Frank also resulted in new insights with regard to the manoeuvrability and seaworthiness of an expanded boat. Hence, it seems likely that expanded boats were primarily used on inland waters, such as lakes,

---

21   Ravn (forthcoming), 28-29
22   Rasmussen 1953
23   Crumlin-Pedersen & Jensen 2018, 88-90
24   At the moment (2022) trials with the Tuna in Badelunda-reconstruction are conducted by the experienced mariner Ole Sand and the present author. More trials are planned in 2023.

Vessel-find	Date, AD	Length (L); Width (W) in m.	Tree species	Propulsion	Crew size	Cargo capacity (in kg)
Albæk 2	C-14: 900-1160	L: 1.12 (not full length) W: 0.38 (not full width)	Oak	Paddling or punting	–	–
Albøge	C-14: 880-1160	L: 5.6 W: 0.9	Oak	Paddling or punting	Estimated: 2-4	Estimated: 100-250
Gelsted Nederland	C14: 780-1040	L: 5 (not full length) W: 0.7	Oak	Paddling or punting	Estimated: 2-4	Estimated: 100-250
Gåsekrog	C-14: 900-1160	L: 1.3 (not full length) W: 0.57	Oak	Paddling or punting	–	–
Haddeby 1	C-14: 766-1018	L: 5 W: 0.51	Oak	Paddling or punting	Estimated: 2-4	Estimated: 100-200
Haddeby 2	C-14: 868-1033	L: 3.8 W: 0.76	Beech	Paddling or punting	Estimated: 2	Estimated: 100-200
Kirkebjerg, Gram	C-14: 880-1030	L: 3.18 W: 0.75	Oak	Paddling or punting	Estimated: 2	Estimated: 100-200
Lunden Vrå	Dendro: 854 +/- 25	L: 3.2 W: ?	Oak	Paddling or punting	Estimated: 2	Estimated: 100-200
Mødbjerg	Dendro: 868 +/- 25	L: 4.25 W: 0.70	Oak	Paddling or punting	Estimated: 2-3	Estimated: 100-200
Nr. Kongerslev	C-14: 625-1035	L: 4.4 W: 0.75	Oak	Paddling or punting	Estimated: 2-3	Estimated: 100-200

Table 1.

Examples of C-14 or dendro-dated logboats from the early Viking Age found in Danish waters and wetlands. Data from: Christian Hirte's chapter 'Logboats' in the book Viking-Age Ships and Shipbuilding, *and Karen Bork-Pedersen's book* Stammebåde *(see Bibliography). Table: Morten Ravn, Viking Ship Museum.*

streams and rivers and on fjords and bays. Under favourable conditions coastal voyages may even have been undertaken (table 4).[25]

The plank-built vessels from the early Viking Age came in many designs and sizes. This, of course, influenced the sailing capabilities of these vessels. The small plank-built boats – for example the small and medium-sized boats from the Gokstad-find – could

---

25   A research paper, Use of local nautical technology along the Dnepr & Volga routes, presented 10 March 2022 by Thomas Frank at the Viking Ship Museum in Roskilde. Thomas Frank has kindly allowed me to share the here stated data and insights.

Vessel-find	Date, AD	Length (L); Width (W) in m.	Tree species bottom component	Frames	Planks	Propulsion	Crew size	Cargo capacity (in kg)
Hasnæs 1, Denmark	C-14: 7th-8th centuries	L:? W:?	oak	yes	?	Rowing	–	–
Fiholm, Sweden	C-14: 10th century	L: 3.5 (Not full length) W:?	pine	yes	?	Paddling or punting	–	–
Kazimierz Pomorski, Poland	Dendro: 10th century	L: 9.35 W:?	oak	?	?	Paddling or punting	Estimated: 5-6	Estimated: 300-400
Tuna Badelunda 75, Sweden	Grave context: 9th century	L: 7.0 W: 1,2	pine	Yes	Yes	Paddling, punting and maybe rowing	2-4	Estimated: 200-300

Table 2. *Expanded boats found in Scandinavia and the West-Baltic sea region, dated to AD 700-950. Data from: Ole Crumlin-Pedersen's chapter 'Bådgrave og gravbåde på Slusegård' in the book* Gravformer og gravskikke. Bådgravene, *and Ole Crumlin-Pedersen's and Hanus Jensen's book* Viking and Iron Age expanded boats *(see Bibliography). Table: Morten Ravn, Viking Ship Museum.*

navigate lakes, streams, rivers, fjords and bays, and could be used for coastal sailing under favourable conditions. And since the small plank-built boats often had more freeboard than the logboats and expanded boats, they could even be used for short crossings of open sea, provided that the weather conditions were favourable (Table 4).

The rowing tests conducted with the Viking Ship Museums reconstructions of the small Gokstad Boat show that this lightly-built boat is no easy boat to operate. However, if handled correctly the boat is a fast and seaworthy vessel that can be rowed through the water by two rowers using the boat's four oars. The estimated top speed for oars is 4-5 knots and an average speed is estimated to be 2-3 knots. The rowing tests conducted with the Viking Ship Museum's reconstructions of the large Gokstad Boat demonstrate an even higher potential for speed. With a rowing power of ten oars operated by five rowers and a lightly-built hull, the boat has an estimated top speed for oars of 5-6 knots. Using the boat's sail for propulsion, the top speed is estimated as being 6-7 knots. The average rowing speed is therefore only slightly higher than the small Gokstad Boat, but running by sail, the large Gokstad Boat has an estimated average speed of 4-5 knots.[26]

---

26 Ravn (forthcoming)

Fig. 2.

Saga Oseberg, the newest interpretation and reconstruction of the ship found in the burial mound near Oseberg in Norway. Saga Oseberg was built between 2011-2012. The reconstruction was built based on a previously conducted, large-scale re-documentation of the original ship-find. Both the re-documentation and reconstruction process are presented in Vibeke Bischoff's PhD-dissertation from 2020. Photo: Werner Karrasch, Viking Ship Museum in Roskilde.

With regards to the medium-sized plank-built ships of the early Viking Age – exemplified by the ship-finds from Grønhaug, Hedeby, Tune and Salme 2 – no reconstructions have been built and therefore no rowing tests and test-sailings have been conducted. However, a recently conducted reassessment of the Tune Ship, resulting in a digital reconstruction by Knut Paasche, suggests that this ship's design allows for both sailing in coastal waters and on open sea. Paasche concludes that the ship might have been almost as seaworthy as the Gokstad Ship, and designed for the fast transport of people and cargo, both along the coast and between areas divided by the open sea (Table 4).[27]

---

27 Paasche, 2020

Vessel-find	Date, AD	Length (L); Width (W) in m.	Propulsion	Crew size	Cargo capacity
Gjellestad Ship	Dendro and grave context c. 800	L: c. 23 W: -	Rowing and perhaps a sail	–	–
Gokstad Boat, small	Dendro and grave context: c. 895	L: 6.51 W: 1.38	Rowing	2-3	Estimated: 400-500
Gokstad Boat, medium-sized	Dendro and grave context: c. 895	L: 8.0 W: 1.75	Rowing and sail	Estimated: 4-5	Estimated: 600-800
Gokstad Boat, large	Dendro and grave context: c. 895	L: 9.75 W: 1.86	Rowing and sail	5-6	Estimated: 800-1000
Gokstad Ship	Dendro: c. 895	L: 23.0 W: 5.0	Rowing and sail	32-40	Estimated: C. 10000
Grønhaug Ship	Dendro: c. 780	L: c. 15 W: c. 2,5	Rowing and perhaps a sail	–	–
Hedeby Ship-grave	Grave context: c. 850	L: 17-20 W: 2,7-3,5	Rowing and sail	–	–
Ladby Ship	C-14 and grave context: c. 925	L: 21.54 W: 2.92	Rowing and sail	30-36	–
Oseberg Ship	Dendro: c. 820	L: 21.50 W: 5.0	Rowing and sail	28-35	Estimated: 6000-8000
Salme 1 Ship	C-14 and grave context: 650-750	L: 11.5 W: 2.0	Rowing	Estimated: 12-15	–
Salme 2 Ship	C-14 and grave context: 650-750	L: 17.5 W: 3.0	Rowing and perhaps a sail	Estimated: 22-26	–
Tune Ship	Dendro: c. 910	L: 18.5 W: 4.9	Rowing and sail	24-30	–

Table 3. Table 3. Examples of Plank-built vessels dated to the early part of the Viking Age. Data from: The books Viking-Age Ships and Shipbuilding by Ole Crumlin-Pedersen and Ladby. A Danish Ship-Grave from the Viking Age by Anne C. Sørensen. The PhD-dissertation Reconstruction af Osebergskibet by Vibeke Bischoff. And the following articles: Arne-Emil Christensen's 'Ohthere's vessel', Douglas Price et al.'s 'Isotopic provenancing', Jan Bill's 'The Ship Graves on Kormt', Knut Paasche's 'The Tune Viking Ship Reconsidered' and Terje Planke et al.'s 'The Third Gokstad Boat'. Table: Morten Ravn, Viking Ship Museum.

Vessel types and sizes Boats are defined as smaller than 10 m. Ships are defined as larger than 10 m.	Archaeological examples presented in this chapter	Area of use
Logboats	Albæk 2, Albøge, Gelsted Nederland, Gåsekrog, Haddeby 1 and 2, Kirkebjerg, Lunden Vrå, Mødbjerg and Nr. Kongerslev	Inland waters: lakes, streams, rivers, and, under favourable conditions, also fjords, bays and even coastal waters
Expanded boats	Hasnæs 1, Fannerup, Fiholm, Kazimierz Pomorski and Tuna in Badelunda	Inland waters: lakes, streams, rivers, fjords and bays, and, under favourable conditions, also coastal voyages
Plank-built boats	The three boats from Gokstad	Inland waters: lakes, streams, rivers, fjords and bays, and, under favourable conditions, also coastal waters and short crossings of open sea
Medium-sized and large plank-built ships	Gjellestad, Grønhaug, Hedeby, Ladby, Oseberg, Salme 2 and Tune	Fjords, coastal waters and open sea
Ocean-going, large, plank-built ships	Gokstad	Fjords, coastal waters, open sea and ocean-going voyages, even under difficult weather conditions

The early Viking-Age vessel-types' areas of use. Table: Morten Ravn, Viking Ship Museum. Table 4.

A similar upgrading of a ship-find's presumed manoeuvrability and seaworthiness has also been demonstrated for the large plank-built ship found in the burial mount near Oseberg in Norway (Fig. 2). In a recently defended PhD-dissertation, *Rekonstruktion af Osebergskibet – Form, konstruktion og function*, Vibeke Bischoff concludes that: 'The present work disproves former scepticism and confirms that the Oseberg Ship was originally technically advanced and seaworthy'.[28]

The medium-sized and large plank-built ships were constructed with different designs. Some were built primarily for the speedy transport of a large crew, for example the Ladby Ship, while others, such as the Oseberg and Tune Ships, were built for transporting both people and cargo. Finally, large ships, such as the Gokstad Ship were built in a design that allowed for long ocean-going voyages.[29] This was clearly demonstrated as early as 1893, during the impressive North Atlantic voyage from Bergen to Newfoundland, conducted by Magnus Andersen on board the Gokstad reconstruction *Viking* (Table 4).[30]

---

28   Bischoff 2020, 264
29   Christensen 2007
30   Andersen 1895

Moveable signs of power – some concluding remarks

Erritsø, and other aristocratic sites, are central to the on-going discussions of how power was expressed and maintained in the Scandinavian Iron Age and Viking Age. The aristocratic sites functioned as places for meetings of commercial, competitive, governmental, legal, military and social importance.[31] At some sites, the meetings might have focused mainly on one or two of these activities while other sites provided a venue for all. What really unites the aristocratic assembly sites is the importance of their location. As stated by Carroll, Reynolds and Yorke: "Power might be in the hands of a particular regime, often in the early Middle Ages [c. AD 600-1066] reinforced by military might, but it needed to be enacted at specific places."[32] Location was paramount, and in this respect the location of the Erritsø manor indicates a maritime connection, controlling the waterways surrounding the manor.[33]

It is, however, important to stress that mobile symbols of power also existed. Most significant among these were the large and beautifully built ships. Not only did these ships symbolize the power and wealth of the owners, they also conveyed some of their splendour to the ports and other sites they visited. If magnificent ships, like those from the burial-mounds at Gokstad and Oseberg, would anchor in Gudsø Vig, and the ship's crew guest Erritsø manor, the status of the manor would most likely rise considerably.

However, in order to draw the attention of such fine guests, visibility, design and a well-functioning infrastructure most have been of great importance. The aspects of visibility from a maritime perspective will be dealt with in chapter 15 and the design and layout of the manor in chapters 17 and 18. In regard to the infrastructure required to uphold the manor's functions and to supply the people living in the fortified manor, the many different types of waterways that surrounded the manor[34] surely provided the necessary conditions for transport, and with a little imagination it is possible to picture these waterways teeming with small and large vessels, transporting cargo and people.

Acknowledgements

This chapter is a revised and expanded version of a paper presented at the Jelling Workshop: *Aristocratic residences in Northern Europe* organised by Vejle Museums and the National Museum at Kongernes Jelling in October 2021. I would like to thank the organisers for the invitation to present my paper and the participating scholars at the workshop for good and motivating discussions. Following the workshop, I have been corresponding with Professor Andrew Reynolds which has been truly inspiring for me in regard to understanding the dialectic interaction between power and place – a big thanks to Professor Reynolds. Also, thanks to the editors and reviewer for constructive comments and

---

31 Caroll et al. 2019
32 Caroll et al. 2019, 33
33 Ravn et al. 2019, c. 700-850 AD
34 Lakes and streams in the Elbo Valley, the Kolding Fjord, bays such as Eltand and Gudsø Vig and the Little Belt (Lillebælt).

suggestions to improve this chapter, and finally big thanks to my colleague at the Viking Ship Museum, curator Tríona Sørensen, for correcting the English language of this chapter. Any errors or shortcomings are, however, my responsibility alone.

Bibliography

Andersen, M. 1895: *Vikingefærden: En illustreret Beskrivelse af "Vikings" Reise i 1893*. The Author.

Bill, J. 2020: "The Ship Graves on Kormt – and Beyond", in *Rulership in 1st to 14th century Scandinavia. Royal graves and sites at Avaldsnes and beyond*, edited by Dagfinn Skre. De Gruyter, 305 – 392.

Bischoff, V. 2020: *Rekonstruktion af Osebergskibet – Form, konstruktion og funktion*. Unpublished PhD-dissertation. Royal Danish Academy – Architecture, Design, Conservation.

Bork-Pedersen, K. 2011: *Stammebåde*. Moesgård.

Carroll, J., A. Reynolds & B. Yorke. 2019: "Power and Place in Europe in the Early Middle Ages", *Proceedings of the British Academy*, 224, 1-33.

Christensen, A.E. 2007: "Ohthere's vessel", in *Ohthere's Voyages. A late 9th-century account of voyages along the coasts of Norway and Denmark and its cultural context,* edited by Janet Bately & Anton Englert. Viking Ship Museum in Roskilde, 112-116.

Crumlin-Pedersen, O. 1991: "Bådgrave og gravbåde på Slusegård", in *Gravformer og gravskikke. Bådgravene,* edited by Søren H. Andersen, Birgit Lind & Ole Crumlin-Pedersen. Aarhus Universitetsforlag, 93-266.

Crumlin-Pedersen, O. 1997: *Viking-Age Ships and Shipbuilding in Hedeby/Haithabu and Schleswig.* The National Museum of Denmark, The Viking Ship Museum in Roskilde & Archäologisches Landesmuseum der Stiftung Schleswig-Holsteinische Landesmuseen, Schloss Gottorp.

Crumlin-Pedersen, O. & H. Jensen. 2018: *Viking and Iron Age expanded boats*. Viking Ship Museum.

Hirte, C. 1997: "Logboats", in *Viking-Age Ships and Shipbuilding in Hedeby/Haithabu and Schleswig,* edited by Ole Crumlin-Pedersen. Schleswig & Roskilde, The National Museum of Denmark, The Viking Ship Museum in Roskilde & Archäologisches Landesmuseum der Stiftung Schleswig-Holsteinische Landesmuseen, Schloss Gottorp, 148-168.

Kastholm, O.T. 2018: "Trods skriveborde og eksperimenter – spørgsmålet om jernalderens udspændte både er stadigvæk ubesvaret", *Arkæologisk Forum*, 39, 41-26.

McGrail, S. 2001: *Boats of the World. From the Stone Age to Medieval times*. Oxford University Press.

Müller-Wille, M. 1974: "Boat-graves in northern Europe", *The International Journal of Nautical Archaeology and Underwter Exploration*, 3.2, 187-204.

Nørgård Jørgensen, A. 2002: "Naval Bases in Southern Scandinavia from the 7th to the 12th Century", in *Maritime Warfare in Northern Europe. Technology, organization, logistics and administration 500 BC-1500 AD,* edited by Anne Nørgård Jørgensen, John Find, Lars Jørgensen & Birthe Clausen. Publications from the National Museum, 125-152.

Paasche, K. 2020: "The Tune Viking Ship Reconsidered", *International Journal of Nautical Archaeology* 49,1, 29-48.

Planke, T., S.E. Øya & E. Heide. 2022: "The Third Gokstad Boat: The Documentation and Context of a Viking Age Boat", *The International Journal of Nautical Archaeology,* (published online).

Price, Douglas T., J. Peets, R. Allmäe, L. Maldre & E. Oras. 2016': "Isotopic provenancing of the Salme ship burials in Pre-Viking Age Estonia", *Antiquity*, 90, 1022-1037.

Rasmussen, H. 1953: "Hasselø-egen. Et bidrag til de danske stammebådes historie", *Kuml*, 15-46.

Ravn, Morten. 2016: *Viking-Age War Fleets. Shipbuilding, resource management and maritime warfare in 11th-century Denmark*. Viking Ship Museum in Roskilde.

Ravn, Morten. (forthcoming): "A 14th century Boat from Vordingborg Castle, Denmark – and the Use of Boats in Medieval Military Operations", in *Proceedings after the 16. International Symposium on Boat and Ship Archaeology*, edited by Katarina Batur, Tomislav Fabijanic & Irena Radic Rossi. University of Zadar.

Ravn, Mads, Christian Juel, Charlotta Lindblom & Anne Pedersen. 2019: "Erritsø – new investigations of an aristocratic, early Viking Age manor in Western Denmark c. 700-850 AD", in *Early medieval waterscapes Risks and opportunities for (im)material cultural exchange,* edited by Rica Annaert. Verlag Uwe Krebs, 37-45.

Sørensen, A.C. 2001: *Ladby. A Danish Ship-Grave from the Viking Age*. Viking Ship Museum in Roskilde.

BY JENS ULRIKSEN

Chapter 15
Navigating past Erritsø during the Viking Age

ABSTRACT
Lately, it has been suggested that the Viking Age site Erritsø possessed a dominating and controlling factor related to the seafaring through the nearby strait of Lillebælt. This suggestion is the point of departure for a discussion of the possibilities of controlling the seaways during the Viking Age of Denmark. Given the natural conditions of the Inner Danish Waters meaning the three straits with adjoining archipelagos connecting the Kattegat to the north of Fyn and Sjælland with the Baltic Sea to the south, the article discusses some hypothetical measures that may have secured the travelling ships a safe conduct. An organisation of security controlled by the king or his representative at Erritsø is very hard to back by archaeological or historical evidence and turns out to be no more than a hypothesis. It is concluded that the Erritsø-site does not possess the qualities and possibilities of being a factor of domination to the sea traffic of Lillebælt, and an organisation guaranteeing a safe conduct through fairways of the Kingdom may be anachronistic.

In the legend of the missionary Ansgar it is told that in AD 830 he went by ship – probably from Hedeby to Birka (circa 20 days). Halfway, the ship was attacked by Vikings.[1] The traders on Ansgar's ship fended off the attackers in the first place, but in the second round they were defeated and their ship and belongings including gifts from the emperor Louis the Pious to the king in Birka were taken. To rescue themselves Ansgar and his travel companions jumped into the water and swam to the shore.

This account does not utter a word about safe conduct or expectations of help from anyone in the situation. Therefore, this article explores from a Viking Age navigational point of view on Lillebælt the surrounding landscapes and not least the Erritsø-site with a focus on the term safe conduct. The point of departure is the excavations of the Erritsø-site and the following interpretations lately published by Mads Ravn, Christian Juel, Charlotta Lindblom and Anne Pedersen (2019). Here, the authors suggested that the

---

1   Rimbert, 1926, 62-63

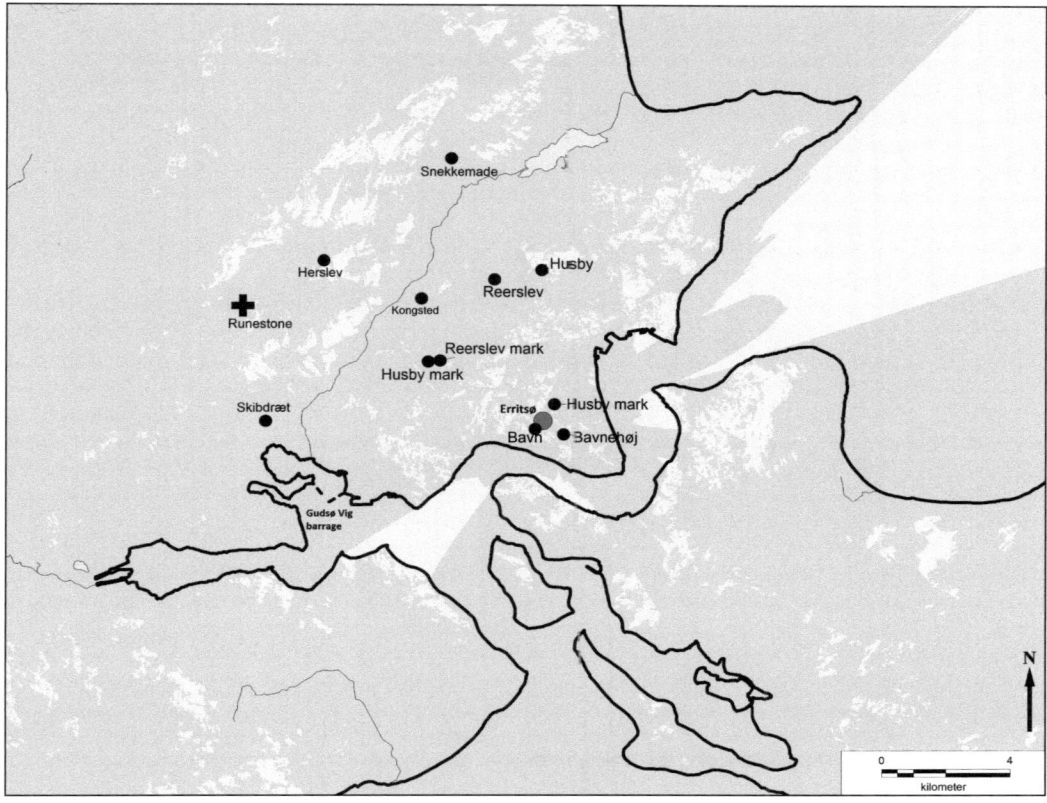

Figure 1. The northern part of Lillebælt. A view-shed analysis of the site of Erritsø based on the 2008 LIDAR scan, with line of sight calculated from the Erritsø hall 2 metres above ground surface. The areas visible from the Erritsø-site are white. Place-names relating to power, armies and ships in the hinterland are indicated. Illustration after Ravn et al. 2019.

Erritsø-site is located on the highest ground in the area overlooking the funnel-shaped northern entrance to Lillebælt as well as the mouth of Kolding Fjord.

At the same time, Erritsø is located by the East-West land-based traffic corridor connected to the assumed crossing point between Jylland and Fyn. Here, Lillebælt is more than 30 m's deep, so the crossing must have been on a floating vessel. The authors are stressing the fact that place names from the surrounding area comprise indications of a military organisation and the presence of a royal estate. In addition, there are a couple of place names related to ships. (Fig. 1.) Overall, there are indications of an area with a concentration of power and it is of course interesting to consider if this force could have been used to control or dominate the seafaring through Lillebælt.

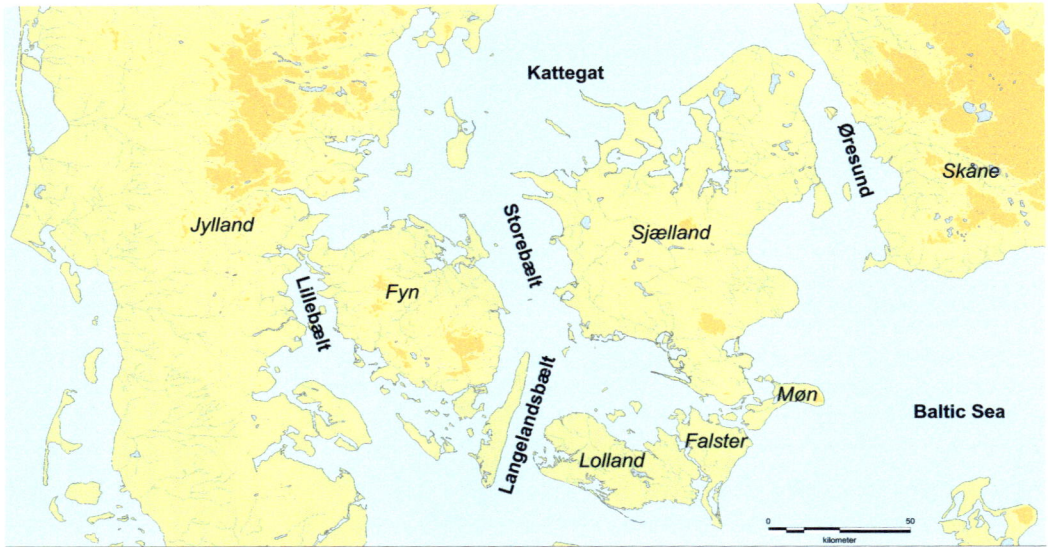

Fig. 2.   *The Inner Danish Waters.*

The natural conditions of the seaways

Lillebælt constitutes one of three fairways connecting the *Seven Seas* to the Inner Danish Waters and the Baltic Sea. (Fig. 2.) Except for Lillebælt, the two other fairways are *Storebælt* between Fyn and Sjælland and *Øresund* separating Sjælland from *Skåne*, Sweden. Looking at an ordinary map it is obvious that sizes and shapes of the three bodies of water are rather different from one another. Øresund is 55-60 kilometres long from *Helsingør* in the north to the southern point of *Amager* (the island southeast of Copenhagen) and where it is most narrow – at Helsingør – there are approximately 4.6 kilometres between the coasts. This is more or less the same distance as between the island of Amager and the island of *Saltholm* to the south. Besides the islands of Amager and Saltholm in the Copenhagen area, the island of *Hven* is situated in the northern part of Øresund. The islands are surrounded by relatively deep waters to a Viking ship type and, thus, constitute no navigational problems.

Storebælt – including *Langelandsbælt* – is approximately 105 kilometres long from a line between the promontory of *Asnæs* on Sjælland and *Fyns Hoved* in the north to a line between the southern cape of *Langeland* and the West coast of *Lolland*. The fairway is rarely less than 20 km wide, but between Langeland and *Omø* there is around 11 kilometres and from Langeland to *Albuen* on Lolland there is approximately 10 kilometres. Taking the small island of *Sprogø* into account it is situated in the middle of the Storebælt around 7.5 km to both Sjælland and Fyn. The islands of *Musholm*, *Agersø* and *Omø* are located close to Sjælland, while *Romsø* is just off the coast of northeastern

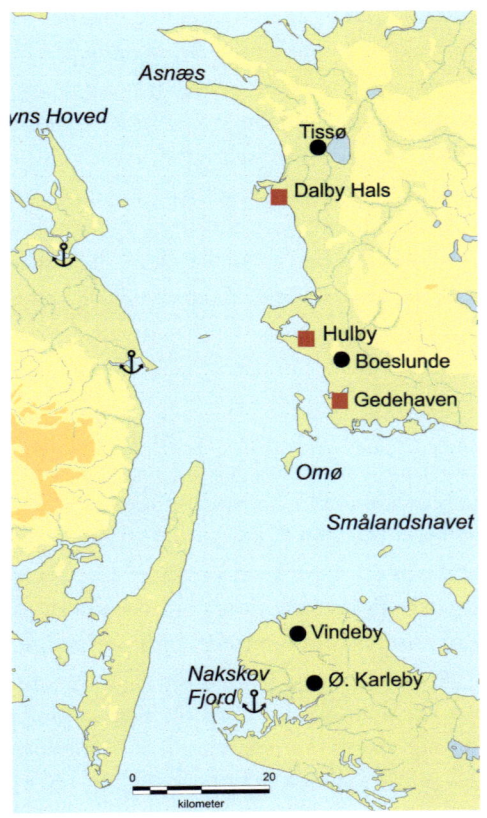

Storebælt and Lillebælt including relevant placenames. Landing sites: (red square) and natural havens (anchor).

Fig. 3.

Fyn. Storebælt offers deep water, also close to the coast, but there are tricky grounds with shallow water between Langeland and Fyn.

Lillebælt is circa 50 km long from the modern town of *Fredericia* in the north to the south point of the island of *Bågø*. Contrasting the other two fairways, the northern part of Lillebælt is winding and narrow – at one place there is less than 600 metres across. Further, there is a variety of islands, capes, promontories and adjoining fjords, especially in the northern part of Lillebælt. In the Southern part, we find shallow water – circa 1 metre deep – around the small islets of *Bastholm* and *Græsholm* to the northeast of the island of *Årø*, but knowing the course it is without consequence since deep waters are close by on both sides of *Bågø*.

Historically, Øresund has been the most important thoroughfare into and out of the Baltic Sea. It offers the shortest distance to all destinations east of *Falster* and uncomplicated sailing conditions.

Sailing to or from the westernmost part of the Baltic is another story. In that case, Storebælt or Lillebælt provide shorter routes. This seems to be confirmed by the written account in the *Old English Orosius* from the late 9th century. Here, Ottar of Hålogaland describes his trip from Northern Norway via *Skiringssal* in South Norway to *Hedeby* on the border between Danes and Saxons.² Because of strange place names like '*Sillende*' as well as a well-known place name like '*Gotland*' in a today unfamiliar way connected to Jylland and imprecise references like '*many islands*' and '*the islands belonging to Denmark*' it has been debated which route Ottar actually followed through the Inner Danish Waters.³ It is agreed, though, that Ottar must have sailed through either Storebælt or Lillebælt, but neither the description nor attempts to establish the shortest distance give us a firm clue of the route. A shorter distance may not have been preferred if it was difficult or risky to navigate compared to a slightly longer distance. Furthermore, the actual weather conditions and wind direction most likely have influenced the choice of route.

A safe conduct

The risky part of sailing is not only a matter of natural obstacles like winds, currents, reefs, sand bars, and grounds. It may also have been a matter of having a safe conduct entering foreign territory, either relying on one's own resources (that is, enough fighting-able men on-board) or aided by guarantees from the significant supremacies in the area. Considering the latter – if it existed how could it have been working? Ottar was underway for more than 30 days and even though his account does not mention stops for the night, it would not have been possible to make the journey without landing several times. Was it necessary to negotiate with each magnate controlling a landing site along the route? Was it a time-honoured privilege handed down through generations to travel along established routes? Or did a king assign the privilege of safe conduct within his realm to foreign traders and consequently a man like Ottar could fly a banner or shield from his mast, or present some kind of token when needed, showing his acquired status to everyone?

That kings had interests in securing safety for traders is illuminated in the *Annals of Fulda*. For the year AD 873 – more or less the time of Ottar – it is noted that peace between King Louis the German of East Frankia and the Danish Kings Halfdan and his brother Sigurd was confirmed so that trade between the kingdoms could continue unhindered.⁴ How this guarantee was proclaimed and secured in real life we do not know. Moreover, neither do we know if it had any influence on the conditions at sea where the Saxon subjects of King Louis were no threat to anyone.

A hypothesis of a safe conduct at sea

However, if we for the sake of argument follow the hypothesis that Ottar had a general guarantee for a safe conduct, where would his ship and cargo be most safe on a sea occasionally roamed by ships loaded with Vikings on the lookout for loot? Sailing in open waters a ship crew would have the opportunity to spot other ships from a distance. But

---

2   Bately 2007
3   E.g., Crumlin-Pedersen 1983, 36-42; Englert 2007; Ulriksen 2009, 135-138.
4   Albrectsen 1976, 98-99

a relatively slow transport ship may have had difficulties outrunning a light, long ship under sail or with oars carrying no other cargo than warriors. In other words, being 7-8 kilometres from the shore in Storebælt under attack from a foe a guarantee of safe conduct would not be of much help. Did the king have ships patrolling the fairways in order to fend off Vikings to the benefit of the traders? This may be a comforting thought, but it would have demanded a number of ships in action and an organisation behind it to be effective in any respect. An example of such a naval organisation is known from the Great Northern War (1701-1720) when in 1711 the Danish Admiralty launched a plan for convoying trading ships in Danish waters. Frigates and smaller vessels should protect convoys sailing to the north of Lillebælt connecting Copenhagen and a number of ports in East Jylland. The northern part of Storebælt was covered by a frigate, while a smaller vessel controlled the Southern part of Storebælt and the thoroughfare in *Smålandshavet*. A minor vessel was patrolling along the north coast of Sjælland and Øresund was under guard too by a frigate. From Øresund to Northeast Falster a frigate and a smaller vessel protected the convoys. Regarding Lillebælt, there was no dedicated protection, but a frigate looking out for privateers from the South coast of the Baltic Sea some 180-250 kilometres away supervised the strait. The Admiralty considered it unlikely that privateers would dare to enter Lillebælt from the north.[5] This means that at least seven vessels would be necessary to patrol the Inner Danish Waters at all times. Making this work, the ships needed provisioning regularly, and written communication with the Admiralty had to be coordinated. This was not an easy task in the 18th century and projecting this set-up back in time to the Viking Age may very well be anachronistic.

The maritime organization of the 12th century, the *leiðangr*, did not succeed in preventing the Slavonic tribes from attacking the Danish coasts for years.[6] Only the mustering of large fleets under the command of the Danish king attacking the Slavs in their homelands and the help and influence from the Duke of Saxony eventually stopped the menace.[7]

Written accounts like the *Annales Bertiniani* and later saga texts indicate that a king was not able to proactively control the enterprises of his subjects, but apparently, he could – and did – punish them with force as a reaction to 'wrong-doings'.[8]

These considerations are of course discouraging for the concept of a safe conduct in the Viking Age seafaring. But would a combination of minor organisation and high visibility be an alternative?

The safety of a narrow strait

Returning to Ottar and his trading mission in the late 9th century, he was bound for Hedeby situated in the southwest corner of the Baltic. We have already established that

---

5   Andersen 2021, 72-74
6   Helmold 1881, 176, 222-223, 278
7   Aggesen, S. 1842, Chapter 8; Albrectsen 2001, 62-65; Helmold 1881, 221, 261, 280-281; Lind 2002, 20-24
8   Albrectsen 1976, 30; Jomsvikingasaga, 91

his route is vaguely described, leaving us with at least two plausible routes for the last two days of his journey.

After following the coast of Halland and Skåne, it is likely that Ottar shifted his course by *Halland's Väderö* off the west coast of Skåne heading towards one of the three passages into the Baltic. A rough estimate indicates that the trip to Hedeby through Øresund is 410 km long, while there are circa 365 km through Lillebælt and 350 km through Storebælt including Langelandsbælt. With a 21st Century mind, it is easy to pick the shortest route. In that perspective, Storebælt is a better choice (Fig. 3). It is spacious enough to beat up against the wind, and there is deep water close to the coast where ships could find a more sheltered route than at the middle of the sea. Along the Sjælland-side, there has been a landing place connected to the residential site of *Tissø*[9] and further south there are two possible landing sites related to the area of *Boeslunde*, rich in metal detected objects.[10] Following the hypothesis, the magnates at both these locations may have played a role in guaranteeing safe passage through Storebælt. South of Sjælland there may have been a haven in *Nakskov Fjord,* maybe controlled by practitioners of power, residing at *Vindeby* some 8 kilometres away. Within an area of 1.5 km² around Vindeby are several locations rich in metal objects dating from the Roman Iron Age to the Late Viking Age.[11] Some kilometres to the South of Vindeby and 5-7 kilometres from the innermost part of Nakskov Fjord, *Øster Karleby* and *Øster Nordlunde* are among other archaeological locations producing a large number of metal objects dating from the 5th to the 11th century AD.[12] This may indicate the presence of a site of local or regional importance that could have controlled the nearby shores and waters.

Lillebælt is a very different story regarding navigability. The current in Lillebælt runs with 3-5 knots. It is shifting in relation to the wind direction, and close to the coast it is pulling in the opposite direction of the main current.[13] This may cause trouble for the unexperienced sailor. But knowing how to manage the currents along the coast, it is an advantage. Further, it is more difficult to go up against the wind through the narrow passage, and it is even risky between the islands in the southern part of Lillebælt if the skipper is unfamiliar with the shallow grounds and sand bars.

On the other hand, a ship is never far from the shore and very visible, and this may have been the advantage of using Lillebælt: The security of being noticed. This presupposes that the seaway was controlled by the king, or by his *lið* or housecarls or of one or more loyal magnates or retainers residing in the area. Additionally, the navigational challenges can be coped with by taking a local pilot on board. If such conditions were

---

9   Holst et al. 2020
10 Nielsen 1991; 1997. Crop marks suggest the presence of pit houses at Korsør Nor, cf. Museum Vestsjælland archive number MVE03559.
11 Museum Lolland-Falster archive numbers MLF00140, MLF01764, MLF01837, MLF01931, MLF02206, MLF02210, MLF02685.
12 Museum Lolland-Falster archive numbers MLF01088, MLF01089, MLF01109, MLF01167, MLF01192, MLF01867, MLF01924, MFL01930, MLF02673.
13 Lyman 2012

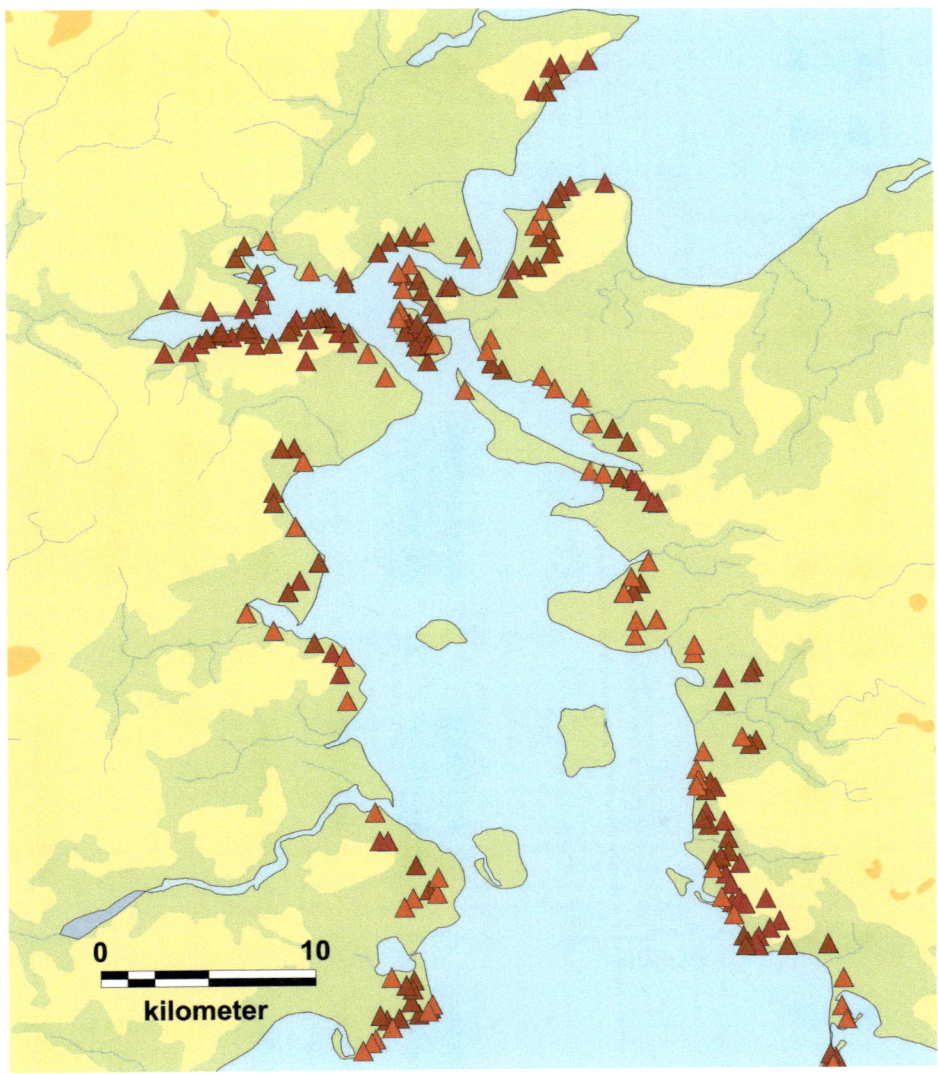

High points in the landscape along the coast of Lillebælt. Light brown triangle: 15-19 m a.m.s.l. Dark brown triangle: 20-29 m a.m.s.l. Red triangle: 30+ m a.m.s.l.

Fig. 4.

reality, it would have been difficult for roaming Vikings to board a ship and get away with it, without being observed and consequently being victims of the king's retaliation. This scenario requires an established presence and visibility of the force of the king, and that the king is backed by enough local power to implement the punishment of the culprits, effectively scaring them off.

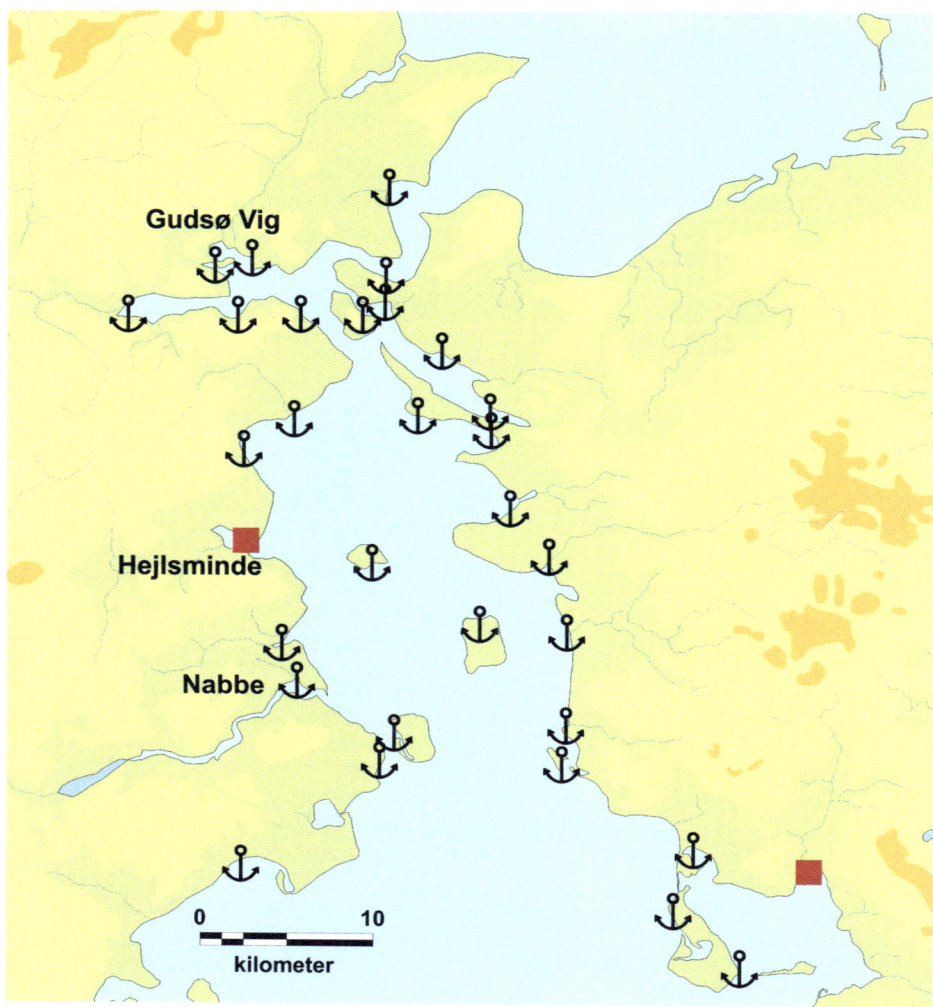

Fig. 5.　　Landing sites (red square) and natural havens (anchor) in the Lillebælt area.

The safety of being noticed
Following the hypothesis of the safety of being noticed there is no need for a large and mustered organisation. The important part would have been to observe the maritime traffic entering Lillebælt. The observers need not be warriors on the watch; instead, they could be those who worked in the fields or pastures on a daily basis. Warnings may have been given by signalling with fire and smoke from high positions, beacons along the coast, using the same model as Thorsten Lemm (2019) convincingly has suggested in relation to the *Schlei Fjord* and Hedeby. Unlike Lemm's survey there are a limited number of place names related to beacons along Lillebælt.[14] Nevertheless, there are

---

14　　Crumlin-Pedersen *et al.* (eds.) 1996, 113, 122-123

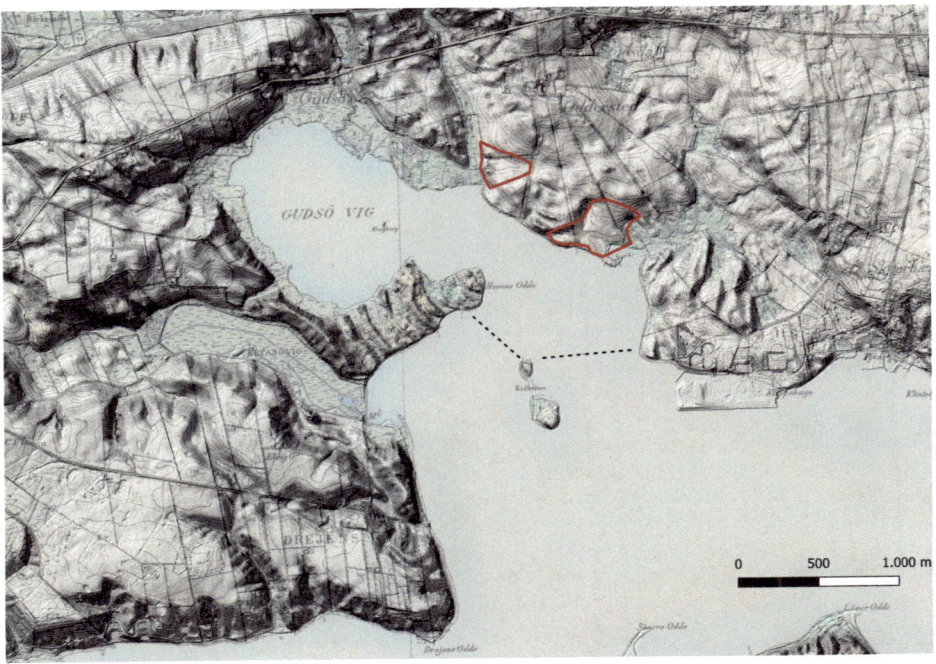

Fig. 6

Gudsø Vig. Barrage: Black dotted lines. Possible area for a landing site: Red polygons. Map: Danish Geodata Agency.

plenty of prominent positions on the coast of both Jylland and Fyn from where signals could have been given, but with no indicative place names given or remembered (Fig. 4).

Ideally, the responsive end of this chain of observations ought to have been ship crews at either end of the strait, alternatively sitting on one of the islands. Regarding the natural conditions, this would not have been a problem. Along the coasts, there is a multitude of natural havens suitable for landing sites (Fig. 5). In the north end of the Lillebælt area is an inviting natural haven called Gudsø Vig. The small kettle-shaped bay is well-protected from the weather by the surrounding terrain rising to 20-25 m above mean sea level close to the shore (Fig. 6). Furthermore, the entrance to the bay has been partly blocked by an underwater barrage. An older phase of the barrage is dated to Pre-Roman Iron Age, while later phases relevant to this paper have been constructed in the late 7th and the early 8th century, followed by maintenance during the late 10th and early 11th century AD.[15] The attraction of Gudsø Vig as something special has been nourished by its name meaning the '*Bay of the God*'.[16] Further, in the river valley of *Gudsø Å*, one kilometre to the North of the bay the place name '*Skibsdræt*' is interpreted as '*the place where you can drag a ship*'. By archaeologists Flem-

---

15   Nørgård Jørgensen 2002, 145-148
16   Jørgensen 2008, 101

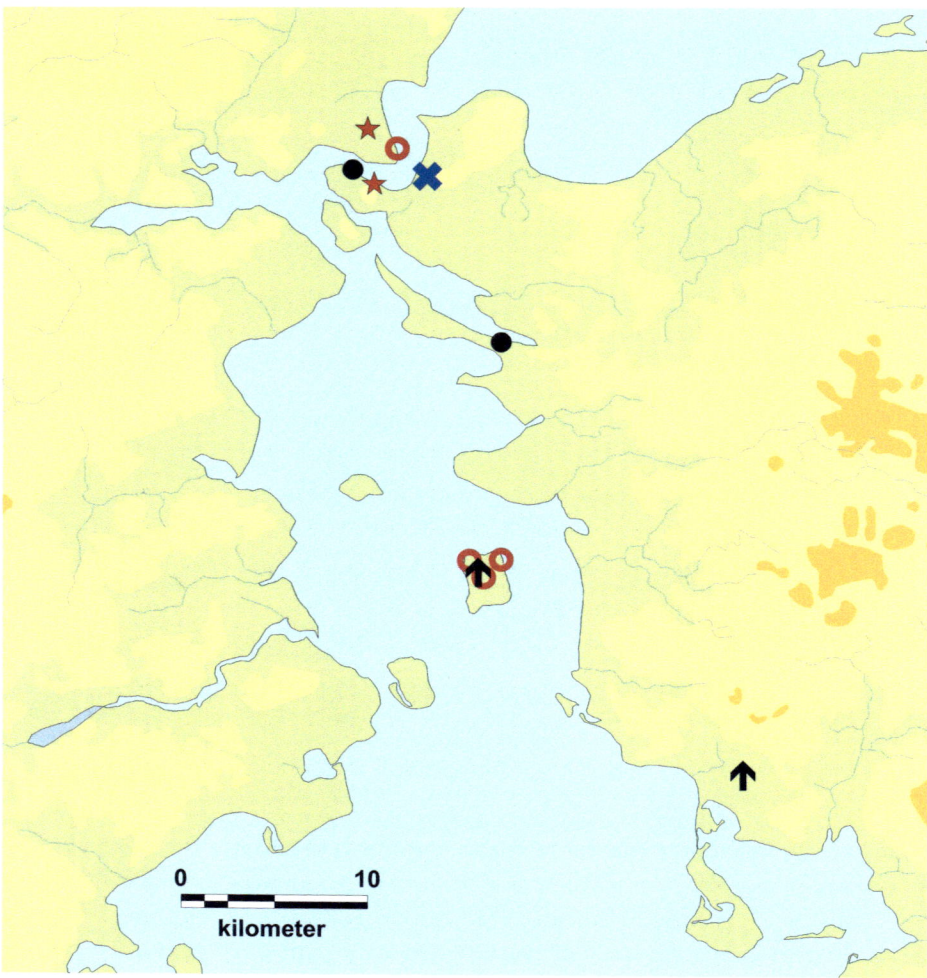

Fig. 7. Archaeological finds of a sacral character on the coasts of Lillebælt. Red circle: gold. Red star: silver. Blue cross: buried horses. Black dot: equestrian equipment. Black arrow: weapon related equipment.

ming Rieck (1992) and Anne Nørgård Jørgensen (2002, 146) Gudsø Vig is understood as '(…) an ideal place for fleet musters.' Mustering of ships before expeditions may have taken weeks and in the meantime, an increasing number of warriors would have gathered.[17] Even though the sagas mention that the Viking Age ship crews slept on their ships, sheltered by cloth, the men most likely got ashore for cooking and convenience anyway.[18] Taking excavated mustering sites into consideration, it is obvious

17   Ulriksen 2018, 349-351, 379, 399-402
18   Kveldulfsønnernes Saga, 55

that this type of activity left a clear mark on the shore, in the form of a landing site with sunken houses for weaving, smithies and other types of workshops.[19] At Gudsø Vig, the inner part of the bay has wetland along its shores and behind the wetland are steep slopes rising to about 25 metres above mean sea level. Access to firm land must have been provided on the eastern side of the bay, close to the barrages. As yet, there is no archaeological evidence of a landing site, though.

Almost midway through Lillebælt a small bay at *Hejlsminde* provides a well-protected natural haven, surrounded by several prominent points. Here, a landing site with sunken houses from the Viking Age have been partly excavated (see Fig. 5).[20]

Further south, close to the mouth of *Haderslev Fjord* is the place name *Nabbe*, situated close by a small creek. The name is connected to fishing hamlets from the Medieval Period, and there are no archaeological finds to support an earlier date.[21] Nevertheless, it offers suitable landing conditions, also for Viking Age ship types.

Even though it is possible to sketch a model to secure a safe conduct through Lillebælt and to point out some of the required elements to make it operational, it is not given that it actually worked this way. The hypothesis of a safe conduct at sea is extremely difficult to prove and it may even be anachronistic to a 9th century Danish society. It presupposes some measures of coordination and organisation, which no contemporary written sources unambiguously can confirm, and archaeological evidence is also either insufficient or lacking.

Would it be possible in AD 890 from a distance to distinguish between traders and Vikings, when both parties would be sailing a ship of the Oseberg- or Gokstad-type having crews carrying weapons? If an attack was observed ahead from the shore, the whole idea that the king could punish the violator could maybe prevent some attacks in waters like Lillebælt.

In addition, there may have been a psychological factor to consider. Along the shores of Lillebælt – especially in the narrow and winding part – archaeological objects and features have been connected to the ritual and cultic sphere. Archaeologist Mogens Bo Henriksen's (2015) survey of Viking Age ritual sites near the sea at Lillebælt, makes him argue that pits with skeletons of horses and dogs or parts of horse's skeletons outside a settlement context may be remains of cultic rituals performed at either the scene or elsewhere (Fig. 7). Either way, the remains have deliberately been placed by the shore either to protect or to warn off at important passageways. Horse's heads – sometimes still attached to the hide including metatarsals and hoofs – put on a *nið* stake were used as an invocation or a curse. Located at the right spot and validated with the correct spell, it may have been believed to secure an area against evil-doers. Put up on the shore of a narrow fairway it would be visible from the ships passing by and thus warning them off.

---

19 Ulriksen 1998, 42-78; 2018
20 Nationalmuseet, Danmarks Oldtid, archive number NM 513/64
21 Christoffersen & Porsmose 1996, 163

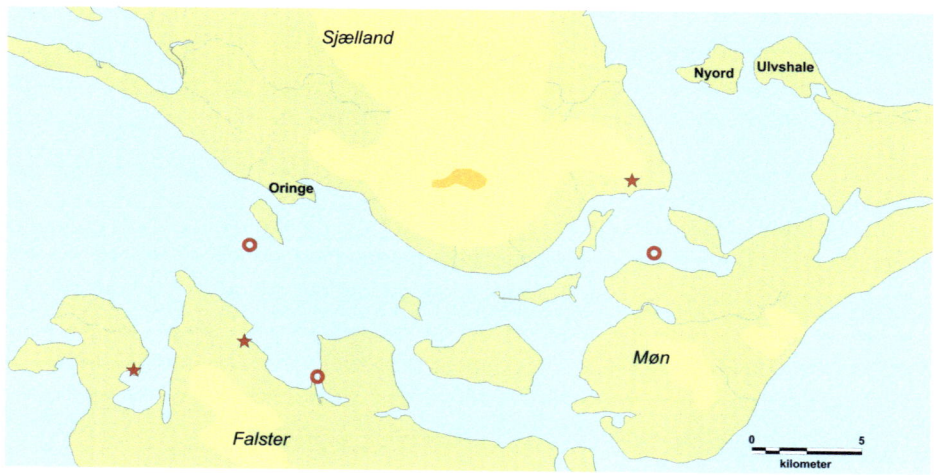

Fig. 8. *Storstrømmen between Sjælland and Falster with finds of a sacral character. Red circle: gold. Red star: silver.*

Connected to the ritual sphere are also single objects of gold or silver, parts of riding gear and mounts related to the warrior found close to the shore. In relation to Lillebælt also the silver treasure from Erritsø must be considered. Further south in Lillebælt – on the island of Bågø – there have been found three gold rings and a fragment of a silver mount from a sword belt. Mogens Bo Henriksen suggests that the coastal cult places might have been used as territorial markers to deter strangers or as places where rituals were practised before venturing out on expeditions of any kind. Following this conclusion, the place name Gudsø Vig comes into mind, maybe referring to a location where rituals were performed in relation to the gathering of ships and their crews before and after expeditions. Cult, rituals and coastal depositions may have constituted a 'sacred passageway' protecting ships and crews in peaceful errands.

The situation described for Lillebælt is not confined to that particular area. Objects and treasures of gold and silver and single objects of copper alloy found on the shore or close by are known from other coastlines of the Inner Danish Waters. An example is *Storstrømmen*, a narrow strait between Sjælland and Falster with a strong current between small islands and grounds. Just like Lillebælt it has not been straightforward to navigate (Fig. 8). Nevertheless, place names like *Oringe* and *Nyord* are related to watch posts flanking the sailing route, and archaeological finds indicate that they are rooted in the Viking Age (Fig. 9).[22] This indication finds some support in Viking Age metal objects found at an assumed landing site on the tip of the peninsula of *Ulvshale*, situated opposite the watch post on the island of Nyord.[23]

22 Jørgensen 2008: Oringe: *Worthyng* (AD 1231), prefix is old Danish *warth* ~ watch post. Nyord: *Nyorth* (AD 1231), suffix is old Danish *warth*.
23 Museum Sydøstdanmark archive number SMV 8437.

Fig. 9. A mount formed as a man's head dating from the Early Viking Age and found on the island of Nyord. Photo: Jens Olsen/Museum Sydøstdanmark.

While the pits with skeletal remains of horses and dogs most likely are the sacrifices by local people, single objects or treasures may also have been deposited by travellers wishing for a good fortune, fair wind and many customers. Whomever, the motive has probably been to promote and secure one's interests by getting the Gods on one's side.

Whether this was the only measure available regarding safe conduct is unclear.

Erritsø and its relation to Lillebælt

The role that the Erritsø-site could have played regarding navigation on Lillebælt may not have been immediate or direct. Despite the elevated position in the terrain, there is only a limited view over the fairway (cf. Fig 1). The viewshed analysis presented in Ravn et al. 2019 visualizes that the northern entrance to Lillebælt can be monitored from Erritsø but closer than c. 6.5 km away the sight is obstructed by the landscape.[24]

---

24   It is unknow if there have been woods limiting the views (Ravn et. al. 2019).

Overlooking the winding part of Lillebælt to the south is possible at a distance of more than 2.8 km, any closer the topography is in the way. This may have been satisfactory in order to spot incoming ships and even identifying them as hostile or not.[25] Turning the point of view and looking from the surface of the sea to Erritsø the magnificence of the main building and the palisade may have been difficult to appreciate from a distance of 2.8 km or 6.5 km. The main building has been c. 39 m long and if we suppose that it was c. 10 m tall at the roof ridge the construction would have been far from impressive in itself. Had it been located by the shore the Erritsø-complex would have signalled power and control to ship crews in a more spectacular way.

An impressive and even intimidating construction from the late 10th century we find at Aggersborg, the ring fortress with an outer diameter of more than a quarter of a kilometre and situated right by the shore. Aggersborg is a monumental signal of power. The Erritsø-complex would not have been neither impressive nor intimidating to friend or foe, thus not scaring anyone off. Controlling and dominating the strait implicates that power is visible. This was true during the Medieval Period (12th-15th century AD), when more castles were built along the coast of the northern part of Lillebælt. The importance of being noticed worked both ways: the strongholds were visible from the sea, and the ships could be observed from the strongholds.

This is not the situation regarding the location of the Erritsø-site itself. Neither does the topographic setting of Erritsø match the magnate's or the king's retired residences in Eastern Denmark, nor the situation of the residence at *Toftum Næs* in Western Denmark. Instead, the noticeability of the Erritsø-site seems to be focused on the land route leading to the crossing at Lillebælt. In that case, the Erritsø-site would have been noticed for what it most likely was: a retainer's base for serving higher powers, most probably the king, controlling and securing the land-based traffic as well as the assumed mustering site at Gudsø Vig.

Conclusion

The hypothesis of a safe conduct in the Viking Age achieved through an organisation with land-based observers and sailing units do not find support in contemporary written sources, nor is it possible to argue satisfactorily based on the archaeological evidence. In the 12th century when a naval organisation was established, the safe conduct for the odd ship was not the task. And even in the early 18th century it was a challenging commission to accomplish.

Returning to the days of Ottar in the late 9th century, ship crews have had to rely in their own strength and hoping for the Gods to be with them on their journey. Likewise, the locals may have sacrificed to the Gods along the seashore wishing to avoid hostile Vikings.

Most of all, during the Viking Age it was just risky business to travel the seas.

---

25   Pommer & Ravn 2019, 115

Bibliography

Aggesen, S. 1842: *Danmarks Krønike*. Oversat og oplyst af R. Th. Fenger, theologisk Candidat. Kjøbenhavn. Forlagt af Universitetsboghandler C.A. Reitzel. Trykt i Bianco Lunos Bogtrykkeri.

Albrectsen, E. 1976: *Vikingerne i Franken. Skriftlige Kilder fra det 9. Århundrede*. Odense Universitetsforlag.

Albrectsen, E. 2001: "700-1523", in *Konger og krige 700-1648. Dansk Udenrigspolitisk Historie. Danmarks Nationalleksikon*, Bind 1, edited by C. Due-Nielsen, O. Feldbæk & N. Petersen. København, 10-215.

Andersen, D.H. 2021: *Den Store Nordiske Krig*. Bind 2. Politikens Forlag.

Bately, J. (ed.). 2007: "Text and translation: the three parts of the known world and the geography of Europe north of the Danube according to Orosius' Historiae and its Old English version", in *Ohthere's Voyages. A late 9th-century account of voyages along the coasts of Norway and Denmark and its cultural context*, edited by J. Bately, & A. Englert (Maritime Culture of the North vol. 1). Vikingeskibsmuseet, 40-58.

Christoffersen, J. & E. Porsmose. 1996: "4.3 Fiskeri og havjagt", in *Atlas over Fyns kyst i jernalder, vikingetid og middelalder*, edited by O. Crumlin-Pedersen, E. Porsmose & H. Thrane. Odense Universitetsforlag, 154-169.

Crumlin-Pedersen, O. 1983: "Skibe, sejlads og ruter hos Ottar og Wulfstan", in *Ottar og Wulfstan – to rejsebeskrivelser fra vikingetiden*, edited by J. Skamby Madsen. Vikingeskibshallen, 32-44.

Crumlin-Pedersen, O., E. Porsmose & H. Thrane. 1996: *Atlas over Fyns kyst i jernalder, vikingetid og middelalder*. Nationalmuseet.

Englert, A. 2007: "Ohthere's voyages seen from a nautical angle", in *Ohthere's Voyages. A late 9th-century account of voyages along the coasts of Norway and Denmark and its cultural context*, edited by J. Bately & A. Englert (Maritime Culture of the North vol. 1). Vikingeskibsmuseet, 117-129.

Helmold. 1881: *Præsten Helmolds Slavekrønike i oversættelse af theol. kand. P. Kierkegaard, udgivet for Selskabet til historiske kildeskrifters overførelse til modersmålet ved H.H. Lefolii*. Kjøbenhavn: Karl Schønbergs Forlag.

Henriksen, M.B. 2015: "Kystens kultpladser – vikingernes rituelle aktiviteter ved havet", *Odense Bys Museer 2015*. Odense, 200-217.

Holst, S., A.B. Gotfredsen & P.S. Henriksen. 2021: "Kultiske fester og blót i sen jernalder og vikingetid ved anløbspladsen til Tissø-residensen", *Glimt fra Vikingetiden*. Danske Amatørarkæologer, 142-145.

Jomsvikingasaga. 1964: *Nordiske Sagaer* I. Tekstgrundlag: C.G. Rafns oversættelse 1829, Det Kgl. Nordiske Oldskriftsselskab. Hasselbalch.

Jørgensen, B. 2008: *Danske stednavne*. Gyldendal.

Kveldulfsønnernes Saga. 2001: *De islandske Sagaer*. Første Bind. [1930] 3. udgave. Gyldendal.

Lemm, T. 2019: "Protecting Hedeby – Reconstructing a Viking Age maritime defense system based on visual Communication", in *Early medieval waterscapes. Risks and opportunities for (im)material cultural exchange. Neue Studien zur Sachsenforschung*. Band 8, edited by R. Annaert, T. Bellens, P. Deckers, F. Theuws, D. Tys, R. van Dierendonck, L. van Impe, J Veeckman & L. Verslype. Published by Braunschweigsches Landesmuseum and Agentur für das Kulturerbe Flanderns, Braunschweig, 101-114.

Lind, J. 2002: "Kirkerne, fyrsterne og vendertogene", in *Venner og Fjender. Dansk-vendiske forbindelser i vikingetid og tidlig middelalder*, edited by A-E. Jensen (Resultater af et forsknings- og formidlingssamarbejde inden for Storstrøms Amt & Indlæg fra et tværvidenskabeligt seminar i Stubbekøbing d. 25.-26. september 2000). Næstved, 17-28.

Lyman, B. 2012: *Komma's havnelods 2011-2013*. Lindhardt & Ringhof.

Nielsen, H. 1991: "Gedehaven at Skælskør – a forgotten site of the late Middle Ages", in *Aspects of Maritime Scandinavia AD 200 – 1200. Proceedings of the Nordic Seminar on Maritime Aspects if Archaeology, Roskilde, 13th-15th March*, 1989, edited by O. Crumlin-Pedersen. Vikingeskibshallen, 207-212.

Nielsen, H. 1997: "Et regionalt rigdomscenter i Sydvestsjælland", in *"... gik Grendel att söka det höga huset ..."*. *Arkeologiska källor till aristokratiska miljöer i Skandinavien under yngre järnålder*, edited by J. Callmer & E. Rosengren (Rapport från ett seminarium i Falkenberg 16-17 november 1995. Hallands Länsmuseers Skriftserie No 9/GOTARC C. Arkeologiska Skrifter No 17). Halmstad, 55-70.

Nørgård Jørgensen, A. 2002: "Naval Bases in Southern Scandinavia from the 7th to the 12th Century", in *Maritime Warfare in Northern Europe. Technology, organisation, logistics and administration 500 BC – 1500 AD*, edited by A. Nørgård Jørgensen, J. Pind, L. Jørgensen & B. Clausen (Papers from an International Research Seminar at the Danish National Museum, Copenhagen 3-5 May 2000. PNM. Studies in Archaeology & History Vol. 6). København, 125-152.

Pommer, R.M.G. & M. Ravn. 2019: "Den sene vikingetids amfibiske militæroperationer. Eksperimentalarkæologiske forsøg med landsætning og kampformationer", *Kuml 2019*. Jysk Arkæologisk Selskab, 93-125.

Ravn, M., C. Juel, C. Lindblom & A. Pedersen. 2019: "Erritsø – new investigations of an aristocratic, early Viking Age manor in Western Denmark, c. 700-850 AD", in *Early medieval waterscapes. Risks and opportunities for (im)material cultural exchange. Neue Studien zur Sachsenforschung,* Band 8, edited by R. Annaert, T. Bellens, P. Deckers, F. Theuws, D. Tys, R. van Dierendonck, L. van Impe, J Veeckman & L. Verslype. Published by Braunschweigisches Landesmuseum og Agentur für das Kulturerbe Flanderns, Braunschweig, 37-45.

Rieck, F. 1992: "Gudsø vig – en vikingetidig samlingshavn", *Ellevte tværfaglige vikingetidssymposium*. Københavns Universitet 8. maj 1992. Forlaget Hikuin, 38-44.

Rimbert 1926: *Ansgars Levned*. Oversat af P.A. Fenger (1910). 5. Udgave gennemset og forsynet med oplysende Noter af Prof., Dr. Phil. Hans Olrik. København.

Ulriksen, J. 1998: *Anløbspladser. Besejling og bebyggelse i Danmark mellem 200 og 1100 e. Kr. En studie af søfartens pladser på baggrund af undersøgelser i Roskilde Fjord*. Vikingeskibshallen. Roskilde.

Ulriksen, J. 2009: "Viking Age Sailing Routes of the Western Baltic Sea – a matter of safety", in *Wulfstan's Voyage. The Baltic Sea region in the early Viking Age as seen from shipboard*, edited by A. Englert & A. Trakadas (Maritime Culture of the North 2). Roskilde, 135-144.

Ulriksen, J. 2018: *Vester Egesborg. En anløbs- og togtsamlingsplads fra yngre germansk jernalder og vikingetid på Sydsjælland*. Bind 1. Aarhus University Press.

PART 4.
THE ERRITSØ LOCATION, ITS CHRONOLOGY, CHOREOGRAPHY AND INTERPRETATIONS

BY BENTE PHILIPPSEN & MARIE KANSTRUP

Chapter 16
Radiocarbon dates and Bayesian modelling of the Erritsø site

Radiocarbon dating of houses and similar archaeological constructions can be challenging, as the available sample material most often comprises charred plant material such as charcoal or cereal grains, found in the fill of postholes, wall ditches and similar features. The samples are retrieved from the sediment by floatation, and short-lived species are selected for radiocarbon dating. Such samples can be problematic due to several reasons (using the example of a house dated by samples from postholes):

1. The postholes can contain older material, which had been present in the soil when the house was constructed.
2. The postholes can contain younger material, which entered the fill through animal activity, root action or frost/drying cracks.
3. Charcoal in the postholes can be from the burning of the original roof-bearing posts. These could potentially have been century-old oak trees or re-cycled timber, and charcoal from the innermost rings can be centuries older than the house construction activity itself.
4. Postholes could have been re-used for other constructions, which potentially were unnoticed during the excavation.

It is not easy to find a sampling strategy that mitigates all these problems. One option is to date a large number of samples and use statistical models to identify outliers. This is a more objective strategy than building an age model and manually removing outliers that do not fit the expectations. We will explain later how this can be realised in an age model.

Calibration of radiocarbon dates

The radiocarbon age is calculated from the measured concentration of ^{14}C atoms in a sample. Due to variations in the atmospheric radiocarbon concentration, this is not identical to the sample's age in calendar years. Therefore, radiocarbon ages need to be

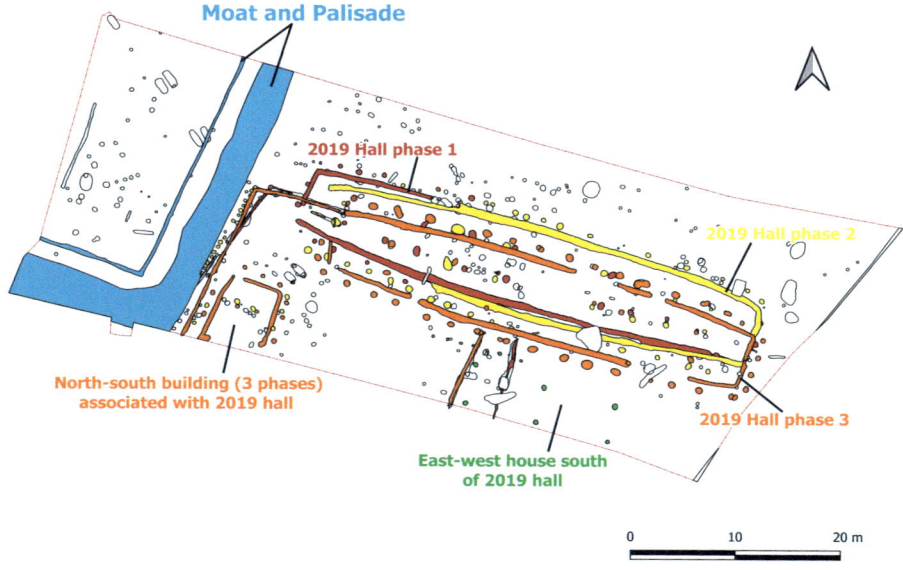

Fig. 1. *Constructions in the eastern part of the excavation, connected to the 2019 hall. The moat/palisade are indicated as well as the three phases of the hall building.*

calibrated to the calendar timescale. This is done by using the so-called calibration curve, which is made by radiocarbon dating dendrochronologically dated wood samples. Depending on the shape of the calibration curve in a given period, the calendar ages can have much broader uncertainties than the measured radiocarbon ages. Often, multiple intervals on the calendar timescale correspond to one radiocarbon age. However, including context information such as stratigraphy can often constrain the broad intervals of the calibrated ages. This is done with Bayesian statistics.

Bayesian modelling

In Bayesian analysis of radiocarbon dates, context information is combined with the radiocarbon dates to produce narrower age ranges than with individual dates alone. This could for example be the fact that several samples derive from the same context, so that their average age can be calculated. Another example is stratigraphic information about the temporal order of features, which can be translated into a sequence of radiocarbon dates. This can result in calibrated age uncertainties down to one or a few decades, especially in cases where single-year radiocarbon events can be found to "anchor" the sequence.[1]

---

1   Philippsen, Feveile et al. 2022

Fig. 2. Constructions in the western part of the excavation, related to the 2007 hall (yellow and brown): Southern house (dark blue), inner fence (grey) and N-S oriented house (red).

A strategy to allow for outliers in the age model, and to identify the outliers, is using the charcoal outlier model in OxCal.[2] The output of this model adds a posterior outlier probability to each date, as well as a distribution of the age offsets.

Materials and methods

In total, 49 samples from the different buildings discovered at the Erritsø site were radiocarbon dated. Six charcoal samples were dated via Aarhus AMS Center situated at Aarhus University in collaboration with DirectAMS in Seattle (AAR-codes) in the context of the Tissø project. The samples were prepared and cleaned with a standard acid-base-acid pre-treatment to remove contamination such as carbonates and humic acids from the depositional environment.[3] Graphitization and measurement took place at DirectAMS in Seattle. The other 43 samples were prepared and analysed in Seattle and marked with D-AMS lab codes.

---

2 Bronk Ramsey 2009
3 Olsson 1976; Philippsen, Feveile et al. 2022 (Supplementary Information)

RESULTS: RADIOCARBON DATES

Table 1 summarises the samples dated for this study, as well as the unmodelled and modelled calibrated ages. The table displays the whole ranges for the calibrated ages for better readability (otherwise, up to six intervals would be necessary for each date).

Most samples have calibrated ages (unmodelled) between AD 700 and 1100. However, there are a few outliers with significantly older ages, even a few with ages BC. This is most probably charcoal from older activities (occupation, agricultural activities or potentially even forest fires), which had been present in the soil before the halls and connected features were constructed.

Lab code	Context	Sample IDs and comments	^{14}C age (uncal. yr BP)	Calibrated age (95.4%), unmodelled	Calibrated age (95.4%), modelled	
					Model 1 (Figure 3)	Model 2 (Figure 4)
AAR-21535	A501/1092, Main hall 2007	x626 Charcoal (3 year rings). Small sample: 0.455 mg C	1369±26	AD 606-771		
AAR-21536	A2193, Main hall 2007	x673 Charcoal, *Fagus* (beech, 1 year ring)	1208±25	AD 705-890		
AAR-21537	A2202, Main hall 2007	x674 Charcoal, *Fraxinus* (ash, 3 year rings)	1355±27	AD 641-773		
AAR-21538	A2194, Main hall 2007	x676 Charcoal, deciduous tree (2 year rings)	1286±27	AD 661-839		
AAR-21539	A2180, Main hall 2007	x679 Charcoal, deciduous tree (2 year rings)	1700±28	AD 255-417		
AAR-21540	A2198, Main hall 2007	x681 Charcoal, *Alnus* (alder, 2 year rings)	1351±28	AD 643-773		
D-AMS 020144	A2309, Fill in moat	x696 Charcoal, *Fraxinus* (ash)	1045±33	AD 895-1114	AD 898-1118	AD 897-1212
D-AMS 020145	A2311, Structure in moat	x697 Charcoal, *Alnus* (alder)	1171±22	AD 774-972	AD 775-975	AD 774-1011
D-AMS 020146	A2275, Southern house	x699 Charcoal, *Corylus* (hazel)	1207±22	AD 707-887	AD 706-944	AD 913-1071

Lab code	Context	Sample IDs and comments	¹⁴C age (uncal. yr BP)	Calibrated age (95.4%), unmodelled	Calibrated age (95.4%), modelled	
					Model 1 (Figure 3)	Model 2 (Figure 4)
D-AMS 020147	A2277, Southern house	x700 Charcoal, *Alnus* (alder)	1239±22	AD 683-873	AD 684-905	AD 912-1071
D-AMS 020148	A2265, Fence associated with main hall 2007	x704 Charcoal, *Fraxinus* (ash)	1231±25	AD 684-882	AD 687-919	AD 913-1070
D-AMS 020149	A2310, Palisade	VKH6810x705 Charcoal	2955±26	1260-1054 BC	1260-1027 BC	AD -1259 --931
D-AMS 020150	A2310, Palisade	x706 Charcoal, *Betula* (birch)	1940±26	AD 11-203	AD 17-212	AD 21-240
D-AMS 020151	A2310, Palisade	x707 Charcoal, *Betula* (birch)	2443±26	750-410 BC	746-398 BC	AD -748 --387
D-AMS 021582	A2309, Fill in moat	x713 Wood, *Fagus* (beech)	1430±49	AD 546-667	AD 547-758	AD 550-864
D-AMS 038540	A2964, Trelleborg type house?	x760 1/2 grain of *Hordeum* sp. (barley)	1183±25	AD 707-950	AD 774-973	AD 709-1012
D-AMS 038541	A2837 Trelleborg type house?	x764 3 plant remains	2101±26	196-44 BC		
D-AMS 038542	A2839 Trelleborg type house?	x765 1 fragment of *Corylus* (hazel)	1198±25	AD 706-893	AD 706-955	AD 707-987
D-AMS 038543	A2638, E-W house south of 2019 halls	x779 2 grains of *Hordeum* sp. (barley)	1027±24	AD 978-1114	AD 989-1126	AD 991-1153
D-AMS 038544	A2643, E-W house south of 2019 halls	x781 1 grain of *Hordeum* sp., 2 grains of *Persicaria* sp.	1115±26	AD 888-993	AD 888-1025	AD 888-1037
D-AMS 038545	A2644, E-W house south of 2019 halls	x782 1 grain of *Secale cereale* (rye)	1028±22	AD 991-1035	AD 991-1115	AD 991-1151
D-AMS 038546	A2641, E-W house south of 2019 halls	x784 1 grain of *Secale cereale* (rye)	1051±23	AD 901-1030	AD 900-1106	AD 901-1158

Lab code	Context	Sample IDs and comments	14C age (uncal. yr BP)	Calibrated age (95.4%), unmodelled	Calibrated age (95.4%), modelled	
					Model 1 (Figure 3)	Model 2 (Figure 4)
D-AMS 038547	A2797, Inner fence connected to 2006 hall	x793 1/2 grain of *Hordeum* sp. (barley), 1 1/2 unid. seeds, 3 unid. plant remains	1001±24	AD 994-1151	AD 994-1160	AD 991-1093
D-AMS 038548	A2993, Inner fence connected to 2006 hall	x794 4 plant remains, 1/2 grain of *Secale cereale* (rye)	2103±24	195-46 BC	195 BC – AD 9	AD 913-1069
D-AMS 038549	A2999, Inner fence connected to 2007 hall	x795 1/2 grain of *Bromus* (brome), 1 fragment of *Trifolium* (clover), 1 fragment of *Danthonia* (oatgrass), ½ fragment of *Galium* (bedstraw), 1 fragment of *Poaceae* (grass), 3 unid. seeds	1158±23	AD 774-977	AD 775-1004	AD 917-1061
D-AMS 038550	A2912, N-S building associated with 2007 hall	x1192 1 fragment of *Galium* (bedstraw), 1 fragment of *Danthonia* (oatgrass), 1 grain of *Persicaria* sp., 1 *Lamiaceae* (mint family), 2 unid. Seeds	2330±30	511-233 BC	468-209 BC	AD 927-1028
D-AMS 038551	A2908, N-S building associated with 2007 hall	x1193 1 grain of *Cerealia* (cereal)	1189±23	AD 707-942	AD 708-957	AD 914-1069
D-AMS 038552	A2902, N-S building associated with 2007 hall	x1194 2 plant fragments	2116±23	335-51 BC	340 BC – AD 4	AD 927-1028
D-AMS 038553	A2955, N-S building associated with 2007 hall	x1196 1 seed of *Hordeum vulgare* (barley), 1 *Secale cereale* (rye)	1056±22	AD 900-1028	AD 898-1090	AD 950-1041

Lab code	Context	Sample IDs and comments	¹⁴C age (uncal. yr BP)	Calibrated age (95.4%), unmodelled	Calibrated age (95.4%), modelled	
					Model 1 (Figure 3)	Model 2 (Figure 4)
D-AMS 038554	A3045, N-S building associated with 2007 hall	x1200 1 seed of *Hordeum vulgare* (barley)	1157±26	AD 774-988	AD 775-1011	AD 943-1046
D-AMS 038555	A3058, N-S building associated with 2019 hall	x1212 1 seed of *Hordeum vulgare* (barley)	1203±24	AD 706-890		
D-AMS 038556	A3053, 2019 hall phase 3	x1213 1 fragment of *Poaceae* (grass)	1100±24	AD 889-995	AD 891-966	AD 895-988
D-AMS 038557	A2338, 2019 hall phase 3	x1216 1 seed of *Hordeum vulgare* (barley)	1208±23	AD 709-887	AD 886-959	AD 892-991
D-AMS 038558	A2354, 2019 hall phase 1	x1218 1 seed of *Cerealia* (cereal)	1222±22	AD 705-882	AD 817-893	AD 774-890
D-AMS 038559	A2356, 2019 hall phase 2	x1219 1 fragment of *Fallopia convolvulus* (wild buckwheat), 4 fragments of *Persicaria* sp. (smartweed)	1158±24	AD 774-977	AD 866-927	AD 776-950
D-AMS 038560	A2361, 2019 hall phase 2	x1222 2 seeds of *Hordeum vulgare* (barley)	1141±22	AD 776-989	AD 871-927	AD 777-950
D-AMS 038561	A2381, 2019 hall phase 2	x1223 1 seed of *Hordeum vulgare* (barley)	1100±28	AD 890-1014	AD 875-924	AD 776-952
D-AMS 038562	A2363, 2019 hall phase 1	x1225 1 seed of *Hordeum vulgare* (barley)	1201±24	AD 706-891	AD 818-893	AD 774-891
D-AMS 038563	A2380, 2019 hall phase 1	x1226 1 seed of *Hordeum vulgare* (barley)	1206±21	AD 707-887	AD 818-893	AD 774-890
D-AMS 038564	A2385, 2019 hall phase 2	x1227 1 seed of *Hordeum vulgare* (barley)	1247±23	AD 680-870	AD 855-916	AD 776-950

Lab code	Context	Sample IDs and comments	¹⁴C age (uncal. yr BP)	Calibrated age (95.4%), unmodelled	Calibrated age (95.4%), modelled	
					Model 1 (Figure 3)	Model 2 (Figure 4)
D-AMS 038565	A2393, 2019 hall phase 3	x1228 1 seed of *Hordeum vulgare* (barley)	1104±29	AD 888-1014	AD 890-966	AD 894-988
D-AMS 038566	A2409, 2019 hall phase 1	x1235 1 seed of *Hordeum vulgare* (barley)	1209±23	AD 706-888	AD 818-893	AD 774-890
D-AMS 038567	A2440, 2019 hall phase 2	x1246 1 seed of *Hordeum vulgare* (barley)	1160±23	AD 774-976	AD 865-927	AD 776-950
D-AMS 038568	A3068, 2019 hall phase 3	x1247 1 grain of *Bromus/Avena* (oatgrass/oat)	1230±23	AD 691-880	AD 887-959	AD 892-990
D-AMS 038569	A2500, Fill in moat	x1261 1.5 grains of *Cerealia* (cereal)	1194±22	AD 707-892	AD 707-953	AD 708-992
D-AMS 038570	A2500, Fill in bottom of moat	x1268 2 grains of *Cerealia* (cereal)	1201±22	AD 707-889	AD 706-948	AD 707-981
D-AMS 038571	A2392, 2019 hall phase 1	x1269 1 grain of *Secale cereale* (rye)	1247±22	AD 681-870	AD 815-893	AD 773-891
D-AMS 038572	A2782, Palisade	x1278 1 plant fragment, ¼ grain of *Cerealia* (cereal)	2117±23	336-51 BC	340-3 BC	337 BC -AD 52
D-AMS 038573	A2782, Palisade	x1279 4 plant fragments, 6 unid. seeds	1986±24	42 BC – AD 114	42 BC – AD 139	42 BC – AD 199

Table 1. *Table 1: Radiocarbon dates of the Erritsø halls. For those samples that were included in the age models, the modelled calibrated ages are given as well. For samples that were not included in the age models, the columns for modelled ages are left blank.*

Age models

We present here two different age models. Both include the possibility of outliers, of radiocarbon dates older than the contexts because of e.g., redeposited charcoal. The 2007 hall is represented here by dates on smaller constructions that were associated with it – a north-south oriented house, an inner fence, and a southern house.[4] The radiocarbon

---

4   See Figure 1 for an excavation plan of the 2007 hall.

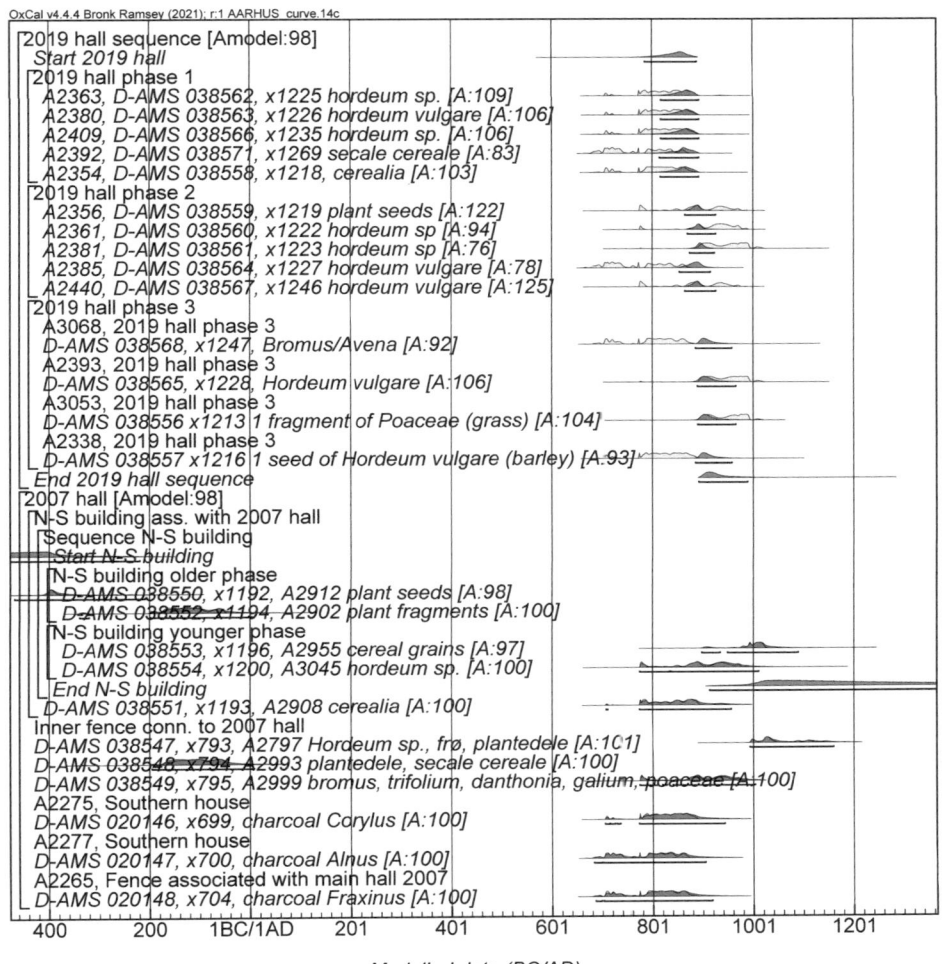

Fig. 3. The first model of the radiocarbon dates of samples associated with the two halls at Erritsø. This model utilises the stratigraphic information of three hall phases that were observed for the 2019 hall as well as two phases that could be discerned in the north-south oriented building associated with the 2007 hall.

dates from the main hall are disregarded in the model, as the samples were obtained under less controlled circumstances than from the other contexts.

For the first model, we only include the context information of the sequence of phases that was observed within each hall. These are three phases for the 2019 hall and two phases for the 2007 hall. For the second model, we include the assumption that the hall excavated in 2019 is older than the 2007 hall, based on archaeological observations and house typology, as a fence from phase 3 in the eastern house excavated in 2019 was cut by the moat (Fig. 1). However, the two halls were on separate locations and did not

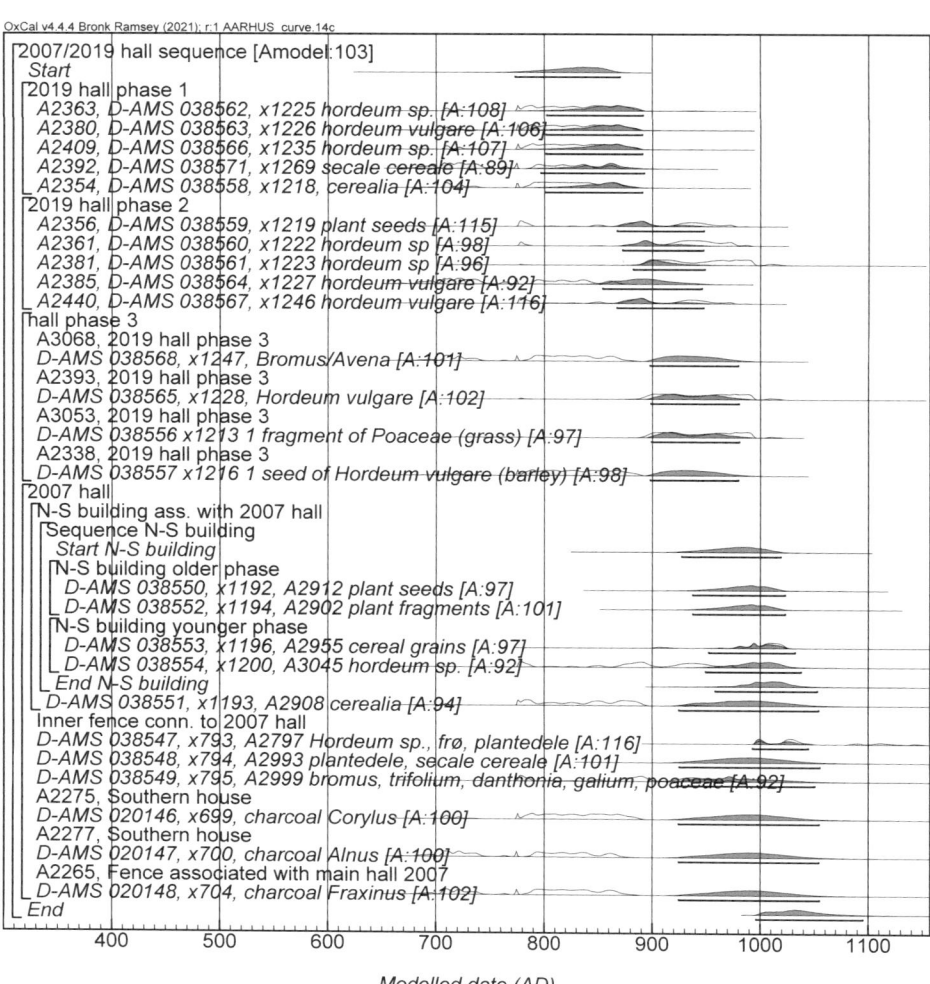

Fig. 4. Radiocarbon dates of samples associated with the two halls at Erritsø. This model includes the assumption that the hall excavated in 2019 is older than the hall excavated in 2007. Furthermore, the model utilises the stratigraphic information of three hall phases that were observed for the 2019 hall as well as two phases that could be discerned in the north-south oriented building associated with the 2007 hall.

cut each other, so a direct stratigraphical relation can only be linked up to the fact that the palisade and moat only had one phase, belonging to the 2007 house, though the moat had several clean-up phases, suggesting that the house from 2007 was younger, as also typology seems to suggest.

The first model results in dates during the ninth century, extending into the tenth century, for the 2019 hall. The dates for the 2007 hall are less well constrained and include several outliers. The more reliable samples associated with the 2007 hall span from the eighth to the 10th/11th centuries. The dates are not able to tell which of the hall buildings (the 2019 hall or the 2007 hall) was earlier.

For the second model, it was assumed that the 2019 hall was constructed earlier than the 2007 hall. Including this assumption in the age model does not change the dates of the 2019 hall significantly; its first phase is still dated to the ninth century, while the second and third phase extend into the tenth century. The dates for the 2007 hall are now constrained to a period from the mid-tenth to the early part of the eleventh century. The transition from the 2019 hall to the 2007 hall would in this model be in the middle of the tenth century.

Bibliography

Bronk Ramsey, C. 2009: "Dealing with outliers and offsets in radiocarbon dating", *Radiocarbon* 51(3), 1023-1045.

Olsson, I.U. 1976: "The importance of the pretreatment of wood and charcoal samples", in *Radiocarbon Dating: Proceedings of the ninth International Conference, Los Angeles and La Jolla*, edited by R. Berger & H.E. Suess. Berkeley: University of California Press, 135-146.

Philippsen, B., C. Feveile, J. Olsen & S.M. Sindbæk. 2022: "Single-year radiocarbon dating anchors Viking Age trade cycles in time", *Nature* 601, 392-396.

BY MADS RAVN & CHRISTIAN JUEL

Chapter 17
The Erritsø Excavations in a Bayesian Perspective

ABSTRACT

This article re-evaluates the Late Iron Age and early Viking Age site at Erritsø, Denmark. Discovered in 2006, the site features significant fortifications including a V-shaped moat and a palisade, suggesting a strategic importance. The study aims to determine the beginning and end dates of the site's use, comparing it with other royal sites like Lejre and Tissø. Two sets of radiocarbon dating scenarios are presented, impacting the interpretation of the site's political and military roles during the 8th to 10th centuries. The site is considered crucial for its strategic location, serving as a defence-in-depth position behind the Danevirke, reflecting its importance in the broader landscape of power and communication in early Denmark

The Erritsø Late Iron Age and early Age Viking site was discovered by chance in 2006, when the developer, *Energinet* needed a centrally placed headquarter for controlling the entire supply chain of power in Denmark. Hence, they chose this slightly elevated hill near the village of Erritsø, today a suburb to the garrison town of Fredericia founded in 1650, four kilometres to the north. Here was a good view over the entire sea-and landscape, centrally placed in the kingdom of Denmark, where communication lines on land and sea from east, west, north, and south convene. As goes with energy so it seems it goes with relations of power of the early kingdoms of Denmark: To rule and defend oneself one needs to be placed where all communication lines meet geographically. This contention will be argued and elaborated upon suggesting that this is the reason for the location of this site in Erritsø: It is here the peninsula of Jutland meets the eastern islands of present Denmark.

Aim of paper

The main research question for the project Royal Power and Landscape was to assess the beginning and end date of function for this site, which in all possible ways looks like similar royal seats in Lejre and Tissø and Järrestad. Therefore, many samples were collected while at the same time, stratigraphic observations on site during many excavation campaigns were conducted. While the main excavation method was to remove the topsoil with machine, there was also systematically metal detector surveys before and during excavations of the topsoil and the excavated surface. One can with some confidence therefore claim that the richness of metal was much less than for example at the Tissø site.[1,2] Combined with two developer-led excavations nearby an area of 33.2 hectares has been revealed (2023) and 34 C-14 dates extrapolated from several soil samples from posts and other interesting features, where only few of them were stratigraphically divided. Another group of C-14 dates from the recently excavated area to the west are still awaiting final processing and dating.

The following is therefore based on two modulations run on the C-14 dates available so far (see also Philipsen this volume). We have chosen to reflect on both sets of modulations, which independently hold quite significant consequences for the interpretation of the site in terms of which political role it played during the turbulent 8th, 9th, and 10th centuries. As for its military function in the landscape of power the interpretation is the same regardless of dates, suggesting that the site and the landscape played a vital political and military role in the defence-in-depth of the kingdom when an enemy broke through the Danevirke, 111 km to the south, a role the garrison town of Fredericia later came to play.

With a focus on the excavation campaigns at the Erritsø site and the revelation of finds, structures and dates there, this paper presents a *Stand der Forschung* of the project 'Royal Power and Landscape' (2024) and outlines future research questions. We will discuss the abovementioned strategic calculations in relation to two C-14 modulations, dendrodates, place names, and the few written sources that we have from this time. But first we need to look at the excavation history.

Discovery and rescue excavations

Little did we know that *Energinet* placed their headquarter on top of, what we suggest from place name evidence and other archaeological finds, to be a royal hall. This is substantiated below, but important here is especially the similarity in detail with significant halls in Lejre, Tissø and Järrestad. Just as important are the differences, being fortifications of a unique type, consisting of a two metre deep, square, V-shaped moat covering 1.2 hectares. Inside that an approximately two to three-metre-high ca 110 × 110 m palisade in one phase is seen from postholes. It fits symmetrically with the moat and is thus considered contemporary with the moat. This phenomenon is not seen around the otherwise identical and contemporary halls in Lejre and Tissø on Zealand. In other words, land defence seems to have mattered more on this location.

Initially in 2007, a developer-led excavation was initiated by the Vejle Museums of

---

1 At the time of writing the Fæsted/Harreby site has not been sufficiently published to make 1:1 comparison, although it is attempted in part below.
2 Also the acidic soil seems to have been bad for metals.

Fig. 1. *The entire area. Research excavations are purple and blue. Developer-led excavations are green and red. All in all 33.2 hectares were excavated. The northern green part reveals the earliest excavation from 2007, whereas the extension towards the west and south is from 2023. The left purple is from 2018. The right purple is from 2019. Graphics: Vejle Museums by Morten Lyngkjær Jensen.*

what we estimate to be the northern part of a fortified hall of Lejre type phase 4[3], leaving the southern part for the future, as it was not immediately threatened. Test trenches, however revealed that there was a larger potential. In 2015, the Ministry of Culture's Research Council donated seed money, which in 2016 led to a small exploratory excavation, funded by the Beckett Foundation; additionally, a DualEM Geo radar survey by the engineering company *Rambøll*[4] revealed significant anomalies, which corresponded with anomalies that had been excavated and identified as archaeological structures, confirming the method, and confirming that the potential of the site was much larger. Thus, we realized that there was a possibility for learning more about this unique site, especially in terms of how similar or different in time and detail it was in relation to the almost identical, so-called royal halls at Lejre, Tissø and Järrestad.[5]

---

3   VKH 6810. see also Lejre type phase 4 which by Christensen is seen as 9th or 10th century, Christensen 2015, 85

4   Thanks to Peter Mejldal and Rambøll.

5   Christensen 2015. See also for excavation history Juel & Ravn 2018. At the time of writing it is unclear how similar it is to recently found structures in Fæsted/Harreby where a significant 10th century gold find and an older cult area was discovered (Grundvad & Albris 2020, 26).

First season of the project Royal Power and Landscape

After the rescue excavation in 2007 and a geophysical survey in 2016, a small excavation of the moat and palisade in 2016 opened up for a larger research excavation in 2018 (Fig. 1).[6] The first season revealed the southern part of the inner court, or possible sacral temple area of the fortified hall complex, as it is called by some.[7] We shall here call the entire complex, hall, inner court and temple, Hall I. Phosphate analyses revealed some activity patterns outside the possible temple building of the inner court.[8] Generally the finds were few, consisting of pottery some bones and few metal finds, most of them in this area fragmented brooches or litter from casting.

Second season

In 2019, geophysical exploration from 2015 and the finds in the original test trenches in concert made us focus on an area only 60 metres to the southeast, where a three-phased, 49 metres long hall, (Hall II) was disclosed. The entire site consisted now of at least five phases of high-status habitation within a radius of 60 metres. Hall II in three phases seemed from stratigraphic observations, the inner fence of the inner court being cut by the moat, to be older than Hall I and moat to the west, a premise which is essential for the **Modulation II** scenario we present which places Hall I in the middle and late 10th century. Also, a dirhem dating from AD 750-815 found in the top layer of the moat, suggests that this moat belonging to hall I has a terminus post quem of AD 815.[9]

It cannot entirely be ruled out that some phases of the eastern Hall II were contemporary with Hall I, as only one phase of an inner court fence is cut by the moat. The latter observation is the basic premise for the Bayesian **Modulation I** C-14 scenario we present. Apparently, and strangely, there were no palisades and moat around the eastern Hall II, a phenomenon we earlier have tried to link up to an event shortly described in the Royal Frankish Annals (hereafter *RFA*) in AD 815, where a penal expedition from Louis the Pious was sent to control King Godfred's sons that had expelled the pretender Harald Klak. (see also Kasper Andersen this volume, chapter 12)[10]

Further rescue excavations

Further non-planned developer-led excavations that can be associated to this royal settlement became necessary in 2020, when 200 m to the southeast a large production area dominated by 34 contemporary sunken featured buildings, so-called *grubenhäuser*

---

6   Ravn & Juel 2019; Juel & Ravn 2018. The western, purple polygon in Fig. 1.
7   Jørgensen 2009, 331
8   Henriksen & Stevnsvig 2020
9   Ravn & Juel 2020
10 Ravn & Juel 2020, 122

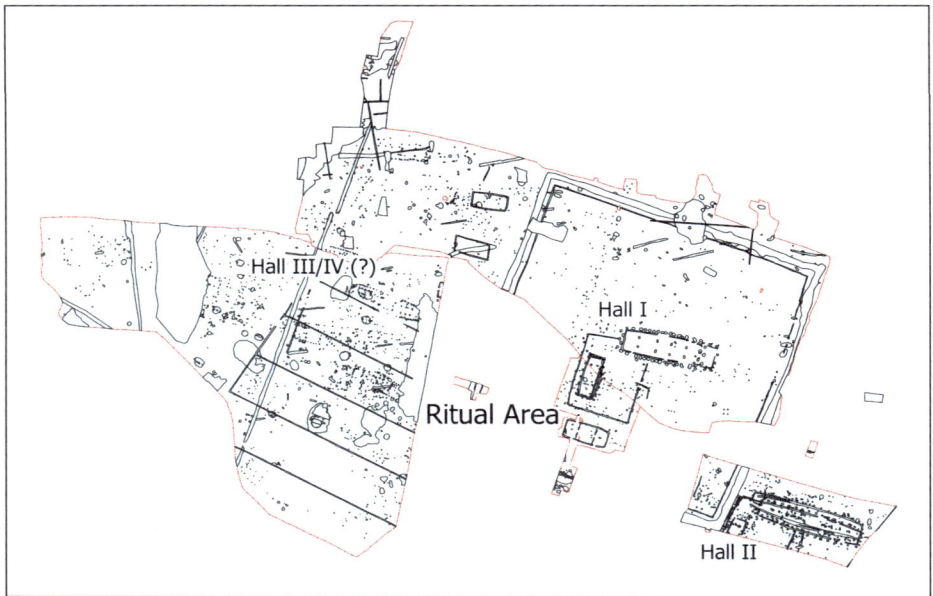

Fig. 2.   *Entire area with Hall I in the centre and Hall II to the east. The production area is to the far east (see Morten Lyngkjær Jensen chapter 18). The area where a possible Hall III is revealed still needs final analyses and dates to be processed. Graphics: Vejle Museums by Morten Lyngkjær Jensen.*

and 30 post-built houses were revealed (Figs. 1 and 2)[11]. The area is however not fully disclosed.[12] In 2020, 2021, 2022 and 2023 also we were able to include students from Aarhus University in this area. It made it possible to design a systematic sampling strategy by sieving calculated parts of the fill in selected *Grubenhäuser*, making us suggest that the general lack of finds is reflecting past activity on the site.[13] Here traces of iron extraction and production, as well as loom weights and spindle whorls appeared, suggesting textile production. The few finds of glass beads suggests that they are lost by accident, questioning the presence of bead production on site. Moreover, postholes from houses built on the surface of a hitherto rare, short, and narrow type indicate that the houses may be dated to the early 8th and 9th century, as also C-14 dates support. We thus seem to have an early, contemporary production and living area with *grubenhäuser* to the east, and a ritual, elite area with large halls (Halls I and II) 200 metres to the west, the latter moving slightly around within a radius of 60 metres.

11 In some texts such huts are called pit huts, a term which incidentally is not generally understood in the English-speaking world (Andrew Reynolds personal communication). We therefore call them sunken featured buildings or Grubenhäuser.
12 Museum journal number: *VKH 7105 Snoghøj*, see also specific paper in this volume by M. Lyngkjær Jensen.
13 Thanks to Aarhus University and Dr. Sarah Croix.

That was the general picture in 2022, when further extension of the present headquarter of the developer was initiated.[14] This time the area to the west of the moat and palisade revealed further 10 grubenhäuser as well as at least three halls, probably of an earlier type, suggesting an even earlier elite residence than the halls we discovered to the east. Typologically these houses seem to be 8th century, when compared to the Lejre chronology, phase 1.[15] We also excavated a well with a well-preserved case of wood, one dendrodate so far revealing a plank that was felled after AD 761 another dating to AD 707 and 718, suggesting at least two phases and certainly occupation as early as in the early 8th century.[16] The well, however could not be directly connected to the houses. Given that a lifespan of a hall may have been 50 years, it indicates with five phases on site already and three new houses that we may be further back in the 8th century maybe even the 7th century or alternatively that there were more coexisting halls.[17] Maybe the life span of the building was not only related to the durability of building materials, but also the possibility that a new king constructed a new building when he came to power, thus suggesting that a hall phase could stand for only a short period of time. In this paper the following two models will present two scenarios. But first we need to look at the location.

Location, location, location

As real estate agents often underline, location matters. Location also mattered in Erritsø. Zooming a bit out from the actual settlement area, one notices that the halls are placed on a hill, which is 32 metres a.s.l.m. The beacon hill 318 metres to the southwest is 28.5 metres high. On older maps, another beacon is located 267 metres to the southeast, being 25 metres high. In comparison to the otherwise flat, Danish landscape this is a significant elevation, and the hill is one of the highest peaks in the Erritsø shire, which for the same reasons conspicuously provided a good view out into the landscape and seascape. To be seen and to have the overview mattered. This contention is substantiated by pollen analyses that suggest that the vegetation of trees was insignificant.[18]

Another pollen analysis from the moat revealed the same[19]. From this location, viewsheds that were generated in collaboration with Aarhus University and Moesgaard Museum have supported the argument that there is a very good view into the narrow Little Belt, which funnels into a 10 km narrow passage of 209 metres at the narrowest point. The passage starts in the North with the present garrison town of Fredericia, founded in

---

14 Ravn & Juel 2020
15 Christensen 2015, 86
16 Jensen 2024
17 In Denmark and Norway there are different suggestion spanning form 30-140 years for post-built houses' potential life span. It all depends on the soil type, see also Løken, T. 2020, 196. We suggest that 50 years is a good possibility for a high-prestige house.
18 Ombashi 2023. VKH 7105 Snoghøj.
19 Sørensen 2017

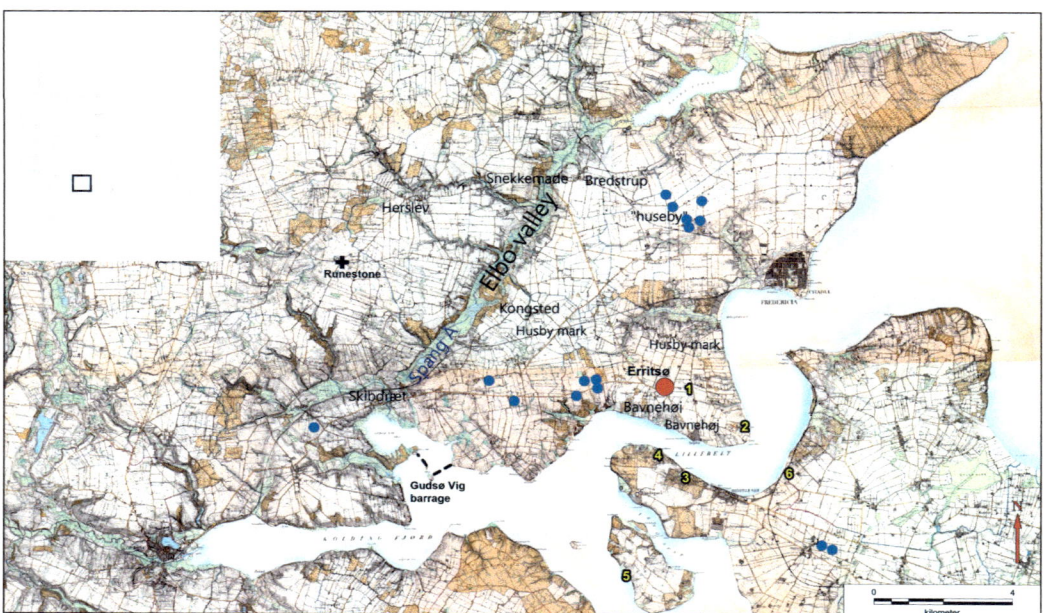

Fig. 3. *Overview of the area on a cadastral map from the 19th century. The halls are located at the red spot. Blue spots are known, contemporary rural late Iron Age and Viking Age settlements. Numbers indicate contemporary prestigious finds. 1: The Erritsø silver hoard. 2: Gold ring. 3: Silvering. 4: Horse fitting. 5: Mould for casting bronze. 6: Cult site. (The numered finds are based on Henriksen 2015, 208).*

1650 on the Jutland side and the ancient fishing village, *Strib* and further south the fishing and whaling town of *Middelfart* on the opposite island of Funen, which is known from written sources back to at least the 13th century, possibly from sagas as far back as the 11th century. On the Jutland side 1.7 km southeast of the halls, the ancient ferry berth of *Snoghøj* is located, a site that can be dated back to at least the 11-1200s. *Middelfart*, or *Melfar* is interpreted as meaning the middle passage by implication suggesting that there possibly were passages further south and north. As indicated by development activity described above, the area is today an important industrial hub where east meets west and north meets south on the essential roads between Copenhagen and Europe where the E20 joins the E45 motorway that extends down into the North and Central European mainland. some of the same transport imperatives seem to be a constant back in time.

Suffice to say is that our recent investigations suggest that in the Viking Age this area was also a hub for the traffic by land and sea. Between the early ninth-century town of Hedeby in present Germany to the south and via Samsø, where a known harbour is contemporary in some of the phases, one could reach the early 9th century town of Kaupang in southern Norway to the north in a few days. It was also at a crossroads of terrestrial routes between the presumed royal seat of the supposed *Scyldings* in Lejre in the east on the island of Zealand and the early town of Ribe in the west of Jutland,

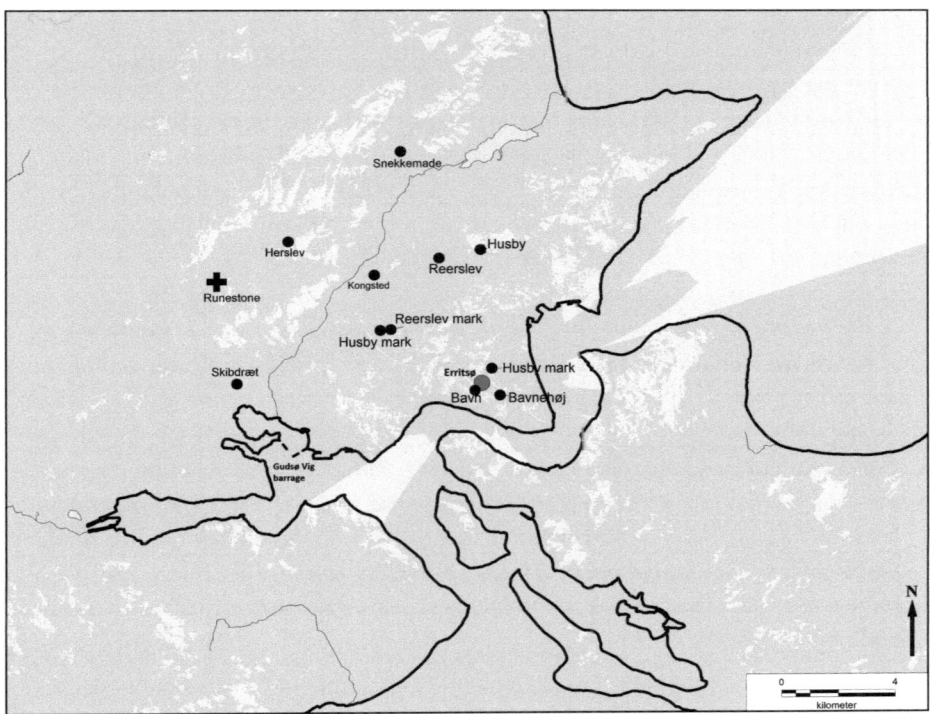

The northern part of Lillebælt. A view-shed analysis of the site of Erritsø based on the 2008 LIDAR scan, with line of sight calculated from the Erritsø hall 2 m above ground surface. The areas visible from the Erritsø-site are white. Place-names relating to power, armies and ships in the hinterland are indicated. Illustration after Ravn et al. 2019.

Fig. 4.

which routes intersect at Erritsø.[20] The rich find complex at Fæsted/ Harreby, where gold and ancient cult activity has been found back into the Iron Age suggests that this location should also be considered a transit point over land to Ribe. Drawing from recent archaeological- and place name analyses by Grundvad and Albris, Erritsø may have been the final passage before turning towards the southwest along the hypothesized, large Farris forest west and south of present Kolding fiord.[21] In that perspective the king or lord would have had to travel far to the west passing north of the Farris Forest via Rødding towards Sønder Hygum parish, a distance of ca. 50 km via Fæsted on the way to Ribe and only in Fæsted they could choose the route further southwards along the Oxen Road. This hypothesized communication line, which needs to be substantiated, however just further underlines that Erritsø was an important land hub in the – then Danish – kingdom of the late 8th and 9th and according to modulation I also the 10th centuries AD, possibly even a strategic fall-back position in a defence-in-depth system,

---

20 Christensen 2015
21 Grundvad & Albris 2020, 20

behind the linear earthwork of *Danevirke*. In that perspective one should bear in mind that Danevirke has recently been dated back to the 5th century.[22]

That the territory of the then Danish kingdom was somehow similar in the early 9th century to the later medieval kingdom is not only indicated by the similarity in detail of the Erritsø halls to the ones in Lejre, Tissø and Järrestad, presuming similarity in architecture. This similarity indicates similarity of ideals by the developer, probably the king, but it is maybe also suggested by the important and quite reliable source of the Royal Frankish Annals (*RFA*) of the year AD 813 that states:

> […] *From the imperial court [in Aachen] some Frankish and Saxon nobles were sent across the river Elbe to the border of the Normans; they should make peace with them according to the desire of their kings and deliver them over to their brother. With them a similar number, namely sixteen, of the great men of the Danes [de primatibus Danorum] met at the appointed place, and after mutual oaths were taken, the peace was confirmed, and the brother of the kings returned to them. They were not at home, however, but had* **gone to Westarfolda with an army, the farthest region to the north-west of their kingdom**, *which overlooks the northern tip of Britain, and whose chiefs and people [cuius principes ac populus] denied them obedience (Our translation and emphasis).*[23]

This passage suggests that southern Norway and thus perhaps *Kaupang* were part of the Danish sphere of interest, at least in the early 9th century, so most likely northern Jutland also was.[24] Also, the presence in the *RFA* in AD 811 of among others a magnate, Osfried from Scania meeting with King Hemming and delegated from Charlemagne at the *Ejder* for a truce seems to suggest that the sphere of interest reached the ancient lands of Scania in present southern Sweden, an area that was yielded to the Swedes as late as in 1658.[25] Being as it may, one should account for different coherence of the realms over time as well as other centrifugal powers that changed this picture especially

---

22 Tummuscheit & Witte 2019, 122
23 See Scholz, Bernard Walther 1972, 99. *Annales Regni Francorum under the year 813 or in Latin Annales Regni Francorum 1895, 138:* Missi sunt de hoc conventu quidam Francorum et Saxonum primores trans Albim x fluvium ad confinia Nordmannorum, qui pacem cum eis secundum petitionem regum illorum a facerent et fratrem eorum redderent. Quibus cum pari numero nam XVI erant de primatibus Danorum in loco deputato occurrissent, iuramentis utrimque factis pax confirmata et regum frater eis redditus est. Qui tarnen eo tempore domi non erant, sed ad Westarfoldam ' cum exercitu profecti, quae regio ultima regni eorum inter septentrionem et occidentem sita, contra aquilonem Brittaniae summitatem respicit, cuius principes ac populus eis subici recusabant.
24 Tummuscheit & Witte 2019, 122
25 Scholz, Bernard Walther 1972, 99. *Annales Regni Francorum*, 1895: de parte vero Danorum inprimis fratres Hemmingi, Hancwin m et Angandeo, deinde ceteri honorabiles inter suos viri, Osfrid ' cognomento Turdimulo q et Warstein et Suomi et Urm et alius Osfrid filius Heiligen et **Osfrid de Sconaowe**… (our emphasis).

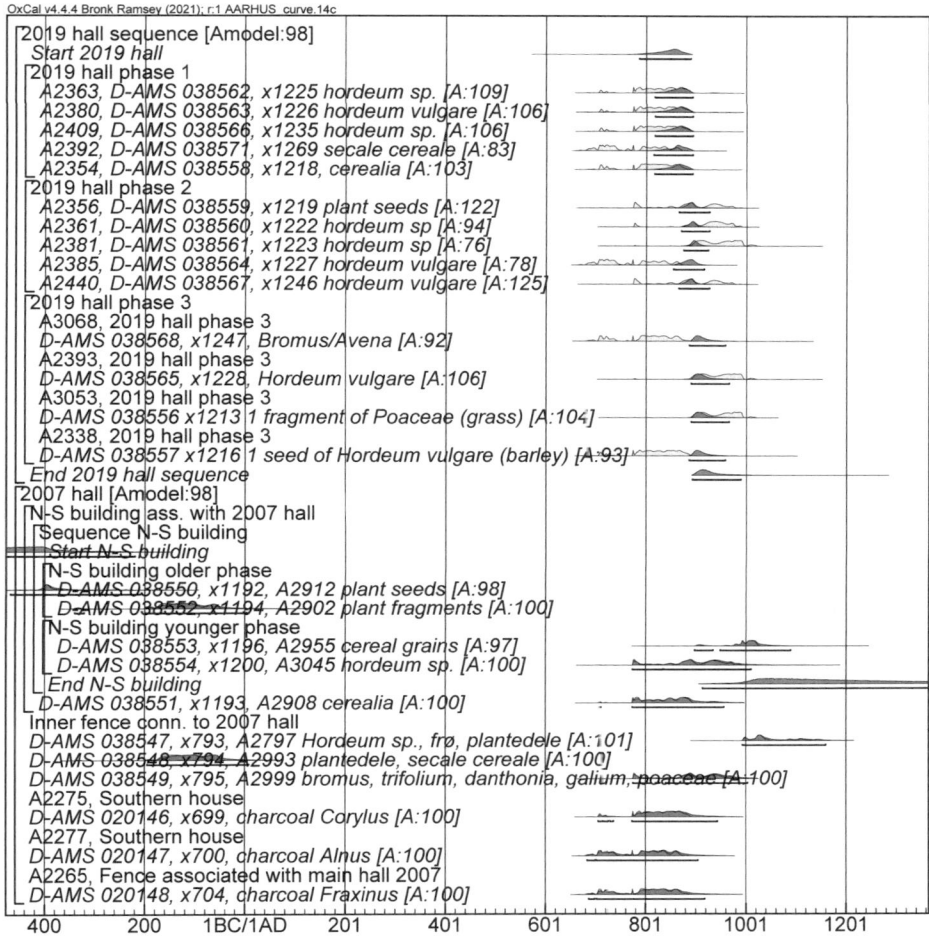

*Modulation I. Fig. 6. Modulation I, **after Philipsen (this volume for further explanation).*** Fig. 5.

during the late 9th and early 10th century. Especially the written sources or the lack of them in this period seem to suggest that.

Details from the Erritsø fortified Hall I in the scenarios of modulation I and II

Given this context, we will, in the following, describe further evidence for the fortified royal Hall I, which during its long continuity at least in one phase may coincide with the above-mentioned events. Whatever kings controlled this fortified hall is difficult to say, but circumstantial evidence suggests that this location at Erritsø was conceived and placed here out of a very specific strategic necessity. But we need first to investigate the details of time to substantiate this contention.

As it looks now, the fortified Viking Age halls at Erritsø to the west of the so-called royal residences in Zealand and Scania was according to Modulation I placed in the middle of the 9th century, in the first phase (Fig. 5). Excavations in the moat also identified a well from which a wooden plank could be dendrochronologically dated to have been felled after AD 779. Most likely this well was older than the moat, thereby providing absolute dating evidence of a terminus post quem for the fortified hall, which must have been placed there after AD 779 and a terminus post quem of the dirhem coin of AD 815.

As mentioned above, despite conforming to the well-known type of buildings in Zealand, this hall complex in Erritsø is also somewhat unique. It is the only example of this type of a hall in southern Scandinavia, where there is also a significant, square defence system, a palisade and moat enclosing the hall measuring 110 × 110 m. A similar but more conspicuous palisade and defence system is found in Jelling, only 30 km to the northwest from the 10th century, however without a moat. As it looks now, defensive aspects around habitations of importance seems so far to be a Jutish phenomenon, probably indicating a war prone region, where the balance of power was not very stable.

Moat and palisade

The moat is up to two metres deep and V-shaped in profile. Layers and analysis of soil samples from the moat clearly showed that the moat was not water-filled. It also showed evidence of several clean-up events, the last refill dating to 10th century, as c-14 dates suggest. Indeed, in Modulation II the complex should be placed in the middle and late 10th century, which makes it contemporary with the similar type of moat at Kovirke known from the Danevirke complex. A few metres inside from the moat there are traces of a palisade that may have been at least two metres high. It has only one phase. Despite several attempts, it has not been possible to C-14 date the palisade, as there was not enough organic material. Both the moat and palisade are placed symmetrically in relation to Hall I, which is in the centre, making us suggest that the hall, palisade and moat were contemporary in both phases of the actual hall. The hall has two phases, suggesting that only the house had been changed once within ca 100 years.

There were significant traces from planks placed on the inside of the moat, maybe to hold the soil of the inner dike between the moat and palisade from filling the moat. On the outside, there were in some places traces of stakes pointing obliquely towards a possible enemy. Both would hinder enemies to cross the moat easily. These suggest a complex defensive cordon designed to make it difficult crossing the moat, a system that was functional and not merely symbolic. It was worthy of a king.

The Western, Hall I may be similar to the phase 4 hall identified at Lejre, suggesting that it was within the 9th or 10th century, in Christensen's chronology from Lejre.[26] Certainly, this hall was in use in two phases. Phosphate analysis of the inner court did not reveal significant activity inside the inner house, as some suggest may have functioned as

---

26   Christensen 2015, 85

a cult house. Just outside the entrance a higher level of phosphate appeared suggesting some activity, which could have included organic material such as milk or blood.[27] It cannot, however, be ruled out that it just reflects activity from a previous house.

Details from the Hall II

But before that we will shortly describe the supposedly earlier Hall II in three phases found 60 metres to the east. Three phases suggest that the hall was renovated at least twice (Fig. 2). Measuring 49 m long and 12 m wide, it is with its 'cigar-form' a type that may be attributed to the slightly earlier phase of the Lejre relative chronology, suggesting a main habitation starting in the 9th century AD. If one adheres to Modulation II that packs the C-14 clearly in the 9th century in phase 1, it also suggests that habitation continues into the first half of the 10th century in phase 3. If each post building stood for 50 years before renovation, the hall may have had a total lifespan of up to 150 years, which represents a significant duration in the landscape. Indeed, taken together, the two neighboring Halls I and Hall II have five construction phases, potentially representing continuous occupation during the 8th, 9th and 10th centuries at the same site within a radius of 60 m.

Through excavation it was shown that one of the fences found around the inner courtyard is cut by the moat from the younger fortified Hall I. In the absence of other dates or observations, this suggests that the hall furthest to the east is older. It also is the basis for Modulation II and its premises set up for making a chronology. It is also interesting that this eastern hall does not have a moat and palisade, as the younger hall to the west does. There is not the same investment in defence applied to the eastern hall (Fig. 2).[28]

Also, in Hall II it was possible to take 37 samples for assessing the presence of botanical material and charcoal. It appears that there is a lot of charcoal in the centre of the house, supporting that it was here the main fireplace was present. But there is also a substantial amount of charcoal in other parts of the house, suggesting that it was affected more generally by fire. Henriksen and Steensvig would not suggest an actual 'burning horizon' from the present data, but a presence of charcoal above the normal is notable.[29]

There is also a significant amount of dominating barley seeds found in the samples, which is a phenomenon Henriksen has observed also at Tissø and Lejre.[30] It could suggest that the making of beer was important in high-status rituals in these sites, as also we see from earlier gold bracteates with runes mentioning 'ale' in several of them, and some even depicting a person drinking from a horn.[31] We also read of this phe-

---

27 Henriksen & Stevnsvig 2020. Investigated with Merck Reflectoquant RQflex 10 reflectometers with phosfate-sensitive test-strips. See also Jørgensen 2009
28 This is stated with the reservation that this area is not totally excavated.
29 Henriksen & Stevnsvig 2020
30 Peter Steen Henriksen: personal communication
31 Ravn 2022: Laursen & Ravn 2022

nomenon of serving beer in the hall from among others the Beowulf poem.[32] However, the overrepresentation of barley could also suggest that the heating of barley for beer production results in an overrepresentation of barley in general. In both cases the presence of beer production is confirmed. The absence of husks suggests that there was no normal agricultural processing of crops taking place in the hall. The overrepresentation of seeds in the western part of the hall indicates that it was here food production took place. There are also seeds from flaks (*Linum usitatissimum*), peas (*Pisum Sativum*), and raspberry (*Rubus Idaeus*), indicating a varied diet. The presence of white goosefoot (*Chenopodium album*) suggest that the fields have been well manured. Bladderwrack (*Fucus Vesiculosus*) is also known from other elite residences and south Greenland. It may have been used as fodder or fuel.[33]

The heap of stones

About 50 metres to the north of Hall II, a heap of cracked stones 8 × 10 metres in diameter and lots of charcoal appeared. It has the last few seasons been investigated with the aim of assessing its function. From similar phenomena in Fæsted, Lejre, Tissø, Uppåkrå and Järrestad, it seems that we so far may interpret those stones like in the other sites as the indication of cult activity and blót where beer and food has been prepared.[34] We await further analysis of the area in order to confirm or reject this hypothesis.

Earlier phases

The most recent developer-led investigations also make it possible to push back the settlement history at least three phases. Estimating a phase to 50 years, this makes it likely that the Erritsø site may be founded already in the 7th or 8th centuries, as it looks now, the earliest dendrodate from a plank in a well is from AD 707. C-14 dates from a recent excavation on site seems to confirm that. This is a scenario not contradictory to Modulation I nor Modulation II.

When did it end?

Including Modulation II in the discussion it seems that activity at Erritsø can be directly related to the rise of Jelling in the 10th century, only 30 km to the northwest, contrary to what we have written earlier.[35] We still maintain that occupation in Erritsø before that was associated to earlier power bases in Denmark, which looked towards the east. It is discussed in scholarship that there could have been several competing dynasties.[36] If this

---

32 E.g., Beowulf verse, 609-621
33 Henriksen 2016, 237-245
34 Jørgensen 2009, 351
35 See Ravn et al. 2019, 37-44; Juel & Ravn 2018, 16-25
36 Skovgaard-Petersen et al. 1977, 149

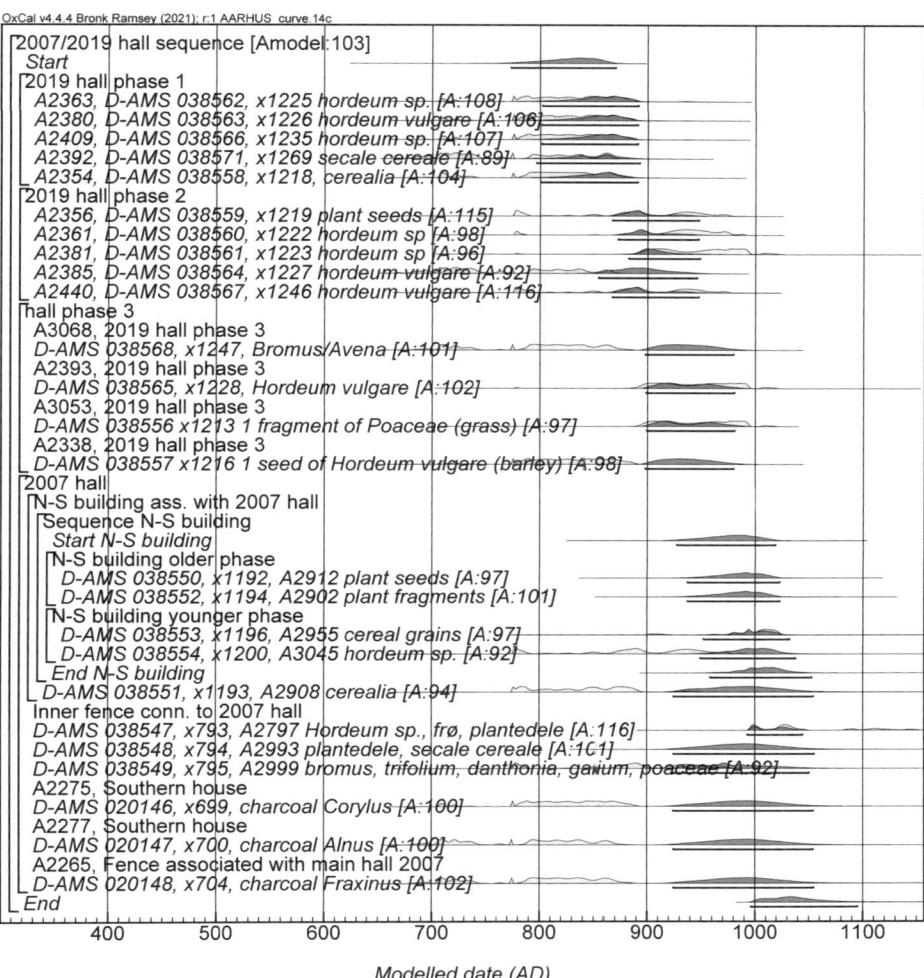

Fig. 6.

Modulation II after Philipsen & Kanstrup this volume.

is so, the identical halls in Erritsø and Lejre could indicate that Erritsø was associated to an hegemony which ruled in Zealand and Lejre first, possibly being a bridgehead in Jutland. In this scenario the presence of a system of itinerant, east Danish kings must be considered.[37] The possible non-permanent occupancy would also explain the relatively few finds located on site, despite intensive detector activity during all campaigns.

In this context, it is worth mentioning that a place name of a possible *Huseby* type has been identified ca. five km to the north of the fortified Erritsø site in *Ullerup* parish, though no elite finds have substantiated this place's importance so far (Fig. 4). Another indication of the presence of the later Jelling Dynasty in the area is a rune

---

37 In the sources probably called North Danes.

stone at *Kongens Kilde,* (literally the King's well) in *Sønder Vilstrup* 10 km to the west of the Erritsø site, bearing the probable name of Harald, supposedly Harald Bluetooth of the Jelling dynasty.[38] Within 876 m to the northeast of the fortified location, the Erritsø treasure, one of the greatest silver treasures from the early Danish Viking Age was found in the late 19th century. It consists of eight silver rings of eastern, Permian origin and two silver bars dating to around AD 900, indicating elite habitation in the immediate surroundings, at least in the 10th century, as also currently the latest dating from the moat does. What speaks against Model II is that there are no obvious finds that are dated to the 10th century, but certainly to the 9th and 8th centuries.

The site and the landscape of power

Regardless of the dates in Erritsø it is significant that the place had an important strategic function and a long place continuity. The moat at Erritsø is reminiscent of the V-shape from the moat, which was excavated at Kovirke close to the Danevirke fortification, near Hedeby.[39] This moat was beyond doubt made with the aim of stopping an invading enemy from the south from entering Jutland. Taken together with these other defensive works, one could imagine that the fortified hall at Erritsø played an important role within the strategic concept of a defence-in-depth, functioning as a fallback position, as we will return to below.

In a paper by Jens Ulriksen (chapter 15), he points out that there are several prominent high points in the Little Belt area, from where one can make early warnings, as evinced on Fig. 7. Here triangles of different shade indicate high points ranging from 19 m, (light) to 30+ a.m.s.l. (dark). In general, Ulriksen's illustration suggests that the sea of Little Belt is not easily accessible from the seaside for the same reason, if the persons on land were hostile. For that reason it need not have been an advanced warning system, as the militarized 10th century system presented by Thorsten Lemm of the Schlei Fjord.[40] Unlike Lemm's study we have so far in Little Belt identified a limited number of place names relating to beacons, indeed only two lying close to the Erritsø site. However, Ulriksen has identified several natural landing sites in the area (this volume).

Further evidence for a strategic place in the landscape

Almost midway through Little Belt, south of Erritsø a small bay at *Hejlsminde* provides a well-protected natural haven, surrounded by several prominent points. Here, a landing site with *grubenhäuser* from the Viking Age has been partly excavated. Furthermore, several important sites dating to the Viking Age seem have occurred in the *Almind* area, 14 km to the west, where there, judging from place names, the so called *Almind Syssel*[41]

---

38 Christensen 2016, 61; see also Moltke 1976, 163
39 Andersen 1998, 154
40 Lemm 2019, 101-114
41 Syssel is best translated as shire, but it is bigger than the later hundreds.

there also was a thing site. At Almind, two excavations west of Almind Church have revealed traces of several Viking Age farms. Also, an Arabic dirhem, sherds from soapstone and a silver tremissis from the Frisian area was found suggesting some luxury imports at the site. Other Viking sites from Dollerup, Viuf, Nr Bjert, Eltang, Sdr Bjert and Sjølund indicate above average Viking habitation in the area.[42] Also on the Funen side there are some important cultic sites and finds, but no clear indication of a harbour.[43] The closest and most significant settlement is, however the *Kirstinebjerg Øst* excavation 2.4 km to the west of the halls in Erritsø. It showed continuity from the Iron Age via the Viking Age in the 8th and 10th centuries, Middle Ages into the Renaissance, indicating an important farm complex with a deep time continuity. Also, abundant finds of wheat in a barn from a Viking Age house (house DG), where it was more normal growing rye and barley would suggest that this site had high status, wheat being prestigious to grow in the Viking Age.[44] One could speculate that this was where the jarl or steward of the king resided in peacetime. From here they could within three kilometres seek refuge or meet with the peripatetic king at the fortified halls in time of war.

That the fortified Erritsø halls could be used in a larger national strategy for a defence in depth is underlined firstly by the halls' position at high points at a distance from the sea along the entire Little Belt, which commands good views at sea and inland and provides a means of defence, as perfect, strategic locales. Defence-in-depth is a military strategy that deploys defenders across multiple sites, including well behind the front line to slow and weaken attackers, cutting off the supply lines while one may hide the actual army at nearby islands, evading a direct confrontation. This strategy was often used to defend Jutland half a millennium later, because the land is flat and difficult to defend. Jutland, however, also has plentiful wetland areas and one needs to follow the few, dry paths that are really directing the way into Jutland. Hence, placing few troops at key positions where the dry paths convene is a good strategic defence strategy.

As mentioned above pollen analyses suggest that there were no large trees, supporting that a good overview was important for the place. To the south-southwest, there was good view of the Stenderup peninsula and thus the entrance to Kolding Fjord and Gudsø Cove (literally Gods' cove). While the place name may also suggest a cultic aspect it is also an obvious place for gathering a larger fleet, with its kettle-shaped bay, well-protected from the weather and placed below hills of 25 metres a.s.l.m. Anne Nørgaard Jørgensen has for Gudsø Cove suggested that it exhibits "all the features that are logistically and strategically important to a fleet-mustering locality".[45] It remains to find clear evidence of harbour facilities and piers. The site's naval importance in the Iron Age and Viking Age in Gudsø Cove has so far only been assessed by place names and wooden barrages, dendrodated between 700-1000 AD. Parts of the area have been

---

42 Hartvig & Sørensen 2021, 46
43 Henriksen 2015, 208
44 Excavation report number: VKH 7087. See also archaeobotanical report by Grabowski 2012
45 Jørgensen 2009, 82

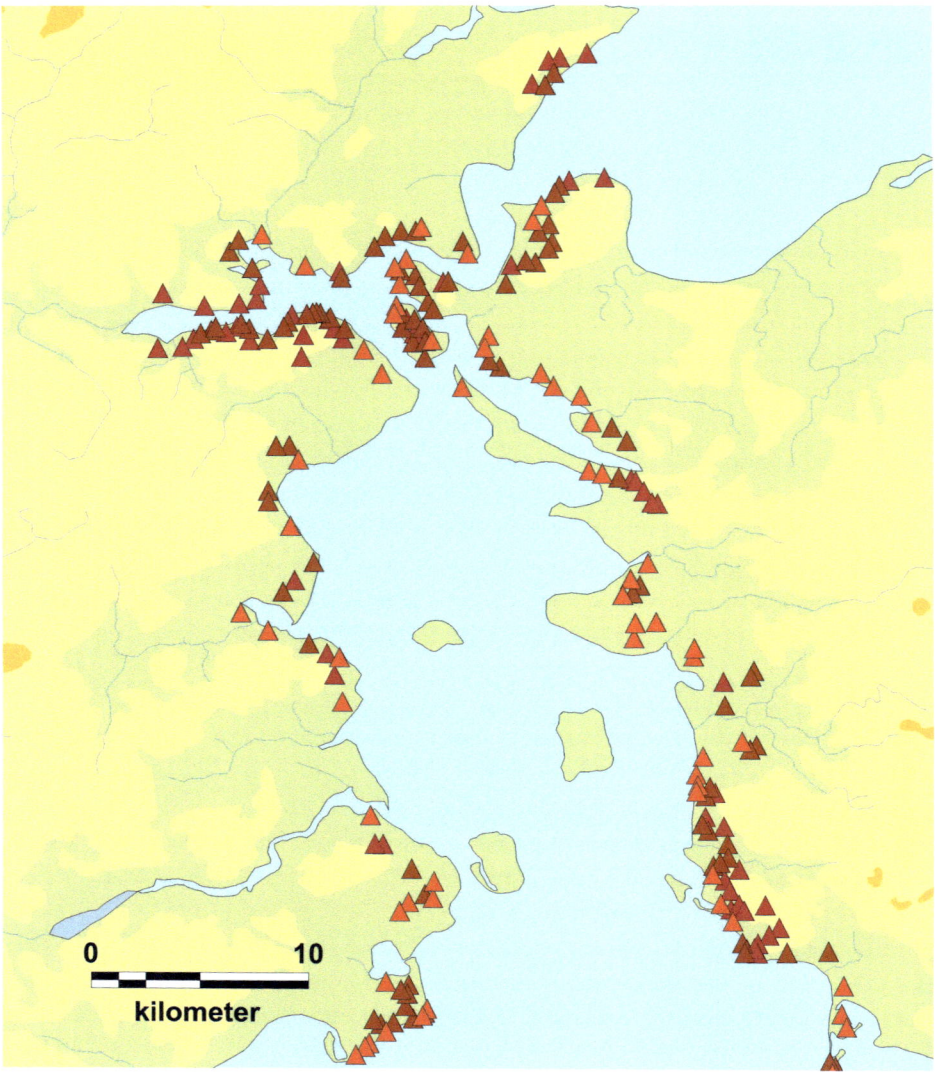

Fig. 7. *Here triangles of different shade indicate high points ranging from 19 m (light) to 30+ a.m.s.l. (dark). By kind permission by Jens Ulriksen, see chapter 15 fig. 4.*

investigated with detectors, so far without luck. Surely, the identified barrage poles in the cove suggest a defensive system, obstructing access to the cove.[46]

Similar sites with a focus on the inland and defence have recently been found in Central Jutland.[47] But the strategic intersection of both land and sea is in Denmark

---

46 Ibid, 83
47 Jessen & Fiedler Terkildsen 2016, 52-71

only seen at Erritsø, which in terms of defence makes this site unique. This may be why the defensive addition, the moat and palisade to a site, otherwise similar to less defensive sites in Zealand and Scania is present. In addition, the ancient country road from Snoghøj towards Kolding passes 70 m south of the fortified Viking halls, funnelling into a narrow, easily defendable, wet passage just west of Gudsø Cove (Fig. 3).

The defensive dimensions of the site are further supported by local terrain in the surroundings. The Elbo Valley of the swampy Spang Stream to the northwest acts as a barrier, making Elbo hundred almost an island, which makes it difficult to cross the Elbo Valley, with hills of up to 40 metres a.s.l.m., all the way up to Rands Fjord (Fig. 3 & 7). Spang stream today looks unimpressive, but by adding layers of landscape data from cadastral maps together with modern LiDAR data, comparing these with military maps of the 17th, 18th and 19th centuries, we get an idea of its potential for defence.

Especially a map from the 17th century, when Sweden invaded Denmark during the Thirty Years' War, shows that Elbo hundred in fact only had three focal passages over the Spang Stream, indicating that a defender had to place only a few troops at three focal passages to defend them. Swedish troops were also present at Kongsted, where there is another possible crossing, as there is, as mentioned above at Gudsø, where the only narrow, passable road west to Kolding is located. The Gudsø Cove being a potential mustering site is supported by cadastral maps and LiDAR data, which suggest that by the depth of the Spang Stream it may have been possible to pull the ships up from there along the Spang Stream. Place names support this idea. The maps show a place name *Schiptrupmuhl*, today called *Skibdræt*, of which the prefix *schip* or *skib*, means 'ship'. Further indications for a possible marine workshop are suggested further north along the stream by the place name *Snekkemade*, suggested by other research to have been related to the making of ships (Fig. 4).[48]

In sum, there seems to be at least a 1000-year continuity for this area functioning to stop invading land armies from the Duchies of Schleswig and Holstein, walking along one of the few dry roads of Jutland past Kolding. In other words, Erritsø needed to be placed exactly where it was, to stop any forces breaking through the Danevirke from moving further north. Those who controlled this area also controlled the passage to Funen and the rest of Denmark. One could only proceed to the islands if one had a substantial navy. Additionally, as in the wars in 1849 and 1864, one could attack the enemy in the flank if they decided to proceed northwards up into Jutland, making the Erritsø location key to a national defence. The persistent strategic weakness of Jutland and its strategic importance is even seen in recent invasion plans from the Cold War, underlining the need for a defence-in-depth strategy, where the area exactly around Erritsø plays a key role.

The defensive dimensions discussed above are also suggested by other place names like *Herslev*, 'a place for the army' (DA: *hær*). It is situated 10 km northwest of the Erritsø site. Incidentally, a *Herslev* is also found 8.6 km north of Lejre in Zealand, a correlation that can hardly be random, suggesting an army of the king could be located

---

48   Christensen 2016, 64. See also Holmberg & Madsen 1998, 197-225

nearby the halls, which however were dedicated more to rituals, than permanently housing an army in time of peace. A Jerslev close to Tissø is not related to the Herslev name, but rather the name Erik, as we shall return to below, but there is also found a Herslev south of Tissø. Also *Kongsted*, literally the 'King's' place' (DA: konge) emphasises the area's significance in terms of defence and power back into the Iron Age, where the suffixes -sted and -lev are suggested onomastically to have been founded, meaning 'the heritage of x' (the prefix).[49] The function may well have continued into the Viking and Middle Ages (Fig. 4).

In addition, as suggested above, place name researchers have also confirmed that a name of the *Huseby* phenomenon is possibly found in the area (Fig. 4).[50] Locations bearing such a name in other parts of Scandinavia have been associated with the presence of a royal or clerical elite.[51] As Christensen puts it, a hypothesis for the presence for a *Huseby*, which is often a late Viking Age phenomenon, may be that it has been broken off a larger estate. This may explain why we have so far not identified habitation at the Erritsø halls later than the 10th century, suggesting that a different organisation of land appeared there, as is also seen in other areas of Scandinavia, where the name *Huseby* is present. Whether the *Huseby* here could belong to the succeeding Jelling dynasty, having a significant presence in Jelling only 30 km to the northwest is a pertinent question. In that case the Huseby site would have defined the Jelling dynasty's presence in the area of Ullerup parish, five km north of the 9th-10th century Erritsø halls. Only future research may show, as the *Huseby* name currently identified in *Ullerup* parish has no clear archaeological evidence of high prestige presence, although there is extensive evidence for long habitation back into the Bronze Age, Iron Age and Viking Age, as well as Viking Age grubenhäuser indicating production.[52] In any case, several important place names suggest the presence of power, royalty, and religious importance in the area.[53]

The sovereign king's place on the hill?

Research by Sofie Laurine Albris reinforces the impression of the presence of royalty in the area.[54] She suggests, based on research made by Swedish scholars that Erritsø may be associated with the royal name '*Erik*', which derives from the Old Norse *ainarīkiaʀ*. This word originally meant the 'almighty sovereign', i.e., a supreme king who

---

49 Albris 2015
50 Christensen 2016, 64
51 Lemm 2016
52 Christensen 2016, 59-64. See also excavation reports VKH 7044, VKH 7403, VKH 6344, VKH 7276.
53 Christensen 2016, 56-57
54 Albris 2015, 26; see also https://arcnames.w.uib.no/2019/11/04/a-name-fit-for-a-king/. (accessed 0706-2024).

is recognized by other kings. Stefan Brink has analysed a similar place name on Öland in Sweden, called Eriksör.[55] Independent of Albris, he interpreted this name to mean: 'the hill where the paramount king lives.'[56] It is therefore reasonable to suggest a similar meaning for Erritsø, that is 'the hill on which the almighty paramount king lives'.[57] In this connection, one should remember as mentioned earlier that the Erritsø site is located at one of the highest points in Elbo hundred, and that its habitation regardless of which model of dating we subscribe to is during the 8th and 9th and 10th centuries, where two King Horiks ruled. Rimbert (dead 888) was following the missionary Ansgar on his mission to christen the Normans and writing about it in Ansgar's biography. He called the king in *RFA* for Horik.[58] Other sources calls him Ericus or Oricus as a later West Francian source does.[59] One may wonder if the outlandish name of Erik in the foreigners' version has become Horik, or whether the H was already silent in the West Francian language, as indicated in the Strasbourg oaths?[60] In this case, the 'Erritsø' name may have stuck to the site, when the two Kings Horik ruled for a long time, and if the name indeed means a supreme king it could have continued regardless of the rise of a different dynasty in the 10th century.

Interpretation and historical context

It is important to know how long the settlement was in activity in the area because it firstly supports the importance of the place in its context, especially when comparing with the sites at Lejre, and Tissø which have a deep time continuity. Recent excavations may also in Erritsø indicate long continuity of power. The more similarity in detail there is, the more likely it is that the site belongs to the same dynasty of kings that have been linked to the early kingdom of the Danes.

One hypothesis in this perspective could be that the Erritsø site was visited by peripatetic kings, a phenomenon one knows among the Franks and from the 7th century in Anglo-Saxon England. The rationale for this could be as quoted here:

---

55 Brink 1999, 431
56 Here Brink 1999, 431, also mentions Eriksgata, "a route a newly elected king in early Sweden had to travel to get acquainted with and accepted by peoples in different lands in this realm."
57 Christensen 2016, 55-67
58 Vita Angari, 24, called Horicum regem danorum.
59 As in Annales Bertiniani, 35 year 847: "Hlotharius, Hlodowicus et Karolus legatos ad Oric Danorum regem destinant, mandantes, ut suos christianorum infestationibus cohiberet, sin alias, bello se inpetendum nullatenus dubitaret". Our translation is: Hlotharius, Hlodowicus, and Charles send ambassadors to Oric, King of the Danes, commanding him to restrain his people from the invasions of the Christians, if not otherwise, he should in no way hesitate to seek war.
60 It is a West-Francian manuscript, and one may wonder if the 'H' is missing because it was already silent in West Francian language. This seems to be the case in the Strasbourg oaths in 842. See also translation by Scholtz, B.W. 1972, 162 and original text https://www.orbilat.com/Languages/French/Texts/Period_02/0842-Le_Serment_de_Strasbourg.htm

Fig. 8. *Arabic silver dirhem found in the top layer of the moat towards the southeastern corner. It dates between AD 750-815.*

"By 650, though, markets were putting new options on the table. Instead of just turning up and eating everything, a king or lord could install an agent on his farm, confiscate the lion's share of its output and then take his cut to Norwich or some similar market to swap for more durable goods. Continental merchants wanted food and drink (and slaves) to sell in the cities back home; Anglo-Saxon elites wanted Continental ornaments, clothes, and weapons to distinguish themselves from their poorer peers. Everybody gained, except the slaves."[61]

If one accepts this highly likely analogy and exchanges Norwich with Ribe or more likely Hedeby, and Anglo-Saxons with Danes, and the 7th century with the 8th and 9th centuries in Denmark, it is most likely that the same happened here. This hypothesis could explain why Erritsø was important and why the construction of the halls was so similar to the ones in Zealand and Scania. The king, as any present leader knows, needed to communicate presence and that the estates belonged to the same dynasty, and that they were ever present while they were not. Architecture can do the job a long way along the line.

Based on that hypothesis one could suggest that as for the Kings Sigfried (777-798), and Godfred (799-810) and Horik I (813-854) and Horik II (death 864), the dates so far substantiate that they on occasion could have been here. That it was not a permanent royal residence could explain the difference between Lejre and Tissø, where the concentration of metal finds in Zealand is much denser. Several attempt to go over the site with detectors have not presented the affluence of metal finds as in Zealand, suggesting

---

61   Morris 2022, 164

a less dense occupation. This model is not contradicted by the C-14 Modulation II, which suggest a continuity into the 10th century. But it could add another layer to the defensive interpretation, as we will return to.

More on defence-in-depth

The position exactly on a visually significant hill may also explain why the organisation and architecture of the site otherwise being so similar to the halls in Lejre and Zealand is also very different with the presence of a military defensive aspect, being the palisade and moat. As discussed above from place names and topographical indications, the Erritsø site could have functioned as a defence-in-depth position, when an invasive enemy had broken though at the Danevirke. And it could have done so several times. The first time we read about is described in the *RFA* in AD 815:

> The emperor commanded that Saxons and Obodrites should prepare for this campaign, and twice in that winter the attempt was made to cross the Elbe. But since the weather suddenly turned warm and made the ice on the river melt, the campaign was held up. Finally, when the winter was over, about the middle of May, the proper time to begin the march arrived. Then all Saxon counts and all troops of the Obodrites under the orders to bring help to Herioldi, marched with the imperial emissary Baldrich across the River Eider into the land of the Norsemen called Silendi. From Silendi they went on and, finally on the seventh day, pitched camp on the coast at …. There they halted for three days. But the sons of Godofrid, who had raised against them a large army and a fleet of two hundred ships, remained on an island three miles off the shore and did not dare to engage them. Therefore, after everywhere laying waste the neighbouring districts and receiving hostages from the people, they returned to the emperor in Saxony, who at this time was holding a general assembly of his people at Paderborn.[62]

---

62 Translation by Scholz 1972, 99. *Annales Regni Francorum*, 1895, 106: "Iussum est ab imperatore, ut Saxones et Abodriti ad hanc expeditionem praepararentur, temptatumque in illa hieme duabus vicibus, si Albia transiri posset, sed mutatione subita aeris emolliti glacie fluminis resoluta negotium remansit inperfectum, donec tandem hieme transacta circa medium fere Maium mensem oportunum proficiscendi tempus adrisit. Tunc omnes Saxonici comites omnesque Abodritorum copiae cum legato imperatoris Baldrico, sicut iussum erat, ad auxilium Harioldo ferendum trans Egidoram fluvium in terram Nordmannorum vocabulo Sinlendi perveniunt et inde profecti septimo tandem die in loco, qui dicitur …, in litore oceani castra ponunt. Ibique stativis triduo habitis, cum filii Godofridi, qui contra eos magnis copiis et ducentarum navium classe conparata in insula quadam tribus milibus a continenti separata residebant, cum eis congredi non auderent, vastatis circumquaque vicinis pagis et acceptis popularium obsidibus XL ad imperatorem in Saxoniam reversi sunt. Ipse enim tunc temporis in loco, qui dicitur Padrebrunno, generalem populi sui conventum habebat".

One hypothesis is that the fortified halls at Erritsø played a role in the above-mentioned disciplinary campaign of Louis the Pious (AD 814-40). The dates from Modulation II, which date the latest Hall I to the 10th century, excludes the possibility that the defensive aspect of the Erritsø halls may be connected to this event. As it looks now, within a frame of 50 years it cannot. In this case it must be the earlier phases at Hall II that must have suffered an attack, as also the high presence of charcoal throughout the hall may be indicating.

But that there was a presence could be indicated by K. Andersen who suggests (this volume) the timing of seven days travel from the Elbe would fit well with the army arriving near Erritsø. Thus, the unknown island omitted in the text could thus be Funen. Accordingly, the Erritsø site, the Hall II may have been ravaged, if it was undefended and belonged to the phase I of Hall II, where we have no evidence of fortification. Indeed there was here found charcoal above the normal in the entire house.[63] In Modulation II the defended Hall I is being constructed *after* the event of AD 815, indeed in the 10th century, where the inhabitants maybe remembering the experience of 815, decided that this site was an important, strategic hub in the future defence of Jutland — a realization that was also reached many centuries later with Fredericia, only five km to the north.

This hypothesis may explain why the occupants moved from an otherwise stable hall, rebuilt at least twice, which had stood there for hundreds of years, 60 m to the west and additionally invested in a massive moat and a 2 m + high palisade. Following model II, the defensive structures could in fact be coincidental with the later invasion by Emperor Otto. Future dates from the one-phased palisade could substantiate this hypothesis. The timing, travel time and other circumstantial evidence certainly makes us suggest that an army was in the area, in the early 800s, as also K. Andersen suggests (chapter 12).

The political background

The historical background for this settlement can be construed in two different ways, which are not mutually exclusive, as there is long settlement continuity. If one adheres to Modulation I, the settlement may be related to the conflicts around the exiled King Harald Klak (death AD 842) in AD 815 who had previously been part of the dual reign of Denmark. He helped incite the conflict on behalf of Emperor Louis who reinstated him as the co-king of Denmark at least twice.[64] The discussion among historians goes whether Emperor Louis' troops while failing in contacting the navy of the sons of Godfred also failed the expedition. This is not necessarily so, as discussed elsewhere, (Andersen chapter 12), because it seems that Harald was reinstated as king, with Horik around four years later from 819-824 where he was again expelled.[65]

The take-away, whether the troops arrived or not in this area is that the inhabitants in Erritsø during the 9th century realized that this site was a strategically important hub.

---

63 Henriksen & Stevnsvig 2020
64 Lund 2002, 45
65 For an elaboration see also Kasper H. Andersen, chapter 12.

The site had by then become a fall-back defence-in-depth position placed in a strategically important place, good for observing and potentially defending the area against an advancing army or navy.

The end of Erritsø

After eight years of campaigns and a number of excavations, both research- and developer-led, two scenarios have appeared in which it is possible that the halls at Erritsø continue up into the 10th century, if one adheres to C-14 Modulation II. In terms of when the settlement began, we are still awaiting the final report from the last campaigns (2023), but from typology and estimation of life spans of houses, being between 50-75 years and a close-by well dated by dendrochronology it seems that the halls go further back into the early 8th and possible 7th centuries, thus looking even more like the settlements in Lejre and Tissø with a long continuity.

We must therefore consider the hypothesis that the settlement at the end of its occupation might have been part of the ascent of Jelling, 30 km to the northwest. That the Jelling dynasty, so to speak overtook power in Erritsø during the 10th century. If that is the case, it must have been when the fortified Hall I was constructed, the one with the moat, 60 metres to the west of Hall II. It could make sense to have a base also facing the sea, not only the Oxen Road, as in Jelling, basing the power in Erritsø by collecting tribute at the Little Belt, surely a very lucrative business for a king who must provide food and weapons for the army. The similarity and continuity in details between the halls at Erritsø, Lejre and Tissø, speak against this hypothesis. Following Modulation II, the moat and last phase at Erritsø may have been constructed during the chaotic years when Emperor Otto I invaded Jutland in AD 973, the Erritsø site again functioning as a defence-in-depth position. In this context one may wonder if the Erritsø location should also be related to the construction of the ring fortresses, that Harald Bluetooth constructed supposedly at this time too. This square defence is certainly different than the round fortresses, but the site also played a different role in many ways. Whether we will succeed in the future to 'square the circle' so to speak is a matter for another discussion another place, meaning whether the sites played part of the same role in a national defensive system in the 10th century. As we see it, it is probably not as simple. However, one should in this connection also bear in mind the above discussion of Huseby, as there has been identified a Huseby only five km to the north and a supposed rune stone mentioning Harald Bluetooth.

Conclusions

The Erritsø settlement can be traced back from possibly as early as the early 8th century, more certainly the 9th and 10th centuries. But if one is to believe Modulation II, it is striking that the highest number of finds including detector finds seem to belong to the 9th century and earlier. In this perspective the settlement at Erritsø may initially have been, as in Lejre and Tissø, royal and cultic, when the peripatetic king visited his jarl or steward claiming his land and riches. It also served, in the 9th century and possibly in the 10th century, a defensive military purpose as a refuge when armies from the south invaded. This happened both in the 9th century and in the 10th century. In this function it was an important node in the defence of Jutland by land and sea, and as in later wars an army could retreat to the here and the islands, as indeed Godfred's sons did in 815. In this way, it was similar to the cultic royal centres in Lejre, Tissø and Järrestad, which is why we suggest a royal presence at times. The lack of many finds suggests that it had not a permanent residence of royalty. A jarl or steward may have been located 2.5 km to the west at *Kristinebjerg Øst*, where we have long continuity and indications of status. Unlike the sites in Zealand the Erritsø site has a more prominent military aspect, suggesting the presence of an army nearby, maybe at Herslev. In this way it seems to be a hybrid between the sites in Zealand and the Füsing settlements,[66]. In terms of the latter which according to the author may have served a pronounced function in relation to the Hedeby and Schleswig urban centres, we cannot identify anything like that in the Erritsø area, where the military, defensive aspect is much more pronounced.

We do not know if the king who came here was called Erik. There is, however, a rune stone 40 km to the south, on which an 'Erik' is named, supporting the idea that the name was in use already in the 8th century.[67] Additionally, various sources suggest that kings named Horik, Ericus and Oricus ruled for most of the 9th century.[68], as indeed also Saxo suggests.[69]

Acknowledgements

The excavations and research at Erritsø have been carried out with kind support from Kulturministeriets Forskningsfond (KFU), the Beckett Foundation and Augustinus Foundation. The project is made in collaboration with the National Museum.

Bibliography

Primary sources

Annales Regni Francorum inde ab a. 741. Usque ad a. 829. Qui dicüntue Annales Laürissenses majores et Einhardi. Ed. Pertzh, Georg, Heinrich. (Hannover: Hannoyerae impensis bibliopolii hahniani) 1895.
See also online: https://archive.org/details/annalesregnifran00anna/page/n5/mode/2up?view=theater. Accessed 2023 January 23.
Saxo Grammaticus. *Gesta Danorum*. Det Kongelige bibliotek. Copenhagen. Online access: http://wayback-01.kb.dk/wayback/20100504153355/http://www2.kb.dk/elib/lit/dan/saxo/lat/or.dsr/9/6/index.htm. Accessed 2023 January 30.
Vita Ansgari: https://archive.org/details/vitaanskariiauc00waitgoog/page/n17/mode/2up?view=theater&q=rex+danorum (accessed july 21 2023).

---

66   Dobat 2022
67   See Albris, Sofie Laurine's blog: https://arcnames.w.uib.no/2019/11/04/a-name-fit-for-a-king/
68   Kramb 2021, 27
69   Saxo Grammaticus, *Gesta Danorum*, liber 9.6.0. http://wayback 01.kb.dk/wayback/20100504153355/ http://www2.kb.dk/elib/lit/dan/saxo/lat/or.dsr/9/6/index.htm

Translation: https://sourcebooks.fordham.edu/basis/anskar.asp (accessed july 21 2023).
Annales Bertiniani auctore prudentio.
https://archive.org/details/annalesbertinianoowait/page/34/mode/2up (accessed july 31st 2023)
Le Serment de Strasbourg: https://www.orbilat.com/Languages/French/Texts/Period_02/0842-Le_Serment_de_Strasbourg.htm (accessed july 31st 2023).

Secondary Sources

Albris, S.L. 2015: "Navnedannelser på -lev og jernalderens samfundsstruktur", *NORNA*, no. 92, 9-35.

Andersen, H.H. 1998: *Danevirke og Kovirke. Arkæologiske undersøgelser 1861-1993.* Aarhus: Moesgaard Museums Skrifter.

Andersen, K.H. 2024: "Failure or success. New Perspectives on the Frankish invasion of Jutland in AD 815", in *Viking Age Aristocratic Residences in Northern Europe,* edited by Mads Ravn. Aarhus: Aarhus University Press.

Brink, S. 1999: "Social order in the early Scandinavian landscape", in *Settlement and Landscape*, edited by Charlotte Fabech & Jytte Ringtved. Jysk Arkæologisk Selskab. Aarhus: Aarhus University Press, 423-439.

Christensen, L.E. 2016: "Husebyer in Denmark – *Husby* in Grejs parish, Nørvang hundred, and *Husby* in Ullerup parish, Elbo hundred", in *Husebyer – status quo, open questions and perspectives. Papers from a workshop at the National Museum, Copenhagen 19-20 March 2014 Publications from the National Museum*, edited by Lisbeth Eilert Christensen, Thorsten Lemm & Anne Pedersen (Studies in Archaeology and History, 20:3. Jelling Series). Copenhagen: University Press of Southern Denmark, 55-70.

Christensen, T. 2015: *Lejre bag myten. De arkæologiske udgravninger* (Jysk Arkæologisk Selskabs Skrifter 87). Aarhus: Jysk Arkæologisk Selskab.

Dobat, S. 2022: "Finding Schliestorp? The Viking settlement at Füsing", *Danish Journal of Archaeology* 2022, Vol. 11, 1-22, https://doi.org/10.7146/dja.v11i.127759

Grabowski, R. 2012: *Archaeobotanical analysis of plant macrofossil material from VKH 7087, Kristinebjerg Øst etape 4, Vejle Amt, East Jutland, Denmark. Environmental Archaeology Laboratory* (Report nr. 2012-027). Department of Historical, Philosophical and Religious Studies. University of Umeå.

Grundvad, L.& L. Albris. 2020: "Afdækning af fænomenet hørg fra yngre jernalder og vikingetid. Nye udgravninger ved Harreby", *By, Marsk og Geest*, 32, 17-43.

Hartvig, A. & Sørensen, M. 2021: "Et indblik i den ældre og højmiddelalderlige bebyggelsesstruktur i Sønderjylland", in *Landbebyggelsen bebyggelsesstruktur. Middelalderens rurale Danmark*, edited by M. Svart & L.C. Bentsen. Aarhus: Jysk Arkæologiske Selskabs skrifter, 33-50.

Henriksen, M.B. 2015: "Kystens Kultpladser". *Odense By Museers Årbog*, 200-217.

Henriksen, P.S. 2016: "Norse agriculture in Greenland? Farming in a remote medieval landscape", in *Agrarian technology in the Medieval landscape*, edited by J. Klápste (*Ruralia* X, 2013), 237-245.

Henriksen, P.S. & A.M. Stevnsvig, 2020: Erritsø VKH 6810. Naturvidenskabelige undersøgelser. Miljøarkæologi og materialeforskning bevaring og naturvidenskab. Nationalmuseet. *Rapport 65/2020. NNU j-nr. A9280*.

Holmberg, B. & J.S. Madsen. 1998: "Da kom en snekke … Havnepladser fra 1000- og 1100-tallet", *KUML* 1997-98 (1998), 197-225.

Jensen. O.J. 2024: VKH 6810 Erritsø (FHM 4296/2270). Dendrokronologisk undersøgelse af brøndtømmer fra Erritsø. Rapport fra Afdeling for Konservering og Naturvidenskab. Moesgaard Museum, nr. 16.

Jessen, M. Dengsø & Terkildsen, K. Fiedler 2016: "Towering above: an interpretation of the Late Iron Age architecture at Toftum Næs, Denmark", *Danish Journal of Archaeology*, no. 5, 52-71. https://doi.org/10.1080/21662282.2016.1248592

Juel, C. & M. Ravn. 2018: "Erritsø – a fortified Early Viking Age manor near Little Belt. New investigations and research perspectives", in *The Fortified Viking Age. 36th Interdisciplinary Viking symposium in Odense, May 17th 2017*, edited by Jesper Hansen & Mette Bruus (Kulturhistoriske Studier i Centralitet, 3). Odense: South Danish University Press, 16-25.

Jørgensen, A.N. 2009: "Danish naval complexes in the Late Iron Age and Viking Age. The Gudsø Vig barrage in perspective", in *The Martial Society. Aspects of warriors, fortifications and social change in Scandinavia*, edited by L. Holmqvist Olausson & M. Olausson. Stockholm: Stockholm University, 79-92.

Jørgensen, L. 2009: "Pre-christian cult at aristocratic residences and settlement complexes in southern Scandinavia", in *Glaube, Kult und Herrschaft. Phänomene des Religiösen in 1. Jahrtausend n.Chr. in Mittel Nordeuropa. Akten des 59. Internationalen Sachsensymposiums und der Grundprobleme der frühgeschichtelischen Entwicklung im Mitteldonauraum*, edited by U. Von Freeden, H. Friesinger & E. Warmers. Bonn: Dr. Rudolf Habelt GmbH, 329-354.

Kramb, K.L. 2021: 700-tallets danerkonger. Unpublished manuscript

Laursen, K.O. & M. Ravn. 2022: "Guldfundet fra Vindelev og Verdens Største bracteat", in *Magt og Guld. Vikinger i Øst*, edited by M. Ravn & C. Lindblom. Aarhus: Turbine, 52-76.

Lemm, T. 2016: "Husby and the equestrian graves in Angeln and Schwansen – Different chronological stages in the development of a royal administration?", in *Aspects of Viking Age Urbanism, c. 750-1100. Ancient Centres, Special Economic Zones and – Restart*, edited by C. Hedenstierna-Jonson, L. Holmquist & S. Kalmring (Thesis and papers in archaeology B:12). Stockholm, 97-113.

Lemm, T. 2019: "Protecting Hedeby – Reconstructing a Viking Age maritime defense system based on visual Communication", in *Early medieval waterscapes. Risks and opportunities for (im)material cultural exchange*, edited by Rica Annaert, Tim Bellens, Pieterjan Deckers, Frans Theuws, Dries Tys, Robert van Dierendonckvan, Luc Impe, Johan Veeckman & Laurent Verslype (Neue Studien zur Sachsenforschung, 8). Braunschweig, 101-114.

Lund, N. 2002: "Horik den Førstes udenrigspolitik", *Historisk tidsskrift*. Bind 102, hæfte 1, 1-22.

Løken, T. 2020: *Bronze Age and Early Iron Age house and settlement development at Forsandmoen, south-western Norway* (AmS Skrifter 28).

Moltke, E. 1976: *Runerne I Danmark og deres oprindelse*. Copenhagen.

Morris, I. 2022: *Geography is Destiny. Britain and the world. A 10.000- year history*. London: Profile Books.

Ombashi, H. 2023: (FHM 4296/2815). Pollenanalyse af en jordprøve fra bundlaget af en brønd. Afdeling for Konservering og Naturvidenskab, Moesgaard Museum Nr. 59, 1-7.

Ravn, M. 2018: "Roads to complexity. Hawaiians and Vikings compared", *Danish Journal of Archaeology* 7 (2018): 119,132. DOI: https://doi.org/10.1080/21662282.2018.1468147

Ravn, M. 2022: "A Warlord's hoard", *Minerva*, November/December 2022, no. 198, 22-28.

Ravn, M., C. Juel, C. Lindblom & A. Pedersen. 2019: "Erritsø – new investigations of an aristocratic, early Viking Age manor in Western Denmark c. 700-850 AD", in *Early medieval Waterscapes. Risk and opportunities for (im)material cultural exchange*, edited by Rica Annaert, Tim Bellens, Pieterjan Deckers, Frans Theuws, Dries Tys, Robert van Dierendonck, Luc van Impe, Johan Veeckman & Laurent Verslype (Neue Studien zur Sachsenforschung, 8). Braunschweig, 37-44.

Ravn, M. & C. Juel. 2020: "En befæstet vikingegård ved Erritsø", in *Glimt fra Vikingetiden*, edited by Iben Skibsted Klæsøe, Jeppe Boel Jepsen, Freddy Arntzen, Benny Staal, Alan Tomlinson, Suzanne Barry, Niels Bødker Thomsen & Severin Tobias Mortensen. DDA Danske Amatørarkæologer. Nordvestgrafik: Danmark, 121-126.

Scholz, B.W. 1972: *Carolingian Chronicles. Royal Frankish Annals and Nithard's Histories*. Translated by Bernhard Walter Scholz. Michigan: The University of Michigan Press.

Skovgaard-Petersen, I., A.E. Christensen & H. Paludan. 1977: *Danmarks Historie*. Bind I. *Tiden indtil 1340*. København: Gyldendal.

Sørensen, M.K. 2017: "Pollenanalyse af en prøve fra voldgraven ved Erritsø", in *Report from MOMO*, Afdeling for Konservering og naturvidenskab, Moesgaard Museum. No. 17.

Electronic documents:

https://arcnames.w.uib.no/2019/11/04/a-name-fit-for-a-king/ (accessed july 21st 2023

https://coldwarsites.net/country/denmark/ accessed 2023 January 23rd

https://arcnames.w.uib.no/2019/11/04/a-name-fit-for-a-king/. Accessed 2023 January 30th.

https://prabook.com/web/horik.horik_ii/2352923 Accessed 2023 January 30th.

http://wayback-01.kb.dk/wayback/20101108105429/http://www2.kb.dk/elib/lit/dan/saxo/lat/or.dsr/ accessed 2023 January 30th

BY MORTEN LYNGKJÆR JENSEN

Chapter 18
Erritsø – the Production Area

The discovery of the fortified great hall complex at Erritsø[1] and the sites similarities to some of the important aristocratic settlement complexes in Southern Scandinavia such as Lejre[2] and Tissø[3] in Zealand and Järrestad[4] in Scania led to a desire to explore other similarities with these kind of sites regarding the overall settlement pattern and structure. At both Tissø[5], Lejre[6] and Järrestad[7] an adjacent area incorporating *grubenhäuser*[8] has been identified, and it was thus relevant to examine if a similar area, including (among other things) grubenhäuser, could be identified in the vicinity of the great hall area at Erritsø. This interest was soon focused on an area just about 200 m east of the great halls, where trial excavations of about 10 hectares in 2008 revealed settlement activity, which initially was interpreted as scattered refuse pits from an earlier part of the Iron Age, while two smaller areas were excavated and interpreted as small post-built houses and pits from ca. 11-1200 AD. But considering the nature of the early Viking Age great hall area immediately to the west, it was considered a possibility that these post-built structures should instead be dated to this same period, and that what was thought of as simple refuse pits were indeed grubenhäuser and so this area could be connected to the great halls as proposed above. To examine if this was the case, a re-interpretation of the results of the 2008 excavation was made in 2018 and three small areas were re-excavated in order to collect material for ^{14}C-datings from the site as well as to establish whether two of the initially supposed pits were indeed grubenhäuser of the early Viking Age. ^{14}C-datings from three grubenhäuser and a single post-built house placed the settlement area in the Late Germanic Iron Age and Early Viking Age around 700-900 AD, which

---

1   Ravn et al. 2019; see also Ravn and Juel this volume.
2   Christensen 2015
3   Jørgensen, L. 2009; Jørgensen, L. 2010; Jørgensen, L. et al. 2019
4   Söderberg 2005, 63ff.
5   Jørgensen, L. et al. 2019, 151
6   Christensen 2015, 46ff.
7   Söderberg 2005, 63ff.
8   The term *Grubenhäuser* is preferred here, but this type of building can also be seen referred to as *sunken featured buildings* og *pit-houses* respectively.

fits very well in the dating frame of the great halls, and as both excavated pits turned out to be grubenhäuser, it was clear that the activity here was indeed associated with the great hall complex at Erritsø, presumably as a production area.

To delimit the Production Area, a supplementary trial excavation was carried out in 2019, covering the western part of the 10 hectares that was initially excavated in 2008. This led to the discovery of an area of just over one hectare with significant settlement traces. This area was excavated in 2020, while an assumed northwestern part of the Production Area, not under threat from immediate construction, was left untouched at the time. It was later possible to examine a portion of this as part of a field school for students of historical archaeology in cooperation with the Department of Archaeology, University of Aarhus, showing that this area had also been part of the same Production Area related to the Great Hall site. It is the results of these excavations that are presented and discussed in this chapter. The grubenhäuser area is broadly interpreted and named as a production area associated with the aristocratic settlement, but as will be discussed below, the interpretation of these kind of sites are still a matter of debate[9].

Topography

The Production Area is placed directly east of the great halls at a distance of about 150 m at the most. We do not have a complete understanding of the area in between the two sites, which has been disturbed in modern times by significant industrial activity. At this place the local topography falls from a level of about 32 m above sea level at the top of the hill at the centre of the fortified area to about 27-29 m for the earlier phases of the great halls. The excavated production area is located even lower at about 23 to 25 m above sea level. At the Production Area specifically the terrain falls from north to south with a local depression at the central part where the character of the subsoil, as well as the presence of three wells of the area, indicate that the terrain must have been at least seasonally wet.

The limits of the Production Area could only be partially established. The area immediately to the north had been dug away completely as a result of modern activity; the southern and western borders are confined by modern roads, but following the results of various investigations in this direction, it seems reasonable to say, that the Production Area has been more or less delimited in these two directions as well as towards the east, where extensive trial excavations have shown hardly any archaeological features for at least 200 m. Only the small area immediately between the Large Halls and the Production Area is still to some degree unexcavated, though this space is to a large extent occupied by modern roads and buildings. The smaller excavations carried out in collaboration with the department of Archaeology, Aarhus University in 2021, 2022 and 2023 in this area have given clear indications that settlement activity undoubtedly associated with the production area are to be found in this general area – the question to what extent and just how close to the great halls the production area goes is still unknown though.

---

9   Jørgensen, A.N. et al. 2010; Jørgensen, L. et al. 2019

Of course, these assumptions regarding the extent and nature of production areas associated with the Great Hall Area can only be seen as referring to the examined area east of the great halls. It is entirely possible that areas of production associated with the great halls at Erritsø could have existed in other places around the Great Halls; when considering the local topography, the areas north, west and south of the hilly fortified site are fairly similar to the eastern Production Area, but unfortunately these areas have today largely been occupied by modern highways, industry and residences. Though hypothetical and yet unproven, such additional grubenhaus-areas would not be surprising considering the longevity of the occupation at the great hall area itself, apparently spanning several centuries, when compared to the relatively short lifespan of the individual smaller post-built houses and grubenhäuser of the excavated Production Area as indicated by the light construction of these as well as the relatively small extent of this area.

Methodology and Results

The buildings at the site

1.1 hectares were examined in the 2020 excavation, in addition to which the adjacent areas of a combined 2650 m² that were excavated in 2008 can be added for a total continuous area of 1.37 hectares. Further smaller areas that are not directly connected to the larger excavated area, but a part of the same overall Production Area has been examined to the northwest in 2018 (330 m²), 2021 (500 m²), 2022 (750 m²) and 2023 (613 m²), the latter three as part of the field school for archaeology students.

The settlement structures that appeared can roughly be divided into two separate groups: 1) post-built houses and 2) grubenhäuser – of which 30 and 34 have been found respectively.

The **post-built houses** are for a large part of a rather light and simple type; most often with just three or four sets of roof bearing posts and with a relatively small, transverse distance between posts. Wall- and entrance posts are only occasionally preserved, although there are a couple of houses with most or nearly all the wall preserved as well as a few where possible entrances can be identified. Of the 30 post-built houses, 28 can be considered a part of this group of small and simple houses with estimated lengths ranging between 10 and 18 m and widths between 4.2 and 6.5 m[10]. A few interesting characteristics can be observed about these houses – for instance the two houses with the best-preserved walls, both of similar dimensions, show a very different form with one being strictly rectangular and the other of a much more rounded form. It can therefore be difficult to assess the original shape of the houses with only the inner roof-bearing posts preserved.

The inconspicuous nature of these small and simple constructions means that they do not necessarily stand out in a larger settlement pattern, and both their function and

---

10 The estimated dimensions for the post-built houses are not certain as walls are rarely found – but by comparing the more well-preserved examples with the rest, an estimated guess can be made.

Fig. 1. The distribution of post-built houses, grubenhäuser and the three wells in the central part of the Production Area at Erritsø. The relation to the great hall-area of Erritsø can be seen in the insert top left.

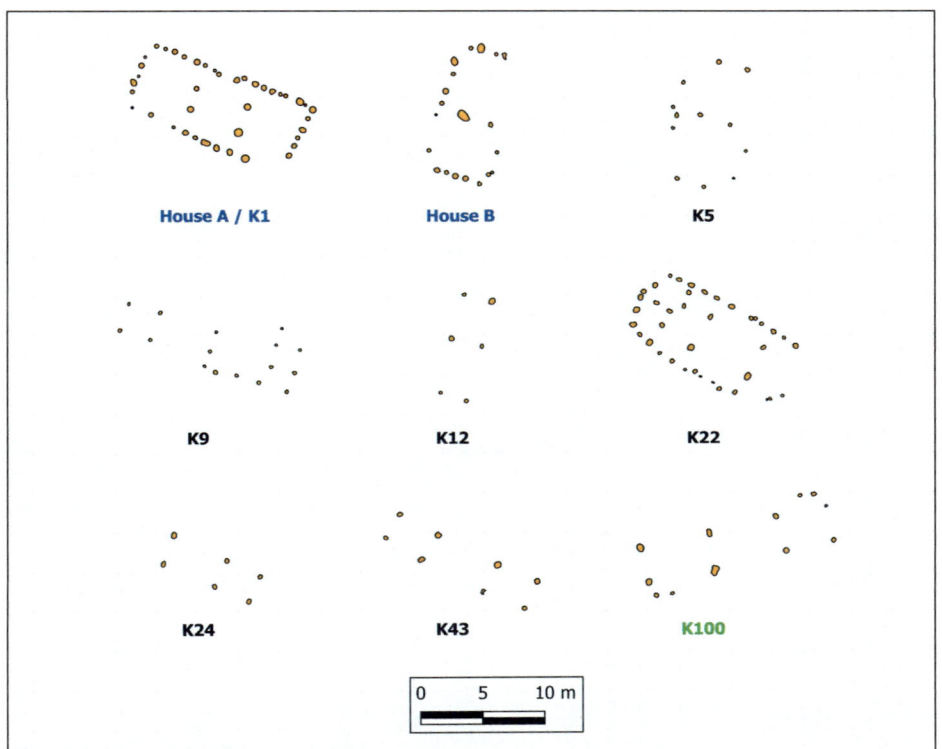

Examples of smaller post-built houses of different types and various degrees of preservation from the Production Area. The houses A and B were originally examined in 2008 with house A slightly re-interpreted in 2018, while K100 were excavated in 2001. The rest are from the 2020 excavation.

Fig. 2.

date can thus be difficult to understand from a purely typological perspective. Similar constructions seem to occur, interpreted as fence-houses at Vorbasse for instance, dating to the 8th and 9th century AD[11] as well as smaller and better-preserved houses from Mørup dating to the 7th century[12]. The best parallel for the small three-aisled houses at the production area at Erritsø though may be found at the coast-bound trading- and production site of Bejsebakken near Limfjorden[13]. At this site 56 three-aisled houses have been examined including a phase from the late 7th to 9th century[14] as well as a very large number of grubenhäuser. The post-built three-aisled houses from Bejsebakken consist of both larger and smaller buildings with particularly the smaller ones being very similar to some of the post-built houses from the production area at Erritsø. At Bejsebakken

---

11   Ethelberg 2010, 328 & 738 (note 391)
12   Hansen et al. 1991, 24
13   Sarauw 2019
14   Ibid, 30ff.

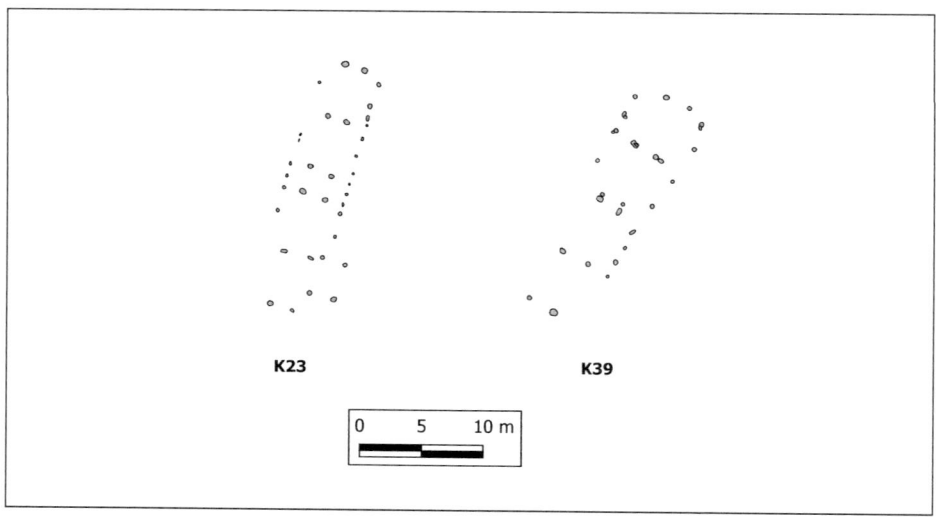

Fig. 3. *The two larger three-aisled long-houses found in the southern part of the Production Area. K23 is shown with a possible windbreak in the southeastern part, but it's uncertain if this interpretation is correct.*

houses with at least four sets of roof-bearing posts, many of which are of a similar size as the small and simple houses from Erritsø, are considered to be "long" or "main houses" in this settlement[15]. The function of the houses at the above-mentioned sites may differ, as does the sites themselves, but it shows that houses of this type were generally known at the transition from Ironto Viking Age, and that both a function as main houses of a farmstead as well as something other than primary housing is a possibility.

Besides the 30 smaller post-built houses there are also two longhouses of a different and more sturdy design with five and six sets of roof bearing posts respectively. With widths of 5.3 and 6.5 m- and lengths of 21 m[16], these are both significantly larger and generally appear notably more substantial and should perhaps be seen as more permanent constructions. Both houses have partially preserved straight walls although the gable-construction is unclear, and one seems to have a windbreak at the southeastern end.

The house type may be associated with what has been named an *early Sædding* house type, dating to perhaps the 8th or 9th century[17]. This seems to be confirmed by the ^{14}C-datings from both houses.

The **grubenhäuser** are represented in 34 examples, all of which can be seen as belonging to the same general type with round- to super elliptical-shaped grubenhaus-pits

---

15   Ibid, 28
16   The widths are measured from wall to wall while the lengths are measured at the roof-bearing sets furthest apart. It's very possible, that these are set in the gables, and that the mentioned lengths are accordingly the real lengths of the houses.
17   Jørgensen & Eriksen 1995, 20

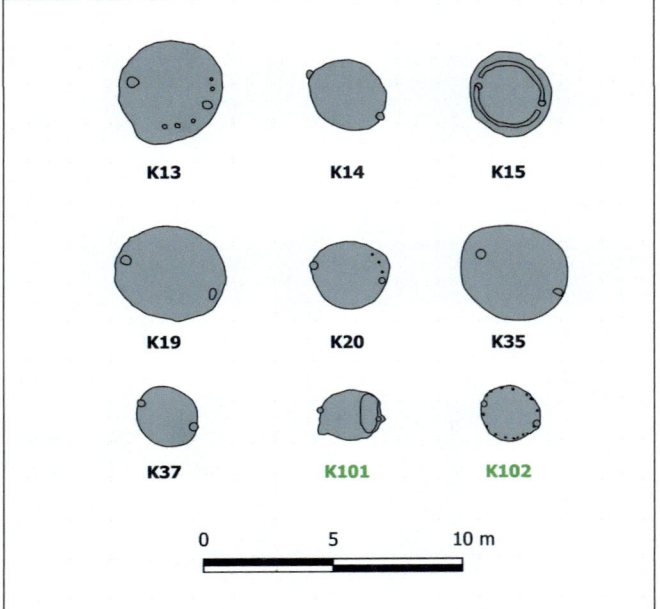

Examples of the grubenhäuser from the Production Area showing the different sizes and variations of these constructions. In some cases stake holes are preserved along the wall-line; the small pit in the eastern part of K101 is interpreted as the original placing of a loom and thus points to a function as a weaving hut for this grubenhaus. The houses K101 and K102 were excavated in 2021, the rest in 2020.

Fig. 4.

each with a ridge post at either end of the gables, giving a general north-northwestern by south-southeastern orientation of the buildings. The pits have depths between 0.12 and 0.81 m and range between 2.2 and 4.1 m in diameter. The sizes of the grubenhaus-pits are to some extent dependent on the degree of preservation of each individual pit – the distance between the two roof-bearing posts of each house gives us a better understanding of the actual sizes of these constructions. Considering the varying degree of the depths of the preserved pits, it is entirely possible that more grubenhäuser have originally existed at the site, but that some have been erased by modern agriculture – a problem also observed in the case of the grubenhäuser at Tissø[18].

In some instances, rows of smaller stake holes can be seen along the edge of the grubenhaus-pit which represents the remnants of an original wicker work wall construction lining the inner part of the pit. This feature or part thereof has only been observed in a few of the grubenhäuser, presumably due to poor preservation, combined with difficulties in distinguishing these stake holes from the abundant natural variations in the subsoil. It seems reasonable to suggest that a wall construction of wattle and daub has generally been used for the grubenhäuser at the site.

The post-built houses as well as the grubenhäuser are evenly spread out over the excavated site, though there may be a slight tendency for the grubenhäuser to be gathered in four small clusters throughout the site with examples of both smaller and larger grubenhäuser being represented in every cluster. It is notable that even though the

---

18   Gotfredsen & Thomsen 2011, 213

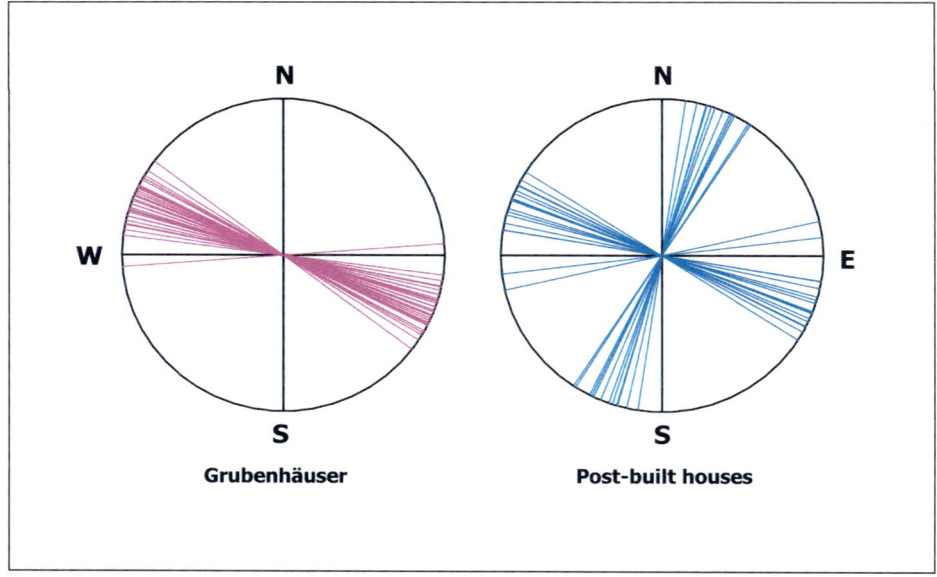

Fig. 5. *The orientation of the grubenhäuser and the post-built houses respectively. The conformity in each group as well as between the two groups is noticeable although with a few outliers in both groups.*

post-built houses are scattered evenly over the site, the two larger and more well-built examples are both situated in the southernmost part. These may be understood as some kind of main buildings at the Production Site or perhaps the sign of more permanent residency at the site which would then have its center here.

Considering the relationship between the various buildings at the site, it is interesting that they have an almost exclusively north-northwest by south-southeastern orientation or perpendicularly to this, a south-southwest by north-northeastern orientation. The grubenhäuser are exclusively oriented towards the north-northwest by south-southeast with just one exception, which is oriented almost completely east-west. The post-built houses are more or less evenly oriented both ways. This large degree of similarity between the various buildings – and various types of buildings – points to a shared and overall understanding of how the site was laid out and used, however deliberate or not this might be, as well as a high degree of continuity of the settlement that is most unlikely to have been disturbed. That we cannot talk of just a single phase of settlement activity, on the other hand it is evident from the fact that there are several examples of buildings being erected at the same spot. In a couple of instances, it seems obvious that this sequence of buildings is the result of a replacement and renewal of already existing buildings, as the sizing, orientation and placing of the different buildings are practically the same[19],

---

19 This goes for the post-built houses K6, K7 and K8 and K10 and K11 respectively which must be considered three and two phases of fundamentally the same construction.

while in other instances buildings of different types overlay[20], or two buildings of the same type but with different sizes are placed at the same spot[21].

Function and dating of the Production Area

As a part of the excavation strategy, a relatively large part of the grubenhäuser-fill was sieved. The degree to which this was done was dependent on time available as this process was time consuming, not least in the cases of larger grubenhäuser, where sieving of the entire fill would be a matter of several days' work, all as it should turn out for a relatively small gain. A strategy was made where it was prioritized to sieve parts of the fill of every grubenhaus of the site, ranging between a quarter and the entirety of the constructions in order to get a good degree of representativity from the site. The purpose of this process, and the large amount of time that was spent on it, was to collect a representative find material from the site that could substantiate the dating as well as the function regarding such activities as trade and exports as well as craft activities.

From 13 grubenhäuser came a total of nine loom weights and six spindle whorls. These are not great numbers, but all in all the Production Area at Erritsø has given relatively few finds and, apart from ceramics, items associated with textile-production are the dominant find group considering the number of constructions in which they were found. Finds connected to textile production were found in 45% of the grubenhäuser at Erritsø and in 63% at Tissø[22]. It is interesting to note that items related to textile production at Erritsø, i.e., loom weights and spindle whorls are solely found in the context of the grubenhäuser, except for a single stray find of a complete loom weight[23]. The loom weights and spindle whorls, though found in grubenhäuser, are almost exclusively found in the fill layers of these constructions. Thus, they cannot with certainty be seen as direct evidence of textile production in the grubenhäuser, but are certainly indicative of the activities carried out nearby.

Another find group of interest when it comes to the function of the Production Area of Erritsø is iron slag, that has been found in the fill of eight different grubenhäuser as well as from a well and a culture layer[24]. It is interesting to note, that the iron slag seems to be concentrated in certain areas, indicating that some local iron smelting was carried out in the vicinity of these constructions. Notably, three of the grubenhäuser containing iron slag also contained loom weights, but it seems implausible that both

---

20   Examples are the post-built house K12 and grubenhaus K21 as well as post-built house K45 and grubenhaus K30.
21   K100 and K104 from the 2021 field school-excavation are an example of this.
22   Thomsen 2010, 112 ff. – It is interesting to note though, that these numbers, high as they may seem, are interpreted as less than usual focus on textile production at this site.
23   Both loom weights and spindle whorls were often found as fragments meaning that as a rule they must have been discarded and displaced items out of their original context.
24   This data does not include the 2022 and 2023 excavations.

Fig. 6. *Three glass beads found in the sieved fill of grubenhäuser during the 2020 excavation. The green segmented metal foiled bead to the left can be dated to the late 8th – mid 9th century AD and was presumably imported from the near east.[25] while the bead to the right might possibly be domestically produced and likely dates from 725 AD and into the 9th century. The yellow glass bead in the middle might also be domestically produced but is difficult to date precisely.[26]*

functions were carried out in the same houses, and the iron smelting must have taken place in the area just outside the particular grubenhäuser.

Of special interest when it comes to iron craft are two grubenhäuser lying close to each other in the northern part of the excavated area. They are among the largest of the grubenhäuser at the site with depths of 0.56 and 0.70 m. One contains a fragment of a spindle whorl as well as a significantly larger amount of iron slag than otherwise found in addition to a single spheroidal hammer scale[27] and some amount of iron flake hammer scale in soil samples taken from postholes as well as the general

---

25   Sode & Feveile, 2002, 7
26   Thanks to Claus Feveile for information regarding the datings and production places of the glass beads.
27   With a size of just a few millimetres in diameter the spheroidal hammer scales are easily overlooked in the field when excavating a grubenhaus, and the single find of one such must be ascribed to mere coincidence. It is entirely plausible that several others might also have been part of the fill, but simply were not found. It is furthermore interesting that a very small clay ball of approximately the same size were also found in this grubenhaus, a type that might be associated with the production of steel (Hansen 2021, 241).

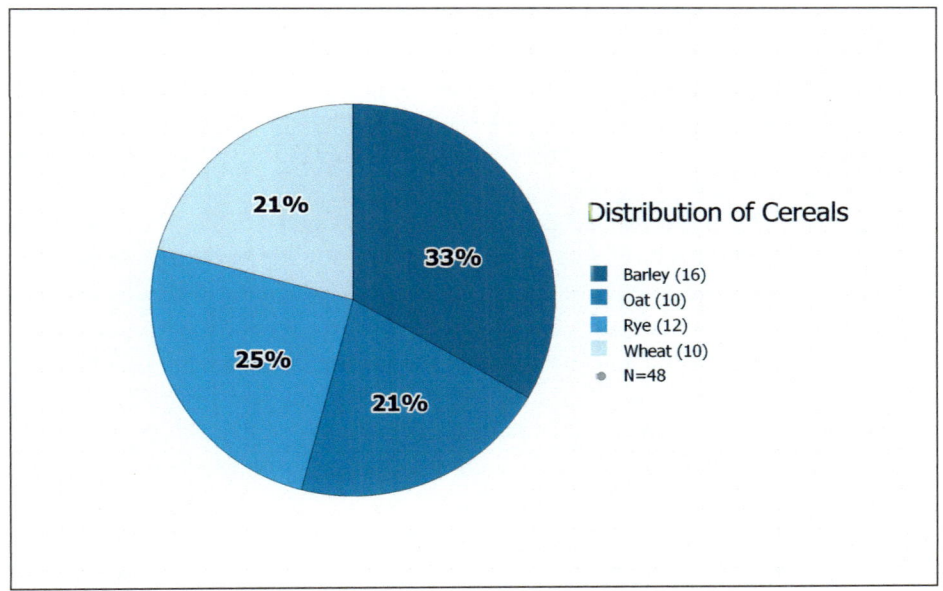

The distribution of the four main cereal types found in soil samples from both post-built houses and grubenhäuser from the Production Area at Erritsø.

Fig. 7.

fill. The neighbouring grubenhaus also contains iron slag in large quantities as well as flake iron scale in the fill. Spheroidal and flake hammer scale can be seen as signs of the grubenhäuser having functioned as smithies, a function that has also been seen at Tissø among other sites[28].

Only a few of the grubenhäuser give a somewhat clear indication of function based on specific details in their construction – in one example a hearth could be observed at the floor level of a grubenhaus[29] meaning that this construction might – at least to some extent – have functioned as a dwelling. Another interesting example was a rather small grubenhaus of just 2.0 × 2.3 m with a low depression transversely spanning the eastern end of the house at floor level that is interpreted as the original placing of an upright loom[30]. Stakes from an upright loom could not be observed in this or any other grubenhaus but considering the difficulties in observing such a trait (as noted above) this is hardly surprising. In the same way it is also possible that other wear-and-tear zones from working on a loom has simply not been made or preserved to a degree where it was possible to detect them during excavation.

---

28 Jørgensen, L. 2003, 202
29 A666 from the 2018 excavation.
30 K101 from the 2021 excavation.

Looking at the botanical remains from the site both rye, barley, oat and wheat species are found as fossilized remains[31] and in addition possibly millet[32]. The four cereal species are all well-known from late Iron Age and Viking Age finds, but the finds at this site may stand out slightly due to a relatively high proportion of wheat, which might be seen as a niche and high-status crop at the time[33], though the few finds (48 samples in all) might make such conclusions uncertain.

The ^{14}C-datings from the 2018 and 2020 campaigns suggests that the Production Area was first established in the late 7th century AD or possibly in the early part of the 8th century. It remained in use through the 9th – and 10th centuries with a few datings indicating, that activity at the site even continued into the start of the 11th century. Thus the Production Area could have been in continuous use through a period of almost 350 years – a long span particularly considering the relatively few constructions at the site compared to other more or less similar sites containing grubenhäuser – as shown in the below. Even though the various radiocarbon datings from the Production Area give an overall timeframe for the activities performed here, the unambiguous dating of individual constructions is more problematic. This is to some extent the result of the fairly broad timeframe each ^{14}C-dating offers (generally ranging between 100 and 200 years) but also because even when it was possible to date constructions by more than a single ^{14}C-dating, these often showed conflicting results. The latter is probably the result of a high degree of contamination due to the longevity of the site – as is indeed also suggested by the ^{14}C-datings as a whole. In a very general perspective though, 9 of the 15 dated grubenhäuser seems to be broadly placed at the transition between the Germanic Iron Age and the Viking Age (ca. 680-880 AD), five in the Viking Age proper (ca. 800-990 AD) and a single one in the very latest part of the Viking Age (ca. 980-1030 AD). Due to the above-mentioned reservations these datings cannot be considered firm evidence, but probably gives us a very general notion of the temporal placing of at least some of the grubenhäuser. The picture is even more vague when considering the smaller post-built houses, who often seem to have a very broad timeframe based on the ^{14}C-datings spanning the period between the second part of the 7th century AD and the end of the 10th century. Two houses excavated in 2018 (K1 and K2). does seem to date to the late Iron Age or early Viking Age and K22 from the 2020-excavation stands out both due to its well-preserved rounded walls as well as a late dating to 10th or even first part of 11th century AD.

The grubenhäuser are harder to date typologically, as this general type has a long continuity through the Iron- and Viking Ages. The relatively few finds from the Production Area do not offer much help in this matter as they either – similarly to the grubenhäuser – are used for a long period of time. This applies to most of the prominent find types such as ceramics of which hemispherical vessels were dominant, as well

---

31   16 examples of barley, 10 oat, 10 wheat and 12 rye respectively.
32   Millet is only known from a single and uncertain find, and generally seem to be a rare if not unknown crop at the time – see Hardt 2000, 43-44; Jensen 2018, 28.
33   Andreasen 2017, 8; Hardt 2000, 45; Jensen 2018, 22

as the loom weights and spindle whorls. Other finds can potentially have a long and complex use-life such as the few finds of glass beads (Fig. 6). From the grubenhäuser, K35 though the find of decorated pottery of Baltic type may point to wider connections of the Erritsø Production Area to the Southern Baltic. This ceramic type generally has a more eastern distribution and is often dated to the 10th century but finds from Southern Jutland including Haithabu have been dated to the 9th century[34].

The metal finds from the production area are also few, and mostly consists of small and simple pieces that do not give much in the way of dating or function of the production area. A clear understanding of the site as a production- or trade site certainly is not substantiated by the finds from the area as could have been hoped for but finds related to crafts such as textile production and iron processing suggests that textile and iron production certainly did take place at the site – at least to some extent.

Interpretation of the Site

Traditionally grubenhäuser of the Southern Scandinavian late Iron Age and Viking Age are often associated with more ordinary farms and villages that constitute a large majority of the settlements at the time. They are typically interpreted as small working huts, often used for weaving, with the primary workspace dug down into the ground and assumably only infrequently and seasonally used for dwelling purposes[35]. This separates them from the grubenhäuser known from the Slavic area of the Southern Baltic where the grubenhäuser are traditionally larger and can seemingly be associated with more permanent dwelling[36].

The grubenhäuser though, are also associated with site types such as the specialized production sites, seasonally used coast-bound landing- and trading sites and in the early towns[37] – and in the context of this paper most interestingly also with high-status aristocratic sites such as Lejre[38], Tissø[39], Järrestad[40] and Toftum Næs[41]. As it is stated elsewhere in this volume[42] there are striking similarities (albeit also differences) between the fortified great hall complex at Erritsø and the aristocratic sites at Lejre, Tissø and Järrestad when it comes to the overall site-layout with their very large halls in several consecutive phases spanning several centuries of settlement and in all these places with an adjacent, enclosed special area surrounding a possibly ritual building lying transversely to the great halls. The site at Toftum Næs distinguishes itself from the

---

34   Madsen 1991, 224
35   Jørgensen, L. et al. 2019, 162; Thomsen 2010
36   Ethelberg 2000, 296-297 and 737 (note 339)
37   Jørgensen, L. 2003, 175
38   Christensen 2015
39   Jørgensen, L. 2009; Jørgensen, L. 2010; Jørgensen, L. et al. 2019
40   Söderberg 2005
41   Jessen & Terkildsen 2016
42   Ravn & Juel this volume

others by not having a separately enclosed special or ritual area adjacent to the halls, which might also be somewhat less monumental than at Lejre, Tissø and Erritsø[43]. On the other hand, this settlement contains a large wooden tower, a trait that has not been seen at any other known locations but give an impression of a fortification that can be related to the moat and palisade at Erritsø. All these sites, which due to their very large halls, longevity and special settlement structure may be labelled as special and aristocratic sites, also contain extensive areas with grubenhäuser as an important feature of the overall settlement layout:

1. At **Lejre** the *Activity Area 1*[44] was placed just east of the great hall area of Mysselhøjgård at a lower terrain down by a local stream. This area is situated under the current modern village and excavation has thus been hampered for most of this area. So far 17 grubenhäuser have been found in addition to pits and postholes at the site[45].
2. At **Tissø** two areas with an estimated minimum of 400-600 grubenhäuser have been identified, of which 84 have been found and 69 excavated. These two areas, which also include postholes, are closely connected to the great hall areas, and are considered related to market- and workshop activities[46]. It has also been proposed though that seasonal dwelling should be seen as the primary function for these sites and that production and craft activities are secondary to this[47]. It is interesting to note, that three grubenhäuser from Tissø, all lying within the main hall area, are interpreted as being related to cultic or special activities[48] – this did not appear to be the case with any of the excavated structures at the Erritsø Production Area.
3. **Järrestad** has only been excavated to a smaller extent, but apart from the striking similarities to the large halls of Erritsø, the settlement at Järrestad also has an adjacent grubenhaus-area with at least 25 and likely more constructions that are thought to be related to both craft activities and accommodation[49].
4. **Toftum Næs** is a recently discovered site with settlement traces including several large halls among other structures. Of special interest is a large wooden tower that stood as part of the settlement structure, which is so far unique in a Southern Scandinavian context. Just north of the large hall area on lower grounds and near a local stream several grubenhäuser has been discovered as well as traces of small post-built houses in an area *"which might cover production units in the pithouses and post built housings spread amongst each other*[50]*"* – this might be a picture very similar to what we see at

---

43 Jessen & Terkildsen 2016, 54 ff.
44 Christensen 2015, 84
45 Ibid., 46 ff. & 54
46 Jørgensen. L 2010, 280 ff.
47 Jørgensen, L. et al. 2019, 150 ff.; Jørgensen, A.N. et al. 2011, 95 ff.
48 Gotfredsen & Thomsen 2011
49 Jørgensen, A.N. et al. 2011, 104
50 Jessen & Terkildsen 2016, 63

the Production Area at Erritsø. The site is interpreted as a supervised, supra-regional trading site[51] and possibly with the grubenhäuser serving as seasonal habitation.

When we consider these four examples of aristocratic sites dominated by large halls and compare them to the site of Erritsø, it is clear that there are striking similarities not only considering the monumental architecture of the halls and their immediate surroundings, but also spatially, in the presence of the adjacent grubenhaus-areas clearly related to the activities carried out at the site. The areas generally seem to include large numbers of grubenhäuser, at least where the extent can be estimated with some probability – sites such as Tissø and Toftum Næs, while the degree of excavation at Lejre and Järrestad does not allow wider conclusions as to the number of grubenhäuser here at this time. Besides grubenhäuser these areas also include postholes which at least at Toftum Næs are interpreted as small houses[52] while at Tissø, where the postholes are found by the thousands, small houses and booths appear[53]. All in all – and despite the differences that also appear between these special, high-status sites, there also seems to be a significant resemblance between them, both regarding the overall site-layout as well as a number of the features that constitutes them. Another site that is interesting when compared to Erritsø is the above mentioned Limfjord site of Bejsebakken, although without the presence of special and monumental buildings like the great halls and enclosed areas of Tissø, Lejre or Järrestad or the tower at Toftum Næs. Apart from the close resemblance between some of the post-built houses of the 8th-9th century at both sites, Bejsebakken also contains at least 442 grubenhäuser and estimated more than 800 for the entire settlement area here with activities connected to trade, textile production and metalworking[54], and is interpreted as a trading site with specialized production[55] though a wider relationship to the central places and possibly early kingdoms of the late Iron Age is also hinted at[56].

A fundamental aspect when trying to understand the grubenhäuser-sites in relation to the aristocratic sites is the question of their use and whether they were continuously- or seasonally used. As stated above, the grubenhäuser are traditionally interpreted as working huts, often associated with weaving. This seems to be corroborated by the finds from Tissø, where 63% have finds associated with textile production and 42% with metalcraft[57] and from Erritsø, where the numbers are 45% and 28% respectively and with only a few at both sites containing fireplaces. At Bejsebakken, which as noted above, seems to represent a different kind of settlement structure, items related to

51	Ibid., 63
52	Ibid., 63
53	Jørgensen, L. 2003, 201
54	Sarauw 2019, 64 ff.
55	Ibid., 242
56	Ibid., 13
57	Gotfredsen & Thomsen 2011, 213

textile production has been found in 35% of the examined grubenhäuser[58]. It must be stressed though that finds from the fill of the grubenhäuser are not necessarily directly related to the function of the house but can come from the immediate surroundings of the constructions. At the sites of Tissø[59] and Toftum Næs[60] trade seems to have taken place, perhaps as a major activity, but little indication of trade has been found at Erritsø[61]. At Lejre and Järrestad the degree of excavation is too limited at this point to make any firm conclusions regarding the specific use of the grubenhäuser.

It has recently been proposed that the grubenhäuser should to a higher degree than previously thought, be considered as multifunctional buildings, and especially the various sites where grubenhäuser are found in large numbers, these should be seen primarily as temporary dwellings for seasonal gatherings or assemblies where relations for a wider society were established and possibly controlled by a newly emerged caste of rulers from the 6th century onwards. Jørgensen et al. write:

> … temporary assembly for undertaking a number of social and societal tasks was the primary function of some of our large pit house sites from the 6th-11th century AD, and that in many cases craft activity was a secondary function carried out during the stay. One function does not definitely exclude the other, and we also have pit house areas where the most important activities are crafts and production. However, a large proportion of the pit house sites may be places of assembly for religious events, trade and political control, which in this case may have been introduced in the 6th century AD. The pit house areas are in this way a clear physical expression of a new control of the society through the utilization of assembly site functions.[62]

This interpretation is proposed for Tissø[63] and Toftum Næs[64], and could be considered for the grubenhäuser area of Erritsø as well. If indeed the large halls of Erritsø should be seen as the seat of early itinerant rulers or otherwise directly associated with a ruling elite, as seems highly likely[65], the presence of the ruler and his retinue would entail people from a wider area around the location. These gatherings could be voluntary as the presence of the ruler also brought with it the possibilities for- and presence of a variety of societal activities connected to ritual/religious-, economic/trade- and political/legal acts and generally social relations of the society that it was desirable or even neces-

---

58 Sarauw 2019, 241
59 Jørgensen, L. 2003, 203
60 Jessen & Terkildsen 2016, 64 ff.
61 A few glass beads, a single dirhem clipping and a lead weight are considered to be too little evidence to make any conclusions in this regard.
62 Jørgensen, A.N. et al. 2011, 96
63 Jørgensen, L. et al. 2019, 162 ff.
64 Jessen & Terkildsen 2016, 62 ff.
65 Ravn & Juel this volume

sary to perform at certain intervals. As part of these assemblies, a variety of crafts and production would surely have been carried out, even though these might be secondary to the assemblies themselves.

It is also a possibility that the activities carried out at the site were at least in part dependent on the ruling elite and that the people that worked and possibly lived at the Production Area were summoned there, possibly as a sort of compulsory or corvée labour. The presence of specialized labourers that might have travelled voluntarily to the grubenhäuser sites to perform highly skilled production such as the production of weapons, jewellery or high skilled weaving at an aristocratic environment are not substantiated at the Production Area of Erritsø though such activities have been proven at Tissø[66].

Conclusion

The Production Area at Erritsø as described above, is characterized by a mix of grubenhäuser and post-built houses that are primarily of a small and light type with only few other constructions or features present. The area is clearly related to the fortified large hall area directly to the east, and the question is how their relationship should be understood. Considering the light construction and presumably temporary nature of most of the settlement traces here, it is possible that it should be seen as a site that was only seasonally occupied and used, probably with some permanent settlement in the form of the two more substantial post-built houses in the southern part of the Production Area.

The specific circumstances of how these gatherings could have been organized, and what practices that were carried out here, are still uncertain, but it does seem clear that crafts and production were to some extent a part of the site – and very likely a highly important one, if not the all dominant part, and that these activities were dependent on the significance of the aristocratic environment around the great halls – either with workers/craftsmen being summoned there or with the site being a natural gathering place for the local population.

If the grubenhaus-site at Erritsø was indeed seasonally used, it would likely be connected to the use of the fortified Great Hall area as a likewise seasonally used seat of itinerant rulers. The activities at the Production Area could either be decided and arranged directly by the ruler, but it is also possible that the gathering of people at the grubenhäuser-site should to a higher degree be seen as a result of the populace of the surrounding area being drawn to the site at their own will in order to exploit the possibilities for trade, worship, or political and legal processes associated with the occasional presence of higher authorities.

The extent of the site seems well understood today and it is interesting to note, that the 34 grubenhäuser and 32 smaller houses represent a more limited settlement then what are seen at Tissø and Toftum Næs, and presumably also Lejre and Järrestad, even though the picture at these two latter sites is somewhat obscured due to the limited

---

66 Jørgensen, L. 2003, 202; Jørgensen, L. et al. 2019, 159 & 167

extent of excavations. It is possible though, that the Production Area associated with the great halls at Erritsø could have been more widespread either with other grubenhäuser at other, yet unknown, places around the great halls or as grubenhäuser that have been destroyed by modern ploughing in the area. Another explanation for this mismatch between the number of grubenhäuser at these sites could depend on the use-life of the Production Area at Erritsø – even though it now seems clear that the large halls at Erritsø had great importance for several centuries, like the comparable sites, it is possible that the gathering of people at a production area with grubenhäuser as the dominant feature were, unlike these other sites, only of importance through a part of this period of time. This latter explanation does not correspond with the available ^{14}C-datings from the site though, and all things considered it seems certain to assume that the Production Area, like the great halls, was in continuous use through a period of time stretching from the end of the late Iron Age and throughout the Viking Age emphasizing the close connection between what must be considered two aspects of an important aristocratic milieu at this time.

Bibliography

Andersen, H.H., P.J. Crabb & H.J. Madsen. 1971: *Århus Søndervold. En byarkæologisk undersøgelse*. Jysk Arkæologisk Selskab, Højbjerg.

Andreasen, M.H. 2017: MKH 1849, Eltang (FHM 4296/2107) *Makrofossilanalyser af grubehuse fra vikingetiden*; Afdeling for Konservering og Naturvidenskab, Moesgård Museum. Nr. 16 2017.
https://www.moesgaardmuseum.dk/media/4144/moes_1716.pdf

Christensen, T. 2015: *Lejre bag myten. De arkæologiske udgravninger*. (Jysk Arkæologisk Selskabs Skrifter 87). Jysk Arkæologisk Selskab, Højbjerg.

Ethelberg, P. 2000. "Gården og landsbyen i jernalder og vikingetid (500 f. Kr. – 1000 e. Kr.)", in *Det Sønderjyske Landbrugs Historie. Jernalder, Vikingetid og Middelalder*, edited by L.S. Madsen & O. Madsen. Haderslev Museum, Historisk Samfund for Sønderjylland, Haderslev, 123-374.

Gotfredsen, A.B. & L.G. Thomsen. 2011: "Three pit-houses of the magnate's residence at Lake Tissø", in *The Iron Age on Zealand. Status and Perspectives,* edited by L. Boye (Nordiske Fortidsminder Series C, volume 8). Det Kongelige Nordiske Oldskriftselskab, 211-220.

Hansen, E.K. 2021: *"*To østjyske smedjer fra middelalder og renæssance: Belyst gennem arkæologiske fund og arkæometallurgiske analyser*"*, *Kuml* 2020. Jysk Arkæologisk Selskab, Højbjerg, 217-258.

Hansen, K.M. & H. Høier. 2000: "Næs – en vikingetidsbebyggelse med hørproduktion*"*, *Kuml* 2000. Jysk Arkæologisk Selskab, Højbjerg, 59-90.

Hansen, T.E., S. Hvass & D.K. Mikkelsen. 1991: "Landbebyggelserne i 7. århundrede", in *Fra Stamme til Stat i Danmark 2. Høvdingesamfund og Kongemagt*. Jysk Arkæologisk Selskab, Højbjerg, 17-28.

Hardt, N. 2000: "Jernalderens og vikingetidens landbrug", in *Det Sønderjyske Landbrugs Historie. Jernalder, Vikingetid og Middelalder*, edited by L.S. Madsen & O. Madsen. Haderslev Museum, Historisk Samfund for Sønderjylland, Haderslev, 17-122.

Jensen, P.M. 2018: *Fynske arkæobotaniske fund fra landbebyggelser i perioden fra romersk jernalder til middelalder*; CENTRUM. Forskningscenter for centralitet (Rapport nr. 2, 2018). Odense Bys Museer, Odense.

Jessen, M.D. & K.F. Terkildsen 2016: "Towering above – an interpretation of the Late Iron Age architecture at Toftum Næs, Denmark", *Danish Journal of Archaeology* vol. 5. Routledge, 52-71.

Jørgensen, A.N., L. Jørgensen & L.G. Thomsen. 2011: "Assembly Sites for Cult, Markets, Jurisdiction and Social Relations. Historic-ethnological analogy between North Scandinavian church Towns, Old Norse assembly sites and pit house sites of the Late Iron Age and Viking Period", in *Arkæologi i Slesvig. Sonderband. Det 61. Internationale Sachsensymposium 2010, Haderslev, Danmark*. Wachholtz Verlag; Neumünster, 95-112.

Jørgensen, L. 2003: "Manor and Market at Lake Tissø in the Sixth to Eleventh Centuries: The Danish 'productive' Sites", in *Markets in Early Medieval Europe. Trading and 'Productive' Sites, 650-850*, edited by T. Pestell & K. Ulmschneider. Windgather Press, Macclesfield, 175-207.

Jørgensen, L. 2009: "Pre-christian cult at aristocratic residences and settlement complexes in southern Scandinavia", in *Glaube, Kult und Herrschaft. Phänomene des Religiösen in 1. Jahrtausend n.Chr. in Mittel Nordeuropa. Akten des 59. Internationalen Sachsensymposiums und der Grundprobleme der frühgeschichtelischen Entwicklung im Mitteldonauraum*, edited by U. Von Freeden, H. Friesinger & E. Warmers. Bonn: E. Dr. Rudolf Habelt GmbH, 329-354.

Jørgensen, L. 2010: "Gudme and Tissø. Two magnates' complexes in Denmark from the 3rd to the 11th century AD", in *Trade and Communication Networks of the First Millennium AD in the northern part of Central Europe. Neue Studien zur Sachsenforschung 1*, edited by H. Jöns, B. Ludowici, S. Kleingärtner, J. Scheschkewitz & M. Hardt. Konrad Theiss Verlag, Hannover, 273-286.

Jørgensen, L., L.G. Thomsen & A.N. Jørgensen. 2019: "Accommodating Assemblies, as Evidenced at the 6th-11th-century Ad Royal Residence at Lake Tissø, Denmark", in *Power & Place in Europe in the early Middle Ages,* edited by J. Carroll, A. Reynolds & B. Yorke (Proceedings of the British Academy 224). Oxford, 148-173.

Jørgensen, L.B. & Palle Eriksen. 1995: *Trabjerg. En vestjysk landsby fra Vikingetiden*. Jysk Arkæologisk Selskab, Højbjerg.

Madsen, H.J. 1991: "Vikingetidens keramik som historisk kilde", in *Fra Stamme til Stat i Danmark, 2. Høvdingesamfund og Kongemagt*. Jysk Arkæologisk Selskab, Højbjerg, 217-234.

Ravn, M., C. Juel, C. Lindblom & A. Pedersen. 2019: "Erritsø- new investigations of an aristocratic, early Viking Age manor in Western Denmark c. 700-850 AD", in *Early medieval Waterscapes. Risk and opportunities for (im)material cultural exchange*, edited by Rica Annaert, Tim Bellens, Pieterjan Deckers, Frans Theuws, Dries Tys, Robert van Dierendonck, Luc van Impe, Johan Veeckman & Laurent Verslype (Neue Studien zur Sachsenforschung, 8). Braunschweig, 37-44.

Sarauw, T. 2019: *Bejsebakken. En nordjysk bebyggelse fra yngre jernalder og vikingetid*. Det kongelige Nordiske Oldskriftselskab – Syddansk Universitetsforlag, København.

Sode, T & C. Feveile. 2002: "Segmenterede metalfolierede glasperler og blæste hule glasperler med metalbelægning fra markedspladsen i Ribe / Segmented metal foiled glass beads and hollow, blown glass beads with a coat of metal from the marketplace in Ribe"; In *By, marsk og geest 14;* Forlaget Liljebjerget, Ribe, 5-14.

Söderberg, B. 2005: *Aristokratisk rum och gränsöverskridande. Järrestad och sydöstra Skåne mellan region och rike 600-1100*. Riksantikvarieämbetet Arkeologiska undersökningar Skrifter No 62, Riksantikvarieämbetets förlag, Stockholm.

Thomsen, L.G. 2010. "Grubehusene som væverum? Overvejelser om funktionsbestemmelse af grubehuse", in *Smedens Rum 1, Værkstedet*, edited by H. Lyngstrøm, M.W. Olesen & L.G. Thomsen (Arkæologiske Skrifter 9, Forhistorisk Arkæologi, SAXO-instituttet, Københavns Universitet). København, 107-122.

Ulriksen, J. 2002. "Håndværksspor på yngre jernalders anløbspladser", in *Metalhåndværk og håndværkspladser fra yngre germansk jernalder, vikingetid og tidlig middelalder*, edited by M.B. Henriksen (Skrifter fra Odense Bys Museer vol. 9). Odense, 7-16.

BY MADS RAVN

Chapter 19
Synthesis of Central Places, Royal Places, Great Hall Complexes and Aristocratic Sites

The late Iron Age (as defined in Scandinavia), Early Medieval (as defined in Britian) and the Viking Age in Northern Europe presents a diverse and complex landscape of settlements and sites. Some stand out namely those categorized as central places, Great Hall Complexes or aristocratic sites or royal manors. These classifications are essential in understanding the socio-political and economic dynamics of the period, especially regarding their geographic distribution and multifunctional roles and should be compared over a larger distance beyond national boundaries, as we do here. But we should not only look at similarities between them but also differences.

Geographic and chronological differences

Central Places: These sites often emerged due to their strategic geographic locations, facilitating trade, communication, and control over surrounding and supra-regional regions. Gudme-Lundeborg on the island of Funen is a prime example, benefiting from its proximity to both inland and maritime routes. This positioning allowed it to serve as a significant hub for economic activities and long-distance contacts for almost 400 years. These sites seem also to be earlier in time and to belong to what others have called first generation central places. Additionally, Jessen et al., seem to suggest that those sites are failed urban developments, or low-density urban places, that somehow ended blindly, a term that we may need to work with more in the future. They bloomed already in the Roman Iron Age in the third and fourth centuries AD and predated the more stratified societies of the 6-10th centuries (Chapter 4). Therefore Gudme-Lundborg remains an enigma.

Aristocratic Sites: Aristocratic residences, like those at Lejre and Tissø, Järrestad and Erritsø and possibly also Munkebo Bakke and Tu/Hauge Borre and Birka Korshamn and early Rendelsham were usually situated in fertile agricultural zones, enabling self-sustaining communities that could support the elite households and their retinues.[1] These locations were chosen for their ability to sustain large populations and support extensive agricultural production. They were most likely also used for peripatetic kings arriving on occasions to collect tribute and perform juridical acts and feasts. The nodal nature of communication lines on sea and /or on land on an interregional level seem essential for all of those phenomena. There are as outlined in several papers in this volume differences between the middle- and southern Scandinavian sites (chapter 8, 9, 11). In Southern Scandinavia there are findings of ritual pits and piles of burnt stones and lots of barley suggesting that also drinking- and eating rituals were performed here, along with cultic activity and production.

Royal Places: Royal sites, such as Jelling, were typically established in areas that allowed for both symbolic and strategic control. These sites were centrally located within their realms, providing a base for royal administration and military operations. Jelling, for instance, was positioned to command land routes, reinforcing its role as a royal centre during the late Viking Age. This type of site probably only starts in the 10 centuries in Southern Scandinavia and seems to be a late phenomenon where the kingdom was more firmly established. Possibly Yeavering in Northumbria and late Rendlesham in East Anglia are compatible as is the emphasis on the phenomenology of power and architecture. The absence of grubenhäuser and other production huts especially in Jelling seems striking.

Similarities and differences in functions

Despite their geographic differences, central places, royal places, and aristocratic sites shared several key functions:

1. Cult and Religion: All these sites, it seems from the interpretations of several finds and buildings, played significant roles in religious activities. Central places like Gudme-Lundeborg featured prominent cultic buildings and ritual spaces, indicating their importance in pre-Christian religious practices. Royal and aristocratic sites similarly integrated religious structures, often associated with the ruling elite's legitimacy, drinking rituals and divine favour and ultimately Christianity.
2. Assemblies and Governance: These sites served as focal points for political gatherings and assemblies. They were most likely venues where laws were made, disputes were settled, and decisions regarding the community were taken. The Great Hall complexes at royal sites like Jelling and aristocratic sites like Lejre may also contain this function, providing spaces for large gatherings and feasts, which were integral to Viking Age governance, but how they relate to other Thing sites such as Almind 20 km west of Erritsø needs to be explored further.

---

[1] At the time of writing a parallel, comparative project between Uppsala and Lejre was not yet published and therefore it was not possible to include these results in the analyses.

3. Tribute Collection and Redistribution: Central places and royal sites were probably crucial in the collection of tribute and redistribution of goods. This system ensured the flow of resources from peripheral areas to the centres, reinforcing the power structures. At sites like Tissø, extensive evidence of tribute collection mechanisms and storage facilities highlights this role.
4. Economic Exchange and Craft Production: These sites were also centres of economic activity, including trade and specialized crafts. The proximity to trade routes and natural resources allowed for vibrant economic interactions. Sites like Gudme-Lundeborg shows significant archaeological evidence of metalworking, trade in luxury goods, and other specialized crafts, indicating their roles as economic hubs for specialized trade, but not urban trade. At Erritsø, however there is mainly evidence of textile production in the numerous contemporary Grubenhäuser, textile production that became very important as the Viking ships and their travels became more important to contemporary society. After an event in 815 the emphasis on defence seems to have developed, especially in Jutland and in Erritsø in particular.

Conclusion

The late Iron Age and Viking Age sites categorized as central places, royal places, and aristocratic sites each had unique geographic attributes that influenced their specific functions and roles. Being placed where important lines of transportation convene seem, however, to be the common ground on which they all are built. The varying emphases serving as centres for cultic activities, political assemblies, tribute collection, and economic exchanges underscore the dynamic and changing nature of socio-political and economic life in the late Iron Age and Viking Age Northern Europe. Understanding these similarities and differences between various locations in time and place in a higher resolution is one way to better understand their commonalities and differences. I believe this book is a first step towards doing exactly that.

Mads Ravn
Vejle 2024

Authors
(in order of appearance in the book)

Trine Louise Borake is a curator at Museum Vestsjælland in Denmark. She holds a PhD in archaeology from Aarhus University and a Master in Medieval Archaeology from Glasgow University. She specializes in detector findings from the Iron Age and Early Middle Ages, focusing on social organization from a bottom-up perspective. She has also been engaged in fieldwork and directed several research excavations centering on early medieval farmsteads with preserved cultural layers.

Mads Runge, Head of development at Museum Odense (Denmark). Until recently he was head of research at the research centre CENTRUM at Museum Odense for 8 years. He holds a PhD in archaeology and has lead several complicated excavations from the Iron- and Middle Ages and published extensively from those. He was a PI on the project that was called from Space to Place.

Mads Dengsø Jessen (PhD) is a senior researcher at the National Museum of Denmark and focusses his research on Iron and Viking Age fortifications, settlements and religious centres, their chronological development, functions and position in the early state formation. Also, the study of the interconnected nature of climatic and cultural development of the period forms part of his research agenda. Of late he has developed an interest for modern warfare history, so-called bunkerology.

Mette Marie Hald (PhD) is senior researcher at the National Museum of Denmark. She holds a PhD in Archaeology, and an MSc in Environmental Archaeology and Palaeoeconomy from the University of Sheffield. Her main research interest is the production and consumption of food, primarily based on archaeobotanical remains, from urban sites in the Near East and Denmark.

Morten Fischer Mortensen is a senior researcher at the National Museum of Denmark. He holds an M.Sc. in biology and a PhD in paleoecology. His research focuses on environmental archaeology, vegetation history, climate change, prehistoric food, Ice Age reindeer hunters, Iron Age sacrificial bogs, pollen analysis, landscape reconstruction, and bog geology. He has authored numerous research and popular science articles

Peter Steen Henriksen (MSc.agriculture) is curator and researcher in archaeobotany and geoarchaeology in the Department of Environmental Archaeology and Material

Science at the National Museum of Denmark. He is an expert on agriculture, foods, and drinks and the natural environment in Danish prehistory. Since 1992 and has published extensively on this subject.

Anders Pihl (Mag.art.) is a PhD-fellow at the National Museum of Denmark studying settlement organization in the 1st millennium AD. His research focusses on the cultural landscape as well as the utilization and mapping of this. Digital visualization of data, be it maps, analyses, statistics, etc. as well as the exploration of new methods in connection with the above. The focus of the past ten years has been particularly on agriculture and settlements from the Bronze Age to historical times.

Sofie Laurine Albris (PhD) is a project senior researcher at the National Museum of Denmark and leader of the DFF Sapere Aude project FORTIS about Iron Age militarisation on Bornholm. She has a PhD in onomastics from the Department of Nordic Research, University of Copenhagen and a Magisterkonferens, (extended MA-degree) in prehistoric Archaeology from the SAXO-Institute, University of Copenhagen. She specialises in interdisciplinary studies between archaeology and onomastics in an Iron and Viking Age context. In 2019-2021, she was a Marie Curie fellow at the University of Bergen, Norway, before returning to Denmark on a Carlsberg Foundation reintegration fellowship.

Anne Pedersen specialises in Medieval archaeology. She holds a PhD from University of Aarhus. She has worked as senior curator at the National Museum of Denmark for many years. Since 2012 she has been P.I. on the Jelling Project and has been engaged in preparing the great special exhibitions about the Viking Age at the National Museum in 2013 and 2021. She is also author of number of important articles on the Viking Age and Medieval period.

Charlotta Lindblom is a curator of archaeology at Vejlemuseerne in Denmark. She holds a Cand. Phil (MA) in Prehistoric Archaeology from the University of Copenhagen. She has worked on several museums in Denmark. She has specialized in Viking Age and has been working on both Danish and international projects related to Viking Age lately in and around the Jelling area.

Katrine Juul Balsgaard holds a PhD from Aarhus University. She was a curator at Vejlemuseerne until 2022 and lead the large Iron Age settlement, Grangaard Allé excavation near Jelling. In 2022 she became head of department at Museum Svendborg. She works today at Museum Horsens (Denmark). She has recently worked with gender archaeology and women's position in academia, archaeology and in the past.

Christopher Scull is a researcher specialising in the early medieval archaeology of north-west Europe. Over the course of his career, he has held academic posts at Durham University and University College London and was Research Director at English

Heritage until 2010. He has been Director of the Society of Antiquaries of London and is currently an Honorary Visiting Professor at the School of History, Archaeology and Religion, Cardiff University, and an Honorary Professor of Practice at the Institute of Archaeology, University College London. He has been involved in the Rendlesham research project as its principal academic advisor since 2012.

Terje Gansum (Fil.Dr.) is the managing director of the Norwegian Institute for Cultural Heritage Research (NIKU) (Norway). He holds a Mag.art. in Nordic archaeology from the University of Oslo (1995) and a PhD from the University of Gothenburg (2004). His leadership includes major roles and projects at Vestfold County and the Midgard Historical Centre (Norway) from where he has also published extensively.

Elna Siv Kristoffersen is professor emerita at the Museum of Archaeology, University of Stavanger, Norway. She holds a PhD from the University of Bergen, where she also has been teaching. In Stavanger she has been working with public outreach and exhibitions as well as research. She is a specialist in Migration Period studies with a focus on female graves, relief brooches, animal art, pottery and textile equipment addressing perspectives on chronology as well as aspects of identity and craft.

Alf Tore Hommedal is a Professor of Medieval Archaeology at the University Museum of Bergen, University of Bergen. He specializes in the archaeology of the Middle Ages, contributing to research on cultural heritage and medieval society. Hommedal is based in the Department of Cultural History and has been involved in various significant projects exploring Norway's medieval past. His work plays a key role in understanding the region's historical development.

Malene Refshauge Beck (cand.mag. [MA]), is curator at East Funen Museums/Vikingemuseet Ladby. She specializes in Bronze Age and Viking Age studies. Since 2015, her primary focus has been the Kerteminde Fjord area and the Ladby Ship grave. She has conducted excavations at the magnate's farm at Munkebo Bakke, and through her analyses of detector finds from the area, she has established a better understanding of the contemporaneous regional context of the ship grave.

Sven Kalmring, born 1976 in Hamburg, studied pre- and protohistoric archaeology in Kiel and in Lund. He specialised in Viking archaeology with a focus on harbours and maritime archaeology as well as on early medieval urbanisation. His doctoral thesis on "Der Hafen von Haithabu" ('The harbour of Hedeby') at Kiel university was granted the faculty price. In the scope of an Alexander von Humboldt-scholarship he took his post doc at the Archaeological Research Laboratory at Stockholm University, where he became associated professor in 2019. As a lector (Assistant professor), he was teaching at Aarhus University in 2016. Kalmring conducted various excavations in Hedeby and Birka, but also on Iceland and Western Scotland. After many years as a researcher at the Centre for Baltic and Scandinavian Archaeology (ZBSA) in Slesvig, today he works as a senior curator of the Younger Iron Age collections at the National Historical Museums (SHM) in Stockholm.

Johan Runer was born in 1973 in Stockholm. For many years he has conducted research on the Scandinavian society of the late Iron Age and Early Middle Ages. Runer received his doctorate in archaeology from Stockholm University in 2006 with a thesis entitled "Från hav till land eller Kristus och odalen" ('From Sea to Land or Christ and the Odal'). The thesis seeks to reconstruct central aspects of the organisation of the Swedish/Scandinavian late Iron Age society and the societal change that the transition to the Middle Ages meant. Runer has also carried out a large number of excavations relating to the period. In 2020, he won the Swedish Archaeological Society's "Golden trowel" award for best archaeological report, for a publication that presented the investigation of a Viking Age burial ground. Presently, he holds a position as a curator responsible for coordinating the archaeological work at the Swedish National and Maritime Museums (SMTM) in Stockholm.

Kasper H. Andersen is a Cultural Historian at Moesgaard Museum in Denmark. He holds a PhD from Aarhus University and is specialized in Viking Age and Middle Ages. His research primarily focuses on urban culture, ethnic identity, migration and mobility, often from an interdisciplinary perspective. He has worked with various collaborative research projects and published approximately 100 academic publications, including five research anthologies and peer-reviewed articles in Danish or English. He has experience in project management of research and dissemination projects, including museum exhibitions and Digital History.

Thorsten Lemm works as senior researcher for the *Leibniz-Zentrum für Archäologie* in Mainz and is stationed in Schleswig, Northern Germany. He holds a M.A. and PhD in archaeology from Kiel University. He specialises in settlement and landscape archaeology as well as military and power-political aspects in Central and Northern Europe in the late Iron Age and early Medieval Period. His main research interests include fortresses and fortifications, the early kingship and royal sites in Scandinavia, and the reconstruction of ancient roads. His research is generally characterised by a certain interdisciplinarity, in that archaeological contexts are considered in combination with written sources, runic inscriptions as well as place and field names.

Morten Ravn is research coordinator and curator at the Viking Ship Museum in Roskilde, Denmark. Holds a PhD in archaeology from Copenhagen University and is specialized in the maritime aspects of the past, primarily from the Viking and Middle Ages. He is associated to both Danish and international universities as a lecturer and was recently a visiting scholar at Sorbonne University in Paris. He is currently conducting two different research projects: about seafaring in the Bronze-Age and about Viking-Age leadership.

Jens Ulriksen (PhD) is Head of Centre for Viking Age Studies and Head of Research at Museum Southeast Denmark. In 1997 he completed his PhD on 1st Millennium AD landing sites in Denmark. His research covers a multitude of facets of the Germanic Iron Age, Viking Age, and Early Medieval Scandinavia.

Bente Philippsen (PhD) is associate professor of radiocarbon dating and leader of the National Laboratory for Age Determination at the University Museum, Norwegian University of Science and Technology (NTNU). She holds a PhD in Physics from Aarhus University and a Diploma (master) in Physics and Archaeology from Heidelberg University. She has worked with dating techniques, biomolecular analyses, scientific archaeology, and field archaeology at Aarhus University and at Danish museums, before she moved to Trondheim in 2023.

Marie Kanstrup specializes in radiocarbon dating and stable isotope analysis, contributing to research projects that span archaeology, geology, and environmental studies. Marie Kanstrup finished a PhD project about Prehistoric manuring practice and holds a Master's degree in archaeology from Aarhus University, where her dissertation focused on dietary studies based on isotope analyses of skeletal remains from Viking Age graves. She currently works at the Aarhus AMS Centre at Aarhus University, specializing in radiocarbon dating and stable isotope analysis, contributing to a range of interdisciplinary research projects in archaeology and environmental science.

Christian Juel is Curator and Team Leader of Archaeology at Vejle Museums in Denmark. He holds a MA and a Magisterkonferens, (extended MA-degree) in Prehistoric Archaeology from the University of Copenhagen. He has previously worked at several museums in Denmark and Norway and has specialized in settlements from the Late Iron Age, Viking Age and Early Medieval periods.

Morten Lyngkjær Jensen is an archaeologist at Vejle Museums, Denmark. He holds a MA in Prehistoric Archaeology from the University of Aarhus. He has led several large-scale excavations among others the economic area of the Viking Age site west and east of the Erritsø halls.

Mads Ravn is head of research at Vejlemuseerne (Vejle Museums) in Denmark. He holds a PhD and MPhil in archaeology from Cambridge University. He specializes in studies of the Iron Age and Viking Age and has worked throughout Scandinavia and around the world in various fieldwork projects. As such, he has worked as an archaeologist and researcher in association with Aarhus University as a Postdoc and associate lecturer, Australian National University as a visiting researcher and as an associate professor and Head of Section at University of Stavanger and University of Oslo before coming to Vejle. From December 1st, 2024, he takes up a new position as head of local heritage at Moesgaard Museum in Denmark.